Laurent Ferrara · Ignacio Hernando
Daniela Marconi
Editors

International Macroeconomics in the Wake of the Global Financial Crisis

Springer

Editors
Laurent Ferrara
Directorate for International
and European Relationships
Banque de France
Paris
France

Daniela Marconi
Directorate for International Relations
and Economics
Banca d'Italia
Rome
Italy

Ignacio Hernando
Associate Directorate General
International Affairs
Banco de España
Madrid
Spain

ISSN 0921-8580 ISSN 2197-1889 (electronic)
Financial and Monetary Policy Studies
ISBN 978-3-030-07720-4 ISBN 978-3-319-79075-6 (eBook)
https://doi.org/10.1007/978-3-319-79075-6

Printed on acid-free paper

This Springer imprint is published by the registered company Springer International Publishing AG part of Springer Nature
The registered company address is: Gewerbestrasse 11, 6330 Cham, Switzerland

Foreword

A decade after the Lehman Brothers collapse set off the most severe global downturn since the Great Depression, we are still coming to grips with the most recent chapter in the world's economic history. Financial factors, of course, have played a leading role in causing the crisis, in generating its effects, and in the policy response–leading to ongoing efforts to synthesize more completely macroeconomics and finance in economists' intellectual paradigms. But even a more conventional focus on macroeconomic variables reveals puzzles aplenty.

And indeed, the years after 2008 have been a distinctive period, following the so-called "Great Moderation" that some economists once believed to have taken firm hold by the mid-2000s. Broad-based global growth has been elusive until very recently, inflation and wage pressures remain muted in much of the world, interest rates remain generally low, and for many countries, medium-term income prospects seem dimmer than in the past. This conjecture has even led some economists to resurrect the specter of Alvin Hansen's secular stagnation. To what extent can the crisis itself explain the singular features of the post-crisis experience? Which of those features continue—while perhaps reinforcing—trends that began before the crisis? And did any of those pre-existing trends contribute to setting the stage for the crisis?

Why do I call the recent decade "distinctive"? The differences from the pre-crisis period are manifold:

- Growth in total factor productivity has been low, and together with low investment, the slow pace has led to lagging in labor productivity. International Monetary Fund projections project lower per capita income growth in the future for much of the world, notably advanced economies, fuel exporters, and—due to its rebalancing process—China. In retrospect, however, productivity growth likely began its decline in the 2000s, partially masked by the global credit boom, while China's torrid growth in the decade, which helped sustain global commodity prices, was not permanently sustainable.

- Real global interest rates are low, and appear likely to remain low for long. Here again the phenomenon is not new, as real rates began their decline around the mid-1980s, receiving a further push downward in the 2000s as some emerging markets ran bigger current account surpluses and accumulated international reserves. But the low levels rates have reached recently are exceptional—several researchers estimate negative values for the "natural" real rates of interest that equate full-employment demand and supply. It is unclear to what degree low real rates are a new "normal," related to population aging and the low productivity growth just mentioned, or a result of elevated debts after the crisis.
- Consistent with low natural real rates of interest, advanced economies have spent a surprisingly long time at or near the effective lower bound on nominal policy interest rates, resorting to unconventional monetary policies to try to lower longer-term bond yields and support anchored inflation expectations. But inflation has been generally below target levels nonetheless, and nominal wage growth has been slow across advanced economies, notwithstanding the general closure of estimated negative output gaps over the decade.
- The slow return of inflation rates to target, coupled with financial actors' reach for yield at low interest rates, has made some central bankers less comfortable with the single-minded pursuit of price-stability mandates. If globalization has made Phillips curves flatter, as some claim, might financial instability set in before inflation targets are reached, setting off a new crisis when monetary and fiscal policy space are both tightly constrained? Or can macroprudential policy somehow square the circle?
- Slow wage growth has taken place against a background, at least in advanced economies, of an increasing inequality trend. Again, this trend began long before the crisis, and reflects technological change, globalization, and a likely downward drift in the relative bargaining power of labor (through, for example, lower unionization density in many countries, less labor-market churn, and more industry concentration). While the resulting political tensions are nothing new, they seem to have combined with cultural and identity concerns, and a resentment of various "elites,' to unleash credible threats to the rule-based, multilateral framework for international economic relations that has underpinned postwar economic growth and convergence.
- The advanced economies' unconventional monetary responses had big effects on exchange rates and capital flows to emerging markets—both in the expansion phase and as exit policies were floated and, in the case of the United States, implemented. One notable spillover recipient was China, which grappled with exchange rate policy—in the process shocking global financial markets—and suffered a period of big capital outflows. Effects of advanced-economy monetary policy on emerging markets have long been studied. There remains considerable debate, however, about the specific effects of unconventional policies on emerging markets, the latter countries' ability to react effectively to the resulting volatile capital flows even when exchange rates are flexible, and the charges some have leveled that unconventional polices inflict beggar-thy-neighbor spillovers.

No single volume can come close to answering all the questions raised by recent international experience, but this volume by research economists from the Banque de France, Banco de España, and Banca d'Italia admirably moves the ball down the field. It collects a set of rigorous and insightful analyses that will do much to inform economists' thinking on a broad range of key macroeconomic topics.

As I write these words at the end of 2017, the world economy is experiencing its most comprehensive cyclical upswing since 2010, a year in which the global economy, advanced and emerging economies alike, bounced back from the initial post-Lehman financial shock. Will the current momentum be maintained, and how can policies prolong it and increase the resilience of recovery? Studies such as those contained here are central to finding the answers.

Bon appetit, buen provecho, and buon appetito!

Washington DC, USA Maurice Obstfeld

Contents

Editors and Contributors

About the Editors

Laurent Ferrara is Head of the International Macroeconomics Division at Banque de France in Paris. He holds a Ph.D. in Econometrics and received a Research Habilitation in Economics from University Paris 1 Panthéon-Sorbonne, and is an Adjunct Professor of Economics at University Paris Nanterre.

He is also Associate Editor of the *International Journal of Forecasting* and a member of the board of directors of the *International Institute of Forecasters*. After working as an economist for a research institute on the behalf of the Chamber of Commerce in Paris, he joined the Banque de France in 2007, where he has held the positions of researcher in the Business Conditions Analysis Division, followed by deputy head of the International Macroeconomics Division.

His research concerns international macroeconomics, business cycle analysis, macroeconomic forecasting and nonlinear modelling. His work has been published in various journals, including the *Oxford Bulletin of Economics and Statistics*, *Journal of Macroeconomics*, *Economics Letters*, *International Journal of Forecasting*, *Journal of Financial Stability* and *Economic Modelling*.

Ignacio Hernando is currently Head of the International Financial Institutions and International Relations Division at the Associate Directorate General for International Affairs of the Banco de España in Madrid. Previously, he was Head of the International Economics Division at Banco de España. He received his B.A. in Economics at Universidad Complutense de Madrid, an M.A. in Monetary Economics at CEMFI and a Ph.D. at UNED.

Since 2010, he is member of the International Relations Committee of the European System of Central Banks. Previously, he was a member of the Eurosystem Research Networks on Monetary Policy Transmission and on Inflation Persistence. His research concerns international macroeconomics and monetary policy. His publications include articles in *Journal of Banking and Finance*, *Oxford Bulletin of Economics and Statistics*, *International Journal of Central Banking*, *European Financial Management*, *Journal of Macroeconomics*, *Economic Modelling*, *Oxford Review of Economic Policy* and *Journal of Financial Services Research*.

Daniela Marconi is Senior Advisor at Banca d'Italia. She graduated in Economics from the University of Rome 'La Sapienza'; she obtained an M.A. in Economics from CORIPE Piemonte (Turin, Italy) and from Duke University (North Carolina, USA). During 2008–2009, she was visiting research fellow at the Department of International Development of the University of Oxford (UK). Since 2002, she has worked in the Bank of Italy's Emerging markets and international trade Division, conducting macroeconomic and structural analysis on emerging markets, particularly on China. Her main academic interests are international macroeconomics, technological progress, economic growth and environmental economics. She has authored numerous papers and articles in these areas. Her publications include article in *The Journal of International Trade & Economic Development*, *Journal of Chinese Economic and Business*, *Asia-Pacific Journal of Accounting and Economics*, *Pacific Economic Review* and *Review of International Economics*. She also edited a book on China, published with Springer Verlag, and several book chapters.

Contributors

Juan Carlos Berganza Banco de España, Madrid, Spain

Alessandro Borin Bank of Italy, Directorate General for Economics, Statistics and Research, International Relations and Economics Directorate, Rome, Italy

Fructuoso Borrallo Banco de España, Madrid, Spain

Ines Buono Bank of Italy, Directorate General for Economics, Statistics and Research, International Relations and Economics Directorate, Rome, Italy

Matthieu Bussière Banque de France, Paris, France

Alessio Ciarlone Bank of Italy, Directorate General for Economics, Statistics and Research, International Relations and Economics Directorate, Rome, Italy

Andrea Colabella Bank of Italy, Directorate General for Economics, Statistics and Research, International Relations and Economics Directorate, Rome, Italy

Riccardo Cristadoro Bank of Italy, Directorate General for Economics, Statistics and Research, International Relations and Economics Directorate, Rome, Italy

Pedro del Río Banco de España, Madrid, Spain

Virginia Di Nino European Central Bank, Frankfurt, Germany

Enrica Di Stefano Bank of Italy, Directorate General for Economics, Statistics and Research, International Relations and Economics Directorate, Rome, Italy

Laurent Ferrara International Macro Division, Banque de France, Paris, France

Sara Formai Bank of Italy, Directorate General for Economics, Statistics and Research, Structural Economic Analysis, Rome, Italy

Vincent Grossmann-Wirth Banque de France, Paris, France

Sophie Haincourt Banque de France, Paris, France

Ignacio Hernando ADG International Affairs, International Economics Division, Banco de España, Madrid, Spain

Iván Kataryniuk Banco de España, Madrid, Spain

Stéphane Lhuissier Banque de France, Paris, France

Michele Mancini Bank of Italy, Directorate General for Economics, Statistics and Research, International Relations and Economics Directorate, Rome, Italy

Daniela Marconi Bank of Italy, Directorate General for Economics, Statistics and Research, International Relations and Economics Directorate, Rome, Italy

Clément Marsilli International Macroeconomics Division, Banque de France, Paris, France

Jaime Martínez-Martín Banco de España, Madrid, Spain

Patrizio Pagano Bank of Italy, Rome, Italy; World Bank, Washington DC, USA

Daniel Santabárbara Banco de España, Madrid, Spain

Massimo Sbracia Bank of Italy, Rome, Italy

Julia Schmidt Banque de France, Paris, France

Fabien Tripier Université Paris-Saclay (EPEE, Univ Evry) & CEPII, Paris, France

Natacha Valla European Central Bank and Paris School of Economics, Paris, France

Javier Vallés Banco de España, Madrid, Spain

Introduction

Laurent Ferrara, Ignacio Hernando and Daniela Marconi

Abstract In the years 2008–09, following the Global Financial Crisis (hereafter the GFC), the global economy experienced its worst economic recession since the Great Depression. Some ten years later, this book examines the macroeconomic dynamics of the global economy in the aftermath of the GFC. The book is split into four sections. First, we look at the supply side of the economy and how potential growth is likely to have been affected by the GFC, against a backdrop of a long-run decline in productivity and rising inequalities. Second, we examine the impact of the GFC on demand, focusing on trends in global trade, household consumption and business investment. Third, we discuss how monetary policy reactions after the GFC were rapid and large enough to sustain the global economy and the international monetary system, but also take a closer look at the challenges ahead for central bankers, notably low inflation regimes, heightened uncertainties and low natural interest rates. The final section points out some stylized facts on the external sector variables of countries such as capital flows, exchange rates and cross-border monetary policy spillovers.

L. Ferrara
International Macro Division, Banque de France, Paris, France
e-mail: laurent.ferrara@banque-france.fr

I. Hernando
ADG International Affairs, International Economics Division,
Banco de España, Madrid, Spain
e-mail: hernando@bde.es

D. Marconi (✉)
Bank of Italy, Directorate General for Economics, Statistics and Research,
International Relations and Economics Directorate, Rome, Italy
e-mail: daniela.marconi@bancaditalia.it

L. Ferrara et al. (eds.), *International Macroeconomics in the Wake of the Global Financial Crisis*, Financial and Monetary Policy Studies 46,
https://doi.org/10.1007/978-3-319-79075-6_1

1 The Slowdown in Global Growth: Supply-Side Factors

A decade after the eruption of the Global Financial Crisis, the world economy has finally returned to a more sustained pace of expansion (see Fig. 1). Yet major challenges still remain, as the engines of long-run growth have still not recouped their pre-crisis power. The subdued growth in productivity in advanced and emerging countries alike, the slow recovery in investment and the persistently low income elasticity of international trade are all casting a long shadow over growth in the medium and longer term, calling for a deeper investigation of their root causes and of the possible policy remedies. At the present juncture, policymakers urgently need to disentangle the cyclical factors from the structural ones, in order to engineer the most appropriate policy responses. However, doing so is proving to be a difficult task because a crisis as deep, long-lasting and widespread as the last one had not been seen since the 1930s. The first section of this book aim to shed some light on the structural and cyclical factors at play behind the slowdown in the supply-side drivers of economic growth. The contribution by P. Pagano and M. Sbracia (Chap. 2) sets the scene by revisiting the debate on the secular stagnation hypothesis. This concept was initially discussed by Alvin Hansen in a speech prepared for the annual American Economic Association meetings in 1938, then put forward by Larry Summers at an IMF conference in 2013. Focusing on the United States, generally identified as the world's technology frontier, Summers noted that, while normal financial conditions were quickly restored in 2009 thanks to aggressive monetary policies, economic output and employment took much longer to recover, systematically falling short of predictions.[1] The secular stagnation hypothesis can be investigated by looking at the secular changes in aggregate demand and its components or by analyzing the developments in the fundamental drivers of aggregate supply—two sides of the same coin. Summers focuses on the first one, examining the idea that secular stagnation occurs when desired levels of savings exceed desired levels of investment and conventional monetary policies are unable to restore the equilibrium by bringing down real interest rates to their natural (or equilibrium) level.[2] Pagano and Sbracia focus instead on the supply-side approach, investigating the secular trends in productivity and the sources of U.S. GDP per capita growth in the post-World War II period. Their analysis stresses that long-run growth can be best predicted by looking at secular trends in total factor productivity (TFP), population and human capital formation, and suggests that some key questions on the factors that will shape future trends have still not been fully answered. A first element of uncertainty is whether there are diminishing returns to R&D, whereby the rate of fundamental inventions decreases as technology advances, as argued by Gordon (2014), or whether the potential of existing technologies has not yet been fully captured, as posited by Mokyr (2013)

---

[1] The underperformance of the United States was not an exception: had the world economy performed as the IMF predicted in 2011, world GDP today would be about 1.6 per cent higher than it is.

[2] The role of unconventional monetary policy in the presence of falling natural interest rates will be investigated by I. Hernando, D. Santabárbara and J. Vallés (Chap. 11).

and Brynjolfsson et al. (2014). A second question relates to population growth and whether national boundaries still make sense today given the growing integration of emerging countries into the global economy. Finally, the assumption that there is an upper bound to the accumulation of human capital, given by the maximum number of years of schooling, can be challenged if we consider that the quality of education and variety of knowledge could in principle keep growing without any upper bound.

The decline in productivity growth in the aftermath of the global financial crisis is also a key concern for emerging market economies (hereafter EMEs, see Fig. 2).

Since the second half of 2011, GDP growth in these countries has progressively slowed, repeatedly failing to meet the forecasts of the leading international organizations. In 2016, overall EME GDP growth stood at 4.3 per cent, well below the 6.7 per cent recorded over the period 2001–07. And according to recent IMF projections (IMF 2017), it should remain below 5 per cent on average over the next five years. Prior to the GFC, favorable external tailwinds, including the integration of trade and production into global value chains, as well as positive income effects stemming from booming commodity prices, helped many EMEs to increase productivity by accumulating more capital and shifting labor to more productive activities (OECD 2014). As a consequence of this rapid development, EMEs' share of world GDP surpassed that of advanced economies in 2010, making it more important than ever that we understand what the future trends in growth and productivity for these countries will be. In Chap. 3, E. Di Stefano and D. Marconi examine the evolution of GDP and labor productivity growth in six major emerging countries, and show that trend GDP growth has fallen on average by almost 2

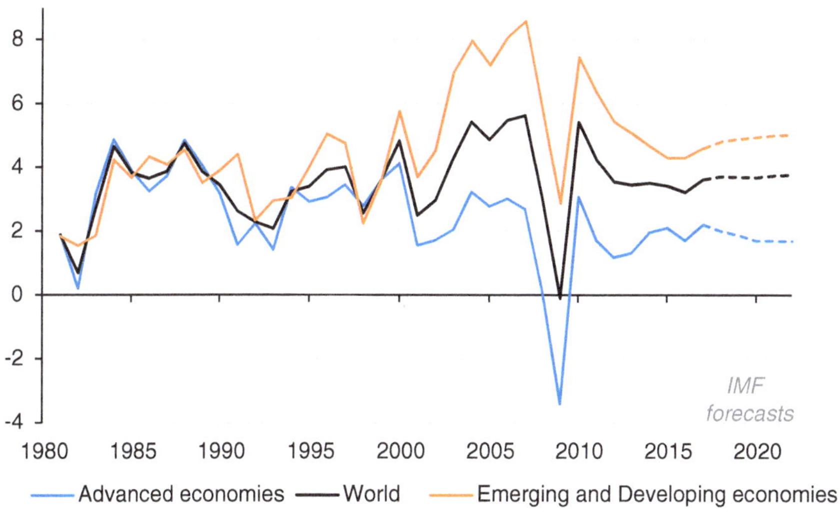

Fig. 1 Real GDP growth for World, advanced and emerging and developing economies (in %, source IMF-WEO)

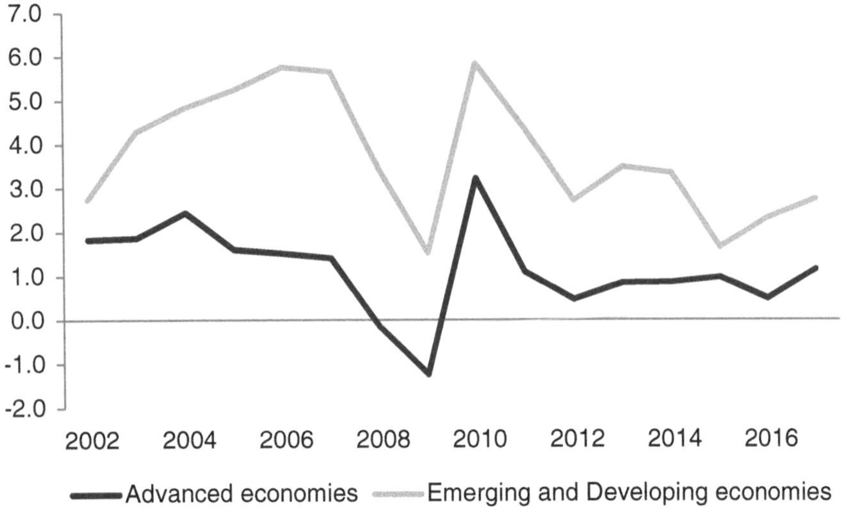

Fig. 2 Labour productivity growth for advanced and emerging and developing economies (in %, source The Conference Board)

percentage points compared with the pre-crisis period. This slowdown has mainly been driven by a deterioration in labor productivity, which followed on from both a reduction in the pace of structural transformation and a slowdown in productivity within sectors. The authors argue that, while the continuing structural transformation of these economies could still give a boost to productivity, major obstacles may be delaying the process, including the quantity and the quality of labor supply. Investigating the determinants of TFP growth for a panel of 41 advanced and emerging economies, I. Kataryniuk and J. M. Martinez-Martin (Chap. 4) reach very similar conclusions. The analysis in Chap. 4 shows that external tailwinds made a substantial contribution to TFP growth in EMEs during the pre-crisis boom years. Moreover, distinguishing between cyclical and structural determinants, the authors find that, although a non-negligible share of the deterioration in growth prospects in recent years may be explained by a negative economic cycle, structural weaknesses are contributing to the slowdown in medium-term growth, especially for emerging countries.

The negative effects of the GFC can also be seen in the increasing discontent over rising income and wealth inequality, especially in advanced economies. Inequality has started to be seen not only as a consequence of the crisis but also as a possible cause of the sluggish recovery (Cynamon and Fazzari 2016). In Chap. 5, R. Cristadoro highlights the current debate over inequality, reviewing its causes and consequences. Although the rapid growth of EMEs with large and relatively poor populations (such as China and India) has certainly contributed to a significant reduction in between-country inequality, inequality among individuals within countries has risen over the last 25 years. Admittedly, inclusive growth and the fight against inequality have become top priorities for policymakers in many advanced and emerging economies. However, the lack of consensus on the root causes of the problem makes it difficult to design appropriate policies to curb it. Trade and financial integration, as well as technology, are widely regarded as the main culprits behind rising wealth and income disparities (Jaumotte et al. 2013). But the paradox is that those same factors have long been recognized in the economic literature as the main contributors to world prosperity (Visco 2015). The real question, therefore, is how to ensure a fairer distribution of the benefits stemming from economic integration and technological advances. As R. Cristadoro argues, the evidence suggests that the main channel through which inequality hinders growth is by undermining education opportunities for those at the bottom of the income and wealth scale, jeopardizing skill acquisition and social mobility. Once again, human capital formation is identified as the key factor that will shape the future of the world economy.

2 The Slowdown in Global Growth: Demand-Side Explanations

The second part of this book is devoted to the analysis of the components of aggregate demand in the wake of the GFC. Chapter 6, by A. Borin, V. Di Nino, M. Mancini and M. Sbracia, investigates the cyclical and structural factors behind the slowdown in global trade volumes over the period 2011–16. There has been intense debate about the causes of the sluggish recovery in global trade volumes and the fall in the income elasticity of trade (IMF 2016). The authors' analysis shows that the income elasticity of trade is highly cyclical, rising above unity during periods of above-trend GDP expansion and falling back to around unity in the long-run. As a consequence, one would expect income elasticity to recover as economic activity, and especially investment, goes back to their long-run trend, returning towards one and only exceeding this value if GDP and investment growth remain persistently above trend.

In the years preceding the GFC, above-trend growth in aggregate demand, and particularly in consumption in the United States, was fueled by the expansion of debt. However, excessive indebtedness eventually resulted in the sub-prime crisis which triggered the GFC. Chapter 7, by V. Grossman-Wirth and C. Marsilli, documents the developments of U.S. private consumption before and after the GFC and underlines the extent to which consumption growth before 2007 was driven by household debt flows. A breakdown of household assets and liabilities shows how the pre-crisis period was characterized by excessive indebtedness, which was a source of both growth (in the short term) and of financial instability. In the current "new normal" situation, private consumption cannot rely on debt flows as much as before the crisis. This is, therefore, an important "demand-side" explanation for the much debated low growth recovery in the United States.

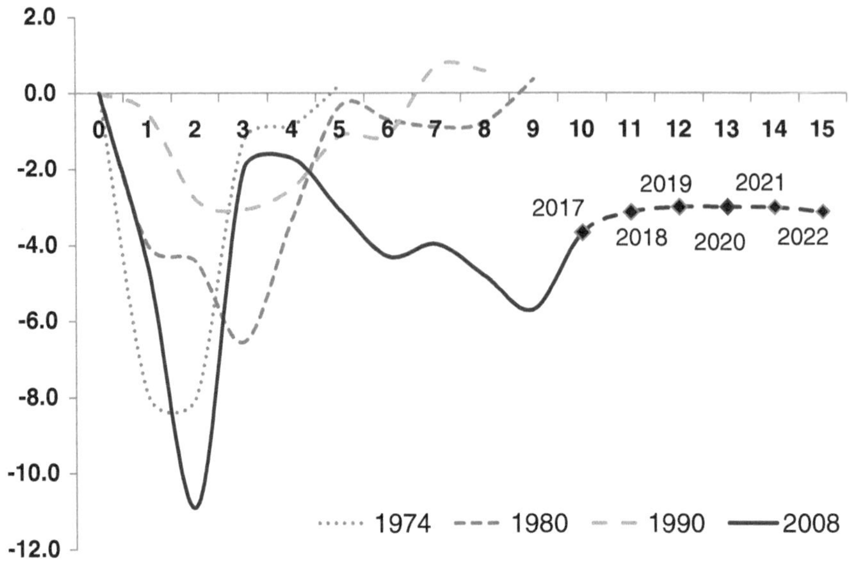

Fig. 3 World gross fixed investment annual growth gaps during and after recessions (source Banca d'Italia based on IMF data)

Alongside trade, and strictly connected to it, as mentioned previously, business fixed investment remained depressed worldwide, particularly in major advanced economies, for a prolonged period of time after the crisis, only showing initial signs of recovery in recent months (see Fig. 3). In recognition of its fundamental role in driving both short and long-term economic developments, Chap. 8, by I. Buono and S. Formai, examines the behavior of business investment for a panel of 19 developed countries over the period 1990–2016. Their analysis shows that the GFC has brought about a structural change in the determinants of investment demand, with financial uncertainty affecting the speed of recovery in fixed capital formation to a greater extent than previously. Moreover, in some countries, most notably the peripheral European countries, business investment has become more sensitive to changes in borrowing costs in recent years. Both findings have significant implications for the conduct of monetary policy, which are discussed in the chapter.

3 Challenges for Monetary Policy After the GFC

In the wake of the GFC, central banking—and, in particular, monetary policy management—in advanced economies went through deep transformations, entering unchartered waters (see, for instance, Bernanke 2011, or Caruana, Filardo and Hoffman 2014). After the collapse of Lehman Brothers, central banks in major advanced economies adopted a number of extraordinary measures to support liquidity and lowered official interest rates to near zero in early 2009. At the same time, they also began implementing so-called unconventional policy measures with the aim of restoring the monetary transmission mechanism, improving access to finance and supporting the sluggish recovery. The toolkit deployed over the post-crisis years included purchases of financial assets, changes in communication policy, including the adoption of what is known as forward guidance, and the provision of credit facilities to the banking system. Moreover, fiscal packages approved in early stages of the global financial crisis helped to stabilize economic activity and support troubled financial institutions, but led to a dramatic increase in average public debt levels in a number of countries. Against this backdrop, fiscal consolidation efforts initiated in 2010 left monetary policy as the "only game in town".

Almost ten years after the critical point in the GFC, the monetary policy stance of many major central banks remains highly accommodative. Admittedly, the Federal Reserve initiated a cycle of increases in its Federal Funds rate in December 2015 after leaving it unchanged for almost seven years, and in October 2017 started the process of normalizing its balance sheet by gradually reducing the reinvestment of the principal payments it receives from the its holdings of Treasury securities, agency debt, and agency mortgage-backed securities (MBS). However, even when the normalization process is complete, market participants still expect the Federal Reserve's balance sheet to remain considerably larger than it was before the crisis, while the median FOMC members' forecast for long–term policy rates is, at the time of writing, 2.9, substantially below the historical mean. Meanwhile, other major central banks—the European Central Bank, the Bank of Japan and the Bank of England, among others—are still relying on the set of unconventional measures put in place in the aftermath of the crisis, and are keeping their policy rates at historically low- and in some cases negative-levels.

In spite of this protracted accommodative monetary policy stance and fiscal support, at least in those economies where it was feasible, growth has been somewhat disappointing. As discussed previously, this sluggish recovery has been the result of a combination of crisis-related headwinds as well as structural deficiencies and underlying trends—such as population ageing and weak productivity growth—which were also present in the expansionary phase before the crisis. All these factors may have contributed to a lowering of expectations of potential output growth as well as to weak current demand and inflation and a lower equilibrium interest rate. The persistence of low inflation rates in spite of the highly accommodative monetary policy stance represents a major challenge for central banks in the main advanced economies. J. C. Berganza, F. Borrallo, and P. del Río (Chap. 10) look at global inflation trends over the last decade and try to disentangle factors that could explain the very low levels of inflation during the recovery from the Great Recession (see Fig. 4). The literature points to possible structural shifts in price and wage-setting processes over recent years, such as the reduced cyclical sensitivity of inflation to domestic economic slack, the bigger role played by forward-looking inflation expectations and the increasing importance of global factors. The authors test empirically whether changes in the coefficients of the Phillips curve in the wake of the GFC can explain the behavior of inflation over this period for a large group of advanced

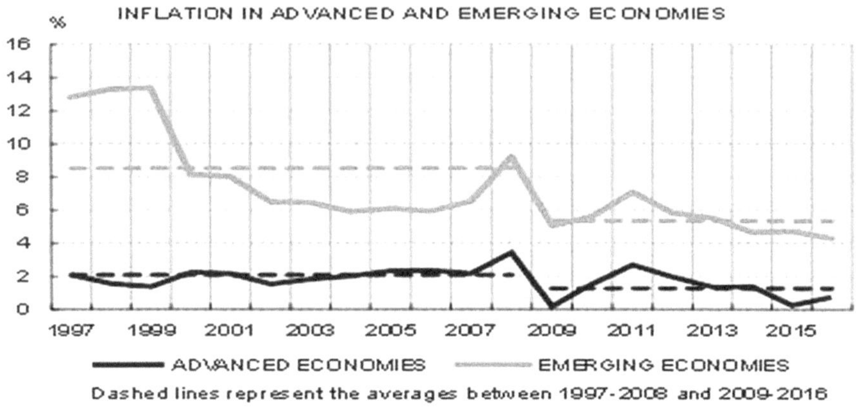

Fig. 4 Headline inflation in advanced and emerging (in %, source: IMF-WEO)

economies. The results show that the persistence of inflation and the increased importance of backward-looking inflation expectations in some countries may pose risks for inflation-expectation anchoring and central bank credibility. Finally, Berganza et al. focus on the adverse effects on the real economy of ultra-low inflation over an extended period and consider the policy options for addressing this problem.

There is ample evidence that real interest rates have progressively declined since the 1980s in most advanced and emerging economies, and currently stand at very low levels (see Fig. 5 and, for instance, Holston et al. 2016). The persistence of this trend, as well as its intensification during the GFC, raises a series of highly relevant questions in different areas. First, to what extent is monetary policy's task of steering interest rates towards their natural level made more difficult by the fact that this natural interest rate may be very low (or even negative), given the current context of persistent low inflation rates? Second, could prolonged periods of very low interest rates have undesirable implications for financial stability? And lastly, could this situation in fact reflect a substantial reduction in potential growth at the global level? In this context, I. Hernando, D. Santabárbara and J. Vallés (Chap. 11) analyze the determinants of this downward trend in real interest rates from a global perspective, discussing the extent to which it is likely to continue in the medium and long term. They argue that the normalization of monetary policies, the change in the growth model of some emerging countries and the socio-demographic and productivity trends would point to a gradual recovery in real interest rates, over a medium-term horizon, albeit with a high degree of uncertainty, both as regards the magnitude of the rise and its timing. Over the longer term, this trend may tail off in a context of limited technological progress, which fails to boost investment, or a sharper-than-expected decline in investment in the emerging economies.

Another feature of the global economic landscape in the last few years is the substantial increase in uncertainty, with significant implications for the conduct of

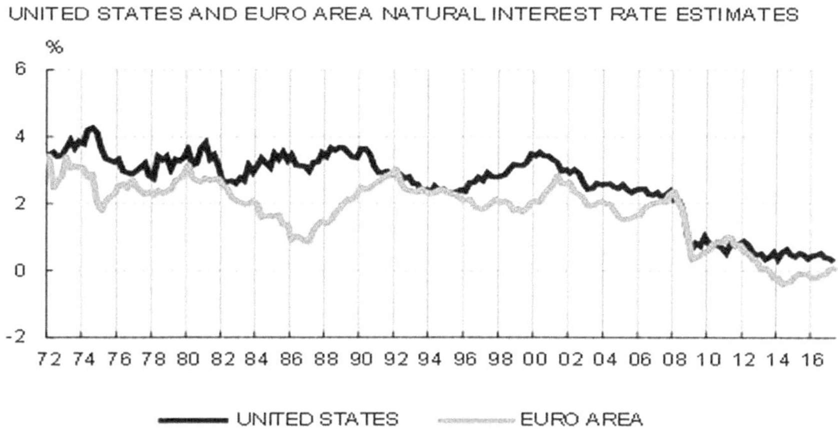

Fig. 5 Natural interest rates in the U.S. and the euro area (in %, source: Holston et al. 2016)

macroeconomic policies. These uncertainty shocks stem mainly from developments in financial systems in some parts of the world and from political and economic policy outcomes. Prominent examples of this latter source of uncertainty are the potential changes in the policy stance of the new U.S. administration, the process leading to the withdrawal of the United Kingdom from the European Union (the so-called Brexit process), and more generally, the developments around the transition process in the Chinese economy. The macroeconomic and financial effects of uncertainty shocks are being increasingly taken into account by policy-makers and integrated into their analysis of current and future conditions. In this vein, there is an increasingly buoyant academic literature on uncertainty. L. Ferrara, S. Lhuissier and F. Tripier (Chap. 9) propose a review of the recent literature, focusing on various aspects. First, they present and discuss several measures of uncertainty that have been put forward in the literature and that are now widely used in empirical analysis. They disentangle financial volatility, economic policy uncertainty, macroeconomic uncertainty and disagreement among forecasters. They then go on to describe the theoretical impact of uncertainty on macroeconomic activity and financial markets and discuss the various channels of transmission. In particular, they consider both domestic effects, on investment, consumption, the labor market or productivity, and international effects, via the impact on exchange rates and capital flows. The theoretical results are supported by empirical results stemming from the recent literature. In the last part of the chapter, they discuss the potential implications of this rise in uncertainty for the conduct of macroeconomic policies and conclude by calling for an extension of economic policies aimed at stabilizing uncertainty in the economy, as well as for greater flexibility in order to adapt policies to periods of uncertainty.

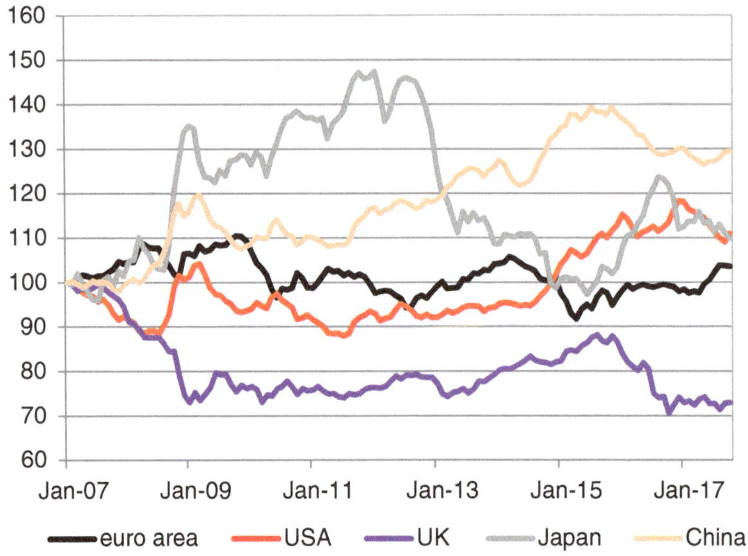

Fig. 6 Nominal effective exchange rates for the main currencies (Base 100 in January 2007, source: ECB)

4 External Developments

The GFC also led to major disruptions in countries' external sectors. As pointed out in previous chapters, the large drop in global trade, slump in economic activity and turmoil on financial markets, as well as the subsequent economic policy reactions, all generated large movements in external variables such as capital flows and exchange rates (see Fig. 6).

Starting with capital flows, we observed wide fluctuations in portfolio flows, banking flows and foreign direct investments before, during and after the GFC. M. Bussière, J. Schmidt and N. Valla (Chap. 13) show evidence of some stylized facts in international financial flows around the GFC, based on an empirical analysis of a large set of advanced and emerging countries. First, they postulate that the "Great Retrenchment" that took place during the crisis has proved very persistent and world financial flows are today down to half their pre-crisis levels. Second, this fall can primarily be related to advanced economies, especially those in Western Europe, while emerging markets, except eastern European countries, have, until recently, been less severely affected. Last, not all types of flows have shown the same degree of resilience, resulting in a profound change in the composition of international financial flows: while banking flows, which used to account for the largest share of the total before 2008, have collapsed, foreign direct investment flows have scarcely been affected and now represent roughly 45% of global flows. Portfolio flows are in between these two extremes; among them, equity flows have proved more robust than debt flows, which should help to strengthen resilience and deliver greater genuine cross-border risk-sharing.

What are the drivers of those movements in capital flows? There have been some tentative explanations, especially regarding the collapse in banking flows. Among the possible drivers, the role of risk aversion and the high level of uncertainty have been put forward, but the correction from a pre-crisis global banking glut, the intensification of the disintermediation process or the impact of the trade collapse on trade credits are also convincing arguments. Focusing specifically on portfolio flows, the main driver is usually considered to be divergences in monetary policy cycles; however, risk aversion and growth differentials are also likely to play a role. There is a buoyant literature on the cross-border effects of monetary policy on portfolio flows, but it mainly focuses on the macroeconomic and financial effects flowing from the United States to the rest of the world, especially emerging economies (see e.g. Eichengreen and Gupta 2015). The 'taper tantrum' episode in 2013 shed light on this topic and prompted numerous research papers, concerned with assessing the impact on and channels of transmission to emerging markets. For example, an NBER working paper by Aizenman et al. (2014) confirms that tapering news was associated with strong exchange rate depreciation and a significant decrease in stock market indices in emerging economies. However, the effects differed widely depending on the economic and international position of the country. Interestingly, emerging markets with current account surpluses and high levels of international reserves were initially more adversely exposed to tapering news than weaker countries, possibly because they were the ones attracting the largest share of financial flows due to quantitative easing. A subsequent research paper by Aizenman et al. (2015) advanced the finding that domestic and international macroeconomic conditions in emerging market economies are important buffers for spillovers from advanced economies. In particular higher levels of financial development, greater financial openness, strong trade ties with the advanced economies, and more stable inflation rates help reduce sensitivity to monetary policy spillovers.

With regard to the international effects of the ECB's monetary policy, the literature is scarcer, especially as concerns the effects of the new unconventional monetary policy tools implemented in the euro area. In a recent speech, Coeuré (2017) shows evidence that the ECB's asset purchase programs (APP) have triggered substantial capital flow across borders. In particular, they have generated large net portfolio investment outflows to countries outside the euro area, flows that peaked at 5% of euro area GDP in 2016. Against this backdrop, A. Ciarlone and A. Colabella (Chap. 14) look at the effects of the ECB's asset purchase programs (APPs) on the financial markets of a set of central, eastern and south-eastern European (CESEE) countries. They show that the implementation of the APPs helped to support cross-border portfolio investment flows to, and larger foreign bank claims on, CESEE economies mainly in an indirect way—i.e. via their impact on liquidity and financial conditions in the euro area—thus revealing the existence of both a portfolio rebalancing and a banking liquidity transmission channel. This means that without the support of such non-standard monetary measures from the ECB, both types of cross-border capital flows would have been weaker and financial conditions in CESEE economies tighter than they actually were. Overall, they support the view that the implementation of the APPs had a positive impact by lowering both policy and long-term interest rates to levels well below those justified by country-specific cyclical positions or global risk factors.

In the open economy literature, there is a close relationship between exchange rates, capital flows and monetary policy, as expressed for example in the Mundell-Fleming world. The Mundell trilemma, which states that it is not possible to have a fixed exchange rate, full capital mobility and monetary independence all at the same time, is at the core of this relationship. In spite of some empirical evidence (see for example Obstfeld et al. 2005), the trilemma has recently been challenged by some researchers, such as Rey (2016), who state that the existence of a global financial cycle reduces the trilemma to a dilemma in the sense that the exchange rate regime does not matter anymore. In this context, it turns out that the causality between financial flows and exchange rate is not that obvious (see for example Coeuré 2017, for a discussion). Yet the identification issue about the nature of the shock that drives fluctuations in exchange rates has been recently put forward in academic and policy circles (see the speech by Forbes 2015). Indeed, the idea is that according to the nature of the shock, the macroeconomic impact of an exchange rate appreciation (or depreciation) is likely to be differentiated. Building on this idea, S. Haincourt (Chap. 12) carries out a model-based simulation using the NiGEM model, an international macroeconomic model developed by the National Institute of Economic and Social Research, and shows that a currency appreciation driven by a fall in risk premium is likely to have less adverse effects on GDP and inflation than one driven by a monetary policy shock. In addition, comparing the United States and the euro area, the model shows that the euro area is more sensitive to a currency appreciation, most likely because of its higher degree of openness. Focusing on the last appreciation cycle for both the U.S. dollar and the euro (2015–16), an identification scheme, based on bilateral contributions to the effective exchange rate, leads to empirical results showing that the euro appreciation had an impact of around −0.2% point on GDP growth for the euro area as a whole, while the impact of the U.S. dollar appreciation on U.S. GDP was broadly neutral.

References

Aizenman J, Binici M, Hutchison M (2014) The transmission of federal reserve tapering news to emerging financial markets. NBER working paper, No. 19980

Aizenman J, Chinn MD, Ito H (2015) Monetary policy spillovers and the trilemma in the new normal: periphery country sensitivity to core country conditions, NBER working paper No. 21128

Bernanke B (2011) The effects of the Great Recession on central bank doctrine and practice. In: Speech at the Federal Reserve Bank of Boston 56th Economic Conference, Boston, Massachusetts, Oct 2011

Brynjolfsson E, McAfee A, Spence M (2014) New world order: labor, capital, and ideas in the power law economy, Foreign Affairs, July–August

Caruana J, Filardo A, Hofmann B (2014) Post-crisis monetary policy: balance of risks. In: Vallés J (ed) Monetary policy after the great recession. FUNCAS, Madrid

Cynamon BZ, Fazzari SM (2016) Inequality, the great recession and slow recovery. Camb J Econ 40(2):373–399

Coeuré B (2017) The international dimension of the ECB's asset purchase programme. Speech at the foreign exchange contact group meeting, 11 July 2017
Eichengreen B, Gupta P (2015) Tapering talk: the impact of expectations of reduced Federal Reserve security purchases on emerging markets. Emerg Markets Rev 25(C):1–15
Forbes K (2015) Much ado about something important: how do exchange rate movements affect inflation? Speech given at the 47th Money, Macro and finance research group annual conference, Cardiff, Sept 2015
Gordon RJ (2014) The Demise of U.S. Economic growth: restatement, rebuttal, and reflections, NBER working paper, No. 19895
Holston K, Laubach T, Williams JC (2016) Measuring the natural rate of interest: international trends and determinants. J Int Econ
IMF (2016) World economic outlook, Apr 2016
IMF (2017) World economic outlook, Oct 2017
Jaumotte F, Lall S, Papageorgiou C (2013) Rising income inequality: technology, or trade and financial globalization? IMF Econ Rev 61(2):272–309
Mokyr J (2013) Technology then and now: why the technopessimists are wrong, Presentation delivered at the Federal Reserve Bank of Atlanta Public Affairs Forum, July
Obstfeld M, Shambaugh J, Taylor A (2005) The trilemma in history: tradeoffs among exchange rates, monetary policies and capital mobility. Rev Econ Stat 87(3):423–438
OECD (2014) Perspectives on global development 2014. In: Boosting productivity to meet the middle-income challenge. OECD Publishing
Rey, H. (2016) International channels of transmission of monetary policy and the Mundellian trilemma. NBER working paper, No. 21852
Visco I (2015) For the times they are a changin' Lecture by Mr. Ignazio Visco, Governor of the Bank of Italy, at the London School of Economics Institute of Global Affairs and London School of Economics Student's Union. Italian Society, London, 11 Nov 2015

Part I
Global Growth Slowdown: Supply-Side Factors

The Productivity Slowdown and the Secular Stagnation Hypothesis

Patrizio Pagano and Massimo Sbracia

Abstract The recent dismal productivity growth in the U.S. and in the global economy has been seen as evidence of a potential return to a period of secular stagnation. Focusing on the U.S.—a proxy for the frontier economy—we consider a standard decomposition of the different sources of post-World War II growth of GDP per capita, and review existing projections. In the next 20–50 years, lower contributions of hours worked and education will negatively affect U.S. economic growth. However, total factor productivity—which some warn will also continue to stagnate—will be key. After showing that similar warnings have been issued after all deep recessions, we argue that such pessimistic predictions were consistently misguided—not because they were built on erroneous theories or data, nor because they failed to predict the discovery of new technologies, but because they underestimated the potential of the technologies that already existed. These findings suggest that we should not make the same mistake today by undervaluing the future effects of current information technology.

1 Introduction

At the IMF Research Conference in November 2013, Lawrence Summers delivered a speech in which he suggested that *secular stagnation* might be "the defining issue of our age" (Summers 2013). Following those remarks, secular stagnation is now at

---

This is a revised and updated version of Pagano and Sbracia (2014). We thank Pietro Catte, Alberto Locarno and Roberto Piazza for comments. Any errors are ours alone. The views expressed in this paper are those of the authors and do not necessarily reflect those of the Bank of Italy or the World Bank. E-mail: ppagano@worldbank.org, massimo.sbracia@bancaditalia.it.

P. Pagano · M. Sbracia (✉)
Bank of Italy, Rome, Italy
e-mail: massimo.sbracia@bancaditalia.it

P. Pagano
World Bank, Washington DC, USA
e-mail: ppagano@worldbank.org

L. Ferrara et al. (eds.), *International Macroeconomics in the Wake of the Global Financial Crisis*, Financial and Monetary Policy Studies 46,
https://doi.org/10.1007/978-3-319-79075-6_2

the center stage in both the research and policy agendas. As Eichengreen (2014) put it, however, secular stagnation is like the Rorschach inkblot test: it means different things to different people.

Summers' original argument focuses first on the natural real interest rate, which in his view may have declined to levels in the order of −2 or −3%, and then on aggregate demand, which is depressed as actual interest rates are higher than the natural rate. An alternative approach to explaining low economic activity rates rests on aggregate supply. In particular, several studies have recently hypothesized that productivity and potential growth in the U.S. may have come to a halt.[1] Some of these studies recall that the world economy stagnated for many centuries until the Industrial Revolution and question the assumption that economic growth can persist forever, predicting a sharp deceleration of productivity and a return to stagnation. The focus of these studies is the United States, the country that has been identified with the world technology frontier since the early twentieth century.[2] In this chapter, we review these recent studies as well as other existing projections, discussing their implications for future long-run economic growth in the U.S.[3]

For insights into the long-run prospects, we examine the *sources of U.S. GDP per capita growth* in the post-World War II period—which is equal to an average annual rate of 2.2%—and review existing projections about future growth rates. Gordon (2012, 2014) predicts that the contribution of *total factor productivity* (TFP), the main source of U.S. economic expansion, will decline from 1.6% points in 1950–2007 to just 1.0 points over the next 20–50 years. The reasons for this prediction are that the positive effects of the diffusion of information and communication technology (ICT) seem to have already peaked; in fact, TFP has decelerated in the last ten years and no other major breakthrough is in sight. GDP per capita will also be negatively affected by other *transitory factors* that are expected to slow down, especially the total number of hours worked and the accumulation of skills. The contribution of these factors, equal to 0.5% points in the post-war period, could become nil in the period until 2060, as a result of baby boomers' retirement, the approaching plateau of years of schooling, and the rising relative cost of higher education. Overall, the lower contributions of TFP and transitory factors imply that the growth of GDP per capita will halve, to 1.1%.

This gloomy prediction seems to be broadly confirmed by other projections. In particular, the fading contribution of the transitory factors defined above is in line with the most recent forecasts based on the findings of Jorgenson et al. (2005) and the OECD (2014a). The OECD also endorses a sharp deceleration of TFP, although at a later stage (the period 2030–2060). Annual TFP growth of just around 1% is also consistent with recent models that split TFP into research intensity (a function

[1] See, for example, Byrne et al. 2013, Cowen (2011), Gordon (2012, 2014), Lindsey (2013), and Vijg (2011).

[2] These studies also argue that other countries, especially the less developed, may still have room for "catch up growth", even in the case of a slowdown in the technology frontier.

[3] Pagano and Sbracia (2014) also discuss the likelihood that the natural interest rate has declined to the levels suggested by Summers.

of the share of workers employed in research and development) and a size effect.[4] In these models, a deceleration of TFP is the result of lower *population* growth, which implies a lower growth in the number of inventors.

Our review begins by stressing that the most important factors for predicting long-term economic growth are *TFP*, *population* (which also contributes to TFP) and *human capital*. We then examine these factors from a broad historical perspective. We argue that the debate on secular stagnation is a *cyclical question*, which has been raised after every deep and prolonged recession. Revisiting the data and theories considered in the past helps us to understand, with the benefit of hindsight, the reasons pessimistic predictions turned out to be wrong.

In retrospect, it emerges that pessimistic predictions based on these studies were flawed not because they built on erroneous theories or data, nor because they failed to predict the development of new technologies, but because they underestimated the potential of the technologies *that already existed*. This analysis also suggests that pessimism about ICT may be unwarranted: its diffusion among U.S. households and businesses has matched quite closely that of electricity in the early twentieth century. Moreover, current research in the ICT sector is turning to the development of consumption devices, like the shift towards home appliances that occurred in the 1920 and 1930s and that anticipated the economic boom observed after World War II.

Historical experience also suggests a number of issues that should be tackled by future research. First, the key question concerning TFP is whether there are *diminishing returns on research*; that is, whether progress becomes increasingly difficult as technology advances. The fact that, historically, the number of patents granted could scarcely keep pace with population growth has often been interpreted as evidence of diminishing returns (see, for example, Merton 1935, or Griliches 1990). This is, however, still a very open issue. *The long-run stability of the growth rate of U.S. GDP per capita since 1870 does not allow us to rule out that technological progress has a "fractal quality"*. In other words, it may well be that the probability of increases does not depend on the TFP level. Interestingly, the Pareto distribution, which is often used to describe productivities in the cross-section of firms, has exactly this property. We suggest, then, that the distribution of productivities across time and across firms should be analyzed jointly.

Second, the relevant population for TFP growth, i.e. the people who can push the technology frontier outward, no longer coincides with the U.S. labor force, as suggested by many indicators (such as the rise in the share of U.S. patents granted to foreign residents). Thus it is worth exploring *the extent to which future TFP growth is likely to benefit from the integration of emerging countries into the global economy*.

Third, the evolution of human capital, usually proxied by the average number of years of schooling and workers' experience, is apparently more worrisome. In the short run, the increasing relative cost of higher education is making it less affordable.

[4]See, in particular, Kremer (1993), Jones (1995a, 2002), and Kortum (1997). In these models, a higher population growth (size effect) translates into a higher growth rate of potential inventors and, in turn, a higher growth of TFP.

In the long run, its accumulation is bounded from above: work experience is limited by the retirement age, and years of schooling by the fact that well before retiring, students must leave school to repay education costs. Of these two problems, rising education costs could be addressed by a variety of public policies, but also by private initiatives, such as the recent proliferation of Internet-based educational resources. One issue that we discuss and suggest for future research is *whether human capital can grow even if the average years of schooling and work experience remain constant.* In fact, human capital could be accumulated by *raising the quality of education (intensive margin) as well as the varieties of knowledge (extensive margin).* If this were the case, human capital could keep contributing to economic growth over and above the mere number of years of schooling and work experience.

The rest of the chapter is organized as follows. In Sect. 2 we review the sources of U.S. GDP per capita in the post-war period and discuss existing projections about their future evolution. Since it emerges that the most important source of U.S. economic growth is TFP, a variable whose ultimate determinants have not been spelled out, Sect. 3 briefly reviews models that explain its growth and discusses their implications. Section 4 is central to our analysis and examines the factors that emerged as the most important for long-term economic growth from an historical perspective. Section 5 concludes.

2 Sources of Post-war U.S. Growth

The growth rate of U.S. real GDP per capita has been very stable since the end of the nineteenth century (Fig. 1, left panel). This finding, together with other stylized facts (such as the absence of a trend in the capital-output ratio), supports the view that the U.S. economy is on a long-run balanced-growth path. The apparent lack of persistent variations in the growth rate despite the many changes that should have altered it (such as the sharp increase in R&D intensity, examined in Sect. 3 below) has also been used to argue in favor of exogenous growth models and against more recent endogenous growth models (Jones 1995b).[5] Therefore, it makes sense to start our analysis by considering the implications of a standard exogenous growth model, while a discussion of some insights from alternative models is deferred to Sect. 3.

Assume that total output produced at time t, Y_t, is given by

$$Y_t = A_t^{\sigma} \cdot K_t^{\alpha} \cdot H_t^{1-\alpha} , \tag{1}$$

where A_t is TFP, σ is a positive parameter, K_t is physical capital, $\alpha \in (0, 1)$ is the share of physical capital in value added, and H_t is the stock of human capital. The

[5] Jones (1995b) gave the following example (suggested by David Weil, who, in turn, credits Lawrence Summers): an economist living in the year 1929, who fits a simple linear trend to the natural log of GDP per capita of the United States from 1880 to 1929 in an attempt to forecast current GDP per capita would make a remarkably precise prediction. At the end of the 1980s, the forecast would fall short by less than 5%.

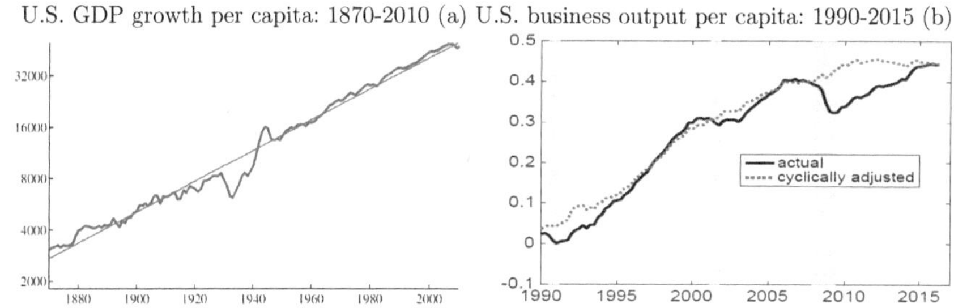

Fig. 1 U.S. economic growth. **a** Annual data; 2009 dollars; log scale. **b** Quarterly data. The solid line is the log of business output per person (i.e. the geometric average of GDP and gross domestic income, excluding government, household, and nonprofit production), normalized to 0in 1991; the dashed line cyclically adjusts those data, following Fernald (2014) and Fernald et al. (2017). *Sources* Bureau of Economic Analysis, Maddison (2008), Fernald and Jones (2014)

last variable has the following standard expression:

$$H_t = L_t h_t \ , \text{with } h_t = \exp(\theta s_t) \ , \tag{2}$$

where L_t is the total number of hours worked, h_t is human capital per hour worked, s_t is the amount of time spent accumulating human capital (usually proxied by the average number of years of schooling and workers' experience), and $\theta > 0$ is the Mincerian return to education. From (1), we can write GDP per capita as:

$$\frac{Y_t}{P_t} = \frac{L_t}{P_t} \cdot A_t^{\sigma/(1-\alpha)} \cdot \left(\frac{K_t}{Y_t}\right)^{\alpha/(1-\alpha)} \cdot h_t \ , \tag{3}$$

where P_t is total population.

Using (3), the growth rate of GDP per capita can be decomposed into the growth rates of its four main components: the *employment ratio* (hours worked over total population), *total factor productivity*, the *capital-output ratio*, and *human capital per hour worked*. A quantification for the period 1950–2007 is reported in Eq. (4) using data gathered by Fernald and Jones (2014); in this equation, we denote the growth rates of GDP per capita ($y_t = Y_t/P_t$), the employment ratio ($e_t = L_t/P_t$), TFP (A_t), capital output ($k_t = K_t/Y_t$), and human capital per hour worked (h_t) with, respectively, $\dot{y}$, $\dot{e}$, $\dot{a}$, $\dot{k}$, and $\dot{h}$:

$$\begin{array}{ccccccccc} \dot{y} & & \dot{e} & & \frac{\sigma}{1-\alpha}\dot{a} & & \frac{\alpha}{1-\alpha}\dot{k} & & \dot{h} \\ 2.2\% & = & 0.1 & + & 1.6 & + & 0.0 & + & 0.4 \\ \scriptstyle(100\%) & & \scriptstyle(6\%) & & \scriptstyle(74\%) & & \scriptstyle(0\%) & & \scriptstyle(19\%) \end{array} \cdot \tag{4}$$

Equation (4) shows that between 1950 and 2007 GDP per capita grew at an annual rate of 2.2%. The exogenous growth rate of TFP has been by far the most important factor, increasing at a rate of 1.6% per year and accounting for about 75% of U.S. economic development in the post-war period.[6] Human capital, measured by years of schooling and workers' experience, contributed almost 20%, growing at an annual rate of 0.4%. The contribution of the employment ratio was small (6%), as this variable grew at a rate of just 0.1% per year. Physical capital increased at the same rate as output; hence, its contribution to the growth of GDP per capita has been nil.[7]

The view that U.S. economic growth will continue to be a straight line (on a log scale) even after the 2008-09 crisis has been recently challenged by Fernald et al. (2017). Using a cyclically-adjusted measure of business output per person (i.e. a geometric average of GDP and gross domestic income, excluding government, household, and nonprofit production), they find that economic growth ceased to take place as a straight line in the mid-2000s and rose much more slowly thereafter (Fig. 1, right panel). In the following section, we review existing projections about the four determinants of the growth rate of GDP per capita, in order to shed some light on these two views about U.S. growth.

2.1 *Total Factor Productivity*

In two recent papers, Gordon (2012, 2014) warns about a possible decline in TFP growth. Taking a very long-run perspective, he recalls that the Industrial Revolution was preceded by several centuries of stagnation, in which the growth rates of GDP per capita and of TFP were almost nil. In particular, Gordon (2012) focuses on GDP growth per capita in the *frontier economy*, which is identified with the U.K. from 1300 to 1906, and with the U.S. thereafter. Noting that growth almost stagnated from 1300 to about 1750, at about 0.2% per year, he then identifies three key phases of the Industrial Revolution[8]:

- In the first phase, the annual growth rate of GDP per capita gradually rose from 0.2% (before the year 1750) to almost 1% at the end of the nineteenth century. In

[6]The parameter α is calibrated at 0.32. An estimate of σ is not needed, since the contribution of $\sigma\dot{a}/(1-\alpha)$ is obtained as a residual.

[7]An alternative decomposition of output per capita considers *capital per worker* instead of the *capital-output ratio* (i.e. $y_t = e_t \cdot A_t \cdot (K_t/L_t)^{\alpha} \cdot h_t^{1-\alpha}$). As capital per worker increased significantly between 1950 and 2007, while the capital-output ratio remained broadly constant, this alternative decomposition suggests a somewhat smaller role for TFP. Although any growth accounting exercise is arbitrary, we prefer the one reported in Eq. (3), because it focuses more closely on the sources of economic growth that, in these models, are supposed to be "autonomous", i.e. TFP and human capital. In endogenous growth frameworks such as the AK-model, instead, physical capital is also an autonomous source of economic growth (see Sect. 3).

[8]According to other studies, economic stagnation dates back at least to the end of the Roman Empire, as shown by the fact that the standard of living in ancient Rome was similar to that of Europe in the eighteenth century (Temin 2006).

this period, the most important innovations were the steam engine and the railroads, which were developed between 1750 and 1830, although their economic effects peaked after about 150 years.

- In the second phase, GDP growth per capita rose to a record-high annual rate of 2.5% during the 1960s. The main inventions characterizing this phase were the internal combustion engine and electricity. They were developed between 1870 and 1900, but it took about 100 years before their full effects fed through to the economy.
- The third phase took off with the invention of the computer and the Internet revolution, from 1960 onwards. Their impact on TFP peaked in the decade between 1995 and 2005, when GDP growth per capita averaged 1.8%, before declining thereafter.

Gordon's projections draw on the fact that the effects of ICT on TFP seem to have already peaked and no other major breakthrough is in sight. In particular, he claims that research efforts are currently focused on the development of consumption devices (mostly in the areas of entertainment and communication), rather than on labor-saving innovations. Other findings corroborate this analysis. For example, the decline in the price index for ICT equipment, which ranged between −10 and −15% per year in the mid-1990s, attenuated thereafter, and in 2012 ICT prices barely fell at all. This result is presumably due to a sharp slowdown in TFP growth. Data from the National Income and Product Accounts (NIPA) also show that the declining trend in computer prices has attenuated; similarly, the more recent estimates of quality-adjusted computer prices carried out by Byrne and Corrado (2016) confirm that even though the discrepancy with official prices has grown in recent years, the fall in computer prices is slowing down (Fig. 2).

Based on these findings, Gordon (2014) projects that future TFP growth will fluctuate around the same average rate it has recorded since 1972, which is 0.6% points lower than the annual growth rate observed in the post-World War II period. This view is apparently shared by many others (see, inter alia, Cowen 2011; Vijg 2011; Fernald 2015), including international organizations such as the OECD. In projecting long-run economic growth, the OECD (2014a) predicts that TFP growth will be temporarily equal to 1.7% in the period 2012–2030 and that it will then decline to 1.1% in the subsequent 30 years.

2.2 *Human Capital*

Human capital accumulation has been a significant contributor to U.S. economic growth. The main factor behind its increase is the exceptional rise in the years spent in school by U.S. residents. Overall, the average number of years of schooling completed by Americans aged at least 25 years old rose by about two-thirds between 1900 and 2010, from 8 to almost 14 years (Fig. 3, panel *a*).

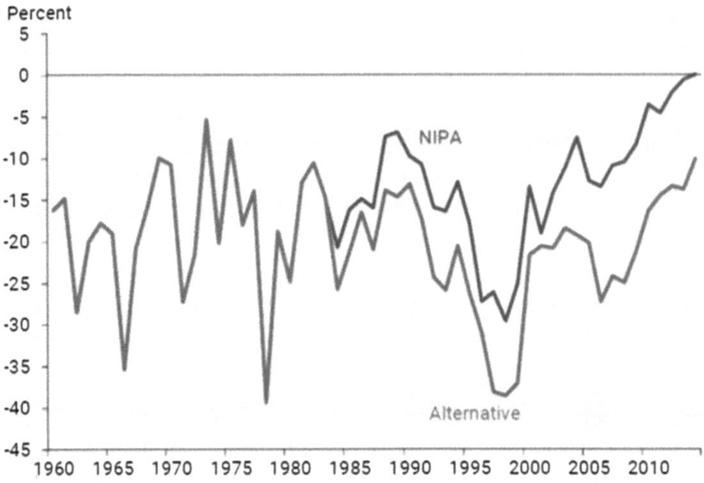

Fig. 2 Computer and peripheral price inflation. Annual growth rate; percentages; quarterly data. Computer price inflation from the National Income and Product Accounts ("NIPA") and from Byrne and Corrado (2016) ("alternative"). *Source* National Income and Product Accounts, Byrne and Corrado (2016), Byrne et al. (2017)

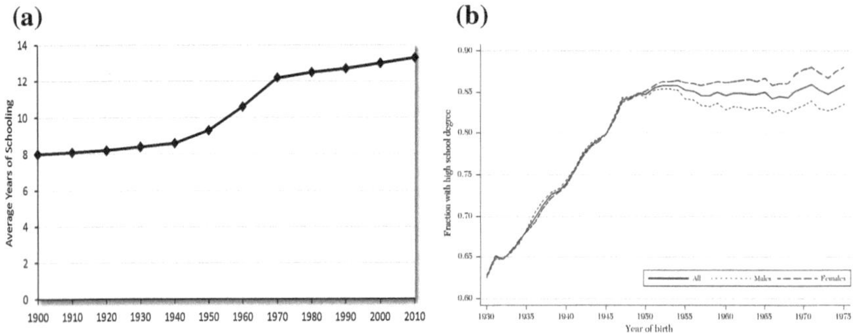

Fig. 3 Average years of schooling and high school completion rates. **a** Annual data. **b** Average years of schooling of U.S. residents aged 25 and older. High school completion rates by birth cohort: 1930–1975. *Sources* Lindsey (2013) and Acemoglu and Autor (2012), based on U.S. census data

Educational attainments, however, seem to be close to a plateau. Consider, for example, the ratio of high-school graduates to 18-year-olds. This ratio, which was only 6% in 1900, had climbed to about 80% by 1970[9]; very recent estimates, however, find that the share of 18-year-olds with high-school diplomas flattened in the

[9]Goldin and Katz (2008) report a U.S. high school graduation rate equal to 77% in 1970, while Heckman and LaFontaine (2010) find a rate of 81%. As noted by Murnane (2013), estimates of graduation rates are sensitive to the choice of the data source and to the treatment of recent immigrants, and General Educational Development (GED) certificates. The GED program, in particular, is a test designed to certify the possession of high-school-level education. It was started as a small-

subsequent 30 years (Murnane 2013). U.S. census cohort data confirm that the share of high-school graduates does not show visible signs of improvement since the class of people born in the early 1950s (Fig. 3, panel *b*). The picture is similar for college attainment rates. The ratio of college graduates to 23-year-olds, which was only 2% in 1900, had risen to 24% by 1980; by 2010, it had risen to 30%, but only thanks to the strong increase in women's attainment rates, while for men it remained at roughly the same level as in 1980.

Many authors believe that the contribution of human capital accumulation to U.S. economic growth will slow considerably in the next few decades. One obvious reason is that graduation rates cannot grow above 100%, so the sharp rise observed since the start of the twentieth century and continuing after World War II cannot go on forever. In addition, education cannot last people's entire lives: at one point, students must leave school and start working to pay back schooling costs and take advantage of their education. From this perspective, the current maximum years of schooling (those achieved by doctoral and post-doctoral students) appear to be close to a ceiling and, as a consequence, average years of schooling may have limited margins for further increase in the U.S. Furthermore, some graduation rates including those for high school, already seem very close to a physiological maximum, despite being still below 100%. For example, Murnane (2013) finds that high-school graduation reached almost 85% in 2010 and, as Heckman and LaFontaine (2010) also point out, a significant portion of the remaining 15% is explained by the higher dropout rates among the military, minorities (blacks and Hispanics), as well as by young people sent to prison.[10]

Another reason for the possible slowdown of human capital accumulation is that since the early 1970s the cost of university education has more than tripled with respect to the overall rate of inflation, making enrollment inaccessible for many young people. Increasing difficulties in finding college-level jobs after graduation are also making college tuition and fees less affordable. Gordon (2014) suggests that although a college degree still pays off in terms of higher income and lower risk of unemployment, about one-fourth of college graduates do not obtain college-level jobs in the first few years after graduation.

According to Jorgenson et al. (2005), the annual growth rate of human capital due to both increased schooling and the rising level of worker experience will decline to about 0.1% in 2010–2020 (from 0.4% per year in 1950–2007)—almost a complete halt.[11] Similarly, the OECD (2014a) projects that human capital will increase at an annual rate of just 0.1% in 2012–2030 and by 0.2% in the following 30 years.

---

scale program for military veterans and has now become a substitute for high school graduation, especially among minorities, as it is generally accepted for college admissions.

[10] A significant portion is also explained by the gender gap, which reflects the higher graduation rates of females common to most OECD countries.

[11] The projections on human capital accumulation, based on the methodology of Jorgenson et al. (2005), were updated by Dale Jorgenson in 2012 and reported in Byrne et al. (2013) and Gordon (2014).

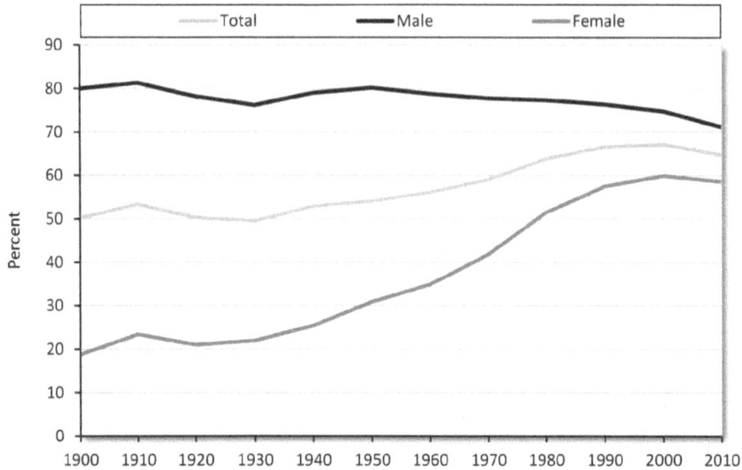

Fig. 4 Labor force participation rate by gender. *Source* Lindsey (2013), based on *Historical statistics of the United States*

2.3 Employment Ratio

The rise in total number of hours worked per capita accounts for 6% of U.S. post-war economic growth. This figure is the result of different trends, dependent on demographic sub-groups.

The first and most important factor supporting the rising employment ratio has been the movement of women into the labor force, which occurred mostly between 1950 and the early 2000s (Fig. 4).[12] The female participation rate rose from less than 20–60% during the twentieth century, before declining somewhat in the last 10 years. The baby boom, which started in 1946 and lasted almost 20 years, was the second factor supporting the growth of the labor force, especially between the 1970s and the early 2000s when baby boomers were in their prime working years (aged 25–54) and the participation rate reached its highest level.

On the other hand, the growth of the employment ratio was dampened by a reduction in the participation rate of men, which started as early as 1950, and—most

[12]As argued by Gordon (2012), innovations such as running water and indoor plumbing were key determinants of this phenomenon. Before their diffusion, in fact, water for laundry, cooking and indoor chamber pots was hauled by housewives. For example, Strasser (1982) reports that in 1885 the average North Carolina housewife walked 148 miles per year carrying 35 tons of water. Running water and indoor plumbing spread into all American houses between 1890 and 1930. Further research, however, would be needed to explain why these inventions, which were already present in Mesopotamia and Egypt over 2,500 years BC and were extensively used in the Roman Empire, did not spread to North America until at the beginning of the early twentieth century. In other words, one cannot exclude a reverse causality issue: running water and indoor plumbing, which were introduced 4,000 years earlier, perhaps spread to North America in the twentieth century because only at that time were women ready to move into the labor force.

importantly—by the decrease in the number of hours worked. The average number of weekly hours worked, equal to about 60 in 1890, had fallen to 37 in 1950, ending up at less than 33 in 2012.[13]

Thus, as for human capital, which was sustained by the rapid spread of education to all American workers, the employment ratio was sustained by a big "one-time event", namely the participation of women in the labor force. On a balanced-growth path the contribution of this variable should be nil, but since 2008 baby boomers have started to retire and this demographic trend is expected to continue to negatively affect the employment ratio over the next two decades. As a consequence, even if participation rates were to stabilize for any age, class, and gender, the retirement of baby boomers would make the size of the labor force decrease relative to the total population, resulting in a negative trend for the employment ratio over the next two decades.

According to the OECD (2014a), the employment ratio, which had already started to diminish before the Great Recession (at an annual rate of −0.2% in 2000–2007), will decline further in 2012–2030, at a rate of −0.3% per year. In particular, the participation rate of people aged 15 and older is forecast to decline by almost 4% points, to 58.5%. The employment ratio is projected to recover somewhat in 2030–2060, when it will grow at 0.1% per year.

2.4 *Capital-Output Ratio*

The contribution of the capital-output ratio to U.S. economic growth has been nil over the post-World War II period. However, many economists have recently started to fear that this contribution could become negative, given that investment rates have declined substantially since the Great Recession (see, for example, Lindsey 2013, and BIS 2014, OECD 2014b). Low investment is also considered worrisome because less physical capital could imply a limited diffusion of new technologies among firms, with a negative effect on both labor productivity and TFP growth.

After collapsing in 2008-2009 to the lowest values since World War II, the share of *nominal* investment over *nominal* GDP—the indicator that is most often used for cross-country comparisons—stood at just 16.3% in the first quarter of 2017 (Fig. 5). This is among the lowest levels observed since the 1970s during business cycle expansions.

However, this indicator is biased due to the well-known declining trend of capital good prices relative to overall prices (Gordon 1990). The share of *real* investment in *real* GDP—which is not affected by relative prices—was equal to 17.2% in the first quarter of 2017 (Fig. 5). This is the same value that the OECD (2014b) estimates as the steady-state level of the real investment-to-GDP ratio. Thus, the slow growth of the real investment share during the economic recovery seems to be entirely

[13]The estimate for the number of hours worked in 1890 refers to the manufacturing sector; this is a slightly higher figure than in other sectors, such as construction and railroads (www.eh.net).

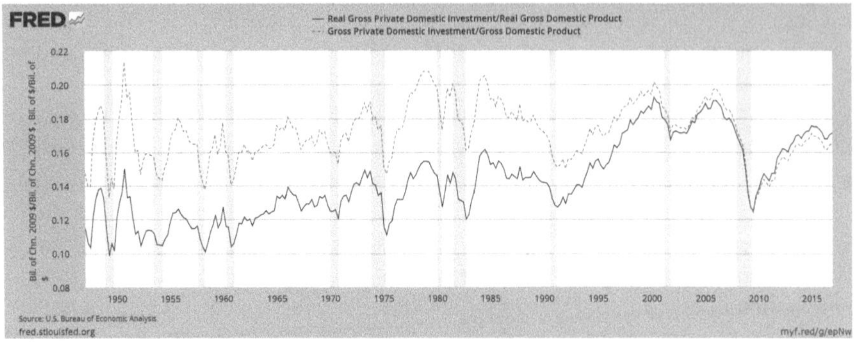

Fig. 5 U.S. investment shares. Real investment as a share of real GDP and nominal investment as a share of nominal GDP. Quarterly data, seasonally adjusted annual rate. *Source* Federal Reserve Bank of St. Louis

ascribable to the severity of the last recession. In fact, the drop in this share during the Great Recession was much larger than for all the previous contractions, equal to almost 7% points against an average drop of less than 3% points in the previous ten recessions. Even without resorting to a precise statistical analysis, the current rise in the investment share does not appear to be less steep than in the past expansionary phases of the business cycle. Thus, the gradual return of the real investment share toward its steady state suggests that the capital-output ratio should not pose an obstacle to long-run labor productivity growth.

The OECD (2014a) projects that the growth of the capital-output ratio will continue to be approximately nil over the next 50 years. The contribution to U.S. economic growth will be marginally positive in 2012–2030 (when it will increase at an annual rate of 0.1%), as physical capital will be rebuilt after the Great Recession, and marginally negative thereafter (−0.1%).

2.5 *Summing Up*

The rise in the employment ratio, human capital accumulation, and the stability of the capital-output ratio contributed 0.5% points to the growth of GDP per capita in the post-war period. According to the OECD (2014a), this contribution could turn negative, at −0.1% points, over the next two decades and then return to positive, at 0.2% points, in 2030–2060. This is in line with Gordon's projection that the contribution of these factors would be nil in the next 20–50 years. Therefore, the growth rate of GDP per capita could be lower by about 0.5% points until 2060.

As Gordon predicts, if the acceleration of technology improvements forecast by the OECD for the period 2012–2030 does not materialize and TFP growth remains equal to the rates observed since 1972 (1.0%, as against 1.6% in 1950–2007), then the growth rate of GDP per capita will be lower by a further 0.6% points. The OECD substantially shares this projection for the period 2030–2060.

Overall, then, GDP per capita could increase at a rate of only 1.1% until 2060, against a rate of 2.2% recorded in 1950–2007.

3 Growth, Research Intensity and Size Effect

The results of the previous section have shown that the most important source of economic growth (in the U.S., but also in most other advanced and developing countries) is TFP, a variable whose dynamic is assumed to be exogenous, estimated as a residual, and whose ultimate determinants have not been spelled out. This is clearly unsatisfactory.[14]

The finding that the search for innovation—as measured by the number of scientists and engineers engaged in research and development (R&D) or by expenditure on R&D—has grown very sharply is another challenge to growth models. For example, the share of U.S. workers employed in R&D, which was 0.25% in 1950, had risen fourfold by the mid-2000s, to 1%.[15] To come to grips with this phenomenon, Jones (2002) assumes that TFP growth has the following functional form:

$$\frac{\dot{A}_t}{A_t} = \beta \cdot \bar{R}_t \cdot A_t^{\phi-1} \tag{5}$$

where $\beta > 0$ is a constant, ϕ a parameter that specifies the returns (decreasing, constant or increasing) on research activity, and $\bar{R}_t$ the number of researchers (where we put a bar to mean that the relevant number of researchers may include foreign researchers, as we explain below). The rationale of Eq. (5) is the following: first, TFP increases because workers employed in R&D develop non-rival ideas on how to organize inputs to produce more output. Because of non-rivalry, income per capita depends on the *total number of ideas* in the economy and not on the *number of ideas per person*. On a balanced-growth path, the number of researchers is a constant share of the labor force; the latter, in turn, is a constant share of total population and, therefore, *the level of TFP depends on the size of the population*. In other words, more population means more potential inventors so that the long run growth of income per

[14]Results from endogenous growth models, which explore the factors that can potentially explain long-run economic growth, are similarly unsatisfactory. These models identify several possible determinants of productivity growth, such as trade openness, government policies, the strength of property rights, competition and regulatory pressures. Permanent changes in these variables, which have frequently occurred throughout U.S. history, should lead to permanent changes in economic growth rates. The theoretical relevance of these changes, however, contrasts with the aforementioned empirical stability of long-run growth.

[15]The increase in the share of researchers for the average of the five largest OECD economies (France, Germany, Japan, U.K. and U.S.) is equally striking: it rose from 0.16% in 1950 to 0.95% in 2007.

capita is driven uniquely by population growth. Second, the growth rate of TFP also depends on the level of TFP, in order to account for potentially non-constant returns to scale in the search for ideas. In particular, $\phi < 1$ ($\phi > 1$) implies diminishing (increasing) returns to the research activity, while $\phi = 1$ implies constant returns.

Simple algebra shows that, if TFP evolves according to Eq. (5), on a constant-growth path the decomposition (3) transforms into:

$$\frac{Y_t}{P_t} = \frac{L_t}{P_t} \cdot \left(\frac{\bar{R}_t}{\bar{L}_t}\right)^{\gamma} \cdot \bar{L}_t^{\gamma} \cdot \left(\frac{K_t}{Y_t}\right)^{\alpha/(1-\alpha)} \cdot h_t \,, \tag{6}$$

where $\gamma = \sigma\,[(1-\phi)\,(1-\alpha)]^{-1}$ and $\bar{L}_t$ is the total number of workers (in terms of heads, while L_t is the number of hours worked). This is the same decomposition as in Eq. (3), except that now, due to (5), the exogenous growth of TFP is split into two terms that together correspond to the stock of ideas. The former is $\bar{R}_t/\bar{L}_t$, which represents *research intensity*, i.e. the strength of the hunt for new ideas. The latter is a *size effect*, measured by the number of workers, which is the denominator of the research intensity.[16]

The relevant researchers—those who can help push the technology frontier outward—do not necessarily live in the U.S. Therefore, $\bar{R}_t$ and $\bar{L}_t$ may refer to researchers and workers who are also in other countries. For example, Jones (2002) assumes that the researchers able to extend the frontiers of knowledge are residents of the five largest OECD countries (France, Germany, Japan, the U.K., and the U.S.).

The growth rate of TFP between 1950 and 2007, equal to 1.6% (Eq. (4)), can thus be decomposed into the growth rate of *research intensity* and the *size effect*. In the following quantification, in which we use data from Fernald and Jones (2014), we retain the same notation as Eq. (4) and we also denote with $\dot{r}$ and $\dot{l}$ the growth rates of, respectively, the share of researchers ($r_t = \bar{R}_t/\bar{L}_t$) and the labor force of the countries where researchers live ($\bar{L}_t$):

$$\begin{array}{ccccc} \frac{\sigma}{1-\alpha}\dot{a} & & \gamma\dot{r} & & \gamma\dot{l} \\ 1.6\% & = & 1.2 & + & 0.4 \\ \scriptstyle(74\%) & & \scriptstyle(54\%) & & \scriptstyle(20\%) \end{array} \,. \tag{7}$$

Equation (7) shows that the exogenous growth rate of TFP, which was equal to 1.6% per year during the period 1950–2007, can be decomposed into a rate of 1.2% due to *research intensity* and of 0.4% due to the *size effect*.[17] The value of γ resulting from the decomposition implies that ϕ is smaller than 1 and, therefore, that there are diminishing returns to scale on research.[18]

---

[16]In Eq. (5), ideas arrive in a deterministic fashion. Kortum (1997) builds a general equilibrium model in which the flow of ideas is stochastic, which yields the same implication that a growing number of researchers generates a constant productivity growth.

[17]We recall that 74% is the share of the contribution of TFP to the overall annual growth of GDP per capita (see Eq. (4)).

[18]Since the parameter σ can be normalized to 1 and given that $\dot{r}$ and $\dot{l}$ are equal to, respectively, 3.1% and 1.1%, it follows that γ is equal to 0.38.

The results reported in Eqs. (4) and (7) highlight that between 1950 and 2007 80% of U.S. economic growth reflected transitory factors. As mentioned above, in these models population rise is the key determinant of long run economic growth; therefore, only the size effect can generate sustainable growth. The employment ratio and research intensity are shares, and as such cannot grow forever. Moreover, as discussed in the previous section, many authors also believe that human capital cannot increase indefinitely. Some of these factors, especially the share of researchers and human capital, may still have margins to increase for some time, but in the very long run, this theory implies that economic growth should revert to the growth rate of the population.

Gordon's projection of an increase of TFP at an annual rate of 1.0% for the next few decades appears consistent with the outlook for research intensity and the size effect. We can assume that research intensity will continue to grow until 2030 at the same rate of 1.8% as the one observed since 1972 (the time period that Gordon labelled the "Third Industrial Revolution")[19]; moreover, census forecast data indicate U.S. labor force annual growth of 0.8% until 2030, which is consistent with the projections of the OECD (2014a). By applying the value of γ derived above, we obtain a prediction for the sum of $\gamma \dot{r}$ and $\gamma \dot{l}$ of 1.0%, which confirms Gordon's projection.

4 Insights from Economic History

The analysis developed in the previous sections has shown that the most important factors to consider in predicting long-term economic growth are *TFP*, *population* (which, in turn, contributes to TFP), and *human capital*. In this section, we examine these factors from a broader historical perspective.

The debate on secular stagnation seems to be, in fact, a *cyclical question*. Figure 6 shows the frequency of mentions of the term "secular stagnation" in books written in English gathered by Google Books and published between 1938 and 2008, which is the last year covered by the dataset. It provides some suggestive evidence that the issue has been raised cyclically, after almost any deep and prolonged recession.[20]

Economic history confirms that this is indeed the case. Among the most famous instances, consider the following examples. In the aftermath of the Long Depression of 1873–1879, Wells (1891) discussed the tendency to pessimism about economic changes that prevailed at his time, even though stagnations only occurred periodically. Following the Great Depression of 1929–1933, Hansen (1938, 1939) introduced the first theory of secular stagnation, which was later resurrected by Summers (2013).

---

[19]This would bring the share of researchers to 1.4% in 2030, which seems a reasonable figure.

[20]The natural continuation of Fig. 6 would be to look for the frequency of the searches of the term "secular stagnation" in Google, which is available from Google Trends. The results, not reported here, would show that the term had an essentially nil number of searches from 2009 to 2013 and then rose sharply until 2015, when it started to decline. Thus, even after the Great Recession, the "prominence" of the issue of secular stagnation has displayed a cyclical behavior similar to that observed in the aftermath of other deep recessions cum slower-than-expected recoveries.

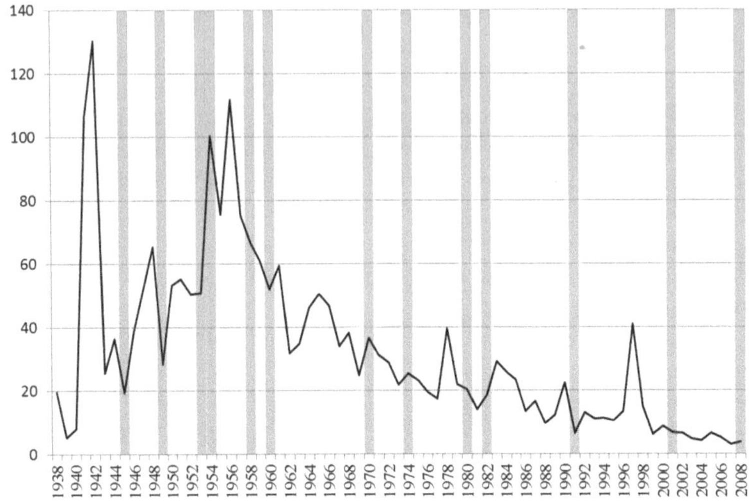

Fig. 6 Mentions of "secular stagnation": 1938–2008. Frequency of mentions of the term "secular stagnation" (case sensitive search) in the books written in English and gathered by Google Books, published from 1938 to 2008. *Source* Google Books Ngram Viewer

As discussed by Sweezy (1943) and as shown in Fig. 6, the debate on the theoretical and empirical premises of secular stagnation started to intensify towards the end of World War II. Thirty years later, Nordhaus (1972) noted the sharp slowdown in productivity during the stagnation of the late 1960s and eary 1970s, predicting a continuation and possibly an intensification of the trend. The issue of productivity slowdown was once again revived in the late 1980s (see Baily and Gordon 1988, and Krugman 1990), on the eve of the sharp acceleration that took place with the ICT revolution.

Given the recurrence of the issue of secular stagnation in economic debates, it may be useful to briefly review the data and arguments analyzed in the past in order to understand why pessimistic predictions turned out to be wrong. As exemplified in particular by the work of Alvin Hansen during the 1930s, the debate has often revolved around the issues of technical change and population growth.[21] Therefore, after revisiting these "older concerns", we turn to one feature that has emerged only more recently—human capital—and examine from a longer-run perspective.[22]

---

[21] Alvin Hansen (1887–1975), often referred to as "the American Keynes" (Nasar 2012), was a professor of economics at Harvard and an influential advisor to the government who helped create the Council of Economic Advisors and the Social Security System. He introduced Keynesian economics in the United States, clarifying its implications (Hansen 1936). He was the mentor of Paul Samuelson, who credited him for inspiring the formalization of the multiplier-accelerator model (Samuelson 1939).

[22] Other factors that have often been identified as posing significant threats to economic growth are pollution and a possible depletion of natural resources (see, for example, the famous study by Meadows et al. 1972, and the criticism by Nordhaus 1992).

4.1 TFP and Population

Many alarming signs identified today are quite similar to those considered by Alvin Hansen in 1938, during the recovery that followed the Great Depression. Like others Hansen was especially worried about the development of two key factors: technical change and population.

As regards technical change, Hansen acknowledged that *inventions* were the main determinants of economic growth and related their development to capital deepening.[23] His worries stemmed from the fact that, in his view, the period 1934–1937 had been a "consumption recovery", with insufficient investment. His analysis was also grounded in the apparent prospects of U.S. industries. In particular, he claimed that the main drivers of growth in the nineteenth century—steel, textiles and railroads—had been exhausted; on the other hand, the newest drivers of innovation—automobiles and the radio—had already become mature.[24]

Population was considered a key determinant of inventions for two reasons: indirectly, because it stimulated capital deepening, and directly, because it "facilitated mass production methods and accelerated the progress of technique". This view, in the tradition of Adam Smith, is very similar to the modern view of Kremer (1993) and Jones (2002), and contrary to the Malthusian theory. Hansen (1939) observed that the population growth rate had halved, and estimated that in the second half of the nineteenth century population growth had contributed to about 60% of the increase in the capital stock.[25] Therefore, he deemed that "a rapid cessation of population growth" could have a strong negative impact on capital formation and TFP. Moreover, in the emerging tradition of Keynesian economics, Hansen was convinced that the combined effect of the decline in population growth and the lack of innovations of significant magnitude were not only the premises of a prolonged stagnation, but also explained the failure of the recovery to reach full employment.[26]

As we know, the stagnation did not materialize. Thus, it may prove useful to review the reasons Hansen's predictions failed in spite of their reliance on sound evidence and arguments: data did support the slowdown of TFP and population, and lower population growth was correctly identified as a factor weakening incentives to innovate. There were, however, a few oversights that led to his conclusions.

The first three oversights concern technology. In particular, first of all *the contribution of electricity to TFP was surprisingly neglected*. Yet, the "electrification

---

[23]Hansen distinguished between *capital deepening* and *capital widening*, depending on whether physical capital grew at a rate, respectively, higher or equal to that of output.

[24]Merton (1935), for example, showed that the number of patents issued for inventions related to the automobile and the radio industry had started to decline in the early 1920s; in the aeroplane industry, the decline had started even earlier, in 1918.

[25]Following similar remarks by Keynes (1937), Hansen (1939) noted that U.S. residents had increased by 16 million during the 1920s (17 million according to the most recently revised data), while in the 1930s the rise was estimated to be in the order of 8 million (9 million using modern data).

[26]Fifty years later, Samuelson formalized this argument in the Keynes-Hansen-Samuelson multiplier-accelerator model of secular stagnation (Samuelson 1988).

of America" was one of the main developments of the early twentieth century (Nye 1990). For example, in 1899 electric lighting was used in a mere 3% of all U.S. residences; in the following two decades, electrification had already reached 50% of all residences and establishments. After 1917, when its cost declined substantially, the diffusion of electricity became almost universal (David 1990). With the wide coverage achieved by electricity, inventors turned to the development of consumer goods: by the 1930s, the commercialization of many home appliances had already begun, although the boom did not occur after World War II. Second, *the assessment of the maturity of the automobile industry turned out to be incorrect.* The production of automobiles increased further after the 1930s and spread to other countries. This phenomenon continued to fuel the growth of inventions into our day: in 2012 the automobile industry was still the third highest-ranking industry for patent generation (preceded only by "telecommunications" and "computers and peripherals"). Third, it is also surprising that *the possibility that television would replace radio was altogether ignored.* Although television was popularized at the New York World Fair in 1939, in the late 1920s its commercialization had already begun. The ancestors of CBS and NBC (WRGB and W2XBS, respectively) started broadcasting in 1928; in 1932 Telefunken sold the first televisions with cathode-ray tubes in Germany, soon followed by other manufacturers in France and the U.K.; and the BBC began broadcasting in 1936.

The fourth oversight regards population. *The annual rate of growth of U.S. residents turned out to be less predictable than previously thought*: after averaging only 0.6% during the entire recovery of 1934–1937, in 1941 it was already above 1.0%; once the baby boom started in 1947, population grew at annual rates of almost 2.0% for twenty years.

Hansen's example, in which sound reasonining nevertheless led to flawed conclusions demonstrates how it is far easier to underestimate the potential of *existing* technologies than to predict the emergence of *new* technologies. This suggests that pessimism about ICT may be unwarranted. *The spread of computers among U.S. households and businesses has matched that of electricity quite closely*: in less than four decades since the early 1970s, computers have entered almost all U.S. houses and workplaces, just as electricity did at the start of the twentieth century. Moreover, research in the ICT sector is currently turning to the development of consumption devices, resembling the shift towards home appliances that occurred in the 1920 and 1930s and that anticipated the economic boom observed after World War II.[27]

The skepticism about the contribution of ICT to TFP growth and its possible maturity also seems unjustified. As shown by Crafts (2002), the contribution of ICT to capital deepening and TFP growth in the U.S. in 1974–2000 was greater than the early contributions of the two other main general-purpose technologies developed during the Industrial Revolution, i.e. electricity (for the U.S. in 1899–1929) and steam

[27] The commercialization of most home appliances—including refrigerators, washing machines, televisions, air conditioning, electric vacuum cleaners, electric toasters, etc.—started in the 1920 and 1930s (see Vijg 2011, for a list of inventions).

(for the U.K. in 1780–1860).[28] Moreover, long periods of productivity slowdown occurred frequently during past expansionary phases, such as in 1890–1913, after the Great Depression, and between the mid-1970s and mid-1990s. After these phases of lower growth, the U.S. economy has always entered periods of sharp upturn in productivity. While one cannot take for granted that such an acceleration will happen again, the current weakness of TFP growth is likely due to a process of resource reallocation across sectors induced by the Great Recession that is still incomplete, and that may turn out to be only temporary. Finally, we should not forget that general-purpose technologies have always taken many decades to exert their full effects on the economy.[29] The technologies, tools and resources with the highest economic impact may have already been invented, but it may take time before they change our lives.[30]

More generally, *the key question concerning TFP is whether there are diminishing returns on research activity*; that is, whether making progress becomes increasingly difficult as technology advances. The fact that, historically, the number of patents granted could scarcely keep pace with the growth of population or with R&D expenditure has often been interpreted as evidence of diminishing returns (see, for example, Merton 1935, or Griliches 1990). This is, however, still a very open issue. *The stability of the growth rate of GDP per capita in the long run does not allow us to rule out that technological progress has, rather, a "fractal quality"*. In other words, it may well be that the probability of TFP increases does not depend on its level. Incidentally, it is worth noting that the Pareto distribution, which is often used to describe productivities in the cross-section of firms, has exactly this fractal property.[31] The alternative paths of TFP represented in Fig. 7 seem equally plausible, and

---

[28]Crafts (2002) estimates that ICT has been responsible for 30% of the overall growth of GDP per capita in its first 15 years and 55% in the following 10 years. The contribution of electricity was broadly similar (28% in the first 30 years and 47% in the following 10 years), while that of steam was much smaller.

[29]As Joel Mokyr (2013) put it, 50 years after its invention the steam engine was probably viewed as a machine that "made a lot of noise, emitted a lot of smoke and stench, and pumped some water out of few coal mines". Similarly, as remarked by Paul David in 1990 (rephrasing Robert Solow's famous quip), many observers living in 1900 might have asserted that electric dynamos were "everywhere but in the productivity statistics".

[30]Brynjolfsson and McAfee (2014) discuss several promising innovations, including recent developments in robotics, 3D-printers, self-driving cars, computer-aided diagnosis in medicine, possible offsprings from genome sequencing, etc. Gordon (2014) and Vijg (2011), however, question the economic impact of most of them.

[31]A truncated Pareto distribution is still, in fact, a Pareto distribution. To understand why this matters, assume, for example, that the TFP evolves stochastically, following a Pareto distribution; namely, $A_t \sim Pareto(1, \theta)$, where t is time (with A_t i.i.d.). Suppose, also, that technological progress is an increase in the level of TFP from a value of at least a' to a value of at least $a'' > a'$. Then, the probability that technological progress occurs is $\Pr\left(A_{t+1} > a'' | A_t > a'\right) = \left(a'/a''\right)^{\theta}$. As a consequence, raising a' and a'' proportionally does not change the probability that technological progress will occur.

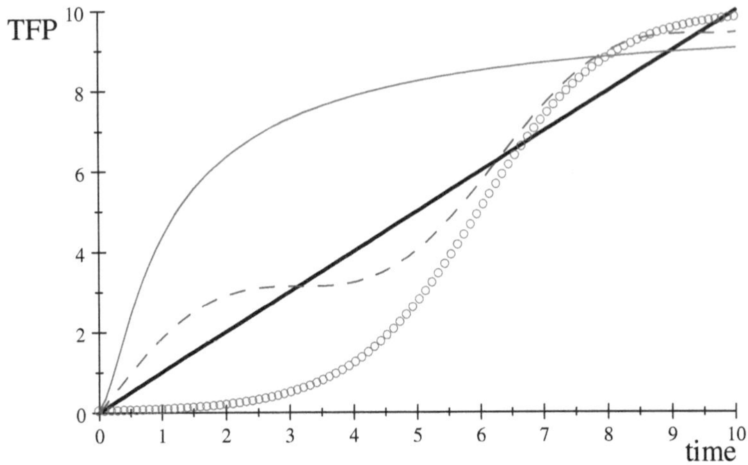

Fig. 7 Alternative paths of TFP growth. Thick solid line: constant returns to scale in the research activity; thin solid line: decreasing returns to scale; dotted line: first increasing and then decreasing returns to scale; dashed line: "variable" returns to scale

more research is needed to explore the properties of both the evolution of aggregate TFP over time as well as those of TFP in the cross-section of individual firms.[32]

The experience of the twentieth century suggests that in the medium to long term population growth rates may fluctuate in a rather unpredictable way. More importantly, the theory presented in Sect. 3 implies that *the relevant population for TFP growth is the people who can actually help push the technology frontier outward.* Many indicators, such as the increase in the share of U.S. patents granted to foreign residents, signal that this population no longer coincides with the U.S. labor force. Thus, the magnitude of the size effect for future TFP growth is likely to be magnified by *the integration of emerging countries into the global economy and their future contributions to the technology frontier.*

4.2 Human Capital

Although the improvement of workers' skills as a source of economic progress goes back at least to Adam Smith, it was not until after World War II that neoclassical models of growth incorporated human capital. From this perspective, the cornerstone in the quantification of human capital is Mincer's (1958, 1974) theoretical and empirical analysis of wages. As a result of his work, human capital is still measured using data on schooling and workers' experience, as in Eq. (2).

[32]Finicelli et al. (2014) show, for both closed and open economies, that aggregate TFP is a specific moment (whose order depends on consumer preferences) of the distribution of TFP across firms.

To the extent that schooling and experience are the most relevant factors for workers' skills, however, two main problems emerge (see also Sect. 2). In the short run, the increasing (relative) costs of higher education are making it less affordable, thereby hampering human capital. In the long run, human capital accumulation is bounded from above: work experience is limited by the retirement age, years of schooling by the fact that well before the retirement age students must leave school to repay education costs.

The problem of rising education costs could be effectively addressed by a variety of policies. In this case projections for human capital growth could turn out to be pessimistic if they do not take this problem into account. For example, the "*higher education initiative*" of the U.S. government aims to keep costs down and make college education affordable. But private initiatives are also helping to address the problem. One important and currently emerging phenomenon is *the rapid proliferation of Internet-based educational resources*. In particular, lecture videos and other online teaching tools are making education almost "non-rivalrous". Acemoglu et al. (2014) have recently built a theoretical model to understand the possible consequences of this phenomenon. Their model predicts that in the future lectures could be provided by a handful of "superstar global teachers", while local teachers, freed from lecturing, would be allocated to other complementary activities. An important result of this model is a "democratization of education", in which high-quality educational resources will be more equally distributed.

The main question that arises in the long-run is whether measuring human capital by means of average number of years of schooling and work experience is still appropriate. One issue that also affects the measurement of physical capital concerns the quantification of the *quality of capital (i.e. its intensive margin)*. Analyses of data on school resources and test scores as proxies for the quality of education—used to augment quantity-based measures—have not produced conclusive evidence. For example, according to Caselli (2005) these augmented measures of human capital are not helpful in explaining cross-country income differences. On the contrary, the World Development Report 2018 (World Bank 2017) shows that there is a strong relationship between test scores and economic growth even after controlling for years of schooling. The Report also suggests that providing basic cognitive skills to all students could significantly boost incomes, especially in developing countries.

An important issue that has been neglected in the economic literature on human capital is the explosion of specializations in all fields of knowledge. It would be worth examining, therefore, whether human capital can grow by extending *the varieties of knowledge (extensive margin)*, even if the average years of schooling remain constant. In fact, it is possible that the competencies of college graduates 60 years ago were more similar to each other than they are today, given the much higher numbers of faculty, types of college degree and university courses that are currently offered. Thus, even though the average years of schooling for college graduates is the same as 60 years ago, a larger variety of competencies in newer college graduates may provide an additional boost to economic growth. Given this, human capital could keep contributing to economic growth over and above the mere number of years of schooling. More generally, one could question the practice of measuring the aggregate stock of human capital simply as the sum of individual stocks. Further research is needed to understand if the aggregate stock of human capital depends on the varieties of knowledge. We also need to understend whether the impact of human capital on economic growth depends also on the way individuals interact with each other.[33]

5 Conclusion

Recent studies have conjectured that the U.S. economy may soon return to a phase of secular stagnation. There is some consensus on the fact that in the next 20–50 years the growth of U.S. GDP per capita—equal to an average annual rate of 2.2%—will decrease due to "transitory factors" (mainly education and hours worked). The contribution of these factors, equal to 0.5% points in the post-war period, could become nil in the years ahead up until 2060, as a result of the retirement of baby boomers, the approaching plateau in years of schooling, and thw rising relative costs of higher education. Some studies add that TFP could also sharply decelerate, as the effects of ICT seem to have already peaked, TFP has already started to slow down, and no other major breakthrough is in sight. Its contribution to GDP per capita could decline from 1.6% points in 1950–2007 to just 1.0 points over the next few decades. Thus, due to slowing TFP and fading transitory factors GDP per capita growth may halve, increasing at a rate of just 1.1%.

However, the debate on secular stagnation seems to be a cyclical question, which has been raised after every deep and prolonged recession. Revisiting past arguments suggests that pessimistic predictions turned out to be wrong not because they built on erroneous theories or data, nor because they failed in predicting new technologies, but because they underestimated the potential of technologies that already existed. This suggests that we should not make the same mistake today and undervalue the potential effects of information technology.

Historical experience also suggests that future research should deepen the analysis on a number of issues including: (i) the properties of TFP across time and across firms, to examine if there are diminishing returns to research or whether technological progress has a "fractal quality", so that the probability of increases does not depend on the TFP level; (ii) the extent to which the integration of emerging countries into the global economy can contribute to the growth of the world technology frontier; (iii) the extent to which human capital can grow even if years of schooling and work experience remain constant, by extending the quality (intensive margin) and the varieties (extensive margin) of knowledge.

[33]See Lucas (1988). Studies focusing on the importance of social capital—defined as the expected collective benefit derived from the way in which individuals interact, cooperate, and trust one another—express a similar view.

References

Acemoglu D, Autor D (2012) What does human capital do? A review of goldin and katz's the race between education and technology. J Econ Lit 50:426–463
Acemoglu D, Laibson D, List JA (2014) Equalizing superstars: the internet and the democratization of education. NBER working paper, 19851
Baily MN, Gordon RJ (1988) The productivity slowdown, measurement issues, and the explosion of computer power. Brook Pap Econ Act 2:347–431
BIS (2014). Recent developments in the global economy. Bank for International Settlements, January
Brynjolfsson E, McAfee A (2014) The second machine age. Norton, New York
Byrne DM, Oliner SD, Sichel DE (2013) Is the information technology revolution over? Int Product Monit 25:20–36
Byrne DM, Corrado C (2016) ICT Asset prices: marshaling evidence into new measures. The conference board working paper, vol 6
Byrne DM, Fernald JG, Reinsdorf M (2017) Does growing mismeasurement explain disappointing growth? Economic letter, vol 4. Federal Reserve Bank of San Francisco
Caselli F (2005) Accounting for cross-country income differences. In: Aghion P, Durlauf S (eds) Handbook of economic growth. Elsevier, North Holland
Cowen T (2011) The great stagnation: how america ate all the low-hanging fruit of modern history, got sick, and will (Eventually) feel better. Dutton, New York
Crafts N (2002) The solow productivity paradox in historical perspective. CEPR discussion paper, vol 314
David P (1990) The dynamo and the computer: an historical perspective on the modern productivity paradox. Am Econ Rev 80:355–361
Eichengreen B (2014) Secular stagnation: a review of the issues. In: Teulings C, Baldwin R (eds) Secular stagnation: facts, causes and cures. Centre for Economic Policy Research, London
Fernald JG (2014) A quarterly, utilization-adjusted series on total factor productivity. Working paper, vol 19. Federal Reserve Bank of San Francisco
Fernald JG (2015) Productivity and potential output before, during, and after the great recession. In: Parker JA, Woodford M (eds) NBER macroeconomics annual 2014. University of Chicago, Chicago
Fernald JG, Jones CI (2014) The future of US economic growth. Am Econ Rev 104:44–49
Fernald JG, Hall RE, Stock JH, Watson MW (2017) The Disappointing recovery of output after 2009. Mimeo, Federal Reserve Bank of San Francisco
Finicelli A, Pagano P, Sbracia M (2014) Trade-Revealed TFP. Mimeo, Bank of Italy
Goldin C, Katz LF (2008) The race between education and technology. Cambridge, Belknap
Gordon RJ (1990) The measurement of durable goods prices. NBER, Chicago
Gordon RJ (2012) Is US economic growth over? Faltering innovation confronts the six headwinds. NBER working paper, 18315
Gordon RJ (2014) The demise of US economic growth: restatement, rebuttal, and reflections. NBER working paper, 19895
Griliches Z (1990) Patent statistics as economic indicators: a survey. J Econ Lit 28:1661–1707
Hansen AH (1936) Mr. Keynes on Underemployment Equilibrium. J Political Economy 44:667–686
Hansen AH (1938) Full Recovery or Stagnation?. Norton Company, New York
Hansen AH (1939) Economic Progress and Declining Population Growth. American Economic Review 29:1–15

Heckman JJ, LaFontaine PA (2010) The American High School Graduation Rate: Trends and Levels. Review of Economics and Statistics 92:244–262
Jones CI (1995a) R&D-based models of economic growth. J Polit Econ 103:759–84
Jones CI (1995b) Time series tests of endogenous growth models. Q J Econ 110:495–525
Jones CI (2002) Sources of US economic growth in a world of ideas. Am Econ Rev 92:220–239
Jorgenson DW, Ho MS, Stiroh K (2005) Productivity: information technology and the american growth resurgence. MIT Press, Boston
Keynes JM (1937) Some economic consequences of a declining population. Eugen Rev 29:13–17
Kortum S (1997) Research, patenting, and technological change. Econometrica 65:1389–1419
Kremer M (1993) Population growth and technological change: one million BC to 1990. Q J Econ 108:681–716
Krugman P (1990) The age of diminished expectations: US economic policy in the 1990s. MIT Press, Cambridge
Lindsey B (2013) Why growth is getting harder. Cato Institute, Policy Analysis, p 737
Lucas RE Jr (1988) On the mechanics of economic development. J Monet Econ 22:3–42
Maddison A (2008) Statistics on world population, GDP and per capita GDP, 1-2006 AD. http://www.ggdc.net/maddison/oriindex.htm. Accessed 8 Nov 2017
Meadows DH, Meadows DL, Randers J, Behrens WW (1972) The limits to growth. Universe Books, New York
Merton RK (1935) Fluctuations in the rate of industrial invention. Q J Econ 49:454–474
Mincer J (1958) Investment in human capital and personal income distribution. J Polit Econ 66:281–302
Mincer J (1974) Schooling, experience and earnings. National Bureau of Economic Research, New York
Mokyr, J. (2013) Technology then and now: why the technopessimists are wrong. Presentation delivered at the Federal Reserve Bank of Atlanta Public Affairs Forum, July
Murnane RJ (2013) US high school graduation rates: patterns and explanations. J Econ Lit 51:370–422
Nasar S (2012) Grand Pursuit: The story of economic genius. Simon & Schuster, New York
Nordhaus WD (1972) The recent productivity slowdown. Brook Pap Econ Act 3:493–536
Nordhaus WD (1992) Lethal model 2: the limits to growth revisited. Brook Pap Econ Act 2:2–43
Nye DE (1990) Electrifying America: social meanings of a new technology. MIT Press, Cambridge
OECD (2014a) Long-term projections for the economic outlook. Organisation for economic co-operation and development, February
OECD (2014b) Policy considerations in the current economic situation. Organisation for economic co-operation and development, January
Pagano P, Sbracia M (2014) The secular stagnation hypothesis: a review of the debate and some insights. Occasional papers, vol 231. Bank of Italy
Samuelson PA (1939) Interactions between the multiplier analysis and the principle of acceleration. Rev Econ Stat 21:75–78
Samuelson PA (1988) The keynes-hansen-samuelson multiplier-accelerator model of secular stagnation. Jpn World Econ 1:3–19
Strasser S (1982) Never done: a history of American housework. Pantheon, New York
Summers, L. (2013) IMF economic forum: policy responses to crises. Speech delivered at the IMF annual research conference, 8th Nov
Sweezy A (1943) Secular stagnation? In: Harris SE (ed) Postwar economic problems. McGraw Hill, New York, London
Temin P (2006) The economy of the early roman empire. J Econ Perspect 20:133–151

Vijg J (2011) The American technological challenge: stagnation and decline in the 21st Century. Algora, New York

Wells DA (1891) Recent economic changes and their effect on production and distribution of wealth and well-being of society. Appleton, New York

World Bank (2017) World development report 2018: learning to realize education's promise. the World Bank, Washington DC

Growth Potential in Emerging Countries

Enrica Di Stefano and Daniela Marconi

Abstract We examine the growth performance of six emerging economies (Brazil, China, India, Indonesia, Russia and Turkey) over the last two decades to discuss whether domestic structural constraints are affecting their present and future growth potential. In order to better assess the determinants of the recent synchronized slowdown of these economies, we concentrate on the dynamics of labour productivity and of employment. We find that the ongoing slowdown in EMEs is largely structural, but there is still ample room for catching up in terms of output composition, reallocation of labour across sectors and within-sector productivity improvements. The scope for further reform and reform priorities differs across countries. In the longer run other structural factors will weigh on potential growth, particularly the evolution of the size and quality of the labour force.

1 Introduction

In the aftermath of the financial crisis, global growth declined by almost 1.5% points (from 4.5 per cent on average in the period 2000–07 to 3.1 per cent in 2016); in emerging markets and developing economies (EMEs), after a quick recovery in 2009–10, the fall was even more marked (2.5% points on average, from 6.6 to 4.1 per cent in 2016). Slowdowns in individual EMEs or regions are not unusual. In the 1980s and 1990s their GDP growth was quite volatile, including in the largest and most successful countries, and pronounced accelerations were often followed by deep and at times protracted slowdowns. However, what makes this time different is that, after an extended period of almost synchronized and rapid growth (2000–07), which

E. Di Stefano · D. Marconi (✉)
Bank of Italy, Directorate General for Economics, Statistics and Research, International Relations and Economics Directorate, Rome, Italy
e-mail: daniela.marconi@bancaditalia.it

E. Di Stefano
e-mail: enrica.distefano@bancaditalia.it

L. Ferrara et al. (eds.), *International Macroeconomics in the Wake of the Global Financial Crisis*, Financial and Monetary Policy Studies 46,
https://doi.org/10.1007/978-3-319-79075-6_3

doubled per capita GDP, EMEs experienced an almost synchronized slowdown since the second half of 2011, reversing the long trend of rapid convergence that started at the beginning of the last decade.

EMEs as a group have become the major contributors to global GDP.[1] It is therefore extremely important to understand how much of the slowdown is cyclical, i.e. temporary, rather than structural and thus more persistent.

This chapter examines the growth performance of six emerging economies (Brazil, China, India, Indonesia, Russia and Turkey) over the last two decades and discusses whether *domestic* structural constraints are affecting their present and future growth potential. Disentangling cyclical from structural components is no easy task, as it requires estimating potential output—a time-varying, pro-cyclical concept that depends on unobservable factors, and for which there is a variety of estimation methods and models (Anand et al. 2014, among others). The recent empirical literature shows that a large portion of the drop in potential GDP growth can be explained by slower productivity growth (IMF 2017). Hence, in order to better assess the determinants of the recent synchronized slowdown of these economies, the chapter focuses on the dynamics of labour productivity (a synthetic measure of capital deepening, labour quality and total factor productivity) and employment.

The analysis shows that trend GDP growth has fallen on average by almost 2% points in the selected group of countries compared with the pre-crisis period. The slowdown has been driven mainly by a deterioration in labour productivity. Half of the change in labour productivity is due to a slowdown of the structural transformation process towards more productive sectors. The other half is due to a slowdown of productivity within sectors.

Nonetheless, output composition and labour productivity gaps indicate that the structural transformation of these economies is far from complete and there is still ample room for catching up. Several obstacles may be delaying the upgrading of these economies, including the quantity and the quality of labour supply, two elements that will shape the structural transformation in the longer run too.

2 The Recent Growth Phases of EMEs

Three growth phases can be identified since the beginning of the last decade.

The first one, between 2000 and 2007, is a protracted and broad-based period of robust growth driven by strong external tailwinds during which the EMEs' aggregate growth averaged 6.7 per cent a year, 2% points higher than the average observed during the previous decade. In particular, the six countries in our sample (Brazil, China, India, Indonesia, Russia and Turkey) grew by 8.1 per cent, more than 3% points faster than in the previous decade. According to Cubeddu et al. (2014), about 25 per cent of the increase in growth registered between those two periods in the group

[1] The EME's share of global GDP at purchasing power parity hit 58.1% in 2016 and has been above 50 per cent since 2008 (WEO database).

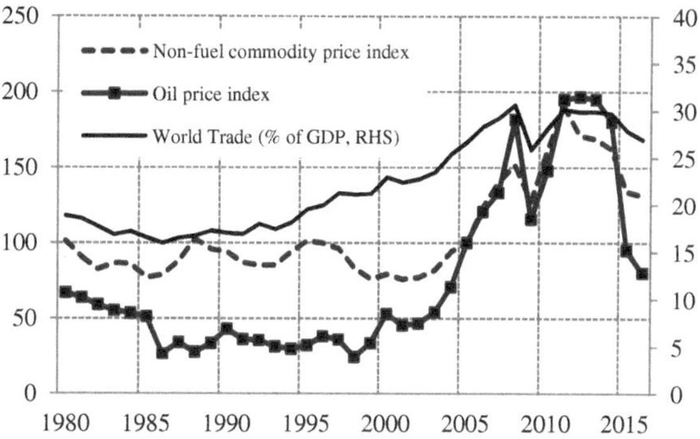

Fig. 1 Trade and commodity prices development. *Source* IMF, WEO database, April 2017

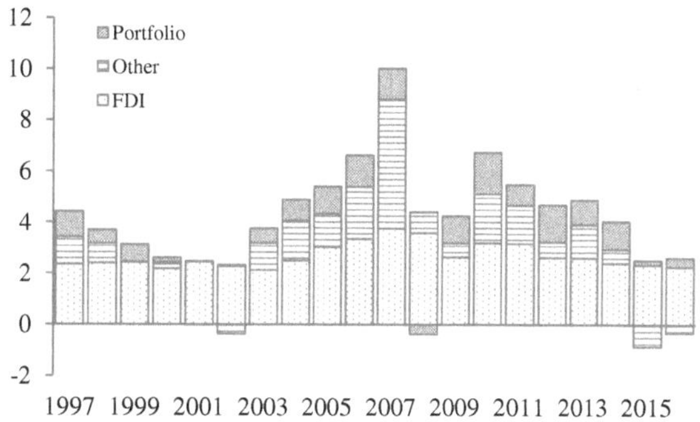

Fig. 2 Gross capital inflows to emerging economies. *Source* IMF, WEO database, April 2017

of non-commodity EMEs was due to the contribution from external demand. After China joined the WTO, the development of global supply chains spurred global trade which increased by more than 10% points of GDP, while inflows of foreign capital into EMEs, particularly in the form of foreign direct investment (FDI), doubled in terms of GDP to more than 8 per cent. For the group of commodity-exporting EMEs, about a quarter of the higher growth seen in the 2000s is instead explained by the improvements in the terms of trade induced by the surge of commodity prices due to the faster growth in rapidly industrializing countries (Figs. 1 and 2).

The second phase (2008–10) saw a sudden reversal in the underlying trends of the aforementioned variables brought about by the global financial crisis which, however, was followed by a very fast recovery in EMEs. This recovery, driven by domestic fiscal and monetary expansion and invigorated by abundant global liquidity, was indeed faster than had been envisaged in 2009. As a consequence of these stimulus policies, however, macroeconomic domestic imbalances deepened almost everywhere, and financial vulnerabilities built up, notably in China, but also in Brazil, India, Indonesia, Russia and Turkey, where corporate leverage increased substantially (IMF 2014).

After 2011 the upside surprise of the previous two years was followed by a downside one, as EMEs entered a (third) phase of unexpected synchronized slowdown. The effects of domestic fiscal and monetary stimuli faded, while external drivers did not return to pre-crisis levels. In this less favourable external environment, domestic impediments to growth became more evident.

Before turning our attention to the factors that impede growth, we first assess the weight of cyclical and structural factors during the synchronized slowdown.

3 Cyclical and Structural Components of the Slowdown in Major EMEs

In order to assess to what extent the observed slowdown is structural or cyclical we compare the changes in *trend*, i.e. *potential*, GDP growth with the changes in actual GDP growth.

Conceptually, potential output is the maximum level of output that an economy can produce (at a constant inflation rate) given its productive capacity, technology, capital stock and potential supply of labour. When the economy is hit by a shock, actual GDP deviates from its potential. From a methodological point of view, the concept aims to separate the real GDP of an economy into a long-term trend (potential output) and a short-term cyclical component. The estimation can be accomplished using different models and assumptions on trend capital, labour and total factor productivity. Different models and assumptions produce different estimates, hence it is sometimes useful to supplement those estimations with simpler and more transparent statistical techniques, such as statistical filters applied to real GDP time series.[2] In what follows we take into account estimates of potential output provided by the IMF and the OECD, as well as those obtained by applying simple statistical filters to real GDP times series for the six countries considered. Sometimes, the estimates of potential output growth differ significantly between the IMF and the OECD, as for example in the case of Brazil, Turkey and Russia, reflecting methodological differences as well as the difficulty of evaluating potential GDP in real time, particularly when structural adjustment processes are at play.

Trend growth estimates obtained by applying a standard Hodrick-Prescott filter to the annual GDP series at constant prices for the period 1980–2015 lie between those of the IMF and OECD estimates, the only exception being a tendency of the filtered series to amplify the growth rates for Brazil and China in concomitance with the 2006–07 peak (Fig. 3).[3]

Estimates show that potential GDP growth has not declined everywhere. Compared to the pre-crisis peak, trend growth has declined markedly in Russia (5.2% points), China (2.8) and Brazil (1.7), while remaining more stable in India, Indonesia and Turkey. Figure 4 reports the breakdown into the cyclical and structural components of the change in GDP growth rates between the period 2011–15 and the

[2]For a brief review of the most popular approaches to estimating potential output, see Anand et al. (2014).

[3]Similar results are obtained by applying other time-series filtering techniques, such as the Christiano and Fitzgerald (2003) filter. Results are available upon request.

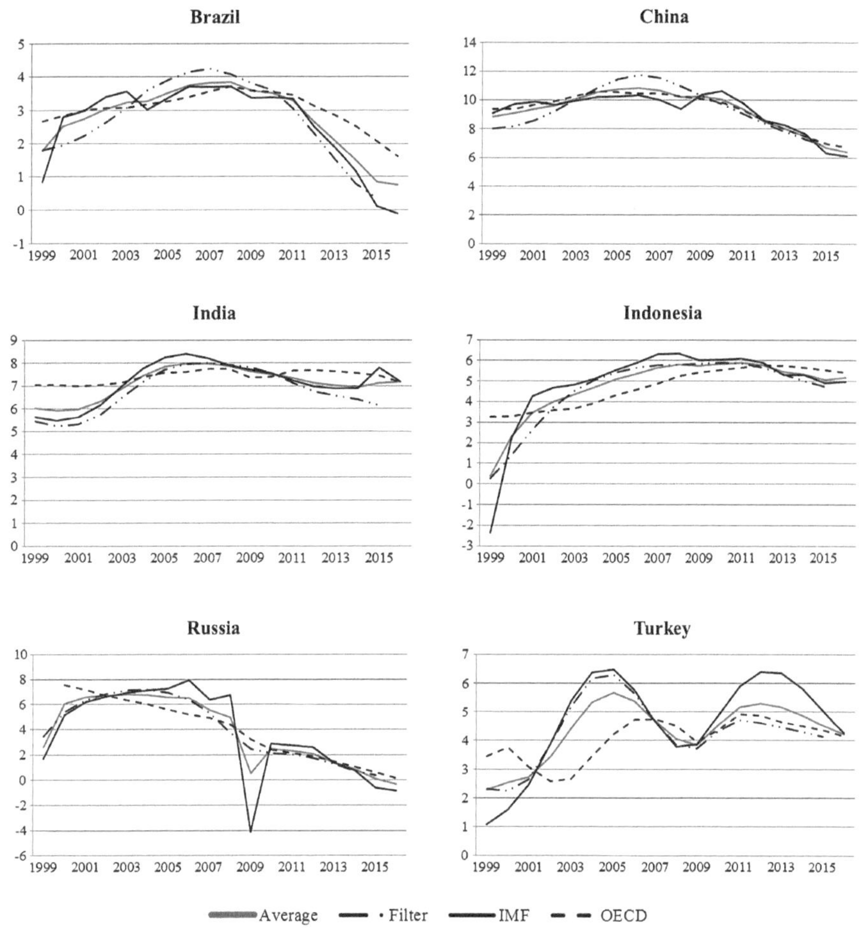

Fig. 3 Comparison of alternative potential GDP growth rate estimates. *Source* IMF, WEO database, April 2017; OECD, Economic Outlook n.100, 2016; authors' estimations based on World Bank, World Development Indicators database. *Note* The IMF adopts a production function approach; the OECD a model-based approach (NAIRU). The 'Filter' figures are obtained by applying a Hodrick-Prescott filter to GDP data over the period 1980–2015, with a smoothing parameter $\lambda = 6.25$

2006–07 peaks.[4] Results indicates that in Russia structural factors played a decisive and negative role, accounting for more than 60 per cent of the slowdown. In China, where GDP growth experienced the largest slowdown, structural factors appear to have accounted for about half of the change. In Brazil, where the potential rate of growth was already relatively low at the peak, structural factors accounted for little

[4]The structural component is derived from the average between the HP-filtered series and the IMF and OECD estimations, while the cyclical component is the difference between the actual GDP growth change and the change in potential GDP growth over the two periods.

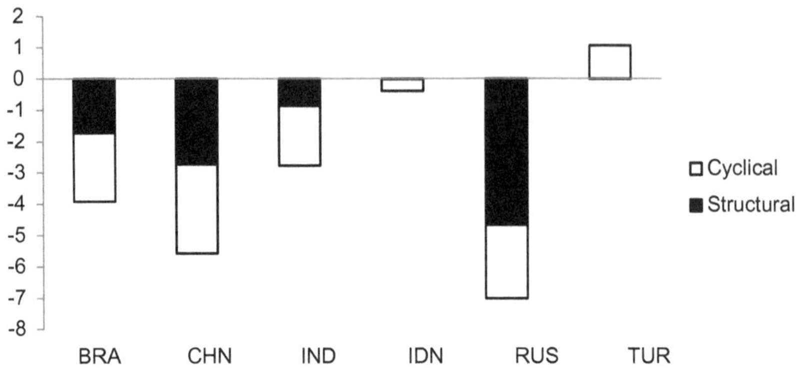

Fig. 4 Cyclical and structural components of the change in GDP growth between 2006–07 and 2011–15. *Source* Authors' calculations based on World Bank, World Development Indicators database; ILO, ILOSTAT database; IMF, WEO database, April 2017; OECD, Economic Outlook database, April 2017. Decomposition based on the 'Average' reported in Fig. 3

more than 40 per cent. In India the slowdown in potential GDP has been less pronounced, accounting for about 30 per cent of the actual one. Two notable exceptions are Indonesia and Turkey, where potential GDP in 2011–15 did not change compared with pre-crisis levels.

4 Labour Productivity

To assess the determinants of the slowdown in trend GDP, this section focuses on the behaviour of labour productivity and employment. Consider the output identity:

$$Y_t \equiv \frac{Y_t}{L_t} * L_t \tag{1}$$

where Y_t and L_t indicate total value added and employment, respectively.

To evaluate the role of labour productivity in explaining the slowdown, the HP filter is applied to the aggregate labour productivity to extrapolate the long-run trend. The trend GDP growth obtained with the HP filter is then decomposed into the growth rate of labour productivity (which reflects the combined effect of capital deepening, labour quality and TFP improvements) and the growth rate of employment.

Table 1 shows that labour productivity recently slowed down everywhere, generally by more than employment growth, which remained positive everywhere and was even quite strong in some countries, such as in India, Indonesia and, above all, in Turkey. As a consequence, productivity explains much of the slowdown in trend GDP growth in all countries (Fig. 5).

Table 1 Decomposition of trend GDP growth into labour productivity growth and employment growth (*HP filter; % changes*)

Country	Period	Trend GDP	Of which	
			Labour productivity	Employment
Brazil	2006–07	4.2	1.6	2.6
	2011–15	1.6	0.4	1.2
China	2006–07	11.6	11.0	0.7
	2011–15	7.9	7.4	0.5
India	2006–07	8.0	7.0	1.0
	2011–15	6.6	5.4	1.2
Indonesia	2006–07	5.7	3.4	2.3
	2011–15	5.3	3.5	1.8
Russia	2006–07	5.8	4.8	1.0
	2011–15	1.2	1.2	0.0
Turkey	2006–07	5.1	3.1	2.1
	2011–15	4.4	1.5	3.0

Source Authors' estimations based on World Bank, World Development Indicators database and ILO, ILOSTAT database

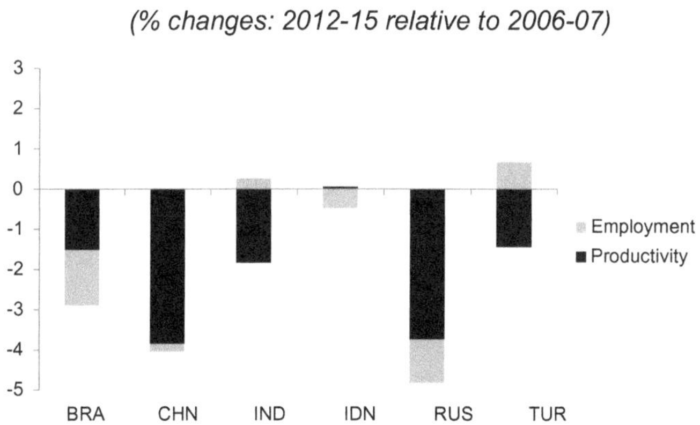

Fig. 5 Contribution of productivity and employment to trend GDP growth (*% changes: 2012–15 relative to 2006–07*). *Source* Authors' calculations based on World Bank, World Development Indicators database and ILO, ILOSTAT database

5 Labour Productivity Gains: Within- and Across-Sector Effects

We have shown that compared with pre-crisis peaks, the trend growth rate of labour productivity has fallen across EMEs and this is the single biggest cause of the GDP slowdown. By contrast, labour productivity was an important driver of growth in the previous period. It follows that in order to understand what factors could help sustain growth in the years to come, the analysis should focus on this component.

Several factors may have contributed to the slowdown of labour productivity. According to a standard Cobb-Douglas production function representation with physical capital (K), human capital (h) labour (L) and technological progress (A), labour productivity reflects the combined effect of capital deepening (K/L), labour quality (h) and total factor productivity (A):

$$\mathrm{Y_t} = \mathrm{A_t K_t^{\alpha}} \left(\mathrm{h_t L_t}\right)^{1-\alpha} \;\rightarrow\; \frac{Y_t}{L_t} = \mathrm{A_t} \left(\frac{K_t}{L_t}\right)^{\alpha} \left(\mathrm{h_t}\right)^{1-\alpha} \tag{2}$$

Recent analyses (IMF 2017) show that the slowdown in labour productivity can largely be traced back to the marked slowdown in total factor productivity (TFP). An economy's TFP depends on the TFP of its component sectors and their weight. The more capital and labour are channelled towards the most productive sectors, the higher the TFP for the entire economy. Among the most widely studied causes of negative TFP performance is the inefficient allocation of capital and labour among the various productive sectors owing to economic distortions (Di Stefano and Marconi 2017; Marconi and Upper 2017).

One simple way to gain insights into the role played by within-sector productivity gains and reallocation forces in driving aggregate productivity is to perform a shift-share analysis (Bosworth and Collins 2007; OECD 2014) which decomposes the aggregate labour productivity growth into these two components. We consider three broad sectors: agriculture, industry and services.[5] Let $LP_t \equiv \frac{Y_t}{L_t}$, then:

$$\begin{aligned}\frac{\Delta LP_t}{L_{t-1}} &= \sum_i \frac{\Delta LP_{it}}{LP_{it-1}} * \frac{Y_{it-1}}{Y_{t-1}} + \sum_i \frac{LP_{it-1}}{LP_{t-1}} * \left(\frac{L_{it}}{L_t} - \frac{L_{it-1}}{L_{t-1}}\right) \\ &+ \sum_i \frac{1}{LP_{it-1}} * (\Delta LP_{it}) * \Delta\left(\frac{L_{it}}{L_t}\right)\end{aligned} \tag{3}$$

The first term is the *within-sector component* of labour productivity, which measures the contribution of productivity growth within each sector on aggregate productivity growth, assuming that sector labour shares are unchanged. The second term measures the *reallocation* (or *between-sector*) *effect*, which measures the impact on aggregate productivity resulting from the shift of labour between sectors, assuming that the level of productivity in each sector is unchanged. The last term (*cross term*)

[5]Results are sensitive to industry details. If the number of sectors is small the within-industry component gets magnified, as within-sector shifts go unaccounted However, for the countries considered in this study, timely and reliable data on value added and employment are readily available only for the three broad sectors; by using this information we can get an idea of productivity performance in relation to broad structural changes in these economies.

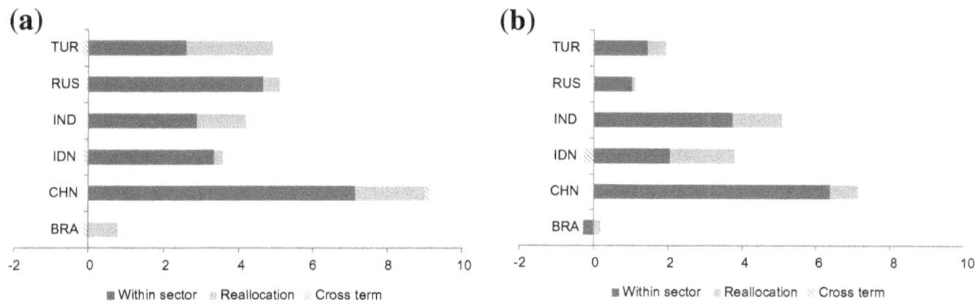

Fig. 6 **a** Shift-share decomposition of productivity growth, average annual growth over 2000–07 (%). **b** Shift-share decomposition of productivity growth, average annual growth over 2011–15 (%). *Source* Authors' calculations based on World Bank, World Development Indicators database and ILO, ILOSTAT database

measures the interaction between the changes in the *within*- and the *between-sector* components.

Figure 6 summarizes the main findings. During the period of rapid growth (2000–07) we observe a generalized shift of workers from less productive to more productive activities, in particular out of agriculture and toward the service sector (reallocation or shift effect), which made an important contribution to the overall productivity improvements.

On average, for the selected countries as a group, half of the change in labour productivity growth between the 2011–15 period and the 2000–07 period is attributable to slower productivity growth within individual sectors and half to the reduced contribution of labour reallocation to more productive sectors. Average numbers mask large differences across countries. In India and Indonesia the reallocation effect is gaining weight, making an important and positive contribution to labour productivity growth. On the contrary, the positive contribution of the reallocation effect dropped quite considerably in all other countries. Labour reallocation can still play a very important role in many emerging countries since they still have ample room for structural transformation.

As a first approximation, the scope for further gains in productivity arising from labour reallocation can be judged from simple sector shares of value added and employment. Despite the important transformations that our selected sample of EMEs have been through in the last 20 years, the share of employment in agriculture is still high everywhere, even when compared with that of the US in 1950 (Table 2) and the labour productivity gap with respect to the US remains quite high across sectors but particularly so in agriculture (Table 3). It is to be expected that shifts of workers out of agriculture towards more productive sectors will continue to play a very important role in productivity gains.

The big question is, however, whether the drivers of transformation have definitively lost power, especially where they had been fuelled primarily by external demand. If this were the case, the catching-up process might be at risk, calling for appropriate policies to revive those drivers and to avoid a *middle-income trap*.

Table 2 Shares of agriculture, industry and services in value added and employment in 2015

	Agriculture		Industry		Services	
	VA	Employment	VA	Employment	VA	Employment
Brazil	5	15	25	22	70	63
China	8	29	47	24	45	47
India	16	46	32	24	53	30
Indonesia	14	33	42	22	44	45
Russia	5	7	34	27	61	66
Turkey	9	20	26	28	66	52
USA (2015)	***1***	***1***	***19***	***17***	***80***	***81***
USA (1950)	***7***	***5***	***35***	***35***	***58***	***60***

Source Authors' calculations based on World Bank, World Development Indicators database ILO, ILOSTAT database, and Bureau of Economic Analysis

Table 3 Labour Productivity gap in 2015 (at 2010 PPP)

	Total economy	Agriculture	Industry	**Services**
Brazil	27.0	11.6	26.0	28.4
China	27.7	7.8	37.0	21.4
India	17.5	5.8	14.1	23.0
Indonesia	25.8	11.1	37.1	19.5
Russia	38.5	31.9	42.0	37.0
Turkey	53.2	25.6	38.7	62.6
USA	**100**	**100**	**100**	**100**

Source Authors' calculations based on World Bank, World Development Indicators database and ILO, ILOSTAT database

The low-hanging fruits arising from global integration processes may have been exhausted, leaving EMEs more vulnerable to domestic structural constraints weighing on the efficient allocation of resources.

Several obstacles may be delaying the reallocation of resources and factors across sectors in EMEs, e.g. price-setting policies and exchange rate regimes that distort internal and external competition, labour market rigidities and underdeveloped financial markets that impede the efficient allocation of capital (Marconi and Upper 2017). In a context of weaker external drivers, such obstacles tend to become more manifest, and targeted structural reforms to remove them can no longer be postponed. Challenges across countries vary and policy priorities differ according to national peculiarities. For instance, in some countries the priority is to expand domestic consumption and upgrade the service sector (China and Indonesia); in others it is more urgent to build up infrastructures and to remove supply-side bottlenecks by diversifying the production structure and expanding the manufacturing sector (Brazil, India, Russia and Turkey). Furthermore, countries differ considerably in terms of physical and human capital endowment, as well as in market structures, financial market development, labour market participation, demographic features and social safety nets.

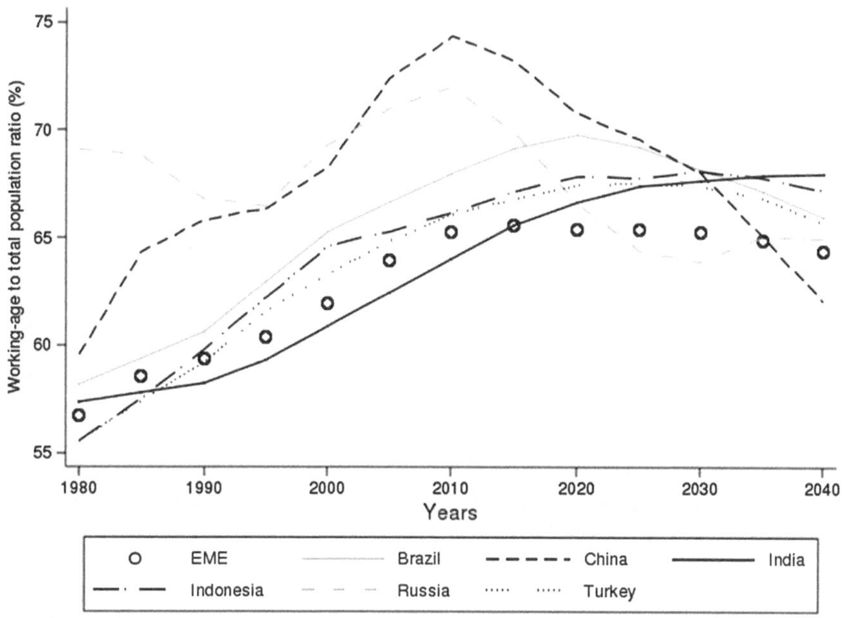

Fig. 7 Demographic transition in selected EMEs. *Source* United Nations, World Population Prospects. *Note* Working age is 15–64

6 Labour Supply: Quantity and Quality Issues

The process of economic upgrading depends crucially on the quantity and quality of labour available in each country. Since the mid-1990s EMEs have been enjoying important demographic dividends as the share of working-age population to total population has increased rapidly, allowing the rapid expansion of manufacturing and service activities while keeping wages relatively low and stable. Moreover, the increasing weight of the working-age population has facilitated domestic saving and capital accumulation, particularly in China (Cristadoro and Marconi 2013). However, declining fertility rates imply a progressive reduction of such dividends. According to the projections of the United Nations, in China and Russia, where fertility rates are remarkably low, the share of working-age population peaked around 2010 (surpassing 70 per cent of the total population; Fig. 7) and started declining thereafter. In EMEs like India and Indonesia, with higher fertility rates, the demographic transition remains favourable, as the share of the working-age population continues to grow, albeit at decreasing rates.

Population ageing can reduce economic growth through its impact on labour supply and saving. Those negative effects can be alleviated by either increasing labour force participation or human capital, or both (Bloom et al. 2010).

Table 4 Female labour market participation, fertility and GDP per capita (latest available data)

	Female Participation rates (%, Female 15+)	Fertility rates/1	Life expectancy at birth (years)	Per capita GDP, PPP (2011 international $)
Brazil	56	1.8	74.1	14,533
China	63	1.6	75.4	13,572
India	27	2.5	67.5	5,733
Indonesia	51	2.5	68.6	10,385
Russia	57	1.7	69.8	24,124
Turkey	30	2.1	74.8	19,460
Memo:				
United States	*56*	*1.9*	*78.9*	*52,704*

Source World Bank, World Development Indicators database; United Nations, World Population Prospects
/1: average number of children that the actual generation of women would have under the hypotheses of no child mortality and constant fertility

In countries like Turkey and India there is still plenty of room to increase female participation (Table 4) while in others, e.g. China and Russia, this margin is tighter; Brazil is somewhere in the middle, both in terms of fertility rates and participation rates. Moreover in several countries, including China, labour supply could also grow by bringing the unemployed or under-employed working-age population into the labour market. Finally, as life expectancy increases, working life duration can be extended as well.

Nonetheless, as technological change is increasingly biased towards high-skilled labour, increased labour force participation per se may not be enough to raise a country's growth potential, as it needs to be complemented with greater investment in human capital (Aghion and Howitt 2006; Acemoglu et al. 2006). There is plenty of evidence (Soares 2005) of the growing complementarity between technological progress and human capital, known as skill-biased technological change (Acemoglu 2009). The lines in Fig. 8 fit the non-linear regressions, for several years, of the log of the human capital index (taken from the Penn World Tables) on the log of per capita GDP, over a sample of 134 countries. The upward shift of the positively-sloped relationship between the two variables suggests that the level of human capital associated with a certain level of per capita GDP has increased over time.

Looking at this relationship in the most recent year for which data are available (2014), it is possible to assess the relative position of the EMEs analysed in this chapter (Fig. 9). Russia is best positioned in terms of human capital endowment, suggesting that it could more easily absorb advanced technologies and speed up the catching-up process, thereby compensating, at least in part, the negative effects of population ageing. The Brazilian endowment appears to be in line with the predicted relationship. By contrast, in China, India, Indonesia and Turkey, human capital

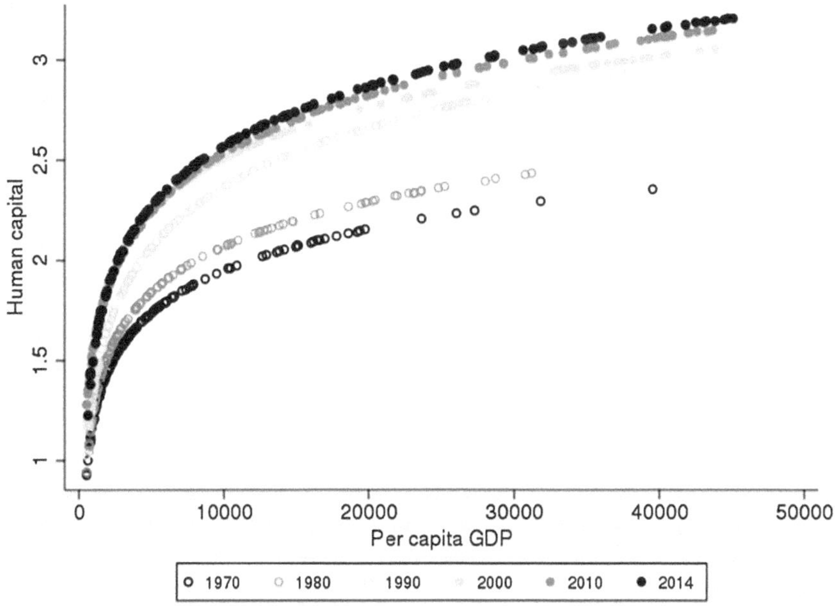

Fig. 8 Human capital and per capita GDP: 1970–2014. *Source* Feenstra et al. (2015), Penn World Table; *Note* HC=b0*ln(b1+b2*PILpc)

endowment appears low relative to their stage of development; in these countries, skill shortages could inhibit the catching-up process.

Investing in human capital is crucial but the results presented above suggest different priorities. In countries closer to the technological frontier, such as Russia and Brazil, investment should concentrate on improving tertiary education. In countries at earlier stages of development, primary and secondary education should take priority, in order to favour the absorption of more basic technologies (Aghion and Howitt 2006).

7 Conclusion

This chapter shows that following the global financial crisis, most of the slowdown in the selected EMEs was structural, except for India, Indonesia and Turkey where the cyclical component played a larger role. The dynamics of labour productivity declined everywhere, contributing negatively to GDP growth potential.

In the period of rapid growth (2000–07) labour productivity increased, driven by within-sector improvements, particularly in the service sector, and by the shift of workers out of agriculture mainly toward the service sector. The crisis has hit the within-sector component particularly hard.

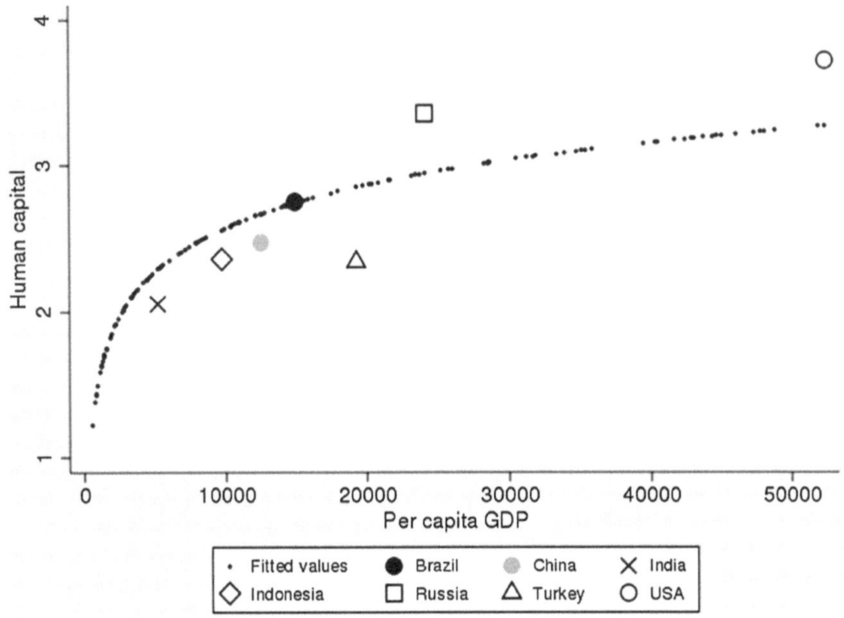

Fig. 9 Human capital and per capita GDP: Selected countries in 2014. *Source* Feenstra et al. (2015) Penn World Table. *Note* HC=b0*ln(b1+b2*rgdpe_pc)

The structural transformation of these economies is far from complete. There is still ample room for catching up in terms of output composition, reallocation of labour across sectors and within-sector productivity improvements. The scope for further reform and reform priorities differs across countries.

In the longer run other structural factors will weigh on potential growth, particularly the evolution of the size and quality of the labour force. As regards labour force size, the population is ageing fast in China and Russia, given low fertility rates; the margins for avoiding a reduction in the labour force appear limited, since both male and female participation rates are already rather high. In contrast, labour force prospects are more favourable in India, Indonesia and Turkey, in terms of demographic dividends as well as female participation. Brazil is somewhere in the middle as far as both fertility and participation rates are concerned.

As regards labour quality, the increasing complementarity between technological progress and human capital accumulation (skill-biased technological change) implies that whenever a country's endowment of human capital is high relative to its stage of development, advanced technologies can be more easily absorbed and greater productivity improvements obtained; in the long run, human capital accumulation is another key factor for continued productivity gains. In Russia, population ageing is partially mitigated by a relatively large endowment of human capital. By contrast, China, India, Indonesia and Turkey lag behind as their endowment of human capital is small compared to their stage of development and could weigh negatively on their catching-up process.

References

Acemoglu D, Aghion P, Zilibotti F (2006) Distance to frontier, selection and economic growth. J Eur Econ Assoc 4(1):37–74
Acemoglu D (2009) Introduction to modern economic growth, Princeton University Press, Oxford, Princeton
Aghion P, Howitt P (2006) Joseph schumpeter lecture. appropriate growth policy: a unifying framework. J Eur Econ Assoc 4(2–3):269–314
Anand R, Cheng KC, RehmanS, Zhang L (2014) Potential growth in emerging Asia. IMF working paper series, 14/2
Bloom DE, Canning D, Fink G (2010) Implications of population ageing for economic growth. Oxf Rev Econ Policy 26(4):583–612
Bosworth B, Collins SM (2007) Accounting for growth: comparing China and India. NBER working paper series, 12943
Christiano LJ, Fitzgerald TJ (2003) The Band Pass Filter. Int Econ Rev 44:435–465
Cristadoro R, Marconi D (2013) Urban and rural household savings in China: Determinants and policy implications. In: Gomel G, Marconi D, Musu I, Quintieri B (eds) The Chinese Economy—recent trends and policy issues. Springer, Berlin
Cubeddu L, Culiuc A, Fayad G, Gao Y, Kochhar K, Kyobe A et al (2014) Emerging markets in transition: Growth prospects and challenges. IMF staff discussion notes series, 14/06
Di Stefano E, Marconi D (2017) Structural transformation and allocation efficiency in China and India. Bank of Italy working paper series, 1093
Feenstra, RC, Inklaar R, Timmer MP (2015) The next generation of the penn world table. Am Econ Rev 105(10):3150–3182. www.ggdc.net/pwt. https://doi.org/10.15141/s5np4s
IMF (2014) Global financial stability report. International Monetary Fund, Apr 2014
IMF (2017) World Economic Outlook. International Monetary Fund, Apr 2017
Marconi D, Upper C (2017) Capital misallocation and financial development: a sector-level analysis. Bank of Italy working paper series (series, 1143) and BIS working paper series, 671
OECD (2014) Perspectives on global development 2014: boosting productivity to meet the middle-income challenge. http://dx.doi.org/10.1787/persp_glob_dev-2014-en
Soares R (2005) mortality reductions, educational attainment, and fertility choice. Am Econ Rev 95(3):580–601

What are the Drivers of TFP Growth? An Empirical Assessment

Iván Kataryniuk and Jaime Martínez-Martín

Over time, productivity growth is the key determinant of improvement in living standards

J. Yellen, Chair of the Board of Governors of the US Federal Reserve System, June 6th, 2016.

Abstract This chapter builds upon the related research that grapples with determinants of TFP, as the driving force of potential growth. In particular, we empirically estimate, in a homogenous and systematic manner, cross-country contributions of cyclical and structural determinants of aggregate TFP growth. Under a growth accounting framework, we compute TFP growth estimates for 41 economies over the 1992–2014 period. After selecting its main drivers by means of a Bayesian Model Averaging (BMA) approach, we exploit panel estimates to conclude that a substantial share of the growth underperformance in recent years was related to cyclical factors, mainly the output gap, but also: (i) over-indebtedness for advanced economies; and (ii) the decline in commodity prices for commodity exporters. In addition, the growth of IT capital and the convergence towards the technological frontier appear to be significant structural drivers of TFP productivity growth in emerging market economies.

We would like to thank Ángel Estrada, Sonsoles Gallego, Ignacio Hernando, Enrique Moral-Benito, Pedro del Río and seminar participants at the Banco de España for their helpful comments. Many thanks as well to Abdul Erumban and Klass DeVries for providing ICT and non-ICT capital stock series from the Conference Board. Finally, we are especially indebted to Marina Sánchez del Villar for her excellent research assistance. All the remaining errors are our own responsibility.

I. Kataryniuk (✉) · J. Martínez-Martín
Banco de España, Alcala 48, 28014 Madrid, Spain
e-mail: ivan.kataryniuk@bde.es

J. Martínez-Martín
e-mail: jaime.martinezm@bde.es

L. Ferrara et al. (eds.), *International Macroeconomics in the Wake of the Global Financial Crisis*, Financial and Monetary Policy Studies 46,
https://doi.org/10.1007/978-3-319-79075-6_4

1 Introduction

Total Factor Productivity (TFP) has been identified as the driving force of economic growth, especially once growth by means of factor accumulation, both in labour and in capital, is subdued (Easterly and Levine 2001). As a result, many advanced and emerging economies are undergoing a process of adjustment of their potential output growth, which coincides with a decline in current TFP growth (see Fig. 1).

Therefore, one of the main suspects behind downward revisions in potential output growth would be a persistent and global slowdown in TFP growth, both in advanced and emerging economies (EMEs).[1] We contribute to the current debate by computing and decomposing TFP growth at an aggregate level for a panel of 41 emerging and developed economies, based on a standard growth accounting framework. To this end, we construct original series of labour and capital, both public and private, and use this framework to capture structural and cyclical determinants of the deceleration of TFP growth in the most recent years. Two challenges remain to researchers aiming to explain these differences: on the one hand, TFP growth becomes empirically hard to measure; and on the other, model uncertainty hampers consensus on its key determinants.

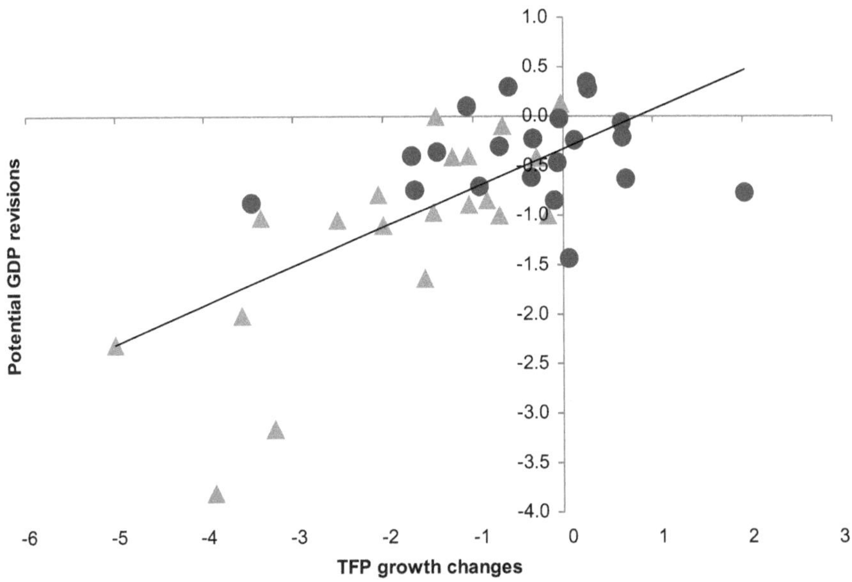

Fig. 1 Potential GDP growth revisions (2011 vs. 2015) and % of TFP growth (2003–2007 vs. 2010–2014). (*Sources* IMF (2015) and own calculations. *Notes* Triangular points refer to EMEs and circle points to advanced economies)

[1]See Basu and Fernald (2009).

With the aim of capturing the main determinants of TFP growth, we follow the related literature that emphasises the need for agnostic priors on the expected results and adopt a twofold empirical strategy. First, we use a Bayesian Model Averaging (BMA) approach following Danquah et al. (2014). We select—in an objective and transparent manner—the most statistically significant predictors from a pool that follows the empirical literature. This framework allows us to choose a statistical model out of several coexisting theories. In this regard, we use the BMA estimates to specify an economic model robust to omitted variable bias. Second, and for the sake of clarity, we build the contribution of each driver behind TFP growth over time and arrange them in a "cyclical versus structural" classification.

The results indicate that a substantial share of the TFP deterioration in recent years may be explained by a negative economic cycle (as predicted by the importance of the output gap and time-specific effects). However, other cyclical factors have contributed to the recent weakness, such as the credit gap for advanced economies—which may be explained by excessive leverage in such economies—and the decline in commodity prices for commodity exporters (Kataryniuk and Martínez-Martín 2017).

From the structural side, our empirical findings suggest that the most robust TFP growth structural determinants in the whole sample are: (i) the growth of IT capital; and (ii) the convergence between emerging and advanced economies, which we model as a factor of both the distance to the frontier and the human capital, as in Benhabib and Spiegel 1994.

The structure of this chapter is as follows. Section 2 sets out the growth accounting methodology and briefly summarises the dataset. Section 3 addresses the related literature highlighting academic and policy research with a special focus on TFP determinants. Section 4 defines our empirical strategy, while Sect. 5 highlights the main empirical results, including a specific subsection devoted to building contributions to TFP growth. Finally, Sect. 6 concludes. In the Appendix, further details on the commodity export price index and TFP convergence computation are to be found.

2 Growth Accounting Methodology and Data

Traditional growth accounting models characterise (real) Gross Domestic Product (GDP) of the economy (Y) by means of a Cobb-Douglas production function, relating the inputs used to generate it (capital K and labor L), while a third variable is included to capture the part of observed production that is not explained by the recorded accumulation levels of the primary inputs (Solow 1956). This last factor proxies the technical efficiency with which the productive factors are used and its behaviour is often related to technological progress. It is commonly known as Total Factor Productivity (TFP, denoted by A).

$$Y = AF(K, L) \tag{1}$$

assuming constant returns to scale and perfect competition in the input and product markets, it can be written as

$$\Delta y = (1 - \alpha)\Delta k + \alpha \Delta l + \Delta a \tag{2}$$

where the lower-case letters represent the natural log of the corresponding upper-case variables, Δ is the difference operator and α is the share of labour income in nominal production. The calculation of the rate of growth of TFP requires data on labour quantity, capital stock and GDP.[2] In this chapter, GDP was obtained in constant terms from national accounts and transformed into 2005 PPP—using GDP PPP from the International Comparison Program (ICP).

Regarding the labour component, we have obtained total hours worked in the economy combining different international sources. Our primary source for the number of persons employed is the International Labor Organization (ILO). When not available, we have relied on data from the Total Economy Database (TED) from The Conference Board. In order to calculate the average hours worked per year, we have used data from TED.

The (time-varying) share of labour in the economy, α, is drawn from Penn World Tables (version 8.1). For the more recent observations, we keep α as time-invariant. The capital component is calculated as the sum of the public and the private capital stock per year. Each stock is calculated using the perpetual inventory method:

$$K_{t+1} = (1 - \delta)K_t + I_t \tag{3}$$

The gross fixed capital formation I_t is taken from national accounts data, compiled by UNDATA. The data are transformed using the price level of investment as a deflator and GFCF-specific PPPs. The depreciation rates are increasing from 1970 to 2010 and constant thereafter, after Arslanalp et al. (2010).

For the initial capital stock, we take the first year available in the Penn World Tables (PWT) and calculate its corresponding public and private capital stock by applying the average shares of each sector over the entire covering period. With this initial capital, we calculate each capital stock until the last period using the previous formula. For the years where no public/private disaggregation is available, we use the depreciation rate provided by the PTW.

The annual dataset employed in this chapter covers 41 countries from 1992 to 2014.[3] Initial country-specific growth accounting results indicate that there are serious grounds for considering high levels of heterogeneity between countries.

---

[2]Bear in mind that one caveat of our empirical strategy has to do with sectoral data constraints. We are not able to construct TFP series at a sectoral level but at an aggregate, country-specific level, observing the output of resource reallocation (if any).

[3]The emerging countries included are ARG, BOL, BRA, CHL, CHN, COL, CZE, ECU, HUN, IDN, IND, KOR, MEX, PER, POL, ZAF, TUR, and URY. In addition, advanced economies under consideration are: AUS, AUT, BEL, CAN, DNK, FIN, FRA, GER, GRE, IRL, ISR, ITA, JPN, NDL, NZL, NOR, PRT, RUS, ESP, SWE, CHE, GBR, and the USA.

3 TFP Growth Determinants

The empirical literature on determinants of TFP growth is vast. Regarding the relatively wide potential set of indicators that could be selected in the analysis, we have only considered those usually employed in the related literature in addition to the basic factors of production considered to calculate our TFP measure and its components. Thus, the number of regressors suggested in the literature as potential determinants of economic growth is huge. For example, Durlauf et al. (2005) survey the empirical growth literature and identify 145 proposed regressors. In this chapter, however, we consider a subset of them to analyse how they affect economic growth through the channel of TFP, which we argue might be a relevant one. Against this backdrop, Ciccone and Jarocinski (2010) and Danquah et al. (2014) found that small-scale models led to the higher robustness of the results in the Bayesian averaging framework. Like them, we avoid the inclusion of several variables as proxies of the same theory. In the empirical specification, we consider data on 19 candidate drivers of TFP growth, described below. Precise definitions of the covariates, how they are measured and their original sources are included in Table 1.

The related empirical literature highlights factors behind TFP growth, which could affect short and long-run productivity growth differently. The determinants considered in the estimation to control for short-run growth (usually related to cyclical movements) are: (i) the output gap, in order to capture the procyclicality of TFP growth; (ii) the credit gap and growth, to account for the process of development of financial markets in most economies; and (iii) growth in commodity prices.[4]

To test for the determinants of productivity growth, in the long run, a wide range of structural variables based on Durlauf et al. (2005) are included. Some TFP growth potential drivers covering social dimensions (income inequality, dependency ratios), transmission and absorption of knowledge (FDI inflows as a % of GDP, trade openness, human capital in terms of % of population with secondary studies), factor supply and efficient allocation (investment, government expenditure and IT capital growth) financial deepening (credit); and finally, other dimensions such as institutions (government quality). Moreover, we also consider a proxy measuring TFP convergence, both in levels (as a distance to the frontier) and interacting with human capital. This approach allows us to distinguish whether the slowdown in TFP growth has been related to a lower TFP growth rate in the frontier or a convergence towards the frontier for some economies. Some variables were not considered owing to data limitations. For instance, R&D as a % of GDP ceased to be available for the whole covering period. In order to tackle this issue, we used as an imperfect proxy the Economic

---

[4]Both variables are computed by applying a two-sided HP filter with a λ parameter of 100 over the annual GDP, in the case of the output gap; and over credit-to-GDP, in the case of the credit gap. In this chapter, we do not attempt to find a causal relationship between the different cyclical variables and TFP growth. For an extended view in this matter, which adds an identification strategy based on the theoretical DSGE framework of Ferraro and Peretto (2017), please refer to Kataryniuk and Martínez-Martín (2017).

Table 1 Variable definitions and sources

Variables	Measure	Source
TFP computation		
GDP	PPP (2005) from the Int Comparison Program (ICP)	National accounts
K (capital stock)	As a % of GDP	National accounts
Share of capital	Time-varying share in the economy	Penn World Tables (PWT) 8.2
L		
Total hours worked	Number of hours	International Labor Organization (ILO) & Total Economy Database (TED)
Share of labour	Time-varying share in the economy	Penn World Tables (PWT) 8.1
Cyclical determinants		
Output gap	As a % of GDP	Own estimates, based on IMF, WEO Database
Credit gap	As a % of GDP	Own estimates, based on BIS Database
Credit growth	As a % of GDP	World bank development indicators (WBDI)
Commodities export price index growth		Own estimates
Structural determinants		
Economic complexity index	Index - Lagged	Atlas of economic complexity
IT capital growth	Year-on-year growth rates	Total economy database (TED)
Trade openness	(X+M)/GDP	World bank development indicators
FDI Inflows	As a % of GDP	United nations (UN)
Urban population	As a % of Total population	World bank development indicators (WBDI)
Gini Index	Index: 2010 = 100	SWIID database
Dependency ratio	As a % of Total population	World bank development indicators (WBDI)
Government quality	Index	Quality of government database (QoG)
Investment	As a % of GDP	National accounts
Government expenditure	As a % of GDP	World bank development indicators (WBDI)
Commodities export price index level		Own estimates

(continued)

Table 1 (continued)

Variables	Measure	Source
Convergence (distance to frontier)		Own estimates
Absorption	(Distance * pop. aged>25 with secondary studies)	Own estimates, based on Barro-Lee database
Population with secondary studies	As a % of Total	Barro-Lee database
Credit	As a % of GDP	World bank development indicators (WBDI)

Complexity Index (ECI) developed in Hidalgo and Hausmann (2009)[5], given its high correlation with R&D investment.

For the sake of clarity, in the Appendix we define how both (i) the commodities export price index (CEPI) and (ii) the distance to the TFP frontier (in order to measure convergence) have been obtained.

4 The Econometric Strategy

The econometric specification of TFP in our panel set-up responds to the following specification:

$$\Delta TFP_{i,t} = \alpha + \tau_t + \beta X_{i,t,t-1} + \mu_{i,t} \tag{4}$$

where α is a constant, $X_{i,t,t-1}$ is a matrix of potential TFP determinants and τ_t is a common yearly shock affecting all countries at the same time.

This specification suffers from several potential problems. On the one hand, country-specific fixed effects may be driving the differences in TFP growth rates. However, we choose not to include them in our main equation, at least for two reasons. First, the presence of country-specific fixed effects would indicate a different interpretation of convergence, in which each country would converge to a country-specific TFP level. Although such a hypothesis could be plausible, we favour an interpretation of convergence based on the absorption of international knowledge, with fixed effects being proxied by observable variables. Moreover, the presence of several variables in our vector of determinants with little time variation will work, to an extent, as an observable fixed effect. As long as they correlate to a potential

[5]The Economic Complexity Index (ECI) is a holistic measure of the production characteristics of a country. The goal of this index is to explain an economic system as a whole rather than the sum of its parts. The ECI aims to explain the knowledge accumulated in a country's population and that is expressed in the country's industrial composition. It combines metrics of the diversity of countries and the ubiquity of products to create measures of the relative complexity of a country's exports. For further details, see Hidalgo and Hausmann (2009).

unobserved fixed effect, the bias would be mitigated (see Appendix 2 for further details). On the other hand, the estimation of the coefficients corresponding to the vector $X_{i,t,t-1}$ is prone to an issue of variable selection. The economic growth literature is very prolific in finding potential determinants of growth, as mentioned in the previous section. Against this background, we use an agnostic method of variable selection, Bayesian model averaging (BMA), to correct for the potential concerns on over-fitting and model selection, as in Danquah et al. (2014). The variables included in $X_{i,t,t-1}$ are already summarised in Table 1.

4.1 Bayesian Model Averaging (BMA)

To begin with, assuming that traditional statistical practice may be ignoring model uncertainty—since the data generating process (DGP) is unknown—and that it may lead to over-confident inferences on information selection, we conduct a Bayesian model averaging (BMA) approach based on Hoeting et al. (1999) to weight variable inclusion.[6] For the sake of simplicity, let us assume a combination of predictors such that: $y = \alpha + x_i\beta_i + \varepsilon$ where $\sim\ N\left(0, \sigma^2 I\right)$, and for each model, i, the parameter space is defined by α and β. Thus, the posterior distribution of the annual TFP growth, Δ, given data D is:

$$p\,(Z|\,D) = \sum_{K=1}^{K} p\,(Z|\,M_k,\,D)\,(M_k|\,D) \tag{5}$$

This is an average of the posterior distributions under each of the $M_1, \ldots, M_k$ models under consideration. Therefore, the posterior probability for model M_k is given by:

$$p\,(M_k|\,D) = \frac{p\,(D|\,M_k)\,p\,(M_k)}{\sum_{l=1}^{K} p\,(D|\,M_l)\,p\,(M_l)} \tag{6}$$

where $p\,(D|\,M_k) = \int p\,(D|\,\delta_k,\,M_k)\,p\,(\delta_k|\,M_k)\,c\delta_k$ is the integrated likelihood of model M_k, δ_k. It assumes that the posterior distribution is proportional to the marginal probability by the prior probability assigned to each model, in our case, a uniform variable.

We apply the BMA approach to the specification described in Eq. (4), in order to test not only the probability of inclusion of our potential determinants of TFP but also the convergence assumption in our model. As a result, we obtain (and show in the next section) the cumulative model probabilities of our predictor's selection based on the whole space of model combinations.

---

[6]For an overview of model averaging in economics, see Moral-Benito (2015).

5 Empirical Results

5.1 BMA: Pooled OLS

In Table 2 we summarise the main results of the BMA estimation. Given that we use a prior inclusion probability of 1/2, our threshold for variables selection in the model is for the posterior inclusion probability (PIP) to be above 1/2. We find that there is a strong cyclical behaviour in TFP growth, characterised by the high inclusion probability of the output gap. The credit gap is included with a negative sign, meaning that TFP growth behaves counter-cyclically with respect to the credit cycle. This behaviour could be explained by, for example: (i) the catching-up effect of countries with underdeveloped financial systems; and/or (ii) the presence of credit bubbles in sectors with low productivity growth. In addition, we also find a higher probability of inclusion of a high significance for the non-linear convergence, but not for the linear convergence. This result suggests that there is a cut-off point (around 20-25% of the population with secondary studies in our sample) above which a country starts to converge on the global frontier. The growth of commodity export prices in commodity-exporting countries is also included with a relatively high probability. The proxy for innovation in this chapter, the Economic Complexity Index (ECI), is playing a substantial role.

In light of these results, the selected "optimal" model considers six variables (in bold). The posterior model probability of the top model is fairly high, at 37.3%.

In the next subsections, we split the sample into regions and try to disentangle the contribution of cyclical as opposed to structural drivers to TFP growth over time.

5.2 Advanced Versus Emerging

In order to test whether there are differential effects between advanced and emerging economies, we split our sample into these two groups. The results are highlighted in Table 2. Our empirical findings suggest that, for emerging economies, the main cyclical determinants are the output gap (similarly to the pooled estimation) and commodity prices. With respect to the structural determinants, there is a high probability of inclusion of investment in new technologies (measured as the change in the proportion of capital devoted to IT). Such evidence is in line with an investment-led strategy of convergence for emerging economies, as in the 'catching-up' model of Acemoglu et al. (2006) and Basu et al. (2006). Our results also suggest some evidence of group-convergence based on human capital improvements for emerging economies, but not in advanced economies, where human capital levels are much less spread. Additionally, for the advanced economies, the credit gap inclusion becomes an extremely robust cyclical determinant along with the output gap. The negative sign of the credit gap suggests that credit growth above the trend might be harmful for productivity. From the structural side, there is a positive effect of trade openness, which is not significant in the emerging sample.

Table 2 Determinants of TFP Growth (BMA estimates)

	Pooled		Advanced		Emerging	
	PIP	P. Mean	PIP	P. Mean	PIP	P. Mean
	[1]	[2]	[3]	[4]	[5]	[6]
Output gap	**1.00**	59.24	**0.99**	21.86	**1.00**	72.97
Credit gap	**1.00**	−0.03	**0.97**	-0.02	0.48	−0.02
Commodity prices growth	**1.00**	0.04	–	–	**0.76**	0.03
IT Share on capital	**0.99**	4.15	0.05	−0.03	**0.92**	4.88
TFP distance * education	**0.98**	0.00	0.17	0.00	**0.96**	0.01
ECI	**0.58**	0.18	0.44	0.11	0.07	0.00
Dependency ratio	0.46	−0.01	0.12	0.00	0.20	−0.01
Openness	0.11	0.00	**0.75**	0.00	0.07	0.00
FDI	0.10	0.00	0.05	0.00	0.06	0.00
Investment	0.08	0.17	0.15	−0.43	0.09	0.25
Government expenditure	0.07	0.00	0.06	0.00	0.07	0.00
Government quality	0.07	−0.04	0.05	0.00	0.10	−0.13
TFP distance to frontier	0.07	0.00	0.19	0.01	0.36	0.10
Gini Index	0.06	0.00	0.05	0.00	**0.95**	−0.07
Human capital	0.05	0.00	0.05	0.00	**0.59**	−0.03
Credit growth	0.05	0.02	0.08	−0.06	0.06	−0.01
Commodity prices level	0.04	0.00	–	–	0.06	0.00
Credit level	0.04	0.00	0.00	0.00	0.27	0.00
Prior inclusion Probability	0.50		0.50		0.50	
Time effects	Yes		Yes		Yes	
Observations	787		519		323	

Notes Columns [1] and [2], refer to the determinants of overall TFP growth of emerging and advanced countries while columns [3] and [4] summarise the results of TFP determinants of advanced countries and [5] and [6] of emerging economies. PIP refers to the posterior inclusion probability of a particular predictor. Given the prior inclusion, the probability is equal for all the variables (i.e. 0.5), those regressors with PIP above 0.5 are considered as robust drivers of TFP growth; P. Mean refers to the posterior mean conditional on the inclusion of a given regressor in the empirical model, which is a weighted average of model-specific coefficient estimates with weights given by the model-specific R-squares. The BMA needs a balanced panel, and therefore there are more years available in the advanced panel when estimating separately

5.3 TFP Growth Decomposition

To shed some more light on the previous results, in this subsection we quantify the contribution of each single driver of TFP growth over time, breaking them down into cyclical and structural components in the following manner:

$$\Delta TFP_{i,t} = \hat{\beta}_c X_{i,t,c} + \hat{\delta}_t + \hat{\beta}_S X_{i,t,S} + \hat{\tau}_i + \hat{\mu}_{i,t} \quad (7)$$

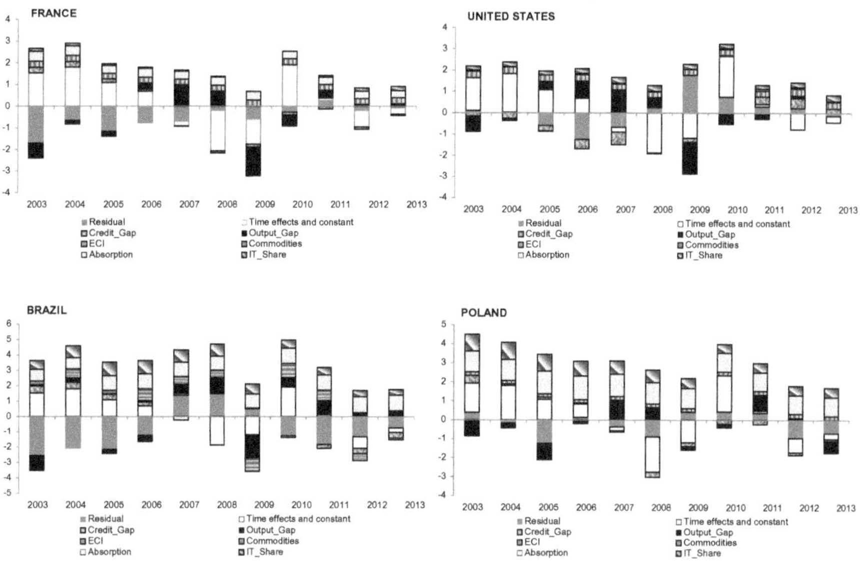

Fig. 2 Contributions to TFP growth. (*Notes* Contribution of each component to TFP growth over the 2003-2013 period, based on Eq. (7) estimates. IT_Share, Absorption and ECI are structural factors. Credit_Gap, Output_Gap and Commodities are cyclical factors)

where $\hat{\beta}_c X_{i,t,c}$ is the so-called cyclical or transitory component of TFP growth and $\hat{\beta}_S X_{i,t,S}$ refers to the structural component. To be more precise, the cyclical factors included in $X_{i,t,c}$ are the output and credit gaps, our measure of commodity export prices and time-specific effects, $\hat{\delta}_t$. On the other hand, the structural factors are those included in the vector $X_{i,t,S}$, already mentioned in the previous section. Finally, we include the estimated residuals $\hat{\mu}_{i,t}$.

Figure 2 evidences the heterogeneity of our panel when plotting the TFP growth decomposition in Eq. (7) for selected countries over the 2003–2013 period. We illustrate some representative cases of advanced economies such as the USA (a frontier advanced economy) and France (a non-frontier advanced economy). Additionally, we show TFP growth contributions of an emerging economy such as Poland and an emerging commodity-exporter such as Brazil.

Several conclusions can be extracted from Fig. 2. First, the importance of cyclical factors in all countries, as much of the time variation is explained by the time dummies and the output gap. Second, the key structural driver of TFP growth is related to innovation. In the previous example with regard to the US, the addition of structural predictors such as IT capital and the economic complexity indicator (ECI) accounts for a TFP growth of 1% per year on average, compared to an observed TFP growth of 1.2% per year on average (incl. cyclical factors). Additionally, it is worth mentioning the increasing relevance of TFP convergence processes of emerging market economies (measured by the "absorption" variable), whose TFP levels are far from those of the frontier. Finally, within commodity-exporting emerging economies, such as Brazil, there is evidence of a booming commodity prices contribution during the so-called "supercycle".

6 Concluding Remarks

A slowdown in TFP growth has been one of the key drivers behind the adjustment of potential output across the world after the Global Financial Crisis. In this chapter, we use an objective methodology to both empirically build on TFP growth drivers in advanced and emerging economies, and to disentangle which part of the deceleration in TFP growth is explained by cyclical and structural factors.

Our empirical findings suggest that the most robust TFP growth structural determinants in the whole sample are: (i) the growth of IT capital; and (ii) the convergence between emerging and advanced economies. In addition, time-specific effects (a global yearly slowdown in TFP growth) and the output gap seem to be the main cyclical factors driving TFP growth in the short run (Kataryniuk and Martínez-Martín 2017). Moreover, we find some differences between advanced and emerging economies. In advanced economies, the credit gap is a crucial cyclical factor, which may be explained by excessive leverage in these economies, while in emerging market economies, especially among commodity exporters, the growth of commodity prices has emerged as the more robust cyclical determinant.

In short, some of the deterioration of the growth outlook in recent years may be explained by a negative economic cycle, but structural weaknesses remain behind the slowdown in medium-term growth, especially for emerging countries. However, there is still room for improvement in several structural determinants, such as investment in IT technologies and in human capital.

Appendix 1. Commodities Export Price Index (CEPI)

In order to build the Commodities Export Price Index (CEPI), we have considered commodities defined by the UNCTAD classification. Each country-specific weight is calculated on an annual basis relative to the value of total exports. To maintain weights constantly, the final weight for each category in the index is the average of each product's weight for all years in the country.[7]

[7] Four different price indices have been employed based on IMF Global Commodities Watch. Each product has been allocated to every single price category: [1] PFANDB: index of food and beverages (base 2005). It includes cereals, vegetables, fruits, oils, meat, sea products, sugar, coffee, tea and cacao. [2] PRAWM: index of raw agricultural materials (base 2005). Includes wood, cotton, wool, rubber and leather. [3] PMETA: metals index (base 2005). Includes copper, aluminium, iron, tin, nickel, zinc, lead and uranium. [4] PNRG: energy index (base 2005). It includes prices for petroleum, natural gas and coal. Consistent data on both prices and export shares are available from 1992 onwards.

We adjust the index for the US deflator (base 2005). Thus, our CEPI measure is calculated as follows:

$$CEPI_{k,t} = \prod_j \frac{w_j * p_{j,t}}{Def_{US,t}} \tag{8}$$

where $w^E_{j,k}$ denotes the weight of each sub-index j and $p_{j,t}$ i s the value of the sub-index at each time t.

Appendix 2. TFP Convergence

As a measure of distance to the productivity frontier, we calculate:

$$Dist_{k,t} = A_{k,t-1} - A_{frontier,t-1} \tag{9}$$

where A denotes TFP in levels using the following approximation:

$$A_t = \frac{Y_t}{L_t^\alpha * K_t^{1-\alpha}} \tag{10}$$

In order to compute the TFP frontier, we have considered the average of the TFP level for the three countries with the highest values at the reference year 2005, CHE, USA and GBR.

While the majority of the countries in our sample have reduced the distance at which their productivity levels stand in the last 10 years, some cases stand out (See Fig. 3a). In particular, Denmark not only outperforms the frontier countries during this period, but its productivity level surpasses the frontier level. Other advanced countries that outperform the frontier growth are Ireland, Korea and Finland. In emerging economies, almost all the countries converge, with the sole exception of Saudi Arabia. Those economies converging faster are mostly from Eastern Europe, with comparatively higher levels of human capital.

To illustrate this point, it is worth mentioning that our baseline convergence path is linear (in logs) while once we add the human capital factor, H_t, the speed of adjustment to the frontier rapidly increases. Additionally, bear in mind that the presence of significant country-specific individual effects (not included in our model) would yield to a non-convergence path as shown in Fig. 3b.

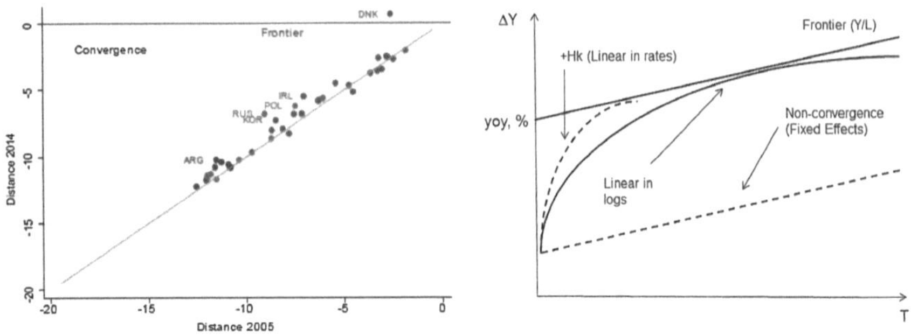

Fig. 3 A (left) Distance to the TFP frontier between 2005 and 2014. B (right) Global and conditional convergence

References

Acemoglu D, Zilibotti F, Aghion P (2006) Distance to frontier, selection and economic growth. J Eur Econ Assoc 4(1):37–74, Mar 2006

Arslanalp S, Bonhorst F, Gupta S, Sze E (2010) Public capital and growth. IMF working paper 10/175

Basu S, Fernald JG (2009) What do we know (and not know) about potential output? Federal Reserve Bank of St. Louis Review, vol 91, no 4, pp 187–213

Basu S, Fernald JG, Kimball MS (2006) Are technology improvements contractionary? Am Econ Rev 96(5):1418–1448, Dec 2006

Benhabib J, Spiegel M (1994) The role of human capital in economic development evidence from aggregate cross-country data. J Monet Econ 34(2):143–173

Ciccone A, Jarocinski M (2010) Determinants of economic growth: will data tell? Am Econ J Macroecon 4:222–246

Danquah M, Moral-Benito E, Outtara B (2014) TFP growth and its determinants: a model averaging approach. Empir Econ 47(1):227–251

Durlauf SN, Johnson PA, Temple JR (2005) Growth econometrics. Handb Econ Growth 1:555–677

Easterly W, Levine R (2001) What have we learned from a decade of empirical research on growth? It's not factor accumulation: stylized facts and growth models. World Bank Econ Rev 15(2):177–219

Ferraro D, Peretto PF (2017) Commodity prices and growth. Econ J (forthcoming)

Hidalgo CA, Hausmann R (2009) The building blocks of economic complexity. PNAS 106(26)

Hoeting JA, Madigan D, Raftery AE, Volinsky CT (1999) Bayesian model averaging: a tutorial. Stat Sci 14:382–417

IMF (2015) Where are we headed? Perspectives on potential output. World Econ Outlook, Apr 2015

Kataryniuk I, Martínez-Martín J (2017) TFP growth and commodity prices in emerging economies, Banco de españa working paper no 1711

Moral-Benito E (2015) Model averaging in economics: an overview. J Econ Surv 29:46–75

Solow R (1956) A contribution to the theory of economic growth. Quart J Econ 70:65–94

The Unintended Consequences of Globalization and Technological Progress

Riccardo Cristadoro

Abstract This chapter reviews the current debate on inequality with a focus on the main global trends and their likely causes. Notwithstanding significant progress, data challenges still limit the degree of confidence one should have on the evidence concerning the evolution of inequality between and, especially, within countries. Finding common causes for the heterogeneous experiences across countries might be unfounded, however it is important to focus on the two main overarching explanations proposed in the literature for the recent evolution of inequality, technology and trade. These two elements are surely and everywhere important drivers of inequality, although their interaction with each country's institutions and policies is an equally relevant factor.

1 Introduction

Over the last 30 years, there has been an unprecedented reduction in global inequality, which over the preceding 150 years had instead been increasing almost uninterruptedly (IMF 2017; World Bank 2016). The driving force of this change in secular patterns has been the economic progress of population-rich countries starting from the late 1980s: China, India, former Soviet Union states and Brazil, to name some prominent examples. This has been a remarkable success of the "high globalization" period (Milanovic 2016) that started with the fall of the Berlin wall and the liberalizations in China and India: more than 1 billion people were lifted from a condition of extreme poverty (defined as living with less than 1.90 USD per day at the 2011 PPP; World Bank 2016).

Arguably, the concept of "global inequality", i.e. income or wealth disparities across the entire world population, is itself a product of the changes in our view of

R. Cristadoro (✉)
Bank of Italy, Directorate General for Economics, Statistics and Research, International Relations and Economics Directorate, Rome, Italy
e-mail: riccardo.cristadoro@bancaditalia.it

L. Ferrara et al. (eds.), *International Macroeconomics in the Wake of the Global Financial Crisis*, Financial and Monetary Policy Studies 46,
https://doi.org/10.1007/978-3-319-79075-6_5

the world, brought about by both globalization and the wider and faster sharing of information across the globe granted by the ICT revolution.

However, as distances *between* countries were shrinking, inequalities *within* countries, especially in advanced economies, increased. It should be immediately added that while the former fact is quite uncontroversial, the actual direction of within-country inequality is less clear-cut (IMF 2017).

It is evident, however, that a significant increase in inequality took place in some advanced economies and that a widespread discontent towards globalization has taken hold in most democracies, leading to mass protests against economic integration and trade liberalization as well as to a rising demand for inward-oriented and protectionist policies (OECD 2015; Autor 2016; Biancotti et al. 2017).

The fight against domestic inequality and for inclusive growth has therefore become a priority in the political agenda of most nations and it is a much-discussed topic in international fora. Former U.S. president Barack Obama stated that income inequality is the "defining challenge of our time" (Obama 2013). In 2017 the World Economic Forum listed "rising income and wealth disparity" as the first of the top five risks to the global economy; the Italian Presidency of the G7 made inclusive growth and inequality reduction a priority and promoted a *Bari Policy Agenda on growth and inequalities*[1]; the G20[2] and other international organizations[3] have published several reports documenting surging inequality trends and pressing nations to act to revert them.

This shift in political priorities follows a slower movement in economic research that has progressively raised the study of inequality from a rather neglected field to a core topic. For a long time, economists considered the study of the distribution of income and wealth among individuals of secondary importance. The predominant attitude toward distributive issues was that the focus of economic research should be on how to increase the size of the pie rather than on how to divide it: "*Of the tendencies that are harmful to sound economics, the most seductive, and in my opinion the most poisonous, is to focus on questions of distribution... The potential for improving the lives of poor people by finding different ways of distributing current production is nothing compared to the apparently limitless potential of increasing production.*" (Lucas 2003). The strong rise in inequality in the United States and in other advanced countries that started nearly four decades ago and, more recently, the fallout from the global financial crisis in terms of household income and wealth, have made "questions of distribution" more relevant. Documenting the observed trends, discussing the causes of rising inequality and proposing measures to reduce it are now high on the research agenda.

Different explanations have been proposed for the surge in income inequality that affected most advanced economies over the past decades. Part of the literature argues that skill-biased technological change is the main factor (Acemoglu 2002) and that

---

[1]http://www.g7italy.it/sites/default/files/documents/Bari%20Policy%20Agenda%20final%20.pdf.

[2]Hamburg Action Plan (link).

[3]The IMF, the WBG and the OECD have all contributed to this call for political action: see IMF (2017), World Bank (2016) and OECD (2015).

the "race between education and technology" (Goldin and Katz 2008) has seen a strong acceleration in the pace of technological progress and possibly a significant change in the mix of skills required (Autor et al. 2006). Some researchers have revisited the evidence on the effect of trade with developing countries on wages in advanced economies (Krugman 2008), partially reverting the dismissive conclusions reached by the first studies in the 1990s.

The relative demerits of technological progress and globalization are at the forefront in the attempts to explain the rise in inequality. Other factors have been investigated too, like the evolution of policies and institutions, with particular emphasis on taxation, and the changes in family structure (OECD 2011; Zucman 2015). Piketty, starting from evidence of persistent high inequality over the last 200 years—interrupted only by the "exceptional" 1950–80 period—, argues against any purely technological explanation of inequality (like the Kuznets curve), maintaining that there is a tendency of the capitalist economy to generate large and persistent disparities, against which changes in social norms, institutional factors and therefore policies play a major role (Piketty 2013).

The lack of consensus in identifying the causes is reflected in the debate concerning the most appropriate policies to curb inequalities, with recipes ranging from better and broader education, to higher taxes, to trade protectionism.

In the rest of the chapter we will first discuss some problems related to the measurement of inequality and the progress made in the recent decades, briefly describing the main databases available for the analysis of income and wealth distribution. We will then illustrate the available evidence on the evolution of global inequality, mainly taking stock of studies by the OECD, the World Bank and by prominent researchers in this field. Finally, we will review the discussion among economists on the likely causes behind the observed trends.

2 Data

In measuring inequality the first, and perhaps foremost, question is "*inequality of what?*", (Sen 1997; Atkinson 2015). Economists have traditionally focused on the *outcomes* of economic activity, such as personal income, consumption and accumulated wealth, rather than on *opportunities* that individuals get to participate in production (e.g. access to basic health or education), or their abilities to transform the fruits of their work into actual wellbeing.[4] This latter consideration is central to Sen's *capabilities and functioning* approach, and leads him to argue that considering solely economic means acquired through the market by individuals provides only a very partial assessment the degree of inequality in a given society (Sen 1997).

Economists' traditional focus on income and wealth is not without reasons, though, and can be defended (Atkinson 2015) since income and wealth are the main means to acquire needed goods and services and they are also highly correlated with

[4]A. Sen (1997), p. 198.

other social and health indicators (Chetty et al. 2014; Cutler et al. 2006; Cannari and D'Alessio 2016; Case and Deaton 2017).[5] Large inequalities in income and wealth tend to reflect similar disparities in other metrics; they are not the sole cause of asymmetries in well-being, but they might still be an acceptable proxy. A second question of particular concern when looking at inequality across the globe is "*inequality among whom?*". Up until about fifteen years ago, economists either measured the dispersion of household incomes within a given country (*within country* inequality) or that of per-capita GDP across a sample of countries (*between country* inequality). Starting with the seminal work by Bourguignon and Morrisson (2002), more studies have been published that look at "global inequality", considering all individuals as inhabitants of the same world, independent of the country where they happen to live (Bourguignon 2015; Milanovic 2016). Such a cosmopolitan view can be challenged as not useful for policy design: redistributive mechanisms are established at the national level; there is no global government responsible and accountable for the wellbeing of world citizens. On the other hand, it can be argued that fast communication and international sharing of information are creating a "global village" in which people's perception of inequality on the world scale is sharpening (Milanovic 2005) and its moral relevance increasing.[6] Large disparities in income and wealth across countries also contribute to the rising tide of migrants. So, on the one hand public conscience is maturing a different attitude toward "global inequality", on the other the dividing line between national and international responsibilities for inequality is becoming blurred.

In any case, the discussion and analysis of "global inequality" relies on the availability of data on which it can be measured. In principle one would like to have a reliable database covering income, wealth, tax and transfers for a representative sample of individuals, including the very poor and the very rich, within as many nations as possible and for a significant time span. This is still a long way ahead, despite the progress made in data collection (and analysis) over the last decades.

Historically, the measurement of income and wealth inequality can be traced back to Vilfredo Pareto and Simon Kuznets. Pareto used tax data collected at the end of the 19th century in a number of European countries to estimate the distribution of income among their citizens. He found an empirical regularity characterizing within-country income distributions across time and space: the richest 20% received about 80% of aggregate income, but he did not suggest any economic explanation for this fact (Milanovic 2005). Tax data (income or inheritance), like those used by Pareto, have long been the main source of information on inequalities.

Starting in the 1950s and 60s, fresh evidence on income and wealth distribution has become available through household surveys,[7] which offer a richer set of individual

---

[5]This is not to say that focusing on these aspects is sufficient to describe, analyse and reduce inequality.

[6]The implicit assumption of perfect symmetry among world citizens implicit in the construction of most global inequality indicators can be relaxed allowing for the fact that "national borders matter and cannot be ignored in setting the principles of international distributive justice"(Brandolini and Carta 2016).

[7]For an historical sketch of household surveys see I. Visco (2015) and the literature cited therein.

data to accompany recorded income or consumption. Kuznets pioneered the use of survey data in the study of income distribution. Contrary to Pareto, he found that inequality does change over time, according to a dynamic law that leads inequality to follow an inverse U curve as a country industrializes (Kuznets 1955). Inequality is low in poor, mainly agricultural countries. Then it soars as industrialization brings rapid growth, hefty profits, rising wage differentials between rural and urban areas and greater job diversification within cities. When the process is over, most people are allowed to share in the higher standard of living produced by industrialization, and inequality returns to lower levels. Kuznets was aware of the limitations imposed by the restricted geographic coverage of his data "In concluding this paper I am acutely conscious of the meagreness of reliable information presented. This is perhaps 5% empirical information and 95% speculation […]".[8]

Since Kuznets' times, the practice of studying inequality with data collected through surveys spread; first in advanced countries, then among developing ones. Survey data on key flow variables, such as income and consumption, are now available for most countries. Conversely, micro-level information on wealth is still scarce and it typically covers shorter timespans. Despite its importance for the measurement of overall wellbeing, it has received less attention because of intrinsic measurement challenges, mostly on the asset side.

The longest standing surveys that cover both income and wealth are the **Bank of Italy's Survey of Household Income and Wealth** (SHIW), launched 1966, and the **Federal Reserve's Survey of Consumer Finances**, launched 1983, with a test run in 1962. Some other OECD countries, e.g. the United Kingdom and Spain, started similar endeavours in later decades. Several national surveys exist that cover income and consumption, but not wealth. Lately, Piketty and his co-authors promoted a revival in studies based on tax-files data (Atkinson et al. 2011; Piketty and Saez 2014). These two sets of data are the modern basis for the analysis of inequality at a global level.

Both data sources have shortcomings. Tax data have been collected for a much longer period, compared to survey data. However, contrary to surveys, they offer little information on personal characteristics that help understand the determinants of inequality, such as household structure, education and income sources, and exclude a large part of the less well off: those that do not file for taxes. These data are also sensitive to legal changes and—especially for the top incomes—might be affected by elusion and other practices to evade taxes. Household survey data do cover a larger set of the population (in terms of income and wealth) and give vital information on personal characteristics. But they also suffer from under-reporting or even refusal to participate in the survey by top income earners.

When computing inequality measures at the global level, some comparability issues exist. As a general rule, information on developing countries is less detailed and less reliable than data from advanced economies. Even for countries that are

[8]Kuznets (1955), p. 26. For the bulk of his analysis, he used data for the United States, the United Kingdom and two German states (Prussia and Saxony) from the end of the 19th century to 1950 (with differences across countries).

otherwise similar, definitions of some items (e.g. gross vs net income) and correction models for non-response and under-reporting may vary widely. Well-documented discrepancies between survey-based data and national accounts (Deaton 2005)[9] add another layer of complication: should the former be adjusted to align with the latter or vice versa? "The practical importance of these choices for the measured level of inequality is significant" (Brandolini and Carta 2016).

There are nowadays several international data sets of income inequality. A first distinction that can be made is between primary and secondary (derived) sources. Primary data sets contain micro-level data on personal income (or consumption) and can be harmonized ex ante or ex post.[10] Secondary dataset report only some key summary statistics on inequality within surveyed countries (typically Gini coefficients and some percentile ratios). The main advantage of secondary datasets is the large number of countries covered and the ease with which they allow comparison among them with ready-to-use summary statistics; on the downside care must be taken since there is little possibility of controlling data quality and consistence across time and space.

Primary sources are, most of the time, collections of harmonized country micro-data from existing surveys. The first attempt at constructing this kind of database is the **Luxembourg Income Study** (LIS), launched 30 years ago, and the **Luxembourg Wealth Study** (LWS). As mentioned above, income and wealth variables are sometimes measured based on different definitions in different countries: in the LIS/LWS database, they are mapped onto harmonized ones. The LIS spans about 50 countries, with data waves starting from 1970, but time coverage varies by country. The LWS so far covers Australia, Canada, Finland, Greece, Italy, the United Kingdom, the United States and Norway.[11] Data are available for research and other non-commercial uses.

The **World Bank's Living Standards Measurement Study** (LSMS) is the richest source of survey-based harmonized micro-data for less-developed nations. Along with income and consumption data, it recently started to record also information on durable assets and on productive capital owned by farming households.

The **European Union Statistics on Income and Living Conditions** (EU-SILC) was launched in mid-2000s. It is a harmonized household survey, coordinated by Eurostat, and carried out by national statistical institutes in European Union member states[12]; it provides a "common framework" to collect data on income, poverty, social exclusion and living conditions. Also in this case, data are standardized ex post.

[9]Typically income or consumption per capita estimated in the national account are higher than the respective mean per capita measured derived from surveys; Deaton argues that the latter are to be preferred over the former for developing countries.

[10]For a more detailed assessment of available data sources for international comparison of income distributions see Forster and Toth (2015).

[11]In 2013, the OECD published non-binding guidelines on the measurement of household wealth at the micro level, followed by the Framework for Statistics on the Distribution of Household Income, Consumption and Wealth.

[12]EU-SILC was launched in 2003 on the basis of an agreement between Eurostat, six Member States (Austria, Belgium, Denmark, Greece, Ireland, Luxembourg) and Norway. It was later expanded to cover all of the EU Member States.

As a rare example of ex-ante standardized primary source, the European Central Bank co-ordinates the euro area **Household Finance and Consumption Survey** (HFCS), that collects comparable results from 20 national surveys mostly run by central banks, based on a common core questionnaire; the first results, covering the 2008–2010 period, were published in 2013.[13] Non-euro area European countries, such as Denmark, soon replicated the effort. The main aim of the HFCS is to gather micro-level structural information on euro area households' assets and liabilities. The survey also collects other data in order to analyse the economic decisions taken by households and to evaluate the impact of shocks, policies and institutional changes.

The **OECD Income Distribution Database** (IDD) is based on data collected from national household surveys and administrative records according to common definitions. It includes 38 countries. The fundamental variable is household disposable income adjusted using an equivalence scale.[14] It does not allow access to underlying microdata, but provides a rather rich set of income distribution and poverty indicators, and the possibility of analysing income dispersion both before and after tax and transfers. In a sense—as Forster and Toth 2015 observe—the IDD "constitutes its own category between primary and secondary data sets." The **OECD Wealth Distribution Database** exploits national sources from 18 OECD members, collecting data on the distribution of real and financial assets and liabilities across households. A subset of these data is available to users.

The following are the main secondary data sources.

The United Nations University World Institute for Development Research (WIDER) **World Income Inequality Database** (WIID), launched in the late 1990s, provides a set of inequality indicators (Gini coefficients, decile and quintile shares, survey means and medians, income shares of the richest 5% and the poorest 5%) for almost 200 advanced, developing, and transition countries and for an extended period, starting in the 1960s in some cases. It builds on the historic Deininger-Squire Data Set (Measuring Income Inequality Database), the first to introduce minimum quality standards. It is a collection of Gini coefficients and cumulative quintile shares for almost 140 countries and includes information on population coverage, whether data are based on income or consumption and so forth. Data only cover the period between the 1960s and early 1990s and are freely available from the World Bank website.

The **All the Ginis** (ATG) data set has been put together by Branko Milanovic and collects harmonized Gini coefficients from seven original sources: the LIS, the Socio-Economic Database for Latin America, the EU-SILC, the World Bank Europe and Central Asia dataset, the World Income Distribution (WYD), World Bank PovCal, and the WIDER.

Recently an international team led by Atkinson, Piketty and other researchers has built a large dataset, the **World Wealth and Incomes Database** (WID)[15] that

[13]The first wave included only 17 countries.

[14]Variables like disposable income or consumption are divided by the square root of the number of family members.

[15]http://www.wid.world/.

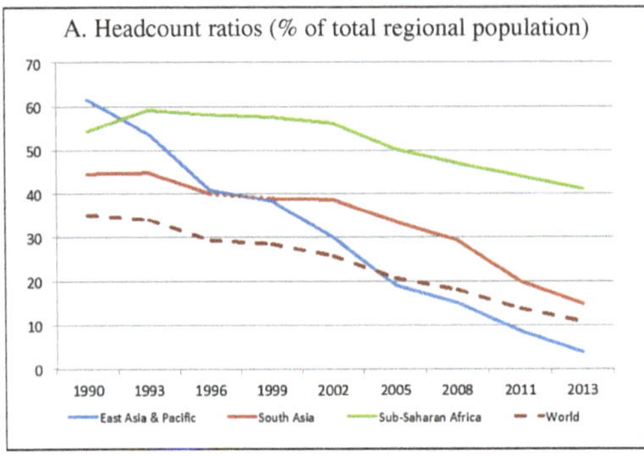

B. Absolute number of Poor (millions)

	1990	2013	Diff.
East Asia & Pacific	983.6	73.9	-909.7
South Asia	505.4	249.1	-256.3
Sub-Saharan Africa	278.1	390.3	112.2
RoW	*100.1*	*55.2*	-44.9
World	1867.2	768.5	-1098.7
% of poor in world population	35.3%	10.7%	

Fig. 1 World and Regional Trends, Poverty Headcount and Headcount Ratio, 1990–2013. (*Note* Author computation on World Bank Data, http://iresearch.worldbank.org/PovcalNet/ (accessed on October 26, 2017) and World Development Indicators (for total world population). Poverty is measured using the US$1.90-a-day 2011 purchasing power parity (PPP) poverty line. Latest available estimates are dated 2013. *RoW* indicates Rest of the World.)

combines national accounts, survey and fiscal data to measure both wealth and income inequality between and within countries for an extended time period (over a century of data). There are still large differences in the quality and amount of data available across countries.

3 Evolution of Global Inequality

Since the 1990s, rapid growth in a number of countries with a large and relatively poor population has greatly contributed to a reduction in the income gap between rich and poor nations and to a decline in global inequality.

The most striking effect of this "high globalization period" has been the sharp reduction in the number of poor in the world. More than 1 billion people escaped extreme poverty since 1990; which is even more remarkable considering that over the same period (1990–2013) the world population increased by almost 2 billion people (World Bank 2016). This reduction has been uneven. The greatest progress has been recorded in South East Asia, with China having the lion's share and in South Asia, with India playing this role. The one exception is Sub-Saharan Africa that now accounts for more than half of the total number of poor, with an incidence on total regional population of more than 40% (Fig. 1).[16]

This remarkable success and the sharp reduction in "global inequality" was reached notwithstanding the increase in inequality among households within many advanced and developing countries. Global inequality results from the composition of *between-country inequality* (differences in mean national incomes, population-

[16]Latin America whose poors' headcount ratio fell by about 10% points (from more than 15% in 1990 to almost 5% in 2013) is included in the "RoW" (Rest of the World) aggregate

weighted) and *within-country inequality* (dispersion of income among citizens of each country, again, population-weighted). Only the first was clearly reduced by globalization. So a sharp fall in poverty headcount and headcount ratios, and a rapid convergence in income levels among (some) developing and developed economies, coexisted with rising inequality is some advanced countries.[17]

A global inequality measure is obtained converting the incomes all world citizens in a common *numeraire*—the international dollar—based on purchasing power parities (PPP).[18] In a seminal paper, Bourguignon and Morrisson (2002) combined national income distributions for almost 180 countries,[19] summarized by the first nine decile income shares and the top two ventile shares, with national account statistics (per capita GDP) expressed in U.S. dollars at 1990 PPP to obtain the aggregate world distribution of incomes. With data covering the 1820–1992 period, they found a steady increase in world inequality up to the 1950s and a subsequent flattening of inequality. Following similar or alternative methods to estimate relative global inequality, several authors have extended and updated Bourguignon and Morrisson's results.

Recently the World Bank (building on Lakner and Milanovic 2016) has published estimates of world inequality updated to 2013. According to this analysis, between- and within-country inequality followed opposite trajectories over the last 25 years: the reduction in between-country inequality largely offset the increase in the "within" component, leading to a fall in global inequality. As stated above, this fall is mainly due to the improvement of living standards in South-east Asia, Russia and parts of Latin America.

It should be kept in mind that the gap between rich and developing economies is still large. Per capita income growth in populous countries like India and China was phenomenal, especially in China where it rose almost 10-fold between 1990 and 2016, greatly contributing to a reduction in poverty rates. However, per capita GDP, measured in 2011 international dollars, is still well below that of advanced countries: about one fourth of US per capita GDP for China, little more than one-tenth for India (Table 1).

While there is little doubt concerning the between-country component of global inequality, there is much uncertainty concerning the actual increase in the within-country component, and hence the final effect on global inequality.

Generally speaking, evidence from survey data suggests that inequality worsened in US, UK and some advanced European nations, and, among emerging economies, in Asia and Eastern Europe; in Latin America the evidence is mixed, and in Brazil inequality declined.

---

[17]As noted in Atkinson and Brandolini (2010) "*people are interested in both world inequality and world poverty, but the two literatures are separate… with an uneasy relationship between them*".

[18]One cannot simply sum income differences by converting all incomes in a common currency, say, the U.S. dollar; to aggregate world citizens in a single global measure one must take into account the differences in what a dollar can buy in different countries. This gives rise to quite complicated measurement issues; the construction of a different *numeraire* can have strong effects on the relative position of citizens of some countries and hence on the global measure.

[19]Some lumped into "country groups".

Table 1 GDP in constant international dollars per person

Country	1980	1990	2000	2016	1990–2016 (1)
China	721.6	1,515.5	3,681.7	14,274.7	9.4
% of US	***2.5%***	***4.1%***	***8.0%***	***26.7%***	***22.6***
India	1,297.2	1,801.7	2,546.4	6,206.9	3.4
% of US	***4.4%***	***4.9%***	***5.5%***	***11.6%***	***6.8***
United States	29,276.5	36,999.1	45,964.2	53,417.0	1.4

Source IMF, World Economic Outlook, October 2017
(1) For per capita GDP level, ratio of 2016 on 1990; for per capita GDP ratio with respect to US level, difference in percentage points between 2016 and 1990

These figures should be taken with a measure of caution because they are likely to incorporate a distortion, but the sign is unknown. On the one hand, inequality estimates from survey data generally suffer from downward bias, because the very rich under-report income and wealth, and the very poor - such as the homeless or undocumented immigrants—are excluded from the sampling frames. Moreover, in developing countries there is a scarcity of income and wealth data so most estimates are based on consumption, which in turn tends to reduce interpersonal differences as affluent families consume a much smaller share of their income compared to poor ones. On the other hand, the practice of aggregating data from different countries using a single PPP exchange rate per country may produce an upward bias: especially in poor countries, imposing the same "price level" on the whole territory may lead to underestimation of living standards in rural areas, and overestimation of inequality (this is the reason why for China and India overall inequality is split into rural and urban population inequality in the World Bank analysis).[20]

Finally, the choice of the index that measures inequality matters, since different indices correspond to different weights given to individuals in the population. In this case, the Gini index (blue line in Fig. 2) suggests a smaller reduction compared to the Theil index (mean log deviation, given by the height of the bars in the same figure).

No widely agreed-upon and fully satisfactory solution to these problems exists. A general caveat is that, while the analysis of overall trends is obviously relevant in a world where economies and citizens are ever more connected, it can be misleading and a deeper look at national microdata is necessary to have a better assessment of inequality dynamics (Atkinson and Brandolini 2000).

Lakner and Milanovic (2016) proposed an anonymous[21] "Growth Incidence Curve" that assesses the increase in real incomes for different percentiles of the world income distribution and attempts to square the evidence on the evolution of

[20]See Lakner and Milanovic (2016) and—for a similar argument concerning the use of the main city price level in the World Bank Doing Business data—Borin et al. (2014).

[21]This curve is "anonymous" as it does not tell what actually happened to people that were in a given decile of the income distribution in 1988 over the next 20 years since the regional composition of the different global income groups changed radically, because growth was uneven across regions.

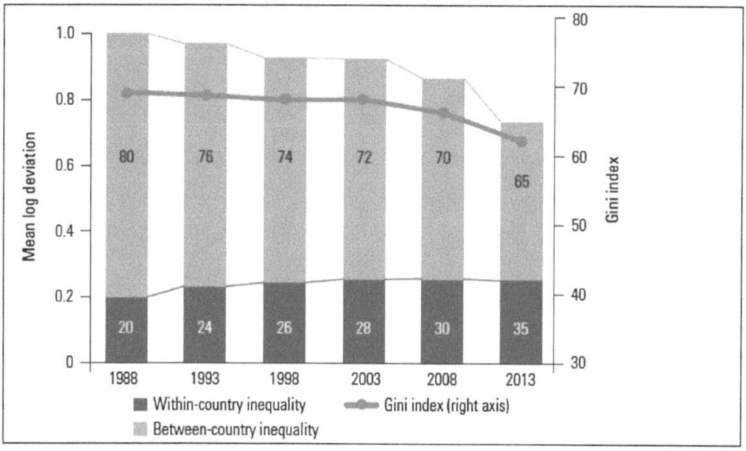

Fig. 2 Global, between and within countries inequality, 1988–2013. (*Source* World Bank. 2016. Poverty and Shared Prosperity 2016: Taking on Inequality. Washington, DC: World Bank. https://doi.org/10.1596/978-1-4648-0958-3. *Note* Household income or consumption per capita is obtained from national surveys and converted with 2011 PPP exchange rates; within-country distributions are based on deciles. The blue line (right axis) shows the level of global inequality measured by the Gini index, the height of the bars shows that measured in mean log deviation (Theil index). The latter is split into inequality within countries, population-weighted (red bars), and between-country (yellow bars), which captures differences in average incomes across countries. Numbers on the bars measure the relative contribution (in %) of these two sources to global inequality.)

between- and within-country inequality in a consistent picture that highlights globalization's winners and losers.

The curve is reported in Fig. 3. It is obtained putting together the results of about 600 household surveys from more than 100 advanced and developing countries,[22] covering the "high globalization period" (1988–2008). Survey data are centred at benchmark years at five years intervals for the period under exam, all after-tax real income data are expressed in international dollars at the 2005 PPPs, and individuals are ranked by their real household per capita income.

On the y-axis is reported the difference between real per capita income[23] of a given ventile of world's population in 2008, with that of the "same" ventile, *that does not necessarily comprise the same people nor the same countries*, in 1988. This computation is repeated for each successive ventile up to the top, singling out the richest 4 and 1% of the world population.

Milanovic (2016) stresses three facts that emerge from the graph (also dubbed "Elephant curve"):

- People around the global median (point A) have made large real income gains. They are, in a proportion of about 90%, from the middle classes of Asian emerging

[22]This dataset covers more than 90% of world GDP and 95% of world population.

[23]Expressed in dollar terms, at 2011 PPP.

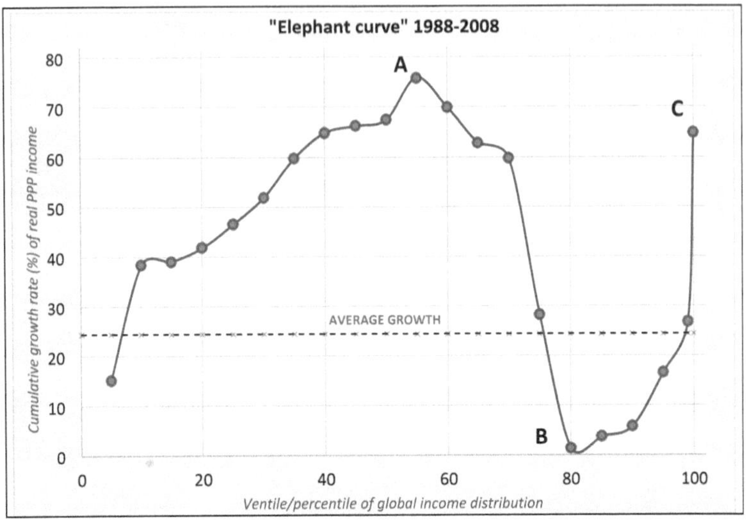

Fig. 3 Cumulative real income growth between 1988 and 2008 at various percentiles of the global income distribution. (*Source* based on Lakner and Milanovic (2016))

economies, mostly China and India. Milanovic labels this the **emerging global middle class**, mainly constituted by individuals resident in "resurgent Asia", but whose per capita income is still low (less than 15 international dollars per day) if compared to the rich-world median income.

- People around the 80–85th percentile of the distribution (point B) have seen little or no increase in their per capita income. About three-quarters of them belong to the "old rich" OECD countries,[24] where they constitute the middle to lower middle class.[25] This group of people can be dubbed the **lower middle class of the rich world**.
- Finally, the very top of the world distribution (point C) saw a rise in real income similar to the middle class in resurgent Asia. This is at least partly consistent with Piketty's claim that much of the action in the rich world has been at the very top of the distribution. People at the top of the world income distribution are mainly the very rich of advanced economies (United States has the lion's share here, accounting for one half of the group), and to a lesser extent the wealthy of some emerging nations (Brazil, South Africa and Russia). This group can be named the **global plutocrats**.

[24]Western Europe, North America, Oceania and Japan.

[25]The concept of "class" here must be interpreted with some care, first of all because the "anonymity" of the clusters does not allow for a clear identification of who is in each income bracket in a given year. Furthermore, to identify in a more convincing fashion a "class", one should examine other dimensions beyond income, like the role of property and of occupations (Atkinson and Brandolini 2011).

The losers of globalization are to be found in the ranks of the lower middle class in the rich world, while the clear winners have been the poor and middle classes of emerging markets (Asian countries in particular) and the very rich (global plutocrats).

The interpretation of these results has been criticized[26] since many other factors might explain the shape of the curve: demographic shifts, stagnation in Japan, and former Soviet Union satellite states that contributed to depress "middle class" incomes. Removing Japan, former Soviet Union satellite states and China results in a substantially flat curve, where most people saw a 40% increase in income apart from the very top (higher increase) and very bottom (lower increase) of the distribution. Considering the different patterns followed across countries by income growth and inequality, it seems difficult to reduce to the unique action of globalization what is more likely due to a combination of global and country-specific factors.

Figure 3—however—summarizes known facts that have been examined separately in the literature and highlights divergences: the unprecedented growth of China and other large countries that were not rich and whose income gap with the West narrowed substantially over the last three decades; the stagnating median income in many advanced countries and the diminished expectations of the middle classes there; the widening gap in those countries with respect to the top 1% of the distribution.

Another indication we can derive from the chart is that, if we take a fully cosmopolitan view treating all individuals the same irrespective of their citizenship, a large share of world population that was in the central clusters of the distribution has fared very well, reducing the gap with respect to the richer world. Valuing a given percentage gain in income more when it accrues to a poor person than to a rich one, and considering that no income group had a decline in real income, we should confirm our positive judgement on the "high globalization period", already suggested when looking at poverty reduction.

The situation changes if one analyses the data from the point of view of nation states in the advanced world: here, working class income has suffered, if not a contraction, a prolonged stagnation. As seen in Fig. 2, within-country inequality rose over the last 25 years and now accounts for about 35% of global inequality, up from 20% in 1980. According to OECD data, income inequality in OECD countries is at its highest level over the past half century. The average income of the richest 10% of the population is about nine times that of the poorest 10% across the OECD, while this ratio stood at 7 to 1 in the 1980s.

The global financial crisis worsened the socio-economic situation of large swaths of the population in most advanced countries, aggravating discontent and pushing up the number of people at risk of poverty. The crisis did not affect all citizens in the same way: manufacturing workers have been more likely to experience displacement and wage cuts; youths have been hit harder than elders, lacking their social protection and suffering the permanent damages coming from unemployment or careers made of temporary, low-quality jobs.

The most striking divergence is portrayed by the evolution of the wealth distribution in the US. According to recent estimates by the Federal Reserve (Fig. 4), wealth

[26]Corlett (2016).

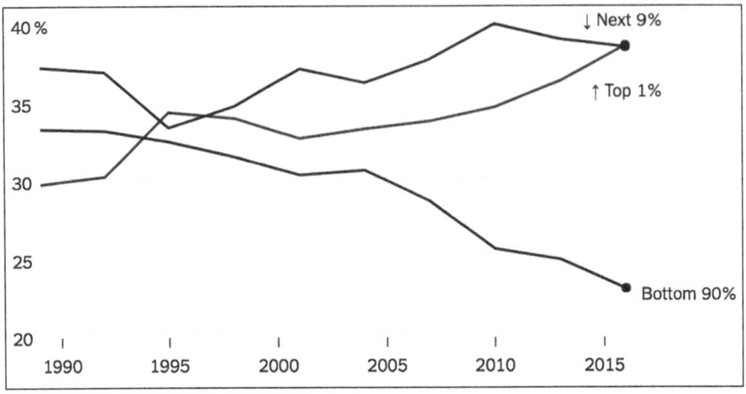

Fig. 4 Wealth shares by wealth percentile in U.S., 1989-2016 surveys. *Source* Survey of Consumer Finances (Federal Reserve Bulletin, Sept. 2017)

of the top 1% accounts for almost 40% of the total (data referring to 2016), while the share of the poorest 90% has been constantly falling since the end of the 1980s. The amount of total wealth accruing on the P90-P99 percentiles has been rising until 2010, then it experienced a fall as a consequence of the global financial crisis.

The rise of income and wealth share at the top is not confined to the U.S. (Piketty and Saez 2014) and also calls into question other factors. The OECD observes (OECD 2015) that in many advanced economies tax and transfers did not reverse the increase in market income inequality, as redistributive measures have been weakened by policies adopted in the past.

The debate among economists is far from having reached a definite conclusion on the effects of the integration of emerging markets in the global economy. Before turning to this topic it is worth stressing once more that—from a global perspective—the overall effect of globalization on the economic wellbeing of world citizens has been clearly positive, irrespective of one's assessment of the relation between gains and losses.

4 Causes of Rising Within-Country Inequality

There is a lively, ongoing discussion among economists concerning the main forces underlying the rise in inequality. No general agreement has been reached on the key causes and on whether these common causes even exist. Country-specific explanations might play a greater role: there are dissimilarities across countries in the evolution of inequality, and one needs to account for different starting points, situations and institutions. A non-exhaustive list of potential drivers of inequality would comprise: (1) globalization and trade; (2) technological change, in particular progress in information and communication technologies (ICT); (3) changes in policies and social attitudes (like tax rates, redistributive policies or pay norms); (4) a reduced role of trade unions.

By far the bulk of the economic literature has focused on the rising skill premium (i.e. the gap between market wages of college and high school graduates) in the US. The US economy offers a very rich and reliable set of data, even compared to other OECD members, and is in many respect the most developed industrial country. In this sense it is a good place to study and compare alternative explanations. However, it is risky to generalise results valid for the US to the rest of the advanced economies, let alone to the emerging ones, that also experienced a surge in inequality. The rising skill premium is less controversial as a focal point since it has been recorded in many advanced economies, and wage dispersion is a natural candidate for explaining rising inequality since almost ¾ of household income in OECD countries consists of labour earnings. This notwithstanding, one should bear in mind that wage dispersion does not map one-to-one with *ex post* inequality of disposable income at the household level, which is the concept adopted in computing statistics on inequality. In fact in the US, after the "great compression"[27] of wage earnings that took place in the interwar period, pay differentials started to widen again, but it was not until the early 1980s that this rising dispersion in market earnings translated into widening inequality.

There are two main explanations of the widening skill premium offered by the literature; the first looks at globalization and trade, the second at skill-biased technological progress. Following the literature, we will consider the two explanations in turn. But a more plausible account would start from considering technical change as endogenous (and related to globalisation) rather than exogenous. Technical change should be thought as the consequence of choices made by firms concerning what to produce and how to produce it. These choices depend on the economic environment in which firms operate, and firms will choose technologies that exploit the opportunities given by a globalized world, in turn changing the pattern of globalization.[28]

A first strand of the globalization literature, originating in the late 1980s and early 1990s, focused on the Hecksher-Ohlin model and the Stolper-Samuelson theorem as a general, simplified framework to analyse the effect on inequality of the entry of developing countries with large endowments of unskilled labour into the international market.

The Stolper-Samuelson theorem shows that in a world where there are two factors of production, skilled and unskilled labour, which can move freely within a country so that wages for each type of labour are the same, and two goods are produced under constant returns to scale with different skill intensity, there is a one to one relationship between the relative price of the goods and that of the labour types:

$$\hat{p}_H - \hat{p}_L = \left(\theta_{H,H} - \theta_{H,L}\right)\left(\hat{w}_H - \hat{w}_L\right)$$

[27] Goldin and Margo (1992).

[28] Technological innovation in products like the iPhones or Boeing airplanes cannot be separated from the fact that their production process is fragmented internationally, thanks to globalization, which enables the exploitation of costs reduction opportunities and productivity gains from increased specialization.

where $\theta_{H,H}$ and $\theta_{H,L}$ are the shares of skilled labour in the production of the two goods, $\hat{p}_H$ and $\hat{p}_L$ the percentage changes in high skill-intensive and low skill-intensive good prices and $\hat{w}_H$ and $\hat{w}_L$ the percentage changes in their respective wages.

In this context, cheaper imports of low-skill labour intensive goods from developing countries into advanced economies would increase the relative price of skill-intensive products and, under Stolper-Samuelson hypothesis, the relative wage of skilled workers, thus increasing inequality.

Several papers, relying on the Stolper-Samuelson framework, have tried to estimate the labour content of imports in advanced nations (mainly the U.S.) to assess its impact on the wage structure of the importing country. Cline (1997) surveyed a number of researches in this strand of literature, concluding that trade could explain only about one fifth of the increase in inequality since the 1980s. Hence, the late 1990s consensus was that skill-biased technological change, rather than North-South trade[29], was the main cause of rising wage inequality in the US.

Later studies, using data for the second half of the 1990s and the first decade of the 2000s, did not reach dramatically different conclusions. However, Krugman (2008) suggested—without computing precise estimates—that the rising importance of US trade with developing countries might have given trade a greater weight in US inequality in 1990s and 2000s.

These conclusions might surprise on the downside, given the magnitude of the underlying changes in the global economy. From the end of the 1980s North-South trade increased dramatically: it can be estimated that by 2001, when China joined the WTO, almost 1.5 billion workers[30] had integrated into the world economy labour force, doubling its size with respect to a decade before (Freeman 2008).

The share of imports from developing countries into the US kept rising over this period, and most of the increase came from imports originating in countries with very low wages compared to the US: as of 2012 China's hourly compensation costs were still below 10% of US costs (Fig. 5).

The increase in imports from countries rich in low-skill labour is not a phenomenon confined to the US: in the generality of advanced economies we can observe a sharp growth of the unskilled labour content in manufacturing goods consumed there. Most of the increase is due to imports from China and India; in 2008 these two countries accounted for almost 80% of total unskilled labour content in goods consumption, up from less than 60% in 1995 (Fig. 6).

From a theoretical point of view, the simplifying assumption in the Hecksher—Ohlin model with 2 goods and 2 countries, used as a reference framework in this literature, are quite strong and might not fully capture some relevant aspects of the effect of trade on inequality. In particular perfect substitution between imported and domestic goods, identical technologies across countries and perfect competi-

[29]Also related phenomena, like immigration and weaker trade unions, were taken into consideration.

[30]These are mainly workers from China, India and former Soviet Union bloc, which up until the late 1980s were de facto excluded from international markets.

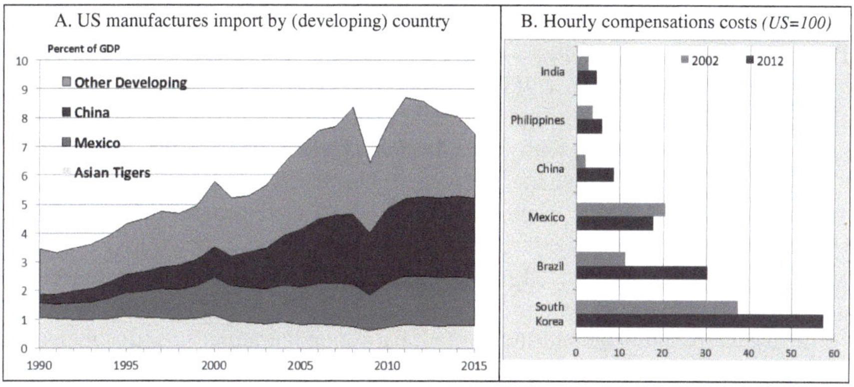

Fig. 5 US manufactures imports by country and relative compensation costs. (*Source* Based on OECD *Bilateral Trade in Goods by Industry and End-use (BTDIxE), ISIC Rev.3* and Conference Board, *International Labor Comparisons program*. *Note*: Compensation costs for China and India are not comparable with each other or with those of other countries.)

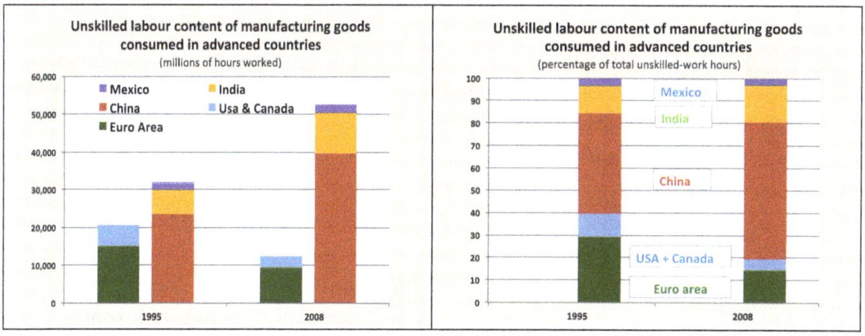

Fig. 6 Unskilled labour content in manufacturing goods consumed in advanced countries, by country of origin. (*Note* Computations on WIOD data, based on the methodology proposed by Borin and Mancini (2015))

tion (which implies no market power since prices are taken as given by agents) can seriously limit the analysis.

A more recent strand of the literature uses different theoretical and empirical approaches to assess the impact of imports from developing countries on income distribution in advanced countries, focusing in particular on the effect of trade on local labour markets.[31] Starting from the clear evidence of a decline in manufacturing employment in import-competing US industries that run parallel to the surge in China's trade, Autor *et al.* (2016) attempt to measure the impact of China's import competition on the employment and wage margin in local labour markets ("commuting zones", CZs). They find that (i) CZs that are more exposed to increased import

[31] Studies on the impact of globalization on inequality in developing economies find—in general—a stronger effect (Goldberg and Pavcnik 2007).

competition from China suffered larger reductions in manufacturing employment; (ii) that job losses for unskilled workers (less than college education) extended to non-manufacturing industries within the same CZ; (iii) proposed estimates of China's competition effects on jobs and salaries vary according to the method used. For manufactures directly competing with China, the China effect accounts for 10%[32] of total fall in manufacturing employment between 1999 and 2011; but the number doubles when the indirect impact is taken into account, and increases further if we move beyond the manufacturing sector (up to 2 million workers in the entire economy); the fall in wages is concentrated in the bottom four deciles of the distribution and outside the manufacturing sector.[33]

The results from this second strand of globalisation literature show that increased import competition from developing countries produced a significant effect in terms of job displacements and wages declines in advanced economies. This is not a direct estimate of the impact on inequality, since job losses and wage declines are—at least partially—compensated by increasing social transfers, but it is suggestive of a non-negligible impact.

The second approach explains the observed rise in the skill premium with skill-biased technical change. Returns to education—measured by the gap between wages of college and high-school graduates—has been increasing for most of the post WWII period in the U.S., suggesting that the demand for college-educated workers has outpaced the supply, that nonetheless grew for most of last century (Tinbergen's race between education and technology). Technological advances—in particular in the ICT sector starting from the 1990s—have increased labour productivity but also displaced low-skill workers, creating an ever-greater demand for higher skills. To gain a better insight into the determinants of the skill premium, researchers refer to the so-called "canonical model"[34] that assumes skilled and unskilled workers produce two imperfectly substitutable goods, technology is "factor-augmenting" (parameterized by a multiplicative factor A_H for high skill and A_L for low skill labour) and the aggregate production function takes a CES form. Assuming H and L are the supply of high and low skill labour respectively, we obtain the following law of motion for the relative wage of skilled versus unskilled workers:

$$ln\left(\frac{w_H}{w_L}\right) = constant + \frac{\sigma - 1}{\sigma} ln\left(\frac{A_H}{A_L}\right) - \frac{1}{\sigma}\left(\frac{H}{L}\right)$$

where σ is the elasticity of substitution between high and low skill labour, $\left(\frac{A_H}{A_L}\right)$ measures changes in the technology skill bias and $\left(\frac{H}{L}\right)$ those in the relative supply of high skill and low skill labour. As long as $\sigma > 1$, which is what is normally assumed in the literature, an increase in the technological skill bias will translate into a raise in the skill premium, holding $\left(\frac{H}{L}\right)$ constant. Goldin and Katz (2008)

[32] About 560 thousand jobs.

[33] The importance in the overall decline of earnings of the job-loss related fall in income is roughly 1.5 times that due to the fall in wages.

[34] See Acemoglu et al. (2012).

argue that the rising skill premium contributed between 60 and 70% to the observed increase in earnings inequality, joining a number of other influential studies arguing that the surge of inequality since the 1980s reflected a rise in the demand for skill that accelerated with the onset of the ICT revolution and met a slowdown in the growth of the relative supply of college-graduate workers during the same period.

But how far can this simple framework explain the skill premium dynamics? Card and DiNardo (2002) argue that the surge in inequality during the 1980s is explained by a fall in the real value of the minimum wage. However, earning dispersion continued to widen over the last two decades, so it is unlikely that a one-off event can explain a prolonged trend.

Assuming that the demand for skills follows a log linear trend ($ln\left(\frac{A_H}{A_L}\right) = a + bt$, t being time), as generally done in the literature, one obtains:

$$ln\left(\frac{w_{H,t}}{w_{L,t}}\right) = constant + \frac{\sigma - 1}{\sigma}bt - \frac{1}{\sigma}\left(\frac{H_t}{L_t}\right)$$

where the subscript t has been added to clarify time dependence. Estimating this model on microdata[35] for the period prior to 1987 produces a remarkably good fit (see Acemoglu and Autor 2012) but extrapolating results for the following years shows that the college—high school wage gap rose less than predicted by the model. This points to some limitations in what the model captures.

In particular, the skill bias story associated with the ITC revolution points to a more complex interaction between skills, labour demand and wages. In the 1980s, consistently with the "canonical model", we observed a monotone surge of inequality with upper incomes rising with respect to mid and lower incomes, and the gap between the median income and the lower percentiles of the distribution also increasing. Starting in early 1990s, the U.S. earnings distribution "polarized": a persistent rise in the gap between top and median incomes was accompanied by a contraction of that between median and low income. This wage polarization was associated with a job polarization, where high- and low-skill employment increasing faster than medium skill jobs.

This suggests that ICT substituted medium-skilled, repetitive routine workers, more than they did displace low-skill jobs. Furthermore, contrary to the implication of the canonical model, whereby only technological regress would produce a fall in real wages, real wages did fall in the case of less educated workers.

[35]CPS is the most commonly used survey for this purpose in the U.S.

5 Policy Options

The last ten to fifteen years has witnessed a noticeable change in attitudes toward economic inequality at both the academic[36] and the political level. This change happened while global disparities between citizens of the developed world and those living in developing countries went through the most remarkable reduction since the start of the industrial revolution.

However, this reduction in global inequality overlapped with a widespread increase in income and wealth disparities within advanced economies and a surge in migration flows from poor to rich countries (IMF 2016). Both phenomena prompted a feeling of insecurity among the weaker strata of population in those countries, an insecurity that has been exacerbated by the effects of the global financial crisis.

While the study of inequality has gained prominence and reached the headlines in the political debate, we are still far from having a shared view on what should be done or—even—on whether anything should be done.

Critics of activist policies to reduce inequality, maintain that the real concern should be fighting poverty[37] and ensuring "equality of opportunities" rather than of outcomes. They argue that in a market economy achievements in business (or sport) are rewarded according to the benefits they provide to the buyers or society at large. Furthermore, high rewards provide incentives for talented entrepreneurs and innovators to devote efforts to what they can do best: "*a well-functioning economy needs the correct allocation of talent*" (Mankiw 2013). So—as long as inequality is efficient—it would be detrimental for society as a whole to try to reduce it. Critics also raise doubts on the soundness of inequality measures from a "moral" standpoint, citing as an example the fact that the most common measure, the Gini coefficient, violates the "Pareto principle", rising when the incomes of the rich increase even if the incomes of the poor remain the same.

A subtler argument stems from the observation that today's inequality in advanced economies is very different from that of last century. Differences in income in a modern advanced economy do not translate in equally large differences in wellbeing. Most of the people ranked poor in our statistics still enjoy a refrigerator and a car, although of lower quality compared to the rich; but the "*lived difference is rather smaller than that between having fresh meat and milk and having none*" or "*between motoring and hiking through the muck*" (The Economist 2007).

Those who argue in favour of a reduction in inequality would normally object that unequal distribution of income and wealth greatly affects equality of opportunity, not least since most empirical studies find a very strong correlation between parents' and

[36]"I was at the World Bank and a commission reviewed our work on inequality for the U.S. Congress or somebody, and the head of the commission said to us: '*You are spending taxpayer money to study issues like inequality? Which goes directly against capitalism and growth.*' That was the perception, that it should not be studied" (Branko Milanovic interview at PBS, Jun 29, 2017).

[37]"A common reaction in the popular press, in political debate, and in academic discussions is to regard the increase in inequality as a problem that demands new redistributive policies. I disagree. I believe that inequality as such is not a problem and that it would be wrong to design policies to reduce it. What policy should address is not inequality but poverty." (Feldstein 1999)

children's achievements in terms of education and income levels achieved as adults. Hence the place in society where one is born is a very strong predictor of one's future fortunes. This argument has an even stronger flavour, from a global perspective, as differences in wellbeing across countries account for about two thirds of global income inequality (OECD 2017). This is what Milanovic dubbed the "*citizenship rent*": the country one is born in greatly affects personal prospects concerning income, education, health and life expectancy.

Concerning the supposed trade-off between inequality and efficiency, the empirical literature has not reached a consensus, but it is fair to say that a growing number of researchers actually argue for a positive relationship between equality and economic growth. Too large a disparity in terms of income and wealth among citizens undermines health and education achievements of the disadvantaged, lowering human capital accumulation and thus affecting long-run growth. Beyond purely economic reasons, when inequalities are perceived as unjustified and too wide, social cohesion might be endangered and political stability weakened. This, in turn, has a negative impact on capital accumulation and growth. Inequality has also led to a demand for inward-looking policies that might damage economic prosperity.

As the IMF writes in its (IMF 2017) Fiscal Monitor: "*Rising inequality and slow economic growth in many countries have focused attention on policies to support inclusive growth. While some inequality is inevitable in a market-based economic system, excessive inequality can erode social cohesion, lead to political polarization, and ultimately lower economic growth.*"

The argument that large income inequalities no longer imply equally big differences in wellbeing might also be criticized. First, it underestimates the fact that, as the domain of the market economy spreads including goods and services once provided within families or by the State, the effect of income disparities is actually magnified, influencing access to healthcare, assistance for old age, education as so forth. Furthermore, on a political level, a very unequal society might mean a society where "the rich" have disproportionate power to influence the political agenda, leaving less space for the others to have their voice heard and taken into account.

With these premises, it should not surprise that proposal to address rising inequality vary widely among researchers and institutions. The IMF (2017) focuses on three key actions that fiscal policy can undertake: modifying tax rates at the top of the income distribution, introducing a universal basic income,[38] and more and better education and health programs. Only the third action is quite uncontroversial. If anything, the current debate is about lowering taxes for the rich and on capital (that, again, mainly affects the wealthier part of the population). Policy advice from the OECD (2011) also includes increasing the marginal tax rate, closing loopholes in the tax system that disproportionately benefit higher income groups and "reconsider" taxation on all forms of property and transfer of assets, including bequest. The G7 Bari Policy Agenda, reflecting a policy compromise, contains a less explicit call for "*higher spending in specific policy areas without necessarily altering the overall budget envelope.*" On the introduction of a universal basic income there is no agreement:

[38] An unconditional transfer paid to all citizens in a given country.

it is controversial for its potential impact on public finances and for its interaction with, and accommodation within, existing social protection schemes. Finally, while the general concept is clear, different solutions are debated for its translation into laws and for its practical implementation. The OECD (2017) concludes that while "a universal basic income is very simple [...] existing social benefits are not, replacing them with a universal flat-rate benefit produces complex patterns of gains and losses." The proposed solution is to keep the door open to changes in existing social protection systems, while avoiding to point to a one-size-fits-all approach like universal basic income as the best policy option for all countries.

Among researchers, Milanovic suggested that to tackle within-country inequality it is best to strive for broader and better education of the labour force, rather than to raise income taxes. This solution would for sure meet less political opposition, but might sound insufficient or unconvincing to some (Piketty, Atkinson). Concerning between-country inequality, Milanovic advocates policies that foster faster growth of poor countries, which is quite uncontroversial. His second suggestion is more challenging: in line with his critique of the "citizenship rent", he favours a large, controlled migration from poor to rich countries.

Atkinson (2016) advocates a form of basic income, a "participation income" distributed to all those who contribute to society, which includes workers, unemployed, persons actively searching a job, caregivers, and those in education or job training programs. The others would be excluded, with the exception of the ill or disabled. He also suggests a stronger redistribution through taxation on both income and wealth and higher minimum wages. Atkinson has some more radical proposals, too. Moving from the consideration that globalization and technological progress are among the main drivers of rising inequality, but that they are not "*exogenous, uncontrollable forces*", he suggests governments should take direct action in those fields too. However it seems doubtful that Governments can effectively influence the direction of technological change, as Atkinson seems to imply.[39]

It is fair to say that some uncontroversial measures are shared by most proponents, while the presence of conflicting interests both within and among countries leaves ample room for controversies on a wider set of redistributive measures.

References

Acemoglu D (2002) Technical change, inequality, and the labor market. J Econ Lit 40(1):7–72

Acemoglu D, Autor D (2012) What does human capital do: a review of goldin and katz's the race between education and technology. J Econ Lit 50(2):426–463

Atkinson AB (2015) Inequality: what can be done? Harvard University Press

Atkinson T (2016) How to spread wealth. Foreign Aff 95(1):29–33

[39]"[...] for instance, to shift priorities from driverless cars, which will likely reduce jobs, to technology that helps the elderly stay in their homes, which would increase the demand for caregivers." (Atkinson 2016 p. 30).

Atkinson T, Brandolini A (2000) Promise and pitfalls in the use of secondary data-sets: income inequality in OECD countries, Banca d'Italia, Temi di Discussione, N. 379
Atkinson T, Brandolini A (2010) On analyzing the world distribution of income. World Bank Econ Rev 24(1):1–37
Atkinson T, Brandolini A (2011) On the identification of the "middle class". society for the study of income inequality, ECINEQ WP 2011–217
Atkinson AB, Piketty T, Saez E (2011) Top Incomes in the Long Run of History. J Econ Lit 49(1):3–71
Autor DH, Katz LF, Kearney MS (2006) The Polarization of the U.S. Labor Market. Am Econ Rev 96(2):189–194
Autor DH et al (2016) Importing political polarization the electoral consequences of rising trade exposure. NBER working paper No. 22637, No. 22637
Biancotti C, Borin A, Mancini M (2017) Euroscepticism: another brick in the wall, Bank of Italy, unpublished manuscript
Borin A, Cristadoro R Mattevi E (2014) Investimenti diretti esteri e qualità delle istituzioni. Bank of Italy occasional paper, N. 230
Borin A, Mancini M (2015) Follow the value added: bilateral gross export accounting. Bank of Italy working paper, N.1026
Bourguignon F (2015) The globalization of inequality. Princeton University Press
Bourguignon F, Morrisson C (2002) Inequality among world citizens 1820–1992. Am Econ Rev 92(4):727–744
Brandolini A, Carta F (2016) Some reflections on the social welfare bases of the measurement of global income inequality. Bank of Italy working paper, N. 1070
Cannari L, D'Alessio G (2016) Socio-economic conditions and mortality in Italy. Politica Econ 2:331–350. https://doi.org/10.1429/83968
Card D and DiNardo JE (2002) Skill-biased technological change and rising wage inequality: some problems and puzzles. J Labor Econ 20(4):733–783
Case A, Deaton A (2017) Mortality and morbidity in the 21st century. Brookings papers on economic activity, Spring 2017
Chetty R, Hendren N, Kline P, Saez E (2014) Where is the land of opportunity: the geography of intergenerational mobility in the United States. Q J Econ 129(4):1553–1623
Cline W (1997) Trade and income distribution. Peterson Institute for International Economics
Corlett A (2016) Examining an elephant. Globalisation and the lower middle class of the rich world, Resolution foundation report
Cutler D, Deaton A, Muney A Lleras (2006) The determinants of mortality. J Econ Perspect 20(3):97–120
Deaton A (2005) Measuring poverty in a growing world (or measuring growth in a poor world). Rev Econ Stat 87:1–19
Feldstein M (1999) Reducing poverty, not inequality. Public Interest 137:33–41
Freeman RB (2008) The new global labor market. Focus 26(1). Summer-Fall, University of Wisconsin–Madison
Forster and Toth (2015) Cross-country evidence of the multiple causes of inequality changes. In: handbook of income distribution. Vol 2B, ch. 19
Goldin C, Katz L (2008) The race between education and technology. Harvard University Press
Goldin C, Margo RA (1992) The great compression: the wage structure in the united states at mid-century. Q J Econ 107(1):1–34
Goldberg PK, Pavcnik N (2007) Distributional effects of globalization in developing countries. J Econ Lit 45:39–82
Krugman PR (2008) Trade and wages reconsidered. Brooking Papers on Economic Activity, 1 (Spring), 103–137
Kuznets S (1955) Economic growth and income inequality. Am Econ Rev 45(1):1–28
IMF (2016) Spillovers from China's Transition and from Migration, chapter 4 in World Economic Outlook, Oct 2016

IMF (2017) Tackling inequality, chapter 1 in Fiscal Monitor, Oct 2017
Lakner C, Milanovic B (2016) Global income distribution: from the fall of the berlin wall to the great recession. World Bank Econ Rev 30(2):203–232. https://doi.org/10.1093/wber/lhv039
Lucas RE (2003) The industrial revolution: past and future. The Region, 2003 Annual report of the federal reserve Bank of Minneapolis, 5–20
Mankiw G (2013) Defending the One Percent. J Econ Perspect 27(3):21–34
Milanovic B (2005) Worlds apart: measuring international and global inequality. Princeton University Press
Milanovic B (2010) The haves and the have-nots: a brief and idiosyncratic history of global inequality. Basic Books
Milanovic B (2016) Global inequality: a new approach for the age of globalization. Harvard University Press
Obama B (2013) Remarks by the president on economic mobility, Washington D.C. https://obamawhitehouse.archives.gov/the-press-office/2013/12/04/remarks-president-economic-mobility
OECD (2011) Divided we stand. OECD, Paris
OECD (2015) In it Together. OECD, Paris
OECD (2017) Basic income as a policy option: can it add up? policy brief in the future of work. OECD Publishing, Paris
Piketty T (2013) Capital in the twenty-first century. Harvard University Press
Piketty T, Saez E (2014) Inequality in the long run. Science 344(6186):838–843. https://doi.org/10.1126/science.1251936
Sen A (1997) On Economic Inequality (Expanded edition). Oxford University Press
The Economist (2007) The new (improved) Gilded Age, Dec 19th issue
Visco I (2015) Fifty years of The Survey on Household Income and Wealth and the Financial Accounts, Seminar on The Bank of Italy's Analysis of Household Finances, concluding remarks
World Bank (2016) Taking on inequality. World Bank Group, Washington DC
Zucman G (2015) The hidden wealth of nations: the scourge of tax havens. University of Chicago Press

Part II
Global Growth Slowdown: Demand-Side Explanations

Trade Weakness: Cycle or Trend?

Alessandro Borin, Virginia Di Nino, Michele Mancini and Massimo Sbracia

Abstract In 2011–2016 global trade volumes systematically surprised on the downside, to a much larger extent than real GDP; in other words, the income elasticity of trade declined and was lower than expected. This finding has generally been interpreted as evidence of the importance of structural factors in determining the weakness of international trade. However, as income elasticity is itself a cyclical variable, the role of cyclical factors has been underestimated. Once the cyclicality of the elasticity is correctly accounted for, it turns out that cyclical forces have provided the main contribution to the unexpected weakness of trade. In addition, the accuracy of existing forecasts on trade growth can be significantly improved by using real-time information about business conditions, given that a large share of the forecast error depends on mispredicted income elasticities.

Keywords Global trade · Trade forecasts · International business cycle

JEL Classification E32 · F1 · F4

The views expressed in this paper are those of the authors and do not necessarily reflect those of the Bank of Italy and the European Central Bank.

A. Borin · M. Mancini
Bank of Italy, Directorate General for Economics, Statistics and Research, International Relations and Economics Directorate, Rome, Italy
e-mail: alessandro.borin@bancaditalia.it

M. Mancini
e-mail: michele.mancini@bancaditalia.it

V. Di Nino
European Central Bank, Frankfurt, Germany
e-mail: Virginia.Di_Nino@ecb.europa.eu

M. Sbracia (✉)
Bank of Italy, Rome, Italy
e-mail: massimo.sbracia@bancaditalia.it

L. Ferrara et al. (eds.), *International Macroeconomics in the Wake of the Global Financial Crisis*, Financial and Monetary Policy Studies 46,
https://doi.org/10.1007/978-3-319-79075-6_6

1 Introduction

In 2016 global trade growth fell short of expectations for the sixth year in a row, fuelling an intense debate about its causes, recently summarized in the World Economic Outlook (IMF 2016). The extent of the forecast error is best illustrated by the predictions formulated by the IMF. For the period 2011–16, the IMF estimated that world trade volumes would grow at an annual average of 5.1%; their actual growth rate, instead, turned out to be just 3.2% per year (Fig. 1). Only a small part of this systematic forecast error has reflected lower-than-expected real GDP growth; the most important part is given by the fall in the income elasticity of trade, defined as the ratio between real import growth and real GDP growth ('income elasticity' hereafter). Income elasticity decreased from the level of 1.3 implicit in the IMF's forecasts (a value close to the historical average) to less than 1.0, thus explaining two-thirds of the forecast error—the rest being explained by lower GDP growth.[1] As a result, the ratio between import and GDP volumes, after growing strongly in the post-war period, has recently flattened.

In order to evaluate how and why trade evolves, it is often implicitly assumed that changes in income elasticity reflect structural factors, such as changing trade barriers. Not surprisingly, the recent dismal performance of international trade has mostly been attributed to different structural developments. For example, using a variety of methodologies, the OECD concludes that two-thirds of the deceleration of trade has been due to structural changes (see Haugh et al. 2016). Several possible causes are frequently mentioned. Some studies have observed that the sectoral and the geographical distribution of trade and production may have shifted towards sectors and countries with lower trade openness; others have focused on a resurgence of protectionist measures, which took place following the financial crisis of 2008–09; another legacy of the crisis has been the weakness of bank credit, which has been persistent in many economies and may have hit exporting firms not only through trade credit, but also by reducing financial support for their internationalization strategies, including foreign direct investment and participation in global value chains; anecdotal evidence, in fact, has pointed to a possible shortening of global value chains.[2]

In a new paper, Borin et al. (2017) show that two standard properties of real trade flows—their high volatility and their procyclicality—imply that income elasticity is itself a cyclical variable. In particular, when real GDP growth is positive but lower than its long-run trend, then income elasticity is lower than its own long-run trend. While Borin et al. (2017) demonstrate this property of income elasticity by building on a theoretical model of international trade (originally developed by

[1] Real GDP growth fell short of IMF projections by an annual average of 0.5% points in 2011–2016. By using the elasticity of 1.3 implicit in the IMF forecasts, lower GDP growth then accounted for 0.7% points of the forecast error. Hence, the remaining 1.2% points are accounted for by the decline of the income elasticity of trade.

[2] See Hoekman (2015) for several explanations for the post-crisis weakness of trade; other views are found in Borin and Mancini (2015), Constantinescu et al. (2015), Del Prete and Federico (2014), IMF (2016), IRC Trade Task Force (2016) and the literature surveyed therein.

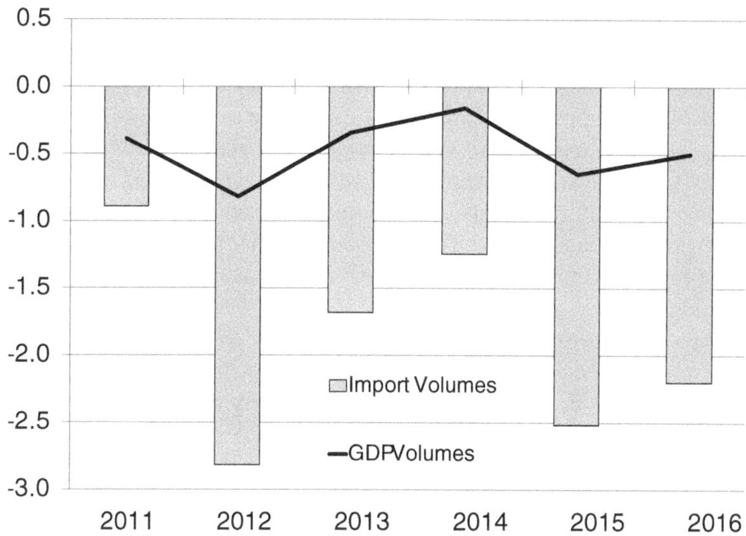

Fig. 1 Forecast errors on the growth of world import and world GDP volumes Percentage-point difference between the growth rate at year t as reported in the IMF WEO (World Economic Outlook) published in October at year $t + 1$ (actual data) and the growth rate at year t as predicted in the IMF WEO published in October at year $t - 1$ (forecast). For the year 2016, actual data come from the IMF WEO Update published in January 2017. *Source* based on IMF data

Bems et al. 2013), in this chapter we use some intuitive examples in order to focus on two important points, which are often a source of confusion in the economic debate. First, even if trade and GDP volumes grow at identical rates in the long run (say over one or more decades), in the short run (such as at quarterly or yearly frequencies) income elasticity can be persistently different from 1. With this assertion we do not just mean that income elasticity can display erratic fluctuations away from 1 in high frequency data; we mean that the different volatility of import growth and GDP growth is such that income elasticity can settle at values that are, for example, always greater than 1 at high frequencies, even though they remain equal to 1 at low frequencies. Second, under conditions that are universally met by trade flows (procyclicality, high volatility and positive long-run growth), the short-run values taken by income elasticity depend on business conditions. In particular, income elasticity is procyclical for both positive and negative growth rates of real GDP, even though this is not across the whole spectrum of growth rates, as it is not defined when real GDP growth is zero.

The cyclicality of income elasticity has very important empirical implications. First, it suggests that a larger share of the weakness of trade may be due to lackluster business conditions and, in particular, to the fact that the recovery of economic activity, especially of investment, has been poorer than expected. Once the cyclicality of income elasticity is correctly factored in, we find that cyclical forces explain most of the unexpected weakness of trade recorded in 2011–2016. Second, the analysis in Borin et al. (2017), which we review and update in this chapter, indicates that, in evaluating the dynamics of income elasticity, one should separate the cyclical from the trend component. By doing so, it emerges that the trend component of income elasticity, which had gradually risen to values well above 2 in the mid-1990s, then started to decline, returning to values close to 1; the cyclical component has become negative in the last few years, bringing income elasticity to below 1 and contributing to a depression of trade. We then discuss the determinants of the trend component over the last 30 years, analyze the consistency of the recent behavior of the cyclical component with the corresponding dynamics of world GDP growth, and then speculate on the possible long-run characteristics of the 'new normal' in international trade.

Thc time-series properties of income elasticity also have important implications for the accuracy of the forecasts for global trade growth. After observing that the IMF's trade forecasts do not account for the cyclicality of the elasticity and using the methodology set up in Borin et al. (2017) to correct these predictions, we use the result to discuss the likely short-term dynamics of global trade.

The rest of this chapter is organized as follows. Section 2 provides some simple examples that clarify some common pitfalls regarding income elasticity and shed light on its dynamic properties. Section 3 focuses on the empirical implications of these properties for the behavior of income elasticity over the last 30 years, with a greater focus on the most recent period. Section 4 deals with the formulation of accurate forecasts on global trade growth. Section 5 summarizes the main conclusions.

2 Building Intuition

Recent studies have argued that income elasticity can be smaller or greater than 1 only to the extent that trade volumes grow more slowly or faster than real GDP, as they do when trade barriers rise or decline; if, instead, trade barriers do not change and trade and GDP grow at the same speed, then income elasticity should lie at its equilibrium level of 1 (see Gaulier et al. 2016). According to this view, the recent fall in income elasticity is interpreted as a return to its equilibrium value, as the secular decline in tariff and non-tariff protectionist measures and in transportation costs is gradually waning.

Although this view is useful in order to evaluate the behavior of trade flows over long time spans, it fails to recognize two important facts about income elasticity. First, if trade barriers do not change and trade and GDP volumes share exactly the same trend growth, then the value of income elasticity over long time horizons is 1 but, in the shorter run, income elasticity can be persistently different from 1; for example, it can take values that are constantly smaller or greater than 1 at quarterly or yearly frequencies, even if it remains equal to 1 if calculated over 10- or 20-year horizons. Second, in the short run, it turns out that the values takes by the income elasticity depend on business cycle conditions. As a consequence, one should separate the trend from the cycle component of income elasticity in order to correctly evaluate what has been depressing trade over the last few years.

How can the short-run values of income elasticity be persistently different from the long-run values? The main reason is related to two standard features of real trade flows (and, in particular, of imports): their *high volatility* and their *procyclicality*. These two features have been well documented in the literature on the international real business cycle. The pioneering paper by Backus et al. (1995) had already documented the high volatility of imports and exports relative to that of GDP. Heathcote and Perri (2002) then added to that, finding a sharp procyclicality in trade flows. Borin et al. (2017) revisited these two using growth rates of trade and GDP volumes instead of HP filtered series of their levels as a method for tackling their time trend.[3] Thus, a *high volatility* of imports means that the standard deviation of real import growth is higher than that of real GDP growth, while a *procyclicality* of imports means that real import growth is positively correlated with the business cycle, as measured by real GDP growth or real investment growth.

To see how high volatility and procyclicality can persistently push income elasticity away from 1, suppose for a moment that the trend growth rates of GDP and import volumes are both nil. If real import growth is more volatile than real GDP growth, then when the latter is positive, the former is either positive and very high or negative and very low. But the positive correlation between import and GDP volumes suggests that the relevant case is the one in which the two growth rates have the same sign. By the same token, when real GDP growth is negative, real import growth is also negative and very low. Thus, a positive (negative) and higher (lower) growth rate of real imports corresponds to a positive (negative) growth rate of real GDP. In other words, the income elasticity can settle at a value that is always greater than 1 at high frequencies, even if trade and GDP share the same trend growth.

Now consider the more important case in which both GDP and import volumes have a positive trend growth and let us provide an example in which income elasticity is not only different from 1, but also affected by business conditions. To separate the 'pure trend effect' on the income elasticity related to declining trade barriers (i.e. to imports growing faster than GDP), suppose that these trend growth rates are identical, say set at 3%. In addition, to build a simple intuition about the reasons why income elasticity is affected by the business cycle, let us also focus only on positive growth rates. As real import growth is more volatile than and positively correlated with real GDP growth, when the latter is above its average (say 4%), the former is even higher (say 5%); when real GDP growth is instead low (say 2%), real import growth is even lower (say 1%). The income elasticity is then greater than 1 when real GDP growth is high, and smaller than 1 when real GDP growth is low (respectively 5/4 and 1/2 in our simple example). Thus, in this example the income elasticity is procyclical.

While this intuitive example works well in a neighborhood of the trend growth rate of real imports and real GDP, in the whole domain of these variables the relationship between the income elasticity and the business cycle is more complex and needs a

[3]Engel and Wang (2011) first put the spotlight on the high volatility and the procyclicality of imports and exports (and on their positive correlation), and analyzed their implications for the *price* elasticity of trade. Borin et al. (2017) followed a similar approach in order to analyze the implications of these two features of trade flows for the *income* elasticity of trade.

full-fledged model to illustrate it. Borin et al. (2017) build a variant of the simple theoretical model from Bems et al. (2013) in which there are two sectors producing, respectively, tradeable and non-tradeable goods, whose volumes change over time with different trend growth rates and different volatilities. The presence of two sectors is crucial, as it causes the differences between imports (which are made up of high-volatility tradeable goods) and GDP (which is more intensive in low-volatility non-tradeable goods).

In particular, denote by $M(S)$ the sector producing tradeable (non-tradeable) goods and, for each sector $j \in \{M, S\}$ of country n, denote by $\hat{d}_{n,t}(j)$ the growth rate (calculated as log-change) of the domestic demand for the goods of sector j by country n at time (quarter or year) t. Assume now that the two growth rates $\hat{d}_{n,t}(j)$ are affected by different long-run trends and by cyclical shocks with different volatility that, for the sake of simplicity, are perfectly correlated. Thus, if we let ε_t be the zero-mean shock hitting the economy at time t, we assume that:

$$\begin{cases} \hat{d}_{n,t}(M) = g_m + \beta \cdot \varepsilon_t \\ \hat{d}_{n,t}(S) = g_s + \varepsilon_t \end{cases},$$

where $\beta \geq 1$ reflects the higher volatility of the demand for tradeable goods and $g_j \geq 0$ is the long-run trend growth of sector j, with $j \in \{M, S\}$.

Under these assumptions, Borin et al. (2017) show that income elasticity has the following expression:

$$\eta_{n,t} = \frac{g_m + \beta \cdot \varepsilon_t}{g_m + \omega_{n,t}(S)(g_s - g_m) + \left[\beta - \omega_{n,t}(S) \cdot (\beta - 1)\right] \cdot \varepsilon_t} \text{ for } \varepsilon_t \neq \bar{\varepsilon}_t\,, \quad (1)$$

where $\omega_{n,t}(S) \in (0, 1)$ is the weight of the sector producing non-tradeable goods on the total expenditure of country n at time t and $\bar{\varepsilon}_t$ is the value of the shock ε_t at which the denominator of Eq. (1) is zero and, therefore, income elasticity is not defined.[4]

Figure 2 shows the behavior of $\eta_{n,t}$ as a function of ε_t from Eq. (1), for $g_m = g_s = 2\%$ and for $g_m = g_s = 4\%$, with, in both cases, $\beta = 2$ and $\omega_{n,t}(S) = 0.5$. The figure provides a visual impression of two different instances of the two intuitive examples discussed above, in which the values taken by income elasticity in the short run were, respectively, always larger than 1 and affected by business conditions. As far as the former example is concerned, in the hypothetical case of a country that, at each time t, is hit either by a shock $\varepsilon_t = 3\%$ or by a shock $\varepsilon_t = -3\%$, it is always $\eta_{n,t} > 1$ at the high frequency t, even though over long time spans (when the shock ε_t is on average nil) the elasticity is 1.[5] Although this example is clearly not realistic, it shows very well how short-term income elasticity can persistently differ from long-term one. As

[4]The exact value is $\bar{\varepsilon}_t = -\left[g_m + \omega_{n,t}(S)(g_s - g_m)\right] / \left[\beta - \omega_{n,t}(S) \cdot (\beta - 1)\right]$.

[5]It is worth recalling that the average of a ratio is not the same as the ratio of the averages: for this reason, the income elasticity over long time spans is not equal to the average of the income elasticities at each shorter horizon. In this example, in fact, the income elasticity would always be larger than 1 at the quarterly or yearly frequency, but would be equal to 1 when calculated over long periods, because $g_{m,t} = g_{s,t}$.

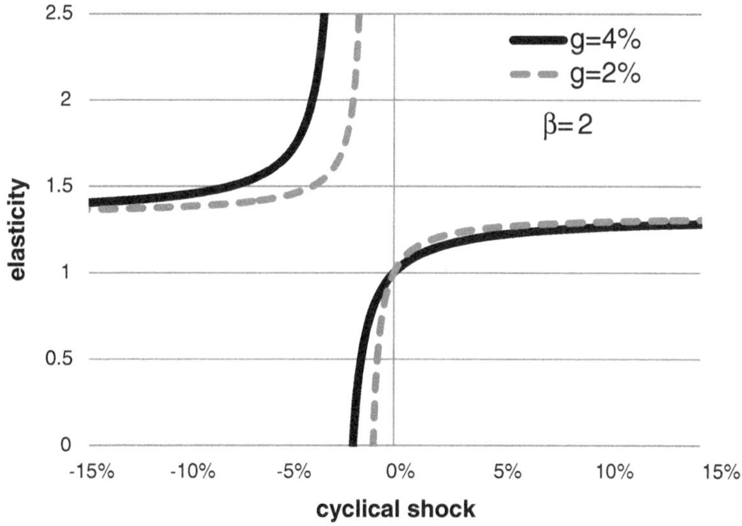

Fig. 2 Income elasticity and cyclical shocks values of $\eta_{n,t}$ (vertical axes) from Eq. (1), for different values of ε_t (horizontal axes), for $g_{m,t} = g_{s,t} = 2\%$ (red line) and $g_{m,t} = g_{s,t} = 4\%$ (blue line), with $\beta = 2$ and $\omega_{n,t}(S)$. *Source* Borin et al. (2017)

regards the latter example discussed above, notice that the elasticity is procyclical in both $(-\infty, \bar{\varepsilon}_t)$ and $(\bar{\varepsilon}_t, +\infty)$, as it is increasing in ε_t in those two intervals, even though it is not procyclical across the whole domain of the cyclical shock.

Two other features of income elasticity are also worth noting: (*i*) income elasticity is always greater than 1, except in the interval $\varepsilon_t \in (\bar{\varepsilon}_t, 0)$, in which GDP growth is positive but lower than its long-run trend; (*ii*) over long time spans, when ε_t is on average nil, it is: $\eta_{n,t} \gtreqless 1$ if and only if $g_{m,t} \gtreqless g_{s,t}$.

Now let us turn to the implications for global trade growth. As world GDP growth is almost always positive, in order to analyze the income elasticity of global trade, the relevant branch of the hyperbola represented in Fig. 2 is the lower one, for which $\varepsilon_t \in (\bar{\varepsilon}_t, +\infty)$. In this branch of the hyperbola, greater values of the income elasticity corresponds to higher values of ε_t, which determine higher world GDP growth. In addition, as is well known, in the last few decades global trade growth has tended to exceed world GDP growth. Thus, in assessing the causes of the fall in the income elasticity and, then, of the weakness of international trade, one should distinguish whether we have been observing a decline in the trend growth rate of trade relative to GDP (as would happen if, for example, g_m/g_s decreases), as is implicitly suggested by the literature focusing on structural factors, or whether we have been observing low realizations of the cyclical shock ε_t, which have brought GDP growth, and consequently income elasticity, below their own trend.

In the next section, we tackle this question and attempt to disentangle the roles played by trend and cycle over the past decades, with a focus on the recent phase of weak global trade.

3 Trade Weakness: The Cycle and the Trend

The theory outlined in the previous section suggests that one can distinguish two main components of income elasticity: (*i*) a long-run component, related to the trend growth of imports relative to GDP and linked to structural developments, such as the dynamics of trade barriers; and (*ii*) a short-run component, related to business cycle conditions. We draw on Borin et al. (2017) to retrieve, using an HP filter, trend, cycle and noise components for the imports and the GDP of the world economy and then build two quarterly series[6]: a 'trend component' of income elasticity, by dividing the growth rate of the trend component of real imports by the growth rate of the trend component of real GDP; and a 'trend-plus-cycle' component of income elasticity, which is the ratio between the sums of the growth rates of the trend and the cycle components of real imports at the numerator, and the sums of the growth rates of the trend and the cycle components of real GDP at the denominator.[7]

Figure 3 shows that for the global economy both these components of the income elasticity are currently declining, contributing to depress trade relative to GDP. Let us first focus on the trend component (solid line). This component rose in the 1980s and early 1990s, determining the acceleration of trade relative to GDP. After achieving a peak in the mid-1990s, it then started to decrease.

To shed some light on the determinants of these long-run changes, it is worth considering the evolution of import tariffs. The most significant liberalization of foreign trade among advanced countries took place between the 1980s and the first half of the 1990s for a variety of reasons: (*i*) according to the Tokyo Round of GATT, import tariffs in the nine most advanced counties were reduced by one third in the 1980s; (*ii*) the European Single Market was created between 1987 and 1993; and (*iii*) in 1994 the NAFTA came into force and the WTO was established. As a matter of fact, as Fig. 4 shows, between 1980 and 2015 the largest reduction of tariffs in both advanced and emerging economies took place in the 5-year period 1990–1995.

One noticeable feature in the behavior of the trend component of the income elasticity is that its peak was achieved in the mid-1990s, before China joined the WTO. This should not be surprising, however, considering that the set of advanced countries was (and still is) much more important than China for world trade. In the mid-1990s, for example, advanced countries accounted for more than 80% of both world trade and world GDP.

Another interesting observation concerns import tariffs, which continued to decline also after 1995. This is consistent with the dynamics of the trend component of income elasticity, which remained above 1, reflecting a higher growth of global

---

[6]The noise component cleans the data for the measurement error that typically affects imports and exports, which is such that these two variables, which should always coincide at the world level, often display significant differences (even though these differences cancel out over time).

[7]As suggested by Borin et al. (2017), income elasticity is not filtered directly because the theory implies that its long-run trend and cyclicality are not 'genuine', but are just the by-product of the long-run trend and cyclicality of imports and GDP.

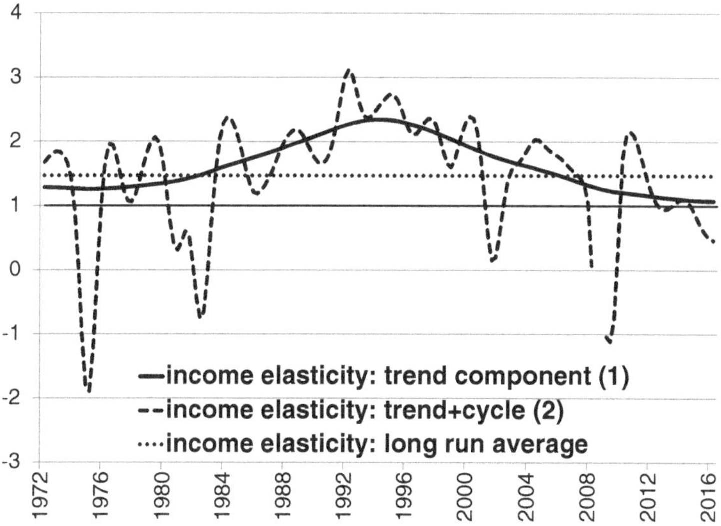

Fig. 3 Decomposition of the income elasticity of world trade, quarterly data, 4-quarter moving averages. The picture excludes three consecutive outliers, from 2008-Q4 to 2009-Q2. (1) Trend component of the income elasticity from HP filtered series. (2) 'Trend+cycle' component of the income elasticity from HP filtered series. *Source* Borin et al. (2017)

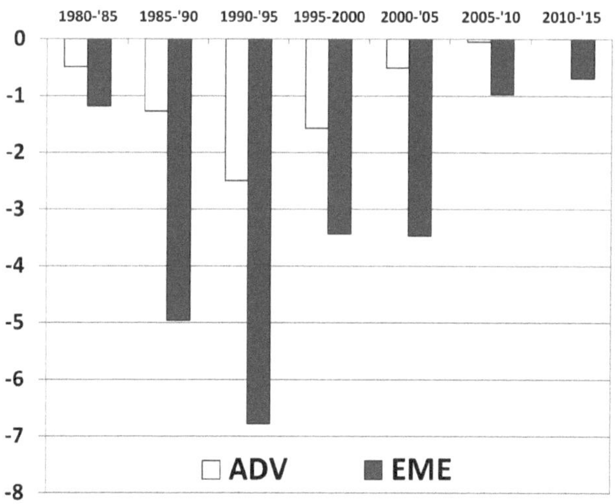

Fig. 4 Changes in the average tariffs on imported goods. Percentage-point changes in the average tariffs on imported goods in advanced ('ADV') and emerging ('EME') countries. *Source* based on data from IMF (2016)

trade relative to GDP. As the decline in import tariffs is waning, however, the trend component of the income elasticity seems to be slowly converging towards 1.

The reduction of trade barriers, along with the decline of transport and communication costs, has also favored the international fragmentation of production, which has played an important role in steering the evolution of the structural relationship between trade and GDP, as documented in Fig. 3. Following the diffusion of global value chains (GVCs), intermediate goods cross borders multiple times, thereby inflating gross trade statistics. In other words, an intensification of the international fragmentation of production pushes income elasticity above its long-run natural level of 1, since it makes trade flows grow more rapidly than final demand. This wedge, however, fades out when GVC intensity stabilizes and it can even turn negative if a reversal of the outsourcing activity occurs. Using data from the Inter-Country Input-Output tables, Borin and Mancini (2015) derive a measure of GVC-related trade in order to assess how the evolution of GVCs has affected the trend component of income elasticity. They decompose the trend component of the income elasticity—which they derive as the ratio between the 5-year average growth rates of trade and GDP—into three parts: the steady-state component, which is always equal to 1; the elasticity of the degree of international fragmentation to GDP; and a residual factor, related to the elasticity of non-GVC trade to GDP. Figure 5, which updates Borin and Mancini (2015) by using the most recent release of the World Input Output Data (WIOD), shows that the contribution of global value chains to total trade elasticity has declined since the late 1990s, reducing the trend elasticity by 0.35 points.

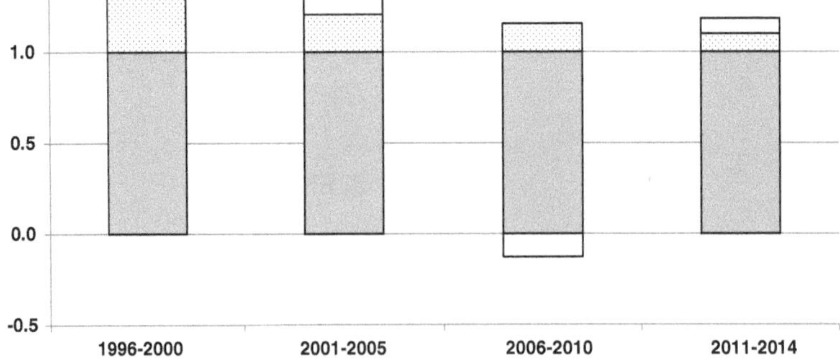

Fig. 5 Decomposition of trend income elasticity of trade. *Source* WIOD and Borin and Mancini (2015)

Now let us turn to the cyclical component of income elasticity, which is conveniently added to the trend component, in order to have an immediate appraisal of the value of the overall elasticity, net of erratic fluctuations (Fig. 3, dashed line). Before the crisis (2002–2008) and in its immediate aftermath (Q3 2009–Q2 2011), the cyclical component pushed elasticity well above its long-run trend, probably hiding the fact that structural factors were already lowering the income elasticity. This 'optical illusion' may explain why the recent weakness of trade has been such a surprise. In the most recent period, however, the cyclical component has started to contribute negatively to global trade, driving the income elasticity below 1.

The reason why the cyclical component turned to negative values is clarified in Fig. 6. World real GDP growth has been on a downward trend since the onset of the global recession (dashed line) but, in the most recent period, it has been running below its trend (solid line), weakening income elasticity due to the mechanisms described in the previous sections.

These findings allow us to provide a simple quantification of the importance of cyclical and structural factors in determining the weakness of trade. Figure 3 shows that, with respect to its historical average of 1.5 (over our sample period), income elasticity fell to 0.7 on average in 2015 with a similar contribution of structural and cyclical factors. But given that lower-than-expected GDP growth has also contributed directly to the forecast error by about one-third (see footnote 1), this back-of-the-envelope calculation suggests that cyclical forces have caused about two-thirds of the forecast error—a result in line with a similar finding by the IMF (2016) and the opposite of those of Haugh et al. (2016) and others.

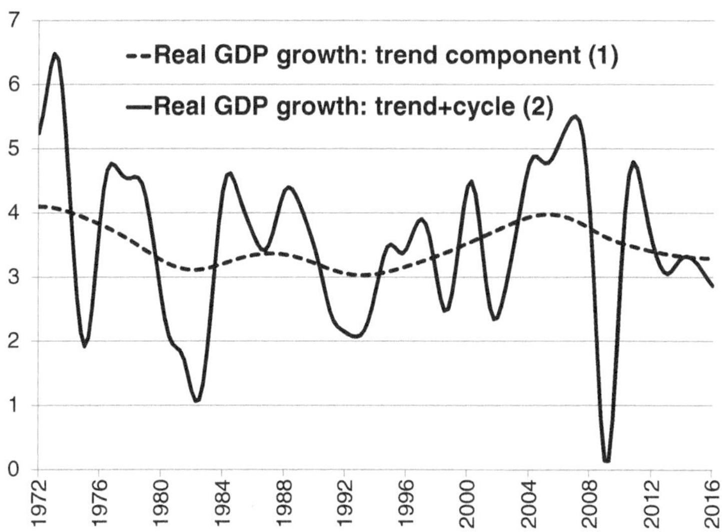

Fig. 6 Decomposition of world real GDP growth. Percentage points, quarterly data, 4-quarter moving averages. (1) Trend component of world GDP growth from HP filtered series. (2) 'Trend+cycle' component of world GDP growth from HP filtered series. *Source* Borin et al. (2017)

Table 1 Within-country trade flows and GDP. Values (billions of domestic currency). *Source* US Commodity Flow Survey and Statistics Canada

United States: domestic commodity flows and GDP			
	Flows (1)	GDP (1)	*Elasticity*
1993	5846	6667	*0.88*
2007	11685	14029	*0.83*
Canada: inter-provincial trade flows and GDP			
	Flows (1)	GDP (1)	*Elasticity*
1993	104	902	*0.12*
2007	164	1566	*0.10*

Figure 3 also shows that the trend component of income elasticity is now converging to 1, a value around which it could lie for some time. Today, a trend-growth of trade equal to that of GDP may seem to be an extraordinary phenomenon, yet it is not unprecedented. Irwin (2002), for example, has documented it for the pre-World War I era (1870–1913), which was characterized by very stable tariff rates (which were also very low in western Europe). More recently, in the period 1993–2007 trade among US states (proxied by total domestic shipments) as well as among Canadian provinces surprisingly grew at a lower rate than domestic GDP (Table 1). In a context of zero tariffs, some have conjectured that this may be the result of a small decline in transport costs which has been more than offset by the fact that the different regions of these two countries are becoming more similar (i.e. they produce similar things). Thus, the trend component of the income elasticity may remain at around 1 (or less, if trade liberalization were to go into reverse), until new impetus comes from a further decline in tariff and non-tariff barriers to trade or technological progress in transportation.[8]

Nevertheless, the exceptional weakness of global trade observed since 2011, which has gradually driven income elasticity below 1, is also the result of lackluster business conditions. Therefore, one should expect that, as real GDP growth returns to trend, global trade growth will recover more strongly, with income elasticity first returning to 1 and then exceeding this long-run equilibrium value once that real GDP rises above its own trend growth.

4 Forecasting Trade

Our analysis of the dynamics of income elasticity has led us to speculate about the future of global trade in the medium-long term, but what about in the very short term? Can we exploit real-time information about business conditions to improve

[8]For the key role of technological progress in the transport sector for the dynamics of international trade, see Estevadeordal et al. (2003).

existing trade forecasts? Following Borin et al. (2017), we can examine these questions by focusing on the forecasts about world import growth formulated by the IMF, undoubtedly the most widely used in the business community and among policy makers.[9] We follow two main steps.

In the first step, we evaluate the contribution of the forecast error on GDP growth and of the forecast error on income elasticity (and the interaction between these two) to the forecast error on world trade growth. The IMF provides data on the actual growth rate of imports and GDP at time t ($g_{M,t}$ and $g_{Y,t}$, respectively) and the predicted values of these variables ($g^p_{M,t}$ and $g^p_{Y,t}$). The forecast error on import growth, $\varepsilon^p_{M,t} = g^p_{M,t} - g_{M,t}$, can then be decomposed into a forecast error on GDP growth, $\varepsilon^p_{Y,t} = g^p_{Y,t} - g_{Y,t}$, and a forecast error on income elasticity, $\varepsilon^p_{\eta,t} = \eta^p_t - \eta_t$, where $\eta_t = g_{M,t}/g_{Y,t}$ and $\eta^p_t = g^p_{M,t}/g^p_{Y,t}$; namely:

$$\varepsilon^p_{M,t} = \varepsilon^p_{Y,t} \cdot \eta^*_t + \varepsilon^p_{\eta,t} \cdot g^*_{Y,t} \, ,$$

where $\eta^*_t = \left(\eta^p_t + \eta_t\right)/2$ and $g^*_{Y,t} = \left(g^p_{Y,t} + g_{Y,t}\right)/2$.

The total mean squared forecast error on import growth (*Total MSFE*) can therefore be written as:

$$\frac{\sum_{t=1}^{T}\left(\varepsilon^p_{M,t}\right)^2}{T} = \frac{\sum_{t=1}^{T}\left(\varepsilon^p_{Y,t} \cdot \eta^*_t\right)^2}{T} + \frac{\sum_{t=1}^{T}\left(\varepsilon^p_{\eta,t} \cdot g^*_{Y,t}\right)^2}{T} + \frac{2\sum_{t=1}^{T}\varepsilon^p_{Y,t} \cdot \varepsilon^p_{\eta,t} \cdot g^*_{Y,t} \cdot \eta^*_t}{T}, \quad (2)$$

where T is the number of years for which actual data and forecasts are available (the period 1986–2015 in our sample). Equation (2) thus shows that the mean squared forecast error on import growth can be decomposed into three terms that measure the importance of: the forecast error on GDP growth (first addendum, *MSFE GDP*), the forecast error on income elasticity (second addendum, *MSFE elasticity*), and the interaction between these two errors (third addendum, *MSFE covariance*).

We perform this decomposition for the forecasts for each calendar year t published by the IMF in the spring and fall of year t.[10] The results show that the MSFE on income elasticity is the largest component at all forecast horizons (dotted area in the first and third columns of Fig. 7). In addition, as the forecast horizon shortens, the IMF significantly improves its forecasts for world real GDP growth (shaded area in the first and third column of Fig. 7), but not its forecast for income elasticity.

In the second step, we formulate an alternative forecast. The importance of the elasticity forecast error and of its correlation with the GDP forecast error suggest, in fact, that we can improve the accuracy of the IMF forecasts by 'adjusting' them to take

[9]Focusing on global trade has another important advantage: because world import growth has generally been positive in the post-war period, observations will be distributed only on the right branch of the hyperbola (see Fig. 2), where the relationship between income elasticity and the cyclical shock is monotonic. We can therefore avoid using more complex non-linear estimations.

[10]Borin et al. (2017) also analyze the IMF forecasts for each calendar year t published in the spring and the fall of year $t - 1$.

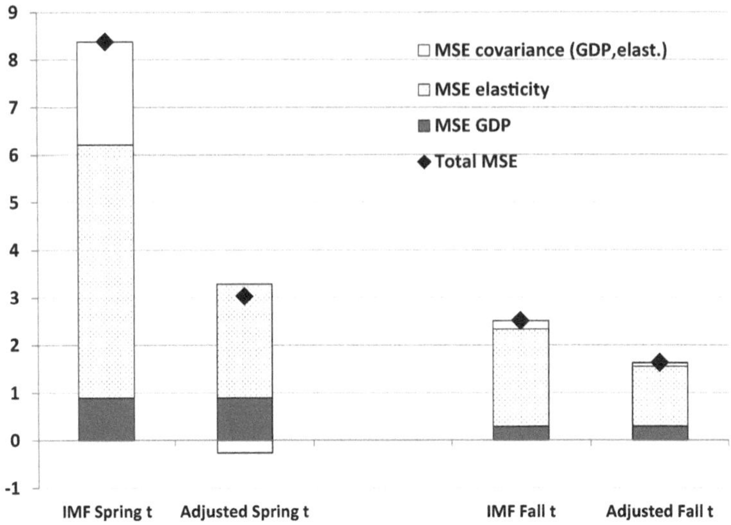

Fig. 7 Mean squared forecast error on world import growth and its components. Total mean squared forecast error on world import growth in year t and its components, for the predictions made by the IMF in the spring and fall of year t and for the corresponding cyclically-adjusted predictions. *Source* based on IMF data

business conditions into account. Hence, we perform an out-of-sample forecasting exercise in the following way. We first estimate the role of the cycle using past data, and measuring the strength of business conditions using a simple 'momentum proxy', available in real time, which is given by the difference between the two most recent forecasts of GDP growth; namely we run the following regression:

$$\eta_t = \alpha + \beta \cdot \eta_t^p + \gamma \cdot cycle_t + \xi_t \ , \tag{3}$$

where η_t is the actual elasticity, α, β and γ are constant, $cycle_t$ is our proxy for the cyclical shock (i.e. the variable denoted with ε_t in the theoretical model) and ξ_t is an error term. The results confirm that information about business cycle conditions is generally neglected by the IMF: the estimate of γ is strongly significant (at the 1% threshold) and with the expected positive sign. The adjusted R-squared is at 60% for both the spring and the fall forecasts against, respectively, 20% and 46% using only the IMF forecasts (i.e. setting $\gamma = 0$).

We then use regression results to 'adjust' the IMF predictions. Specifically, we run the following regression on a 12-year rolling window:

$$\eta_t = \eta_t^p + \gamma \cdot \left(g_{Y,t}^p - g_{Y,t}^{p-1} \right) + \xi_t \ , \tag{4}$$

and then formulate the following out-of-sample prediction for the growth rate of world imports:

$$g^{*}_{M,t} = g^{p}_{Y,t} \cdot \left[\eta^{p}_{t} + \hat{\gamma} \cdot \left(g^{p}_{Y,t} - g^{p-1}_{Y,t}\right)\right], \tag{5}$$

in which $\hat{\gamma}$ is the OLS estimate of γ from Eq. (4); our first (last) forecast $g^{*}_{M,t}$ is produced for the year 1998 (2015), where $\hat{\gamma}$ is estimated using data for the period 1986–1997 (2003–2014).

Figure 7 compares the MSFE using IMF predictions and cyclically-adjusted predictions. Results show that, when using the latter, the forecast error declines substantially. For the forecasts produced in the spring, the total MSFE is cut by 70%, with half of the reduction coming from the improved prediction of elasticity and half from the lower covariance between the elasticity forecast error and the GDP forecast error. For the fall forecasts, the total MSFE is cut by 40%, with the reduction coming almost entirely from the improvement in predicting elasticity. The effectiveness of our correction for the business cycle is reflected by fact that the covariance between the elasticity and the GDP forecast errors becomes essentially nil.

5 Conclusion

The analysis reviewed in this chapter has discussed the role of the structural and cyclical components that drive the behavior of the income elasticity of trade. Since the mid-1990s, the structural component has been gradually declining towards its equilibrium level of 1. This result suggests that income elasticity will probably remain distant from the values of 2 or more recorded in the early 1990s, unless international trade receives new impetus from international integration or technological advances in transportation. Instead, it could even fall below 1 if trade liberalization were to go into reverse.

At the same time, however, the analysis stresses the role of cyclical factors for the slowdown of trade in the current phase. One should then expect that, as real GDP growth returns to its trend, global trade growth will recover more strongly, with income elasticity first returning towards 1 and then exceeding this value once real GDP growth moves above trend.

References

Backus DK, Kehoe PJ, Kydland FE (1995) International business cycles: theory and evidence. In: Cooley T (ed) Frontiers of business cycle research. Princeton, Princeton University Press

Bems R, Johnson RC, Yi KM (2013) The great trade collapse. Ann Rev Econ 5:375–400

Borin A, Mancini M (2015) Follow the value-added: bilateral gross export accounting. Temi di discussione (Working Papers), no 1026, Bank of Italy

Borin A, Di Nino V, Mancini M, Sbracia M (2017) The cyclicality of the income elasticity of trade. Temi di discussione (Working Papers), no 1126, Bank of Italy

Constantinescu C, Mattoo A, Ruta M (2015) The global trade slowdown: cyclical or structural? World Bank Development Research Group working paper, no 7158, Washington, DC

Del Prete S, Federico S (2014) Trade and finance: is there more than just "Trade Finance"? Evidence from matched bank-firm data. Temi di discussione (Working Papers), no 948, Bank of Italy
Engel C, Wang J (2011) International trade in durable goods: understanding volatility, cyclicality, and elasticities. J Int Econ 83:37–52
Estevadeordal A, Frantz B, Taylor AM (2003) The rise and fall of world trade, 1870–1939. Q J Econ 118:359–407
Gaulier G, Mayer T, Steingress W, Zignago S (2016) Aggregation and omitted variable biases in the trade elasticities, *mimeo*, Banque de France
Haugh D, Kopoin A, Rusticelli E, Turner D, Dutu R (2016) Cardiac arrest or dizzy spell: why is world trade so weak and what can policy do about it? OECD economic policy paper, no 18, Organization of Economic Cooperation and Development
Heathcote J, Perri F (2002) Financial autarky and international business cycles. J Monet Econ 49:601–627
Hoekman B (ed) (2015) The global trade slowdown: a new normal?. CEPR, Voxeu Ebook, London
IMF (2016) Global trade: what's behind the slowdown? World economic outlook (Chapter 2), International Monetary Fund, October
IRC Trade Task Force (2016) Understanding the weakness in global trade: what is the new normal? Occasional paper, no 178, European Central Bank
Irwin DA (2002) Long-run trends in world trade and income. World Trade Rev 1:89–100

The Role of Debt Dynamics in US Household Consumption

Vincent Grossmann-Wirth and Clément Marsilli

Abstract This chapter documents why US private consumption, while remaining the key engine of US growth, slowed after the financial crisis. To this purpose, we estimate an error-correction model for US consumption, accounting for the role of household debt flows before and after the crisis. Contrary to an analysis carried out in terms of net wealth, a decomposition of households' assets and liabilities shows how the pre-crisis period was characterized by an excessive indebtedness, which was both a source of short-term growth and of financial instability. In the current "new normal" situation, private consumption cannot rely on debt flows as much as before the crisis. This is, therefore, an important "demand-side" explanation for the much-debated low growth recovery.

1 Introduction

The US economy has experienced an unprecedented leveraging-deleveraging cycle over the last fifteen years. The ratio of household debt to disposable personal income rose continuously in the 2000s, reaching a peak of 133% by the end of 2007, before a sharp decline; with a debt-to-income ratio of around 104% in late 2016. It is thus of no surprise that the relation between household debt and economic activity has been widely discussed over the last few years, in both public and academic fora.

The views expressed in this paper are those of the authors and do not necessarily reflect those of the Banque de France or the Eurosystem. We would like to thank Sophie Rivaud, Clotilde Bureau and Marie Albert for earlier discussions and work on this topic.

V. Grossmann-Wirth
Banque de France, Paris, France

C. Marsilli (✉)
International Macroeconomics Division, Banque de France, Paris, France
e-mail: clement.marsilli@banque-france.fr

L. Ferrara et al. (eds.), *International Macroeconomics in the Wake of the Global Financial Crisis*, Financial and Monetary Policy Studies 46,
https://doi.org/10.1007/978-3-319-79075-6_7

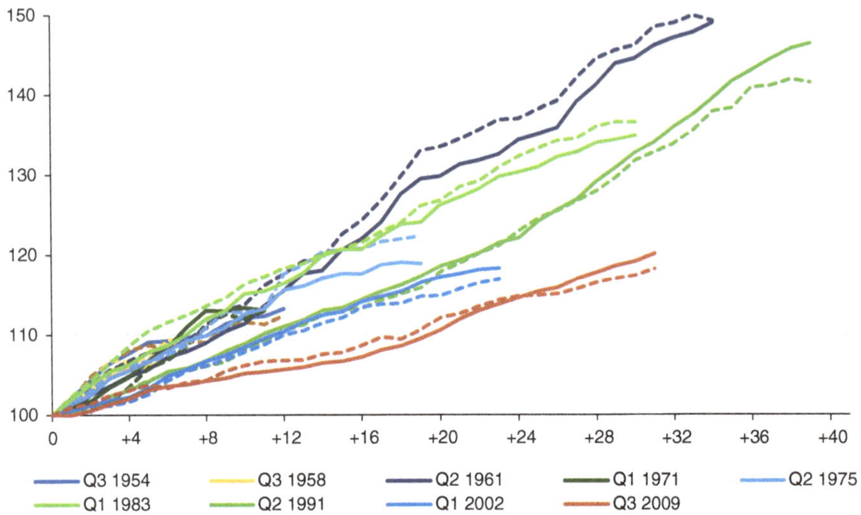

Fig. 1 US consumption (full lines) and GDP (dashed lines) growth during recoveries. *Sources* BEA, NBER.Quarterly data;first post-recession quarter=100

While only a few economists anticipated the Great Recession, which affected almost all advanced economies in 2009–09, most of them quickly realized afterwards that it would have long-lasting effects on the economy. For example, Glick and Lansing (2009) correctly forecasted that "the deleveraging process could result in a substantial and prolonged slowdown in consumer spending relative to pre-recession growth rates". Federal Reserve Chair Janet Yellen also frequently pointed out household deleveraging as one of the headwinds weighing on US aggregate demand after the crisis.

In fact, following the Great Recession, the US economy experienced its slowest recovery since WWII, in terms of both GDP and consumption growth (see Fig. 1). A comparison of pre- with post-crisis growth rates shows that the consumer spending "new normal" has been weak so far (about 35% lower on average).

In a historical perspective, Reinhart and Rogoff (2009) suggested that this deleveraging process following financial crises is typical and tends to be sizable (see also McKinsey 2012). The IMF April 2012 WEO examined earlier deleveraging episodes (across emerging and advanced economies) and found that household deleveraging takes approximately seven years following busts associated with a large increase in household debt, with a decline in the debt-to-income ratio of roughly 23% points.

The macroeconomic consequences of such deleveraging processes have been widely discussed in the economic literature. Reinhart and Rogoff (2009), Reinhart et al. (2015) and Lo and Rogoff (2015) argued that a high debt ratio should generally act as a warning of potential contractionary effects. However, looking specifically at the recent period, Justiniano et al. (2015) estimated that the macroeconomic impact of the leveraging and deleveraging processes in the US remained relatively minor.

From the perspective of their dynamic general equilibrium model, household debt overhang cannot explain, alone, the slow recovery after the Great Recession. On the contrary, Mian et al. (2015) suggest that a rise in household leverage explains a large fraction of the overall consumer default rates during the recession. Mian et al. (2015) broaden this research to find that generally high levels of household debt relative to income are a reliable predictor of low economic growth periods.

Most standard macroeconomic models do not however attribute a large role to debt dynamics and were not very useful to make predictions. As recognized by Krugman and Eggertsson (2011), "one might have expected debt to be at the heart of most mainstream macroeconomic models—(...) however, it is quite common to abstract altogether from this feature of the economy". Furthermore, Sufi (2012) argued that: "household debt played a relatively minor role in mainstream macroeconomic models prior to the recession of 2007–2009". According to him, these models need to be refined by adding various elements such as heterogeneity in the household sector (with financially constrained agents), the possibility of a shock resulting in tightened leverage constraints or some frictions preventing the economy from adjusting. In this vein, Guerrieri and Lorenzoni (2011) and Midrigan and Philippon (2011) proposed various approaches for modelling the effects of a credit crunch on the household sector.

Against this background, some contributions have questioned in greater depth the foundation of macroeconomic models. Recent research in central banks highlighted the need to reflect on how money is viewed in macroeconomic models. For example, Jakab and Kumhof (2015) contrast in a Bank of England working paper the loanable funds model with the "real world" money creation process: "In the intermediation of loanable funds model of banking, banks accept deposits of pre-existing real resources from savers and then lend them to borrowers. In the real world, banks provide financing through money creation." This "endogenous money" view is in line with post-Keynesian critics of mainstream economics and opens the way to new approaches by taking account of money and debt when modelling the economy.

In this chapter we empirically study the relationship between household debt and private consumption in the United States over the pre- and post-crisis periods. More specifically we assess the contribution of debt in consumer spending by developing an econometric model of household consumption that accounts for debt flows. A decomposition of household assets and liabilities shows how the pre-crisis period was characterized by excessive indebtedness, which was both a source of short-term growth and of financial instability that aggravated the recession. While most existing studies and standard models consider net wealth as a determinant of private consumption, we rather identify separately the role of assets (wealth) and liabilities (debt). Using a simple error-correction model approach with both BEA's NIPA and Fed's Financial Accounts data, we quantitatively assess the role of debt flows in private consumption growth over time. We find that about two-thirds of the cumulative difference in private consumption from the pre- to the post-crisis period can be explained by the change in household debt flows. Our analysis also shows that the recovery in consumption could have been even slower if wealth effects, boosted by rising financial gains, had not played such a key role over this period. Overall, our approach offers a "demand-side" explanation to the much-debated low growth recovery in the United States.

2 Illusions About Private Consumption and Debt Sustainability

2.1 A Credit and Asset Prices Boom that Boosts US Private Consumption and GDP

The sharp increase in household debt before the Great Recession, from around 90% of household disposable income in the 1990s to 130% in 2007, came with an even sharper increase in housing and financial wealth (both real housing prices and the SP500 index nearly doubled over the same period). This pattern results in significant changes in the financial system. In particular, while financial deregulation accelerated,[1] banks increasingly made loans with the intention to sell them to other institutions and/or investors, as opposed to holding them to maturity, using the "originate-to-distribute" (OTD) model. Purnanandam (2011) showed that banks with high involvement in the OTD market during the pre-crisis period excessively originated poor-quality mortgages. Previously, successive US governments had also eased the regulation of mortgage lending in order to encourage home ownership[2] (the proportion US homeowners rose sharply from the 1990s onwards).

Hence, as documented by Gorton and Metrick (2012), "the credit boom took the form of asset-backed securities, particularly mortgage-backed securities. There was an explosive growth in securitization in the six or seven years before the crisis. The private-label securitization market grew from under $500 billion in issuance to over $2 trillion in issuance in 2006, the year before the crisis". As securitization enabled lenders to move at least part of the risks associated with the housing loans off their books and homeowners to "extract" more and more value from their home (through "mortgage equity withdrawal"), the leverage cycle went into full swing. US housing prices rose by more than 80%[3] in nominal terms between 2000 and 2006, before starting to fall in the summer of 2007.

---

[1] See, for example, the chronology of the Glass-Steagall Act, from its passage in 1933 to its death throes in the 1990s, as established by the Public Broadcasting Service (PBS), "The Long Demise of Glass-Steagall".

[2] The US Housing Bubble and the Global Financial Crisis: Housing and Housing-Related Finance, Joint Economic Committee, United States Congress, May 2008.

[3] The S&P Case Shiller National Home Price Index rose to 184 in early 2006 against 100 in 2000.

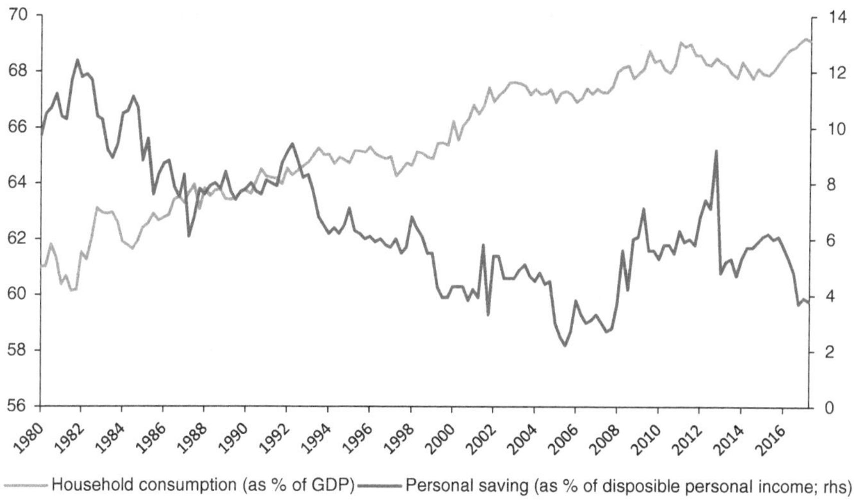

Fig. 2 US household consumption and savings. *Source* BEA

Mian and Sufi (2010) estimated that, from 2002 to 2006, homeowners borrowed between 25 and 30 cents on every dollar of the rising value of their home equity. They argue that this credit was likely used for real outlays rather than to purchase new real estate or pay down high credit card balances. Hence, over the same period, GDP growth rested for a large part on this buoyant household consumption growth and a decrease in the savings rate. Figure 2 shows that personal saving, as a share of disposable income, fell from more than 8% in early 1990s to a low of 2.2% mid-2015. Consumption as a share of GDP increased from around 60% in 1980 to nearly 68% before the crisis and has kept growing since then. More than ever, household consumption is the main engine of US growth. In this respect, its slowdown to an average of 0.6% growth per quarter since 2011, while it averaged about 0.9% over 1996–2007, can be considered to be one of the main factors behind the US sluggish recovery after the Great Recession.

2.2 *An Illusion of Household Balance Sheet Sustainability Caught Back by the Deleveraging Reality*

The strength of US consumption in 2000s was seen to be a result of the increase in net wealth which, at that time, was not considered problematic by most observers of the US economy. As displayed in Fig. 3, the household balance sheet significantly changed over this period. From 1995 to 2006, both house and financial asset prices increased by more than 100% points of disposable personal income. While this simultaneous increase in housing and financial wealth started to attract some attention

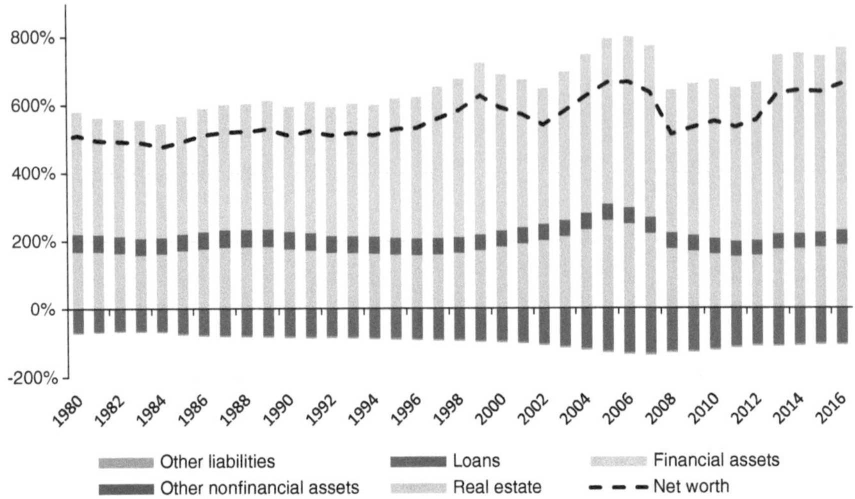

Fig. 3 Household balance sheet (% of DPI). *Source* Financial accounts of the United States, Federal Reserve

in the mid-2000s, many economists downplayed the risk posed by the increase in household debt (on the liability side), as well as by the decrease in the savings rate (see Fig. 2).

For example Garner (2006) would refer to the behavior of households in standard models, suggesting that rational behavior should in principle prevent undesired dynamics: "If households follow the permanent income hypothesis or the life-cycle model, they rationally assess future retirement needs and adjust saving and consumption appropriately as current asset values change". In the same vein, Steindel (2007) recalled the sharp increase in wealth and downplayed somewhat the fears of a slowdown in consumer spending: "Despite the low personal saving rate, aggregate household wealth has risen sharply in the past few years. (…) [We] uncover no strong evidence to suggest that low personal saving today would be associated with lower spending growth tomorrow".

The permanent income hypothesis (Friedman 1957) and the life cycle theory of consumption (Ando and Modigliani 1963) hence provided the theoretical background justifying an increase in consumption growth as long as households could expect higher future income and/or had higher wealth. This approach was and still is, with many variants, a theoretical background for many models used to forecast or study macroeconomic fluctuations.

However, since these approaches generally use a "net wealth" concept (i.e. assets minus liabilities), they have serious drawbacks. They implicitly suppose a symmetric effect of household assets and liabilities on their consumption behavior. Yet, looking at Fig. 3, it is clear that household assets, especially financial assets, are more volatile than liabilities. The value of financial assets mostly depends on their market price, while the change in price is much slower on the liability side. Because of the higher share of financial assets as a percentage of household income and its higher volatility, the change in net wealth is very much in line with the change in financial assets, dwarfing changes in debt. The unprecedented losses and gains in wealth over the recent period were mostly driven by financial asset price movements. Hence, by reasoning in terms of net wealth, the increase in household debt (displayed by the negative red bars in the Fig. 3), and related weakening of the household balance sheet, was masked by the parallel increase in housing and financial assets.

As housing prices started to fall and more and more households defaulted on their debt, it was soon clear that the consequences would not be neutral for private consumption and GDP. Indeed, also impacted by the decrease in stock prices, the fall in private consumption and in GDP was one of the most severe in US history. As the standard approaches do not seem to capture properly the boom and bust cycle, we use another approach for looking at household wealth, by considering separately the asset and liability sides of household balance sheets within a consistent framework.

3 A Consistent Stock-Flow Approach for Debt Dynamics

In order to identify the role of debt dynamics, we focus on the composition of household balance sheet flows. Rather than considering the saving rate to be the share of income that is not spent, our approach uses financial flows including for instance housing spending. In this respect, in order to balance household assets and liabilities it is also necessary to include the net purchase of financial assets as well as the net increase in household debt. Using US national accounts data (NIPA, BEA) and financial accounts data (Federal Reserve) we can write the following macroeconomic accounting identity:

$$DI - C - I = \Delta Fi\,asset - \Delta Debt$$

where DI is the disposable income of households, C is the consumption, I stands for the household investment, $\Delta Fi\,asset$ is the net purchase of financial assets and $\Delta Debt$ is the net indebtedness.

Then we isolate from the previous equation the source of funds, on the one hand, and the use of funds, on the other hand:

$$\underbrace{DI + \Delta Debt}_{\text{Source of funds}} = \underbrace{C + I + \Delta Fi\,asset}_{\text{Use of funds}}$$

This decomposition aims to identify the role of debt flows as a complementary source of income for households. As highlighted in Fig. 4, debt flows increased progressively from the mid-1990s to 2007, growing at a faster rate than disposable income. From 2008, household debt flows reversed abruptly (see Fig. 4 for the stock versus flow debt dynamics) and stopped contributing positively to the overall source of funds until 2011, before contributing again in a more limited way.

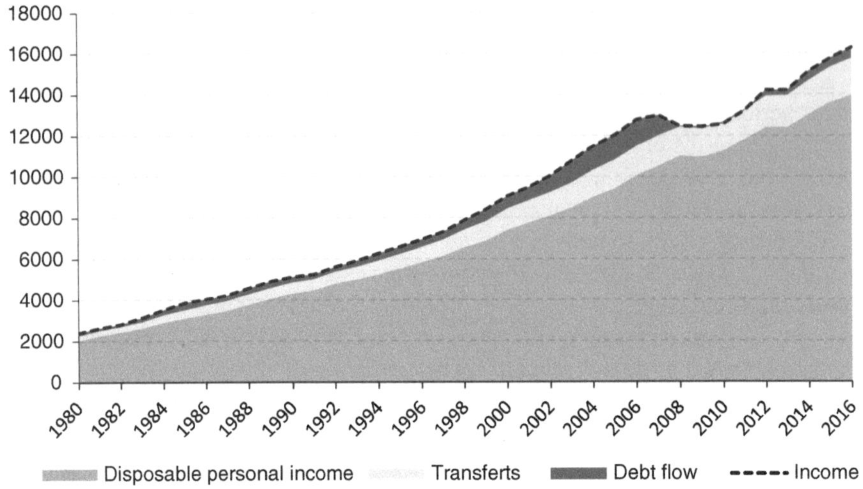

Fig. 4 Source of funds for US households (current USD, billion). *Sources* Federal Reserve, Bureau of Economic Analysis

As argued by the IMF (2012), this significant change in household behavior could stem from various theoretical reasons that American US households faced during this specific period: a tightening in credit standards (Guerrieri and Lorenzoni 2011), a realization that house prices were overvalued (Krugman and Eggertsson 2011), a sharp revision of income expectations, or an increase in economic uncertainty (Baker et al. 2012). In another vein, Minsky (1986) developed a framework allowing for an endogenous shift in debt flows after a period of financial fragility: "over periods of prolonged prosperity, the economy transits from financial relations that make for a stable system to financial relations that make for an unstable system" (Minsky 1992, p 8). Here, the key parameters are the increase in interest burden (for households in our case) and the increase in default rates. At some point, the interest burden becomes too high, default rates increase and debt flows reverse abruptly.

On the "use of funds" side, the accounting identity includes household housing and financial investment in addition to private consumption. Household funds can be used for consumption, but also to invest (housing) and to purchase financial assets. While consumption accounts for most of the use of funds, housing investment represented a growing share from the 1990s onwards, before declining sharply during the crisis (see Fig. 5).

This framework incorporating household income, spending and financial flows, offers a consistent representation of household balance sheets during the boom-bust period. In particular, private consumption seems to be empirically homogeneous to debt flows as theoretically defined in the equation decomposing sources and uses of flows.

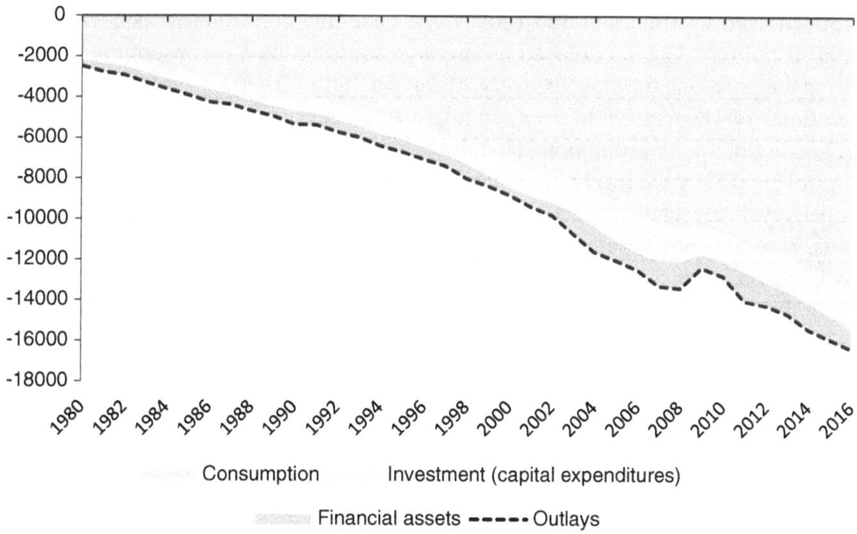

Fig. 5 Use of funds for US households (current USD, billion. *Sources* Federal Reserve, Bureau of Economic Analysis

4 Modelling US Private Consumption with Debt Flows Dynamics

Consistent with the stock-flow framework, we propose an empirical approach to model US household consumption in which debt flows represent an additional source of income. For this purpose, we develop a single equation model that uses the "debt flow" approach we described in Sect. 3.

More specifically, our model is based on an error-correction model (see for example Engle and Granger 1987) in which the long-run co-integrated equation incorporates three additional sources of revenue: labor income, debt flows and financial income. The consumption growth can be explained by both the adjustment to the long-run trend and some short-term factors, including the derivative of stock flows. Thus, the model can be written as follows:

$$\begin{aligned}\Delta \log C_t =& \beta_0 + \beta_1 \left[\log C_{t-1} - \left(\gamma_0 + \gamma_1 \log\left(DPI_{t-1} + \alpha \frac{\Delta\, Debt_{t-1}}{DPI_{t-1}}\right) + (1-\gamma_1)\log Fi_{t-1}\right)\right] \\ &+ \beta_2 \Delta \log DPI_t + \beta_3 \Delta \log Fi_t + \beta_4 \Delta \frac{\Delta\, Debt_t}{DPI_t} \\ &+ \beta_5 Unempl_t + \beta_6 1_{2001q4} + \beta_7 1_{2012q4} + \epsilon_t,\end{aligned} \tag{1}$$

Debt flow augmented model

where C_t reflects personal consumption expenditures, DPI_t stands for disposable personal income, $\Delta Debt_t$ is the flow of debt, Fi_t represents household financial assets value and ϵ_t is the error term.

As showed in Mian and Sufi (2014), the changing consumption behavior over the distribution of income played an important role in the US consumption trends during the crisis and the slow recovery. Mian and Sufi's (2014) estimates suggest that the effects of US household leverage might be larger enough to explain the entire decline in durable consumption. Therefore, we take debt as a percent of income, in order to control by the level of income. The parameter α can be seen as the marginal propensity of households to get into debt for consumption. To take into account capital gains, which are not included in disposable income or debt flows, we also include the stock market index S&P500 as a proxy for financial asset wealth dynamics, denoted Fi_t in the equation. We use well-known macroeconomic data series collected from national sources: the Bureau of Economic Analysis, the Financial Account of the United States of the Federal Reserve and Reuters. The variables are expressed in real terms except the debt-to-income ratio.[4] To estimate the regression model, we use a standard two-step procedure. First, we estimate the co-integration relationship in levels[5]; then the gap between current and equilibrium consumption is incorporated in the model as explanatory variables with the variations of DPI and financial assets, the unemployment and the acceleration of debt over DPI. We also include two dummy variables in 2001q4 (sharp rebound in consumption expenditures after 9–11 attacks) and 2012q4 (the expiration of the payroll tax cut and other fiscal policy measures) that can be considered outlier data points, possibly leading to biased estimations.

In order to compare the debt flow model given by Eq. 1, we also consider a benchmark approach that does not incorporate debt dynamics, neither in long-term nor short-term components, of the error-correction model:

$$\begin{aligned}\Delta \log C_t &= \beta_0 + \beta_1 \left[\log C_{t-1} - (\gamma_0 + \gamma_1 \log (DPI_{t-1}) + (1-\gamma_3) \log Fi_{t-1})\right] \\ &\quad + \beta_2 \Delta \log DPI_t + \beta_3 \Delta \log Fi_t + \beta_5 Unempl_t + \beta_6 1_{2001q4} + \beta_7 1_{2012q4} + \epsilon_t \end{aligned} \quad (2)$$

Benchmark model

We estimate both models by using data from Q1 1995 to Q4 2016. Table 1 reports the estimation results. We note that all coefficients have coherent signs and are statistically significant. In particular, these results indicate that higher indebtedness is associated with higher consumption. These results indicate that model (1) outperforms model (2) in terms of explanatory power, and, as a consequence, suggest that the debt-flow framework succeeds in capturing consumption dynamics.

Using model (1) specification, we decompose the contributions[6] of the various explanatory variables. Figure 6 exhibits this decomposition and highlights the role of debt dynamics in private consumption fluctuations. While the increasing contribution of debt flow over the period from 1995 to 2006 was a clear support for consumption,

[4]To check for the robustness of our results, we also evaluate our single equation model in nominal terms with the consumption price index as an additional element. The results are very similar and hence do not provide significant evidence.

[5]We use a Gauss-Newton optimization to address the nonlinearity involved by constraint on the parameters α and γ_1 within the long-run equation. The equation in differences is estimated using standard ordinary least squares.

[6]This decomposition uses both co-integrated and differenced terms of the Eq. (1). We use a Taylor series approximation to compute the contribution of "debt flow" terms in the long run.

Table 1 Regression results

	(1) Debt flow augmented model	(2) Benchmark model
Long run (β_1)	−0.22***	−0.14***
Intercept (γ_0)	−0.03***	0.10***
Income (γ_1)	0.99***	0.97***
$\frac{\Delta Debt_t}{DPI_t}$ (α)	0.44***	
DPI_t (β_2)	0.20***	0.17***
Fi_t (β_3)	0.01**	0.02**
$\frac{\Delta Debt_t}{DPI_t}$ (β_4)	0.13**	
$Unemployment_t$ (β_5)	−0.08***	−0.11***
$1_{2001q4}(\beta_6)$	0.01***	0.01***
$1_{2012q4}(\beta_7)$	−0.01**	−0.01***
Intercept (β_0)	0.01***	0.01***
R-squared (adjusted R-squared)	0.53 (0.49)	0.44 (0.40)
Log likelihood	371.2	363.4

*, ** and *** denote statistical significance at the 10%, 5% and 1% respectively

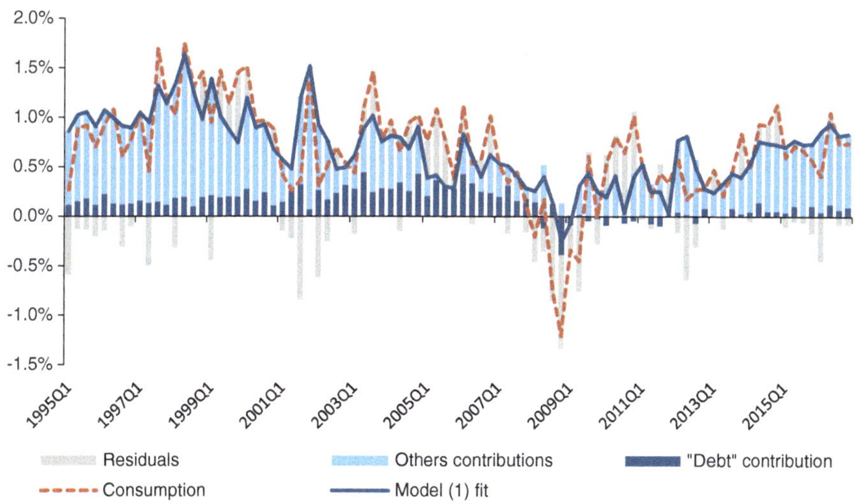

Fig. 6 Contribution of debt flow to consumption growth modelling in model (1). *Source* authors' calculations

it diminished after the Great Recession. In the post- crisis period, the almost non-existent contribution, and even negative contribution in 2010 and 2011, suggests that debt flow was a drag on consumer expenditures.

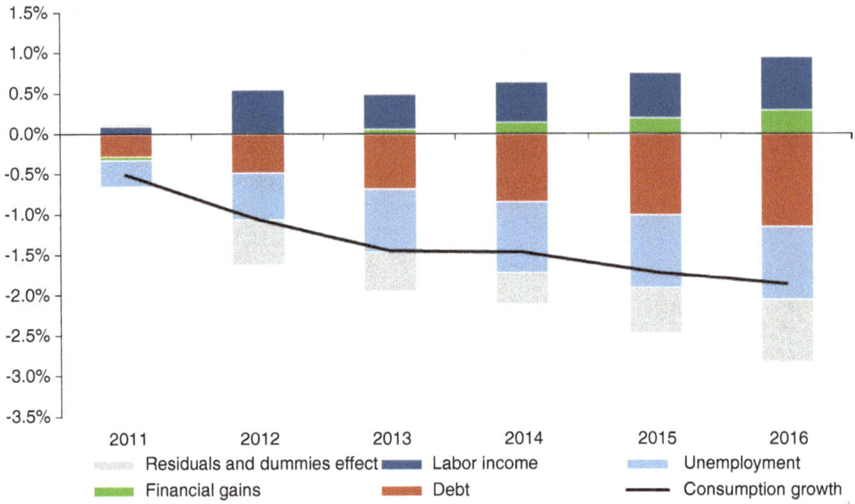

Fig. 7 Cumulative contributions to consumption growth since 2011, relative to 1996–2007 average. *Source* authors' calculations

Conflating the influences of debt, income, unemployment and financial assets, Fig. 7 examines the contributions since 2011 of these factors to private consumption, relative to an average over the pre-crisis period 1996–07.

Several observations can be drawn from these results.

First, Fig. 7 indicates that the model's residuals are slightly negative. This negative "contribution" of residuals could be interpreted as either an overestimation over the period 2011–2016 or an underestimation of the pre-crisis period; in all events, it reflects a change in household consumption behavior.

Then, as regards the contributions of factors, we observe that labor income and financial gains supported consumption growth while both unemployment and debt flows were a drag over the post-crisis period. In particular, these results indicate that the household sector debt flows significantly affected the growth rate of consumption. About two-thirds of the slowdown in private consumption from the pre- to the post-crisis period can be explained by the change in household debt flows.[7] Indeed, as predicted by Glick and Lansing (2009), deleveraging seems to have depressed household consumption.

Finally, looking at others factors, we observe that most of the gain in the contribution of labor income is concentrated in 2012, following which it has been almost stable. This pattern may be related to the sluggish recovery in wage growth which remains well below where it was prior to the Great Recession (see IMF 2017). Due

[7] While consumption growth averages 0.9% over the pre-crisis, it slows to about 0.6% in the post-crisis period. By averaging post-crisis contributions of model (1) we calculate that debt flows contributed about −0.19% point to this slowdown, whereas other variables only accounted for −0.06 (similar to the contribution of residuals).

to the significant improvement over the past years, labor market slack was only absorbed in 2016; as a consequence, the negative contribution of unemployment started to diminish in early 2016. Another interesting feature of this decomposition is the increase in financial gains which gave a positive boost to consumption growth, as an alternative source of revenue.

5 Conclusions

Contrary to an analysis carried out in terms of net wealth, a decomposition of household assets and liabilities shows how the pre-crisis period was characterized by excessive indebtedness. High and increasing debt flows enabled private consumption expenditures to grow faster than disposable income. These dynamics provided a significant boost to US economic growth in the short run. However, after the Great Recession, households were then forced to deleverage in order to repair their balance sheet and rebuild some of their lost wealth, thus putting a strong drag on consumption during the economic recovery.

Using an empirical stock-flow approach, we find that about two-thirds of the cumulative difference in private consumption from the pre- to the post-crisis period can be explained by the change in household debt flows. Going forward, the future behavior of both financial assets and house prices is likely to significantly influence the dynamics of debt and private consumption. While consumer credit picked up, housing debt dynamics remain far from pre-crisis dynamics and private consumption still cannot rely on debt flows as much as before the crisis. Similar approaches based on debt flows could be developed to assess other sources of vulnerabilities within the US economy, like for example in the corporate sector.

References

Ando A, Modigliani F (1963) The life cycle hypothesis of savings: aggregate implications and tests. American Economic Review 53(1):55–84

Baker SR, Bloom N, Davis SJ (2012) Has economic policy uncertainty hampered the recovery? In: Ohanian LE, Taylor JB, Wright IJ (eds) Government policies and the delayed economic recovery, chapter 3, Hoover Institution, Stanford University. https://ideas.repec.org/h/hoo/bookch/6-3.html

Engle RF, Granger CWJ (1987) Co-integration and error correction: representation estimation testing. Econometrica 55(2):251–276

Friedman M (1957) A theory of the consumption function, Princeton University Press

Garner CA (2006) Should the decline in the personal saving rate be a cause for concern? Fed Reserve Bank Kansas City Econ Rev, second quarter 91(2):5–28

Glick R, Lansing KJ (2009) US household deleveraging and future consumption growth. Fed Reserve Bank San Francisco Econ Lett, 2009–16

Gorton G, Metrick M (2012) Getting up to speed on the financial crisis: a one-weekend-reader's guide. J Econ Lit 50(1):128–150

Guerrieri V, Lorenzoni G (2011) Credit crises, precautionary savings, and the liquidity trap. National Bureau of Economic Research working papers 17583, National Bureau of Economic Research, Inc

International Monetary Fund (2012) Dealing with Household Debt, Chapter 3. World economic outlook. International Monetary Fund, Washington, D.C., April 2012

International Monetary Fund (2017) Recent wage dynamics in advanced economics: drivers and implications, chapter 2. World economic outlook. International Monetary Fund, Washington, DC, Oct 2017

Jakab Z, Kumhof M (2015) Banks are not intermediaries of loanable funds—and why this matters. Bank of England working papers 529, Bank of England. https://ideas.repec.org/p/boe/boeewp/0529.html

Justiniano A, Primiceri G, Tambalotti A (2015) Household leveraging and deleveraging. Rev Econ Dyn 18(1):3–20. Elsevier for the Society for Economic Dynamics

Krugman P, Eggertsson GB (2011) Debt, deleveraging and the liquidity trap. Society for Economic Dynamics, meeting papers 1166

Lo S, Rogoff K (2015) Secular stagnation, debt overhang and other rationales for sluggish growth, six years on working paper 482. Bank for International Settlements

McKinsey Global Institute (2012) Debt and deleveraging: uneven progress on the path to growth. McKinsey & Company

Mian A, Sufi A (2010) Household leverage and the recession of 2007–09. Int Monetary Fund Econ Rev 58:74–117

Mian A, Sufi A (2014) House of debt: how they (and you) caused the great recession and how we can prevent it from happening again. University of Chicago Press, Chicago

Mian A, Sufi A, Verner E (2015) Household debt and business cycles worldwide. National Bureau of Economic Research working papers 21581, National Bureau of Economic Research, Inc

Midrigan V, Philippon T (2011) Household leverage and the recession. Centre for Economic Policy Research discussion papers 8381, Centre for Economic Policy Research Discussion

Minsky HP (1986) Stabilizing an unstable economy. Yale University Press, New Haven, Connecticut

Minsky H (1992) The financial instability hypothesis. Levy Economics Institute, Working Paper No. 74

Purnanandam A (2011) Originate-to-distribute model and the subprime mortgage crisis. Rev Financ Stud 24(6):1881–1915

Reinhart C, Rogoff K (2009) This time is different: eight centuries of financial folly. Princeton University Press, Princeton, New Jersey

Reinhart C, Reinhart V, Rogoff K (2015) Dealing with debt. J Int Econ 96(S1):43–55 Elsevier

Steindel C (2007) Household saving and wealth accumulation in the United States. Bank for international settlements IFC bulletin no. 25 (March). In: Proceedings of the conference measuring the financial position of the household sector, vol 1, pp 58–70

Sufi A (2012) Lessons from the great recession: household debt in macroeconomic models. University Chicago Booth School of Business and National Bureau of Economic Research

Explaining Weak Investment Growth After the Great Recession: A Macro-Panel Analysis

Ines Buono and Sara Formai

Abstract Business investment could be dampened by weak aggregate demand, the high cost of capital and macroeconomic uncertainty. The importance of each factor may vary both over time and across countries. In this chapter we use a panel of advanced economies to estimate a model of business investment based on the above mentioned factors. The main objective is to understand, through time-varying parameters estimations, how their relative importance has changed over time, in particular after the global financial crisis. The analysis reveals that all three factors matter for investment, and suggests a key role for countercyclical policies aiming at lowering interest rates, supporting aggregate demand, and restoring confidence on financial markets against unfavorable macroeconomic and financial developments, such as those that followed the global financial crisis and the debt crisis.

Keywords Investment · Uncertainty · Time-varying parameters

JEL classification E22 · C23

1 Introduction

Business fixed investment has been persistently weak in advanced economies since the global financial crisis: nine years after its outburst, the investment-to-GDP ratio was still almost 3% points lower, on average, than its pre-crisis level of 24 per cent.

The views expressed are those of the authors and do not necessarily reflect those of the Bank of Italy.

I. Buono
Bank of Italy, Directorate General for Economics, Statistics and Research,
International Relations and Economics Directorate, Rome, Italy
e-mail: ines.buono@bancaditalia.it

S. Formai (✉)
Bank of Italy, Directorate General for Economics, Statistics and Research,
Structural Economic Analysis, Rome, Italy
e-mail: sara.formai@bancaditalia.it

L. Ferrara et al. (eds.), *International Macroeconomics in the Wake of the Global Financial Crisis*, Financial and Monetary Policy Studies 46,
https://doi.org/10.1007/978-3-319-79075-6_8

Although the downturn was comparable with past experiences of financial crisis, the recovery was highly heterogeneous across countries, and especially slow for those hit by the European sovereign debt crisis in 2011. For some countries investment is therefore still stuck at pre-crisis levels.

Different explanations have been invoked for the puzzling sluggishness of the recovery, and several recent empirical works have tried to identify the relative roles played by different factors in holding back aggregate investment. According to a conventional model combining an accelerator and a neoclassical approach, investment is a function of aggregate output and the user cost of capital, while recent contributions have successfully explored the importance of uncertainty (for instance, Meinin and Roche (2017)).

In this chapter, we take stock of previous results and study whether the response of investment to expected demand, user cost of capital and uncertainty has changed over time, especially after the outbreak of the 2008–2009 crisis. We consider a panel of 19 countries and take semi-annual data from 1990 to 2016. After testing how the benchmark model performs, we go on to study how its main parameters have changed over time. We first test the hypothesis of a structural break, generally during the 1990–2016 period, and specifically in 2008. We then exploit the time dimension of the data and perform a series of analyses in which the parameter of each determinant of investment is allowed to be time-varying. Finally, we check whether our findings are common to all the cross-sectional units, or whether the countries more severely hit by the crisis (peripheral European countries) were characterized by specific dynamics.

We find that the role played by investment determinants has changed over time: while expected demand was the main driver of investment in the first part of the sample, economic uncertainty became the most significant variable during the crisis. Interestingly, even after the crisis uncertainty has continued to play an important role. The elasticity of investment to the user cost of capital has, instead, been remarkably constant across time: however, its magnitude is higher on average for peripheral European countries, especially after the crisis.

As already mentioned, our work relies on a vast empirical literature on the determinants of investment. Recently this literature has focused on identifying which of the main drivers can be held responsible for the weak performance of the last few years, since this would have important implications for the optimal policy responses. Busetti et al. (2016) analyse the severe decline in investment in Italy between 2007 and 2014, finding that, although demand conditions were the most important driver of capital accumulation, uncertainty was an impediment both during the global crisis and in 2013–2014, appearing as one of the main factors behind the delayed recovery of the Italian economy. Meinin and Roehe (2017) first conduct an extensive comparison of various widely-used uncertainty proxies and then analyse the role of macroeconomic uncertainty for gross fixed capital formation in machinery and equipment for the four largest euro-area economies, finding that it accounts for a considerable share of the decline in investment during the Great Recession.

Several other studies, covering broader samples of countries over different time periods, find a predominant role of output decline in explaining the fall in investment: Lewis et al. (2014) who studied 13 OECD countries between 1993q1 and 2013q3; Chap. 4 of the IMF's April 2015 WEO, which uses data for 27 countries during and after the crisis; and Barkbu et al. (2015) who perform country-specific estimations for seven euro-area countries in the period 1990–2013.

Finally, Bussiere et al. (2015), who perform a panel estimation for 22 countries with annual data from 1996 to 2014, find that the main cause of the fall in investment was weak demand, but they show that this is best accounted for when expectations for future demand (measured, in their main specification, as the current-year IMF-WEO GDP nowcast) as opposed to past GDP, are used in the investment model. We will use a similar approach.

Against this background, our work explores whether the relative importance of the determinants of investment has changed over time, an issue that is not addressed in any of the studies referred to above. Our results suggest the existence of a structural break in the aggregate business investment model, induced by the recent crisis.

The remainder of the chapter is organized as follows. Section 2 describes the data set. Section 3 explains the empirical strategy and presents the main results. Section 4 deals with robustness checks. Section 5 concludes.

2 The Model for Investment and the Data

The models most commonly used in the literature to explain the dynamics of private non-residential investment at the aggregate level are: (i) the accelerator model; (ii) the neoclassical model; and (iii) Tobin's q model. The first two are based on the idea that investment I_t is a distributed lag function of changes in the desired capital stock.

The accelerator approach assumes that the level of desired capital stock is proportional to the level of output.[1] In the neoclassical model, instead, investment is determined by the expected return on new capital and the real user cost of obtaining and using this capital.

The main idea in Tobin's q model is that the marginal product of capital is not directly observable, and its best measure comes from the stock-market value of a firm. A firm's investment decision is given by the comparison of this value with the current cost of replacing the capital stock in place. Tobin's q is thus defined as $q = \frac{market\ value\ of\ installed\ capital}{replacement\ cost\ of\ installed\ capital}$.

The empirical literature has often enriched the models mentioned above with additional variables that are thought to affect the dynamics of investment, such as credit risk, liquidity, leverage and, more recently, uncertainty (see for instance Barkbu et al. (2015), Lewis et al. (2014), and Bussiere et al. (2015)). When investment projects are irreversible, uncertainty may restrain the propensity to invest, since waiting for more information can be a valuable option (see Bernanke (1983) and Dixit and Pindyck (1994)). The role of uncertainty in shaping investment decisions has also been analyzed at the micro level: Guiso and Parigi (1999) find that firm-specific uncertainty weakens investment, the more so when capital expenses are less

[1] See Jorgenson and Siebert (1968) for a more detailed description of the accelerator model.

reversible and the greater the firm's market power. Gilchrist et al. (2014) show that, conditional on investment fundamentals, i.e. proxies for the marginal product of capital, increases in idiosyncratic volatility are associated with a substantial decline in the rate of capital formation. The Chap. 4 of the IMF's April 2015 WEO, besides estimating an accelerator model based on aggregate data, employs firm-level data and finds that both credit constraints and uncertainty cause investment to be put off.[2]

We follow the recent empirical literature on the determinants of aggregate investment, in particular Bussiere et al. (2015), and estimate a model that takes into account demand, as measured by output, a proxy for economic uncertainty and the user cost of capital.

We use an unbalanced panel of more than 900 observations with semi-annual data from 1990h1 to 2016h2 for 19 countries.[3] Data on real private non-residential investment and realized GDP come from the OECD Economic Outlook 100 and the OECD QNA dataset.[4] Data on expected GDP comes from IMF-WEO vintages collected in April and October. While other data are available on a quarterly basis, data on expected GDP are only available on a semi-annual basis. We thus transform quarterly into semi-annual data and use half-years as our time-series unit.

Uncertainty is, by nature, not observable and can relate to various dimensions that are relevant for economic agents' decisions. The literature has thus proposed different measures of uncertainty.[5] Measures of uncertainty in financial markets are usually based on the observed or implied volatility of asset prices. The underlying idea is that a greater expected volatility of asset prices presumably reflects greater uncertainty about their determinants. These financial market based measures are commonly used as they are easy to compute from financial market data and are available for most countries, on long time series and with varying frequencies. These measures can be computed either as implied volatility of forward looking financial instruments (the VIX, for instance, is a 30-day option-implied volatility in the S&P500) or as the realized stock market volatility. Although the latter measure is backward looking, it has two important advantages: first, its computation does not require any specific assumption, and second it is free of any risk premium component.[6] In this work we thus use realized financial market volatility, given by the variance over the semester

[2]See Bussiere et al. (2015) and Busetti et al. (2016) for a more extensive review of the literature on both theoretical and empirical investment models.

[3]The countries are Australia, Austria, Belgium, Canada, Finland, France, Germany, Greece, Ireland, Italy, Japan, the Netherlands, New Zealand, Portugal, Spain, Sweden, Switzerland, the United Kingdom and the United States.

[4]For Austria, Belgium, Greece, Ireland, Italy, Portugal, Spain and Switzerland data on non-residential investment are obtained by the QNA dataset by subtracting residential capital expenditure from total (private plus public) gross fixed capital formation. This means that for these countries the dependent variable is total (instead of private) non-residential investment. Notice, however that all results hold when we consider this measure for all the available countries (that is all the countries in the dataset, with the exception of Japan). Moreover the correlation between the two variables is 0.83.

[5]See Ferrara et al. (2018) for a comprehensive review.

[6]See Bekaert et al. (2013) for a decomposition of the VIX into two components, an uncertainty measure and a proxy for risk aversion.

(130 working days) of daily stock returns Δx_{it}. Formally, for each country in our sample, we compute:

$$UNC_{it} = \sqrt{\frac{1}{130}\sum_{i=1}^{130}(\Delta x_{it})^2}$$

Although this measure directly refers to financial markets, it can be interpreted as a broader proxy of macroeconomic uncertainty to the extent that the determinants of stock market prices are closely related to macroeconomic variables. Other measures, instead, are more directly related to non-financial outcomes. A growing literature, for instance, measures uncertainty as reflected in forecasting errors of macroeconomic variables or in the disagreement among professional forecasters. Uncertainty can also be measured using firm-level data. Bloom (2009), for instance, uses US data to compute uncertainty as the cross-sectional standard deviation of firms' profit and TFP growth. In his seminal contribution, the author also shows that stock market volatility is strongly correlated both with these micro-founded measures of uncertainty and with those based on forecasters disagreement. This finding further supports our choice of UNC_{it} as a proxy for economic uncertainty.[7] More recently, Baker et al. (2016) focusing on the uncertainty around the realization of economic programs and reforms, have constructed a narrative measure of Economic Policy Uncertainty (henceforth, EPU) based on the number of times specific words or sequences of words related to economic policy appear in newspapers. Differently from other measures of uncertainty, EPU is less correlated with stock market volatility, thus capturing a different dimension of uncertainty.[8] As a further analysis we thus show results using the EPU index.[9]

Finally, the user cost of capital is measured by using a standard definition which multiplies the cost of capital (given by the real interest rate, $i_{it} - \pi_{it}$, adjusted by capital depreciation δ_{it}) by the relative price of capital (given by the ratio between investment and the GDP deflator), namely:

$$UCC_{it} = (i_{it} - \pi_{it} + \delta_{it}) * \frac{INVdef_{it}}{GDPdef_{it}}$$

From the OECD Economic Outlook 100 we obtain data for the interest rate on the 10-year government bond i_{it} and for the realized annual growth rate of the GDP

[7] On the other hand, the correlation between UNC_{it} and expected demand in our sample is negative and quite low (-0.2), confirming that expected demand does not capture uncertainty.

[8] For instance the correlation between the EPU index and our main proxy for economic uncertainty in our dataset is indeed very low (0.15).

[9] This is however only available for a limited number of countries, so when we include this measure in our analysis, we restrict the sample to G7 countries.

deflator π_{it}.[10] The depreciation rate comes from the European Commission AMECO database, computed from the consumption of fixed capital and the stock of capital.[11]

Table 1 reports summary statistics for the main variables used in the analysis, showing how they differ between the pre-crisis and the post-crisis periods. While uncertainty is higher after 2008, the growth rate of investment and that of both realized and forecasted GDP are on average higher in the pre-crisis period. In the full sample (panel a), investment growth varies from −30 per cent (in Ireland during the second semester of 2012) to +42 per cent (in Greece during the second semester of 1995), with an average of 16 per cent throughout the sample. In order to obtain results which are robust to these extreme values, from the main analysis we exclude six outliers, identified as those observations with the three highest and the three lowest private investment growth rates.[12] Finally, the user cost of capital is characterized by a negative growth in both subsamples, slightly lower after the crisis. Nevertheless, as we discuss shortly, this variable is characterized by a high degree of heterogeneity across countries.

Figure 1 shows the average growth rate of fixed private investment for the countries in our dataset both before and after the crisis, as well as the latest data available for 2016. Notwithstanding a marked heterogeneity in investment growth within our panel of countries, the figure highlights some common interesting patterns. First, after 2008 average investment growth was very low in almost all countries (with the notable exception of Ireland and Switzerland); second, there seems to be no correlation between the growth rates of investment and their fall during the crisis; finally in 2016 there were widespread signs of an upturn.

Figure 2 shows our uncertainty proxy for several countries: not surprisingly, the index displays a strong co-movement, especially during the crisis. Among advanced economies outside the euro area, the pattern for Japan moved away from that of other countries in the period 2013–2014 (as Abenomics set in), while within the euro area, the index for Spain was considerably higher in 2010, as well as between 2012 and 2014.

---

[10]Although firms' borrowing cost may be more accurately reflected by yields on corporate bond, this measure is not available for all the countries in our sample, thus, following previous studies we use 10-year government bond and abstract from the differences between business and government borrowing rates.

[11]Analysis on the determinants of investment at the micro-level have shown the relevance of firm-specific credit constraints (see, for instance, Cingano et al. (2016) and Buono and Formai (2018)). It is unlikely that our aggregate measure of user cost of capital can fully capture the extents of credit constraints restraining firms' investment decisions. Unfortunately it is extremely hard to obtain a micro-funded measure which is comparable across all the countries in our sample. Barkbu et al. (2015) proxy credit rationing for euro-area countries by using results from the European Commission's consumer and business survey. Since, from the supply side, credit constraints may also arise in response to economic uncertainty, it is plausible that their effect is partially captured by our proxy for uncertainty.

[12]These are Greece in 1995h2 (42 per cent), and 2012h1 (−23 per cent); Ireland in 2003h2 (38 per cent), 2012h1 (39 per cent) and in 2012h2 (−30 per cent) and New Zealand in 1991h1 (−21 per cent). We add back these observations in a robustness check.

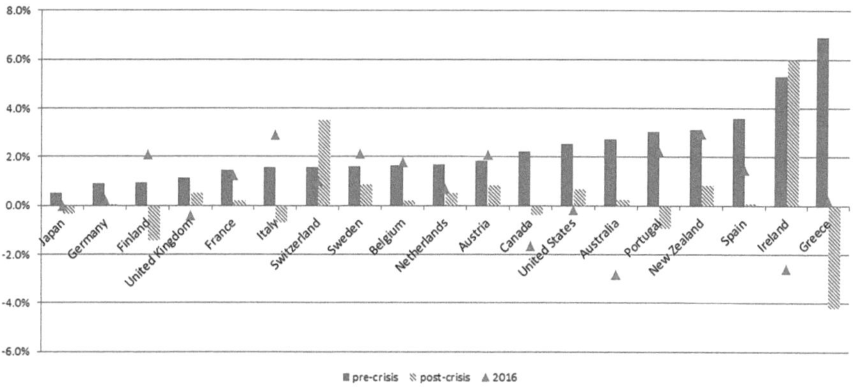

Fig. 1 Fixed private investment growth rates. *Note* Pre-Crisis refers to the average growth in the period 1990h1–2008h1, Post-Crisis to the average growth in 2008h2–2016h2. *Source* authors' calculations based on OECD Economic Outlook 100 and QNA dataset

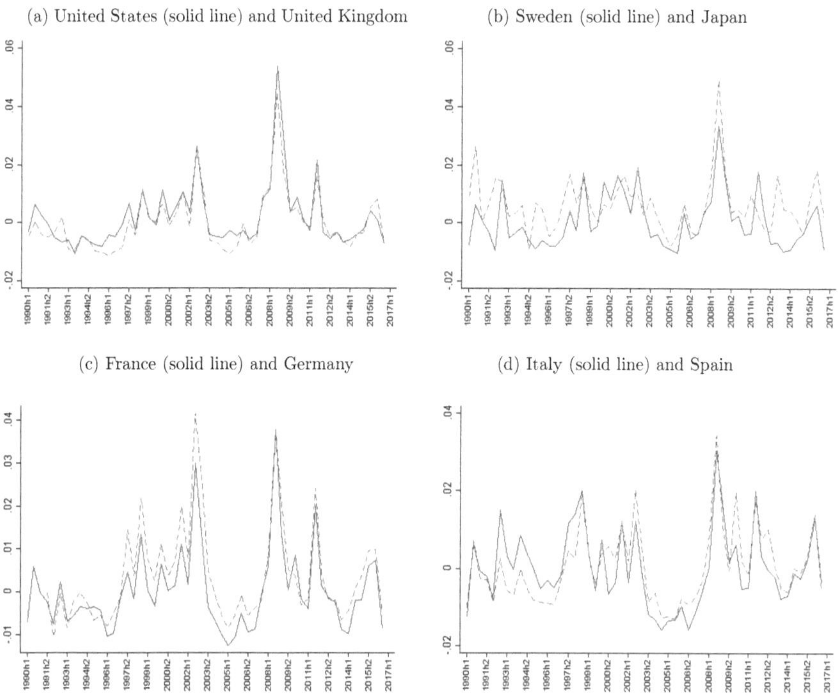

Fig. 2 Realized stock market volatility in some economies of the sample. *Note* Realized financial volatility is computed as the variance over the semester (130 working days) of daily stock returns. *Source* authors' calculations on Datastream data

Table 1 Descriptive statistics

	Obs	Mean	Std. dev.	Min	Max
(a) Full sample					
Investment	921	0.016	0.060	−0.30	0.42
GDP realized	921	0.020	0.033	−0.14	0.46
GDP nowcast	921	0.017	0.020	−0.08	0.09
GDP forecast	921	0.023	0.012	−0.04	0.07
Uncertainty	921	0.012	0.006	0	0.04
User cost of capital	921	−0.001	0.021	−0.10	0.10
(b) Pre-Crisis sample					
Investment	599	0.023	0.054	−0.21	0.42
GDP realized	599	0.026	0.025	−0.10	0.18
GDP nowcast	599	0.023	0.015	−0.03	0.09
GDP forecast	599	0.027	0.010	−0.01	0.07
Uncertainty	599	0.011	0.005	0	0.04
User cost of capital	599	−0.002	0.018	−0.10	0.07
(c) *Post-crisis sample*					
Investment	322	0.003	0.067	−0.30	0.38
GDP realized	322	0.007	0.041	−0.14	0.46
GDP nowcast	322	0.006	0.023	−0.08	0.05
GDP forecast	322	0.014	0.012	−0.04	0.04
Uncertainty	322	0.013	0.006	0.005	0.04
User Cost of Capital	322	−0.001	0.025	−0.10	0.10

Note All variables, except for uncertainty, are expressed in growth rates. The statistics are based on all observations, including outliers. Pre-Crisis refers to the period 1990h1–2008h1, Post-Crisis to 2008h2–2016h2

Figure 3 reports analogous information for the user cost of capital measure. This variable shows a clear downward trend for the UK, the US, Sweden, France, Germany and, to a lesser extent, for Japan. In Italy and Spain the decreasing trend started to reverse in 2003 and 2005, respectively: the user cost of capital reached its highest value during the sovereign debt crisis and then decreased again as the ECB's QE was implemented.

Fig. 3 User cost of capital in some economies of the sample. *Note* The user cost of capital is computed as the real cost of capital $i_{it} - \pi_{it} - \delta_{it}$ multiplied by the ratio between the investment and the GDP deflator. *Source* authors' calculations on OECD Economic Outlook 100 and European Commission AMECO data

3 Results

3.1 Time-Invariant Coefficients: Model Selection

We consider the following model for investment I_{it}:

$$\Delta lnI_{it} = \alpha_i + \beta_1 \Delta lnY_{it} + \beta_2 UNC_{it} + \beta_3 \Delta lnUCC_{it} + u_{it} \tag{1}$$

where Y_{it} is a measure of demand, UNC_{it} is uncertainty and UCC_{it} is the user cost of capital as defined above. The dependent variable is the semiannual growth rate of investment, while the growth rate of demand is yearly, although the data release frequency is semiannual (see below, for further discussion). All our specifications include year fixed effects that account for international macro shocks that affect investment simultaneously across countries (for instance, oil prices), and country fixed effects that account for country-specific determinants of investment.[13] In what

[13]Results are robust when country fixed effects are omitted from the model.

follows we compare some alternatives of Eq. 1, in order to select the main model we will use throughout the rest of the chapter.

While we have already described our measures of uncertainty and the user cost of capital in Section 2, the choice of a suitable measure of demand requires a more thoughtful discussion, being it widely debated in the literature, for both econometric and economic issues. According to an accelerator model, investment depends on the desired amount of capital, which is proportional to the level of output/demand. Many previous works thus make investment depend on realized output, and to avoid the endogeneity stemming from investment being a component of output, this usually enters the model with a time lag. If capital adjusts to meet future demand, however it is reasonable that entrepreneurs choose investments based on their envisaged capacity needs and expectations of future demand, as the micro empirical literature suggests. For instance, Gennaioli et al. (2016) provide empirical evidence about the extent to which a CEO's expectations for earnings growth help explain firms' choices, including investment and production. Their result shows that expectations contain information on investment plans that is not captured by Tobin's q. Bussiere et al. (2015) are the first to apply this idea to a macro panel analysis, and prove it to be correct.

In Table 2 we compare estimates of Eq. 1 using different measures of the demand determinant of investment decisions. We start with the standard lagged realized growth rate of GDP (column 1). This variable is computed as the annualized growth rate from semiannual data, in order to harmonize it with the other measures we use for demand. The estimated coefficient is 0.52, meaning that if (lagged) GDP growth increases by 1 p.p., then the semiannual investment growth increases by 0.5 p.ps. The effect on the annualized growth rate of investment is roughly twice as much.[14]

Following Bussiere et al. (2015), we then replace the realized GDP growth with forecasts taken from the IMF WEO, i.e. the nowcast $GDPnow_{it}$ and the 1-year ahead forecast $GDP1yf_{it}$. As shown in Table 1, both these variables have been on average higher in the pre-crisis than in the post-crisis period. More interestingly, while in the pre-crisis period both forecasts are quite similar to the realized growth rate, in the post-crisis period the 1-year ahead forecast tends to be significantly higher than the other two growth rates. Both forecasts are only available for annual growth rates and are released and updated every six months, in April and October. As for column 2 of Table 2, the semiannual investment growth of the first semester of a given year is regressed on the April WEO's nowcast of GDP growth for that year, while for the investment growth of the second semester the expected GDP growth refers to the same year, but comes from the WEO October vintage. Analogously, in column 3, $GDP1yf_{it}$ refers, for both semiannual observations within a year, to the annual growth rate of the same following year, but it comes from two different WEO vintages. This implies that the explanatory variable in each observation incorporates new information on future demand that is relevant to the current investment decision. On the other hand, the forecast horizons change between observations, and this could

[14]Given g_s a semi-annual growth rate and g_y the corresponding annualized rate, $\Delta g_s = x$ implies $\Delta g_y \approx 2x$, if g_s is small. In our data, the semi-annual investment growth rate is on average 0.02.

Table 2 Main specification: searching for a proxy for aggregate demand

	(1)	(2)	(3)	(4)	(5)
GDP_{it-1}	0.520^{***} (0.141)				
$GDPnow_{it}$		0.958^{***} (0.210)			
$GDP1yf_{it}$			1.183^{***} (0.398)	1.183^{**} (0.533)	
$GDPyf2_{it}$					1.336^{**} (0.521)
UNC_{it}	-0.730^{**} (0.271)	-0.690^{**} (0.270)	-0.656^{**} (0.296)	−0.212 (0.630)	-0.715^{**} (0.292)
UCC_{it}	-0.555^{***} (0.116)	-0.501^{***} (0.129)	-0.501^{***} (0.134)	-0.358^{**} (0.153)	-0.498^{***} (0.133)
Observations	906	915	915	453	915
R^2	0.316	0.300	0.284	0.371	0.283

Note Robust standard errors in parentheses. $^{*}p < 0.1$, $^{**}p < 0.05$, $^{***}p < 0.01$

cast doubts on the interpretation of the coefficients. We tackle this concern in columns 4 and 5.

The nowcast used in column 2 is probably the most endogenous among the different measures, since investment at time t is an important component of contemporaneous GDP. The coefficient for the 1-year ahead forecast for GDP growth in column 3 is 1.2, suggesting that investment reacts significantly to expected demand. If expected GDP growth increases by 1 p.p., then the semi-annual investment growth increases by 1.2 p.ps. The results do not change when we align the forecast horizon across observations: in column 4 we halve the sample and estimate the model by only using observations for the first semester. This requires only using the April WEO forecast for $GDP1yf_{it}$ and all observations have the same forecast horizon. The coefficient for expected demand is unchanged, although the estimation is less precise due to the smaller sample size. As a further check, in column 5 the independent variable $GDP1yf_{it}2$ is given, in the first semester, by the 1-year ahead April forecast and, in the second semester, by the average between the 1-year ahead and the 2-year ahead forecasts for GDP growth rates, both taken from the October WEO. Again the results are basically unchanged.

All the other determinants of investment have the expected signs, as we will discuss later in more detail: increases in the uncertainty proxy and in the user cost of capital both drive investment down. Moreover, with the exception of uncertainty in column 4, the coefficients are always significantly different from zero and similar across specifications. Our preferred measure of demand is thus going to be GDP $GDP1yf_{it}$, as used in column 3.

In Table 3 we show results considering different lag structure of the investment model, using our preferred measure for the expected demand (the 1-year ahead GDP forecast). In the first column we augment the specification with the lagged depen-

Table 3 Main specification: searching for the lag structure of the variables

	OLS	AB	OLS	OLS
Inv_{t-1}	0.025 (0.082)	−0.051 (0.113)		
$GDP1yf_{it}$	1.135** (0.398)	1.133*** (0.348)	1.113*** (0.383)	1.183*** (0.398)
UCC_{it}	−0.506*** (0.136)	−0.508*** (0.153)	−0.486*** (0.133)	−0.501*** (0.134)
UCC_{it-1}			−0.104 (0.100)	
UNC_{it}	−0.661** (0.268)	−0.827*** (0.271)	−0.526 (0.315)	−0.656** (0.296)
UNC_{it-1}			−0.298 (0.265)	
Observations	900	886	902	915
R^2	0.284		0.285	0.284

Note Robust standard errors in parentheses. $^{*}p < 0.1$, $^{**}p < 0.05$, $^{***}p < 0.01$. Coefficients for $GDP1yf_{it}$ and UCC_{it} should be interpreted as elasticities

dent variable which is not significant. To overcome standard endogeneity problems with the lagged dependent variable we show the estimates using the Arellano-Bond estimator in the second column, which confirms that the investment growth at time t is uncorrelated with past growth rates. In the third column, we insert a lag for the user cost of capital and the proxy for uncertainty.[15] Only contemporaneous variables are significant in explaining investment. In particular, even if the joint effect of contemporaneous and lagged uncertainty is significantly different from zero, the effect of the former is estimated with more precision, and thus in subsequent regressions we only keep UNC_{it}.

In order to choose the appropriate estimation technique, we test for the presence of cross sectional correlation and non-stationarity. Macroeconomic variables are notoriously affected by these issues, which can seriously undermine consistency and efficiency. Cross sectional dependence may arise because of common shocks to the cross sectional units, which ultimately become part of the error term. Increasing economic and financial integration makes this issue particularly relevant. To check for cross-sectional dependency, we compute a set of Pesaran (2004) cross-sectional dependence test statistics (CD_P), which are N(0, 1) distributed under the null hypothesis of cross-sectional independence. The CD_P statistic obtained after performing our main regression is 5.8, meaning that cross-sectional independence for all variables is rejected at the 1 per cent significance level. Thus, cross-sectional dependence should be accounted for when performing regressions.

[15]In unreported regressions we also insert the past value of one-year-ahead GDP, which is not significant. We also try a specification with both the GDP nowcast and the 1-year-ahead GDP forecast. In this case we find that only the first is significant. However, we think this variable is seriously flawed by endogeneity: thus in our main analysis we use the one-year-ahead GDP forecast.

Table 4 Test for stationarity

	IPS	Fisher-type
	$Z_{\tilde{t}-bar}$	Inverse $\tilde{\chi}^2$
Investment	-15.70^{***}	273.07^{***}
GDP forecast	-8.16^{***}	136.89^{***}
Uncertainty	-10.51^{***}	168.42^{***}
UCC	-17.97^{***}	847.86^{***}

Note IPS and Fisher-type panel unit root test statistics. Asterisks indicate rejection of the null hypothesis of a unit root at 1 per cent (***)

Table 5 Main specification: solving the cross-sectional dependence

	OLS	PCSE	Driscoll-Kraay
$GDP1yf_{it}$	1.183^{***} (0.398)	1.183^{***} (0.299)	1.183^{***} (0.368)
UNC_{it}	-0.656^{**} (0.296)	-0.656^{***} (0.226)	-0.656^{**} (0.304)
UCC_{it}	-0.501^{***} (0.134)	-0.501^{***} (0.117)	-0.501^{***} (0.112)
Observations	915	915	915
R^2	0.284	0.308	
Country FE	Yes	Yes	Yes
Time FE	Yes	Yes	Yes

Note Robust standard errors in parentheses. $^{*}p < 0.1$, $^{**}p < 0.05$, $^{***}p < 0.01$. Coefficients for $GDP1yf_{it}$ and UCC_{it} should be interpreted as elasticities

In order to test for stationarity, we perform both an Im-Pesaran-Shin (IPS) and a Fisher-type test. Both are panel unit root tests that can account for cross-sectional correlations and preserve the desired properties when performed on an unbalanced panel like ours. The null hypothesis is that all panels contain a unit root. As shown in Table 4, the null is strongly rejected for each variable, suggesting that our series are all stationary.

Table 5 reports the results of our preferred specification when we deal with the presence of cross-sectional dependence. In column 2 we report panel-corrected standard errors (PCSEs) and in column 3 Driscoll-Kraay standard errors, which remain valid also when the cross-sectional dimension grows large compared with the time dimension. The estimates are unbiased and the covariance matrix estimator is consistent under the hypothesis that the cross sectional dependence is caused by common factors which are unobserved but uncorrelated with the included regressors. Overall, this table shows that estimates and significance levels are quite stable across the different methodologies.

To summarize, our preferred model is one where the growth rate of investment is explained by the 1-year-ahead forecast of GDP growth, a proxy of contemporaneous uncertainty, and the contemporaneous user cost of capital. We estimate this model by using OLS with PCSEs, and the result is that aggregate investment increases when expected demand increases, when uncertainty decreases and when the user cost of capital declines. In particular, when the 1-year-ahead forecast of GDP growth increases by 1 p.p., the semi-annual growth rate of business investment increases by 1.2 p.ps. This corresponds to an increase of roughly 2.4 p.ps of the annualized growth rate, a result equivalent to that found by Bussiere et al. (2015), although they use the GDP nowcast as a proxy for future demand. As for the user cost of capital, an increase of 1 per cent implies a decrease in investment equal to 0.5 per cent (compared with 0.7 per cent in Bussiere et al. (2015)). The coefficient for (the standardized) UNC_{it}[16] suggests that a one standard deviation increase in uncertainty implies a reduction of 0.7 p.ps in the semi-annual investment growth rate, which is around half the overall mean growth rate (see Table 1). This estimate is again close to that obtained by Bussiere et al. (2015), although uncertainty enters their preferred specification with a lag. In what follows we investigate whether these average coefficients hide relevant variations in the determinants of aggregate investment over time.

3.2 The Determinants of Investment Over Time: Sample Split

We split our sample into two sub-periods: before and after the Great Recession. The first and third columns of Table 6 report results for the main specification: while the coefficient of the user cost of capital is unchanged between the two sub-samples and with respect to the one obtained for the entire period, the coefficients for the expected demand and uncertainty coefficients show interesting patterns. The first decreases after the Great Recession, the latter becomes economically and statistically significant only afterwards (in the last column it is almost significant at 10 per cent). In particular, after 2008h2, a one standard deviation increase in uncertainty implies a decrease in the semi-annual investment growth rate of around 1.5 p.ps.

The picture that emerges reveals that expected demand is an important determinant of investment over the full sample, even if with a magnitude that changes over time, while uncertainty only became a key determinant of aggregate investment after the Great Recession.[17] It follows that, in the aftermath of the financial crisis, sluggish expected demand, increased uncertainty and, in some countries, a sharp increase in the cost of capital, negatively contributed to investment growth. In the following semesters, expectations on GDP growth, usually above realized values (see Table 1),

[16]In the regressions uncertainty is normalized by subtracting the country-specific mean and dividing by country-specific standard deviation.

[17]An alternative interpretation of our results could be a non-linear, but constant, relationship between uncertainty and investment growth. If uncertainty was increasingly detrimental on investment when getting larger, the higher uncertainty in the second part of the sample would result in a higher coefficient if the non-linearity was not taken into account. To exclude this interpretation, we run the main specification by adding a quadratic term for uncertainty: this is never significant, while the linear term is basically unchanged in magnitude, being higher after 2008h1, and almost significant at conventional levels.

Table 6 Sample split

	1990h1–2008h1	1990h1–2008h1	2008h2–2016h2	2008h2–2016h2
$GDP1yf_{it}$	1.715*** (0.278)	1.848*** (0.267)	1.329** (0.670)	1.400** (0.672)
UNC_{it}	−0.216 (0.218)	−0.181 (0.220)	−1.018* (0.592)	−0.857 (0.599)
UCC_{it}	−0.524*** (0.150)		−0.453*** (0.167)	
$BorrCost_{it}$		−0.611** (0.244)		−0.427 (0.283)
$RelPInv_{it}$		−0.598*** (0.174)		−0.718** (0.281)
Observations	596	596	319	319
R^2	0.325	0.343	0.359	0.377

Note Robust standard errors in parentheses. $^{*}p < 0.1$, $^{**}p < 0.05$, $^{***}p < 0.01$. Coefficients for $GDP1yf_{it}$ and UCC_{it} should be interpreted as elasticities. BorrCost is the borrowing cost as defined in the text; RelPInv is the relative price of investment as defined in the text. Estimates are obtained using OLS and standard errors are corrected for cross-sectional dependence.

positively contributed to investment growth, although with a lower impact compared to the pre-crisis period. On the contrary, high uncertainty had an increasing negative contribution, that in many countries lasted till the most recent period.[18] The user cost of capital, whose effect has been quite constant over time, contributed differently across countries depending, for instance, on the timing of the introduction of non conventional monetary policies.

In columns 2 and 4 of Table 6 we replace the user cost of capital by its two components: the borrowing cost $i_{it} - \pi_{it} + \delta_{it}$ and the relative price $\frac{INVdef_{it}}{GDPdef_{it}}$ (see Sect. 2). Our results show that both components have an important effect on aggregate investment: the relative price coefficient is more stable throughout the sample, while borrowing costs are slightly more relevant in the first part of the sample.[19]

The results in Table 6 point to the presence of a structural break in the relationship under analysis. Now we formally test the hypothesis that the change in the aggregate investment model took place following the global crisis of 2008–2009. For this purpose we first construct a dummy that takes the value 1 starting from 2008h2 (Post-crisis dummy), and we run the main regression on the three dependent variables as well as on their interactions with the crisis dummy. As usual, we insert country and time dummies (which also incorporate the Post-crisis dummy). The results in Table 7 confirm that the determinants of investment have changed since the crisis. In particular, while expected demand and the user cost of capital have a significant

[18]Only for the last observation, 2016h2, uncertainty contributed positively to the investment growth rate of most countries.

[19]There is a lively academic and policy debate on how the decrease in the price of investment goods—due to rapid advances in technology—is shaping labour and the capital share of firms' production function.

Table 7 Post-crisis dummy

	1990–2016
$GDP1yf_{it}$	1.247*** (0.339)
*Post-crisis dummy	−0.281 (0.503)
UNC_{it}	−0.200 (0.281)
*Post-crisis dummy	−0.901** (0.389)
UCC_{it}	−0.552*** (0.167)
*Post-crisis dummy	0.098 (0.236)
Observations	915
R^2	0.314

Note Robust standard errors in parentheses. $^{*}p < 0.1$, $^{**}p < 0.05$, $^{***}p < 0.01$. Coefficients for $GDP1yf_{it}$ and UCC_{it} should be interpreted as elasticities. Estimates are obtained using OLS and standard errors are corrected for cross-sectional dependence

effect throughout the sample (as obtained by testing for the significance of the sum of the coefficients before and after the crisis), our proxy for economic uncertainty enters the model significantly only after the global crisis.

Finally, we test whether the existence of a structural break is common to all countries in the dataset. To do this, for each country we perform a standard structural break test (Chow test) under the null hypothesis that the coefficients do not vary after 2008h2. The null hypothesis of no structural break is tested using a Wald test which is distributed as a Chi-square. In Fig. 4 we report the Chi-square statistic ranked from the lowest (Japan) to the highest value (New Zealand). The horizontal line indicates the threshold above which we reject the null hypothesis: thus the Chow test detects the presence of a break in 2008h2 for nine countries in our dataset.[20]

The evidence collected so far suggests that the aggregate investment model has changed over time and that important transformations may have happened after the burst of the 2008–2009 crisis. In the next section we go a step further and analyse a time-varying coefficient model to back up these findings and obtain precise estimates for each point in time.

[20] In an unreported analysis we find that in each country in the dataset there is at least one structural break (however not necessarily in 2008h2). This result is obtained by performing a series of Wald test over a range of possible break dates in the sample.

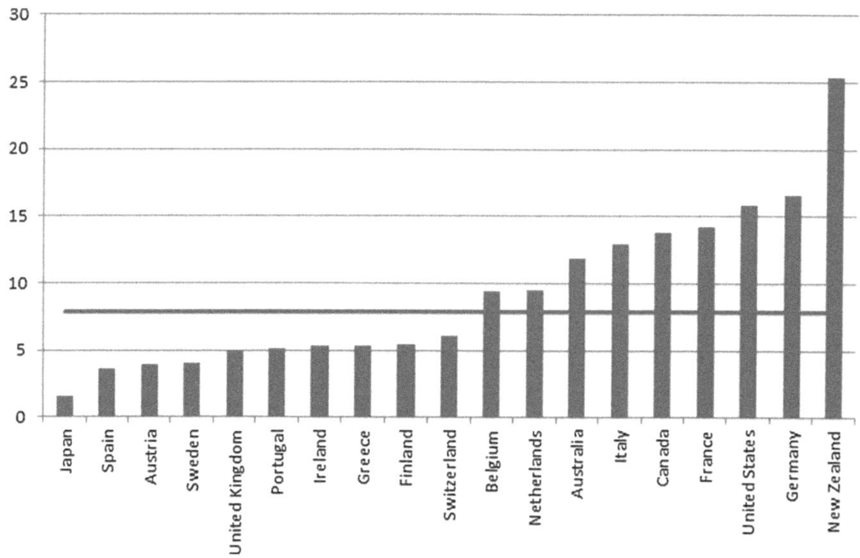

Fig. 4 Structural break test (2008h2). *Note* Chi-square statistic for Chow's structural break test. Bars above the horizontal line indicate the rejection of the null hypothesis of no structural break. *Source* Authors' calculations

3.3 *The Determinants of Investment over Time: Time-Varying Coefficients*

The aim of this section is to estimate the following regression:

$$\Delta ln I_{it} = \alpha_i + \beta_{1,t}\Delta ln Y_{it} + \beta_{2,t} UNC_{it} + \beta_{3,t}\Delta UCC_{it} + u_{it} \quad (2)$$

where all the coefficients are indexed by t. We first employ a rolling window methodology in which, given our sample of semiannual observations from 1990h1 to 2016h2, Eq. 2 is estimated with OLS for all the overlapping backward-looking windows of n observations $[t - n + 1, t]$, with t = 1990h1 + n − 1, ..., 2016h2. This provides a sequence of estimated parameters $\{\beta_{1999\text{h}2}, ..., \beta_{2016h2}\}$. Figures 5, 6 and 7 show, for each explanatory variable, the estimated parameters and the 90 per cent confidence intervals when $n = 20$ as well as the time-invariant coefficient (dotted horizontal lines) from the regression in Table 5, column 1.

The results confirm and qualify the findings from the previous analysis. In particular, Fig. 5 shows that the role of expected demand, with an estimation of around 1.6 before the crisis, became less important after 2009, losing some significance in the following five years. According to Fig. 6, the coefficient of economic uncertainty is zero at the beginning of the sample, decreases as the world slips into global crisis, and remains significantly negative thereafter. Since the crisis, global investment has become significantly reactive to financial uncertainty, which has thus contributed to

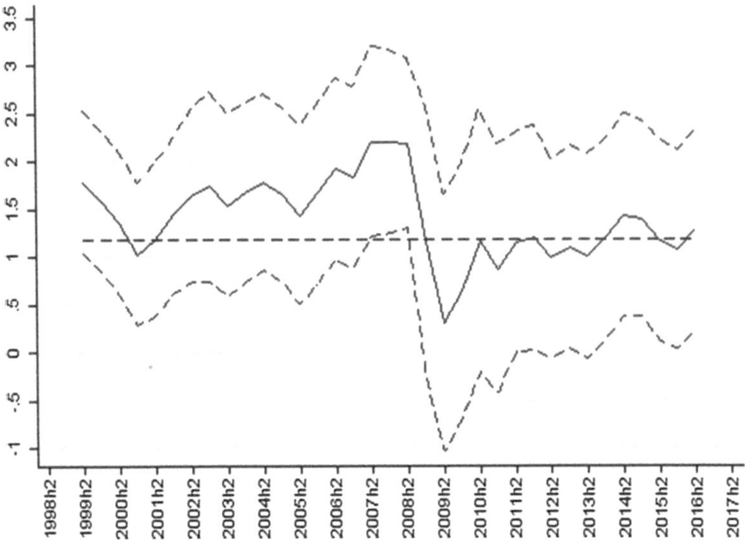

Fig. 5 Expected demand on investment; rolling windows with n = 20. *Source* Authors' calculations

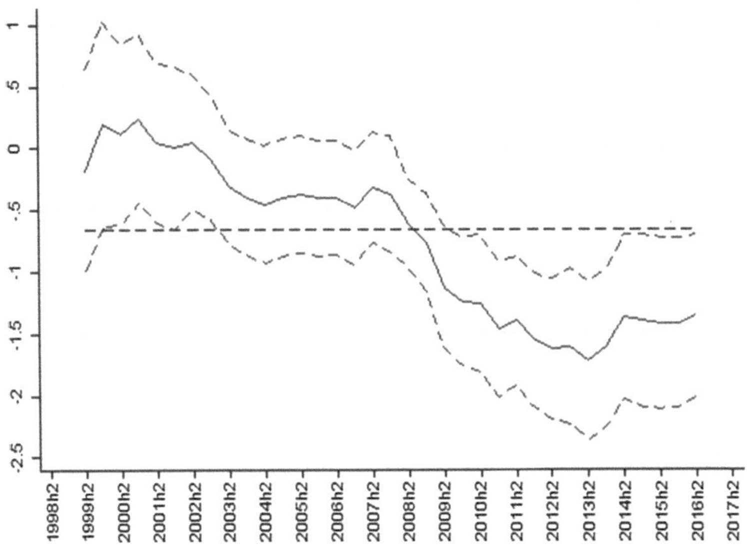

Fig. 6 Uncertainty on investment; rolling windows with n = 20. *Source* Authors' calculations

keeping it al lower levels. The decreasing trend in the uncertainty coefficient seems to have ended by 2014. However, the latest point estimate is still negative and large, which does not suggest a reversal of the trend. Finally, Fig. 7 shows a remarkably stable estimated coefficient for the user cost of capital throughout the entire period.

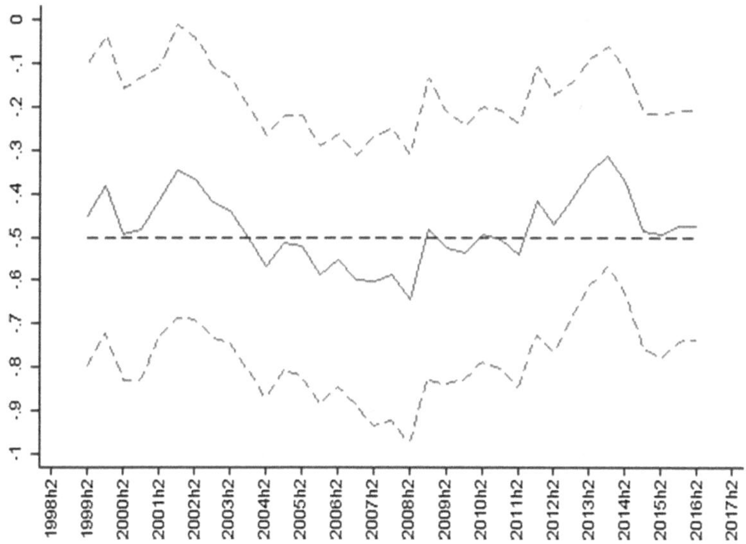

Fig. 7 User cost of capital on investment; rolling windows with n = 20. *Source* Authors' calculations

Of course, rolling window results may be sensitive to the choice of the window length n. In particular, as n increases the graph levels out.[21] Moreover, this methodology applies equal weights to all the past observations n in $[t - n + 1; t]$, and a weight equal to zero to all the remaining ones. Alternatively, one could apply a different weighting scheme: for instance, discounting the more distant past observations would produce a path for β_t that could better capture gradual structural changes in the underlying relationship. To this end, we estimate Eq. 2 by implementing a non-parametric technique whose properties have been discussed by Giraitis et al. (2014). This implies estimated coefficients given by:

$$\hat{\beta}_t = \left[\sum_{j=t-n}^{t} \omega_{j,t} x_j x_j'\right]^{-1} \left[\sum_{j=t-n}^{t} \omega_{j,t} x_j y_j\right], \quad (3)$$

where $\omega_{j,t}$ is the weight and x_j and y_j stand for generic observations of the dependent and the independent variable. This is a weighted-OLS estimate whose weight may be chosen from different classes of distributions. In particular, given the generic weight function

$$\omega_{j,t} = cK\left(\frac{t-j}{H}\right), \quad (4)$$

[21] As a robustness check we estimate the model by imposing $n = 15$ and the results are confirmed.

we will consider both the Exponential Kernel function $K(z) = e^{(-z)}$ and the Gaussian Kernel function $K = (1/\sqrt{2\pi})e^{\frac{-z^2}{2}}$. Both are normalized by the bandwidth H and c is an integration constant such that the weights within each window sum up to 1. While using the exponential weighting scheme implies backward looking weights, increasing up to t, the Gaussian Kernel function implies a scheme that is forward-looking at the beginning of the sample, backward-looking at the end and centred in t for the other observations. In both cases, any variation of H changes the weighting scheme and the estimated parameters: the higher H is, the more uniform the weights (when $H \to \infty$ the estimation becomes an unweighted OLS and corresponds to the rolling windows specification described above).[22,23] Following Giraitis et al. (2014), we set $H = \sqrt{T}$.[24]

Estimates are shown in Figs. 8, 9 and 10, where in panel (a) there are those using the Gaussian Kernel, while those obtained with the Exponential Kernel are in panel (b).[25] The effect of expected demand on investment decreases starting from a coefficient greater than 1.5 to values lower than 1 during the global recession and then remaining at values around the unity thereafter (see Fig. 8). The coefficient of uncertainty is instead insignificant at the beginning of the sample and decreases, reaching a minimum value during the crisis of around −1.5 using the Gaussian Kernel (Fig. 8, panel a) and around −2 using the Exponential (panel b). Interestingly the graphs show that after the crisis the coefficient remains permanently low, even if it shows an upward trend. The effect of the user cost of capital does not reveal any surprises: the time-varying coefficient is quite stable and fluctuates around its mean value (Fig. 10).[26]

Given that the intensity of the crisis and the length of time until the first signs of recovery have been quite heterogeneous across countries, we estimate Eq. 2 using the Gaussian Kernel separately for peripheral European countries as opposed to other countries.[27] The results are reported in Fig. 11 where the solid lines are time-varying coefficients for the peripheral countries. The analysis shows that the effect of expected demand is stable and of a higher magnitude for non-peripheral countries throughout the time sample, while after the crisis it became nil for peripheral European countries. Economic uncertainty instead drags investment down in non-peripheral countries only after the crisis, while for peripheral European countries it has always played a role, with the negative effects only being mitigated around the early 2000s. The most interesting result comes from the borrowing cost of capital ($i_{it} - \pi_{it} - \delta_{it}$) whose

---

[22]See Buono and Formai (2016) for further discussion on these two weighting schemes.

[23]The Gaussian Kernel estimator has recently been used by Riggi and Venditti (2015), to estimate the time-varying parameters of a (backward-looking) Phillips curve and by Buono and Formai (2016) to estimate the de-anchoring of inflation expectations.

[24]Results are robust to different choices of H.

[25]As the Exponential Kernel is backward-looking, the estimates β_t start at $t = 1999$. On the other hand, for the Gaussain Kernel in the first part of the dataset, estimations are obtained by using only future information, and we chose only to show results from 1995 onwards.

[26]When we perform regressions separating the effect of the borrowing cost of capital from that of the relative price of investment, we find quite stable results, without any clear trend.

[27]The peripheral European countries include: Italy, Spain, Portugal, Ireland and Greece.

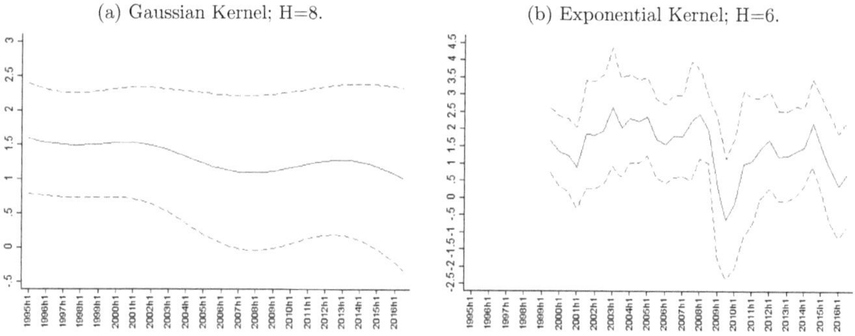

Fig. 8 Expected demand on Investment—time-varying specification. *Source* Authors' calculations

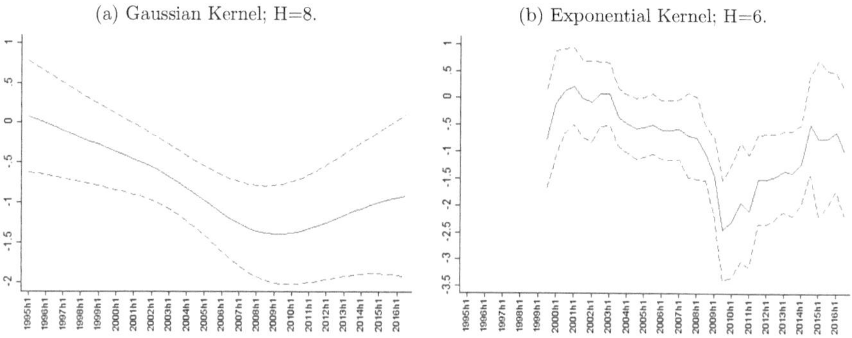

Fig. 9 Uncertainty on Investment—time-varying specification. *Source* Authors' calculations

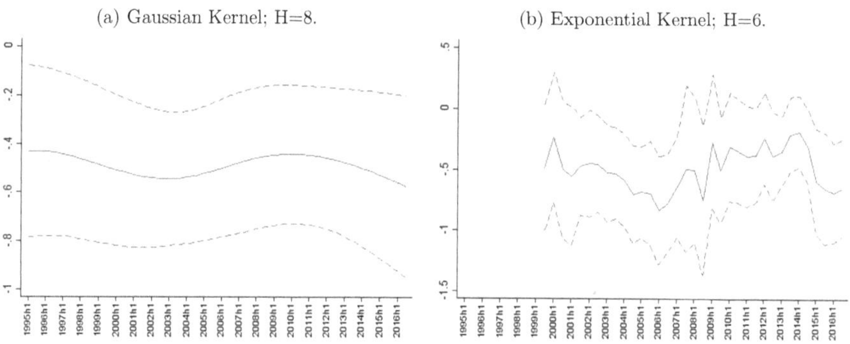

Fig. 10 User cost of capital on Investment—time-varying specification. *Source* Authors' calculations

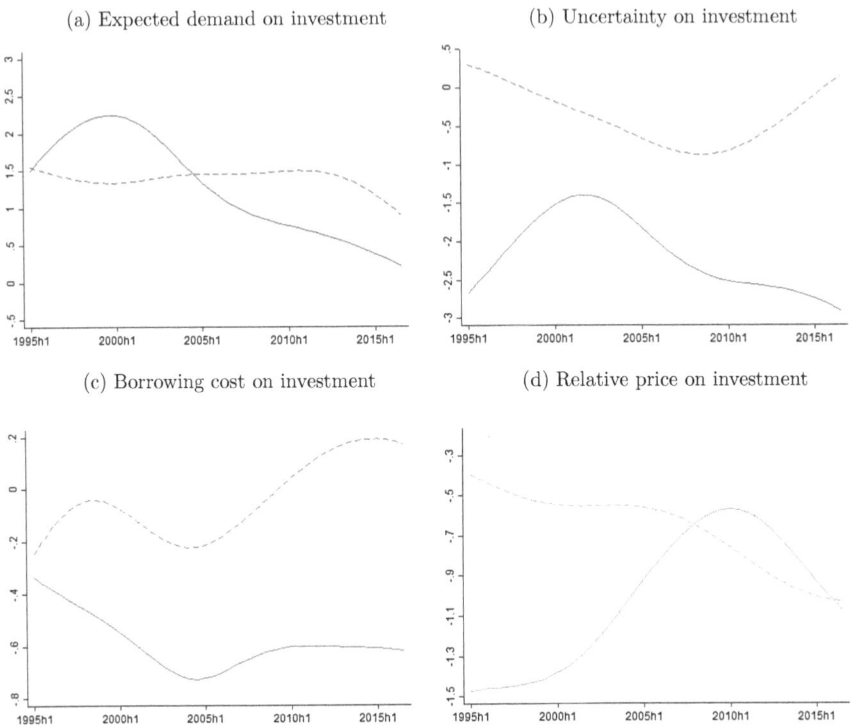

Fig. 11 Periphery European Countries (solid lines), comparison with the rest of the sample (dotted lines)—Gaussian weights; H = 8. *Source* Authors' calculations

effect appears to be larger in peripheral European countries, especially around and after the great recession. This might suggest that the stimulus of European monetary policy may be acting precisely for the countries that need it most, i.e. those where the consequences of the financial and debt crisis have been more severe. Finally, the response of investment to its relative price shows a clear downward trend for non-peripheral countries, where, in absolute value, it has doubled in the last twenty years.

4 Robustness and Further Analysis

The analysis has been so far performed excluding extreme observations, defined as the observations with the three highest and the three lowest growth rates of private investment. Table 8 reports results when these outliers are included too. We find that main findings hold, except for the coefficient of uncertainty losing some significance, although its magnitude is stable.

Table 8 Robustness 1: including outliers

	(1)	(2)	(3)
$GDP1yf_{it}$	1.198^{***} (0.325)	1.344^{***} (0.316)	1.204^{***}
*Post crisis dummy			−0.136 (0.610)
UNC_{it}	-0.797^{***} (0.241)	-0.686^{***} (0.240)	−0.426 (0.301)
*Post crisis dummy			-0.732^{*} (0.450)
UCC_{it}	-0.494^{***} (0.136)		-0.468^{**} (0.199)
*Post crisis dummy			−0.042 (0.274)
$BorrCost_{it}$		-0.510^{**} (0.225)	
$RelPInv_{it}$		-0.752^{***} (0.199)	
Observations	921	921	921
R^2	0.283	0.307	0.286

Note Robust standard errors in parentheses. $^{*}p < 0.1$, $^{**}p < 0.05$, $^{***}p < 0.01$. Coefficients for $GDP1yf_{it}$ and UCC_{it} should be interpreted as elasticities. Column 1 reports results for the benchmark regression; column 2 reports results for regression in which the user cost of capital is replaced by its two components (borrowing cost and investment relative price); column 3 reports results for regression which includes Post-crisis dummy interactions with the main variables. Estimates are obtained using OLS and standard errors are corrected for cross-sectional dependence

The results presented so far are obtained from specifications that include year- and country-fixed effects. It follows that identification relies on the variability of the regressors over time within each country. This greatly reduces the chance that our estimates are biased due to omitted variables. On the other hand, any global trend in both uncertainty and in the relative cost of capital does not contribute to the estimation of the parameters of interests. The same is true for systematic differences across countries in any of the explanatory variables. To check whether this significantly alters the results, in Table 9 we compare the main time-invariant estimations (column 1) with those obtained by omitting year-fixed effects (column 2) and country-fixed effects (column 3). While in the latter case results are basically unchanged, removing year-fixed effect reduces the R^2 and increases the effect of expected demand. On the other hand, the parameters for uncertainty and the user cost of capital are not affected.[28]

[28]We also check whether the estimated year-fixed effects exhibit any time trend, and this in not the case. We also could not find evidence in favor of a liner trend in any of our main variables. This is not that surprising, at least for investment, expected demand and user cost of capital, as they are taken as first differences.

Table 9 Robustness 2: omitting fixed effects

	(1)	(2)	(3)
$GDP1yf_{it}$	1.183^{***} (0.299)	1.492^{***} (0.267)	1.225^{***} (0.249)
UNC_{it}	-0.656^{***} (0.226)	-0.673^{***} (0.248)	-0.682^{***} (0.216)
UCC_{it}	-0.501^{***} (0.117)	-0.495^{***} (0.113)	-0.495^{***} (0.118)
Observations	915	915	915
Country F.E.	Yes	Yes	No
Year F.E.	Yes	No	Yes
R^2	0.308	0.205	0.293

Note Robust standard errors in parentheses. $^{*}p < 0.1$, $^{**}p < 0.05$, $^{***}p < 0.01$. Coefficients for $GDP1yf_{it}$ and UCC_{it} should be interpreted as elasticities. Estimates are obtained using OLS and standard errors are corrected for cross-sectional dependence

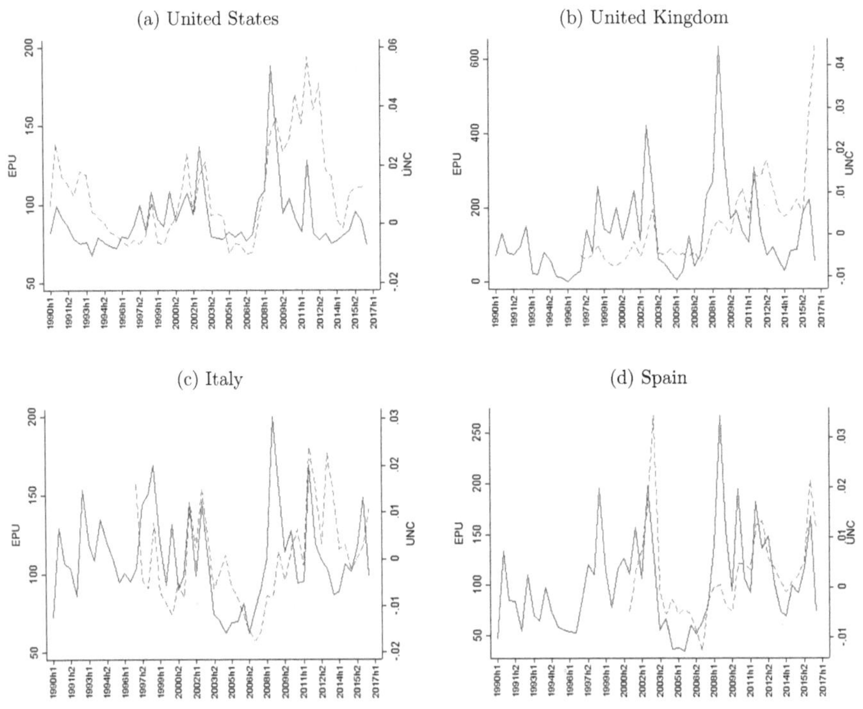

Fig. 12 Economic policy uncertainty Index (EPU, dashed line, left-hand axis) and realized financial volatility (UNC, solid line, right-hand axis.) *Source* EPU Index is from Baker et al. (2016), realized financial volatility is authors' calculation on Datastream data

Table 10 Robustness 3: Political versus economic uncertainty

	(1)	(2)	(3)	(4)	(5)
$GDP1yf_{it}$	1.241*** (0.236)	1.362*** (0.246)	1.228*** (0.237)	1.190*** (0.286)	0.985*** (0.278)
*Post crisis dummy				0.500 (0.478)	0.368 (0.465)
UNC_{it}	−0.655*** (0.222)		−0.641*** (0.224)		0.020 (0.288)
*Post crisis dummy					−1.184*** (0.389)
UCC_{it}	−0.405*** (0.118)	−0.406*** (0.119)	−0.409*** (0.118)	−0.271 (0.173)	−0.268 (0.169)
*Post crisis dummy				−0.265 (0.236)	−0.219 (0.236)
EPU_{it}		−0.003 (0.003)	−0.002 (0.003)	0.003 (0.007)	−0.009 (0.007)
*Post crisis dummy				−0.008 (0.008)	0.008 (0.008)
Observations	343	343	343	343	343
R^2	0.518	0.503	0.518	0.508	0.536

Note Robust standard errors in parentheses. $^{*}p < 0.1$, $^{**}p < 0.05$, $^{***}p < 0.01$. Coefficients for $GDP1yf_{it}$ and UCC_{it} should be interpreted as elasticities. Estimates are obtained using OLS and standard errors are corrected for cross-sectional dependence

As mentioned in Sect. 2, several alternative measures of uncertainty have been proposed by the literature. Here, we consider the EPU index of Baker et al. (2016) as opposed to our proxy based on financial market data, UNC. This measure has become increasing central in the debate as its evolution has started to diverge from that of other more traditional measures of uncertainty. Figure 12 shows that, although in some periods the two measures were capturing uncertainty in a similar way, more recently they have largely diverged in some countries, most notably in the United Kingdom (after the Brexit), but also in Italy both in 2014 and in 2016. More generally, the correlation between EPU and UNC in the sample was 0.26 before the global crisis, −0.009 after it. This may cast doubt on the ability of financial markets to properly account for political and economic policy uncertainty. In Table 10 we thus replicate the analysis for the subset of countries for which the EPU measure is available.[29] First of all, according to column 1 the results for this restricted sample are very close to those obtained for the full set of countries (Table 5, column 1). When we replace the measure of financial uncertainty with EPU_{it} (see column 2), the coefficient for this new variable is zero, while the coefficients for other variables are essentially unchanged. When we have both measures of uncertainty (column 3), only UNC_{it} has a negative and significant coefficient. The picture does not change when we allow

[29] Australia, Canada, France, Germany, Ireland, Italy, Japan, Netherlands, Spain, Sweden, the United Kingdom and the United States.

the effects to be different before and after the crisis. This result is similar to that of Bussiere et al. (2015), who also find that the EPU index does not seem to play a role in explaining investment.

5 Concluding Remarks

This chapter studies how the determinants of business investment have changed over time, using a panel of 19 advanced economies over the period 1990–2016. Taking stock of existing contributions, we consider an empirical model where investment depends on expected demand (1-year ahead), economic uncertainty (as proxied using financial data) and the user cost of capital.

We find that the role played by the various determinants of investment has changed over time: while expected demand, its main driver, has decreased in importance since the onset of the financial crisis, uncertainty has become a much more important variable. These results, which are stronger for peripheral European countries, qualify previous findings in the literature that, based on time-invariant models, stressed the major role played by aggregate demand and missed out the increasing importance of uncertainty. We also find that the elasticity of investment to the user cost of capital has been remarkably constant across the years. Moreover, peripheral European countries appear to have become more sensitive to the borrowing cost component, especially in the last part of the sample.

Our results suggest the following policy implications. First, monetary policy, by curbing interest rates and thus the user cost of capital, retains a key role as a way to stimulate aggregate investment, and this role has probably been crucial in preventing the recent crisis from having even more serious consequences for investment, especially in the hardest hit countries. Second, policies that stimulate aggregate demand (including, of course, monetary and fiscal policies) have an indirect positive effect on capital accumulation. Third, reducing uncertainty on financial markets also helps to create an environment that supports investment. In this respect, the central banks' efforts to re-build confidence after the outbreak of the global financial crisis and the debt crisis may have been key in preventing a much deeper and more persistent collapse on business confidence and productive investment.

References

Baker S, Bloom N, Davis N (2016) Measuring economic policy uncertainty. Q J Econ 131(4):1593–1636

Barkbu B, Berkmen SP, Lukyantsau P, Saksonovs S Schoelermann H (2015) Investment in the euro area: Why has it been weak? IMF working paper WP/15/32

Bekaert G, Hoerova M, Duca ML (2013) Risk, uncertainty and monetary policy. J Monetary Econ 60(7):771–788

Bernanke BS (1983) Irreversibility, uncertainty, and cyclical investment. Q J Econ 98(1):85–106

Bloom N (2009) The impact of uncertainty shocks. Econometrica 77(3):623–685
Buono I, Formai S (2016) The evolution of the anchoring of inflation expectations. Occasional papers 321, Bank of Italy
Buono I, Formai S (2018, forthcoming) Bank credit, liquidity and firm investments. Working paper series, Bank of Italy
Busetti F, Giordano C, Zevi G (2016) The drivers of italy's investment slump during the double recession. Ital Econ J 2:143–165
Bussiere M, Ferrara L, Milovich J (2015) Explaining the recent slump of investment: the role of expected demand and uncertainty. Document de travail, 571
Cingano F, Manaresi F, Sette E (2016) Does credit crunch investment down? new evidence on the real effects of the bank-lending channel. Rev Financ Stud 29(10)
Dixit AK, Pindyck RS (1994) Investment under uncertainty. Princeton University Press
Ferrara L, Lhuissier S, Tripier F (2018) The challenges of rising uncertainty for macroeconomic policy. International macroeconomics in the wake of the global financial crisis. Springer, Berlin
Gennaioli N, Ma Y, Shleifer A (2016) Expectations and investment. NBER Macroecon Annu 30:379–442
Gilchrist S, Sim JW, Zakrajek E (2014) Uncertainty, financial frictions, and investment dynamics, NBER working papers
Giraitis L, Kapetanios G, Yates T (2014) Inference on stochastic time-varying coefficient models. J Econ 179:46–65
Guiso L, Parigi G (1999) Investment and demand uncertainty. Q J Econ 114(1):185–227
Jorgenson DW, Siebert CD (1968) A comparison of alternative theories of corporate investment behavior. Am Econ Rev 58(4):681–712
IMF (2015) Private investment: Whats the holdup? World Econ Outlook 4:71–113
Lewis C, Pain N, Strasky J, Menkyna F (2014) Investment gaps after the crisis, OECD economics department working papers, No. 1168
Meinin P, Roehe O (2017) On measuring uncertainty and its impact on investment: cross-country evidence from the euro area. Eur Econ Rev 92:161–179
Pesaran M (2004) General diagnostic tests for cross section dependence in panels, Cambridge Working Papers in Economics 0435, Faculty of Economics, University of Cambridge
Riggi M, Venditti F (2015) Failing to forecast low inflation and phillips curve instability: a euro-area perspective. Int Financ 18:47–68

Part III
New Challenges for Monetary Policies at a Time of High Uncertainty, Low Inflation and Low Real Interest Rates

Uncertainty Fluctuations: Measures, Effects and Macroeconomic Policy Challenges

Laurent Ferrara, Stéphane Lhuissier and Fabien Tripier

Abstract The world economy is plagued by uncertainties of various kinds from economic policy uncertainty to financial volatility. This chapter presents the main measures for uncertainty referred to in policy debates, explains how uncertainty affects the macro-economy and draws three lessons for policy-makers facing increasing uncertainties. First, macroeconomic policies have a direct role to play in stabilizing policy-related uncertainty. Second, financial uncertainty should be constrained through financial regulation. Third, the effectiveness of economic stabilization policies depends on the state of uncertainty and should be adapted accordingly.

Keywords Uncertainty · Measurement · Macroeconomic impact · Economic policy

1 Introduction

> Today I want to discuss what uncertainty means for the UK's economic performance, and how the Bank of England can best respond to it
>
> Mark Carney, Governor of the Bank of England, speech "Uncertainty, the economy and policy" given the 30 June 2016
>
> The outlook is subject to considerable uncertainty from multiple sources, and dealing with these uncertainties is an important feature of policymaking.

The authors would like to thank Nick Bloom, Christophe Destais, Giovanni Caggiano, Daniela Marconi, Sarah Mouabbi and Simon Sheng for helpful comments and discussions.

L. Ferrara (✉) · S. Lhuissier
Banque de France, Paris, France
e-mail: laurent.ferrara@banque-france.fr

S. Lhuissier
e-mail: stephane.lhuissier@banque-france.fr

F. Tripier
Université Paris-Saclay (EPEE, Univ Evry) & CEPII, Paris, France
e-mail: fabien.tripier@univ-evry.fr

L. Ferrara et al. (eds.), *International Macroeconomics in the Wake of the Global Financial Crisis*, Financial and Monetary Policy Studies 46,
https://doi.org/10.1007/978-3-319-79075-6_9

Janet L. Yellen, Chair of the Board of Governors of the Federal Reserve System, Speech "Inflation, Uncertainty, and Monetary Policy" given the 26 September 2017

And, finally, we need prudence. As the economy picks up we will need to be gradual when adjusting our policy parameters, so as to ensure that our stimulus accompanies the recovery amid the lingering uncertainties.

Mario Draghi, President of the ECB, speech "Accompanying the economic recovery" given the 27 June 2017

There has been a strong focus in recent policy debates, on the various types of uncertainty in the global economy. Those discussions are motivated mainly by the fact that the global economic activity was extremely sluggish in the wake of the Global Financial Crisis (GFC), or at least much slower than most economists expected. Among the possible drivers of this sluggishness, business investment is frequently cited, and it seems that investment rates post-GFC have been much lower than those observed pre-2007. Also, uncertainty is a standard explanation in policy explanations for weak investment. Ten years after the GFC, uncertainty remains at the top of the policy makers agenda as can be seen from the comments made by central bankers, quoted above.

By its nature, uncertainty is an unobservable variable and thus there are various approaches to its measurement. Compared to ten years ago, there is ongoing rich and active research efforts aimed at providing uncertainty measures. For example, the VIX has been extensively used as a measure of uncertainty reflecting the volatility in financial markets. The lack of consensus among forecasters surveyed is another widely used measure of uncertainty; it is assumed that there is a direct positive link between uncertainty about the future and the way opinion surveys diverge. More recently, text-based analyses have been used to assess perception of uncertainty by counting specific words and the occurrence in large databases of newspapers articles. Those new measures have been integrated by policy-makers into policy debates, and are shedding light on the concept of uncertainty leading in turn, to the development of new measures, within a virtuous circle of activity.

Following the GFC, economists have tried to achieve a better understanding of how fluctuations in these measures of uncertainty might influence the economy by offering numerous mechanisms through which uncertainty fluctuations are transmitted to the economy. Some channels are well known, for example the "wait-and-see" investment channel and especially for the most irreversible type of investment, and the precautionary savings channel. However, evidence on other channels is more recent, and we refer for example, to the role played by financial frictions. Uncertainties affect not just domestic activity. Indeed, the increasing integration of finance and trade has generated greater connectedness in the world economy with the result that an uncertainty shock is likely to propagate across borders.

Finally, it is clear that economic policy decisions are affected by the evolution of uncertainty. In a recent speech, Yellen (2017) showed how uncertainties about the economic outlook are related to macroeconomic activities, to the assessment of the slack in the labor market and to measures for expected inflation and how in turn these expectations weigh on monetary policy decisions, particularly in terms of unwinding unconventional monetary policy measures. Similarly, the great uncertainty about upcoming economic activity renders policy-making and policy decisions more complex in the context of the implementation of fiscal measures or structural reforms, whose effects, it is well known, are sensitive to the state of the economy (see, e.g. IMF 2016). At the same time, economic policies have a role to play in reducing the various types of uncertainty by anchoring agents' expectations to a transparent and clear commitment. In this respect, forward guidance used by central banks for the future direction of short-term interest rates or multi-year credible fiscal consolidation plans are efficient ways to conduct economic policy while reducing uncertainty.

In view of the buoyant literature on the topic, this chapter is an attempt to review some recent results. We do not pretend to provide an exhaustive review of the papers dealing with the concept of uncertainty, rather we try to focus on the key challenges raised by the concept:

- How to measure uncertainty?
- Through which channels does uncertainty impact the economy?
- What are the implications of uncertainty for policy makers?

To address these issues, in the first section we present various measures of uncertainty used by practitioners and their advantages and drawbacks. We then discuss the main macroeconomic effects of uncertainty fluctuations and the various channels through which they operate. In the final section, we discuss some policy implications based on our reading of the literature:

- *Lesson 1*: *Macroeconomic policies have a direct role to play in stabilizing policy-related uncertainty.*
- *Lesson 2*: *Financial uncertainty should be restrained by financial regulations.*
- *Lesson 3*: *The effectiveness of economic stabilization policies depends on the state of uncertainty and should be adapted accordingly.*

2 Measuring Uncertainty Fluctuations

There has been a focus in recent policy debates on the uncertainties surrounding the global economy. The concept of uncertainty is not new; for instance, Knight (1921) in a seminal paper makes a conceptual difference between risk and uncertainty, while Bernanke (1983) considers the effect of uncertainty on investment. By its nature, uncertainty is an unobservable variable, and thus, to be estimated using various approaches. What has changed over the last ten years is that a rich and active literature has emerged proposing uncertainty measures. Those new measures have been integrated into policy debates by policy-makers to shed light on the concept of uncertainty which in turn has led to the development of new measures, within a virtuous circle. In this chapter, we do not pretend to provide an exhaustive review of the papers dealing with this concept but rather focus on the most popular measures of uncertainty and the provision of a sensible classification.

First, we need to revisit the conceptual difference between risk and uncertainty proposed in Knight (1921). Risk corresponds to a situation where the distribution of probabilities for a series of events is known. Within this framework, risk assessment corresponds to estimation of the quantiles of the distribution based on learning. On the other hand, uncertainty, sometimes referred to as deep or radical uncertainty, describes a situation in which agents have no way of predicting the probability that an event will occur. Brexit corresponds more to the concept of uncertainty since it is the first time that a country has taken the decision to leave the European Union. However, from an empirical point of view, the recent literature tends not to make this distinction as can be seen from Bloom's (2014) recent review.[1] Therefore, in the rest of this section we consider volatility as one of various measures of uncertainty based on the understanding that it refers to both risk and uncertainty.

2.1 Uncertainty on Financial Markets

Traditionally, uncertainty is defined generally in terms of financial uncertainty, and has been described as stock market volatility in the empirical parts of some influential papers (see Bloom 2009). The VIX index constructed by the Chicago Board of Option Exchange, sometimes called the *fear index* in financial markets, is the most widely used measure in the empirical literature and is aimed at assessing the effects of uncertainty shocks (see Fig. 1). This index is a measure of 30-day volatility in the S&P500 index implied by option bid/ask quotes, and thus, reflects the expectations of agents in the equity market. Therefore, the VIX can be seen as a fairly broad measure of uncertainty since it captures uncertainty related directly to both equity markets and also the macroeconomic environment to the extent that it is related to financial developments. The VXO index which is based on S&P100 stock futures has also been used in empirical analyses, and starts earlier (January 1986 compared to January 1990 for the VIX). The monthly correlation between these two indicators is very high, close to 1. Bloom (2009) proposed to back-calculating the VXO to 1962 by taking the standard deviation of the daily S&P500 index normalized to the same mean and variance as the VXO when they overlap after 1986.

An alternative to the VIX/VXO is realized stock market volatility which has the great advantage that it is model-independent and simple to compute but it does not reflect expectations. For example, Senyuz et al. (2015) use realized volatility to show empirically that it has a large negative impact on economic growth and employment in the US economy.

Lastly, financial volatility can be estimated using an econometric model that explicitly integrates conditional variance or stochastic volatility as in Ferrara et al. (2014) or Carriero et al. (2016). For example, using a mixed-frequency model, Ferrara et al. (2014) find that using daily stock price volatility, estimated using a GARCH-type model, allows significant improvements in output forecasting accuracy for a set of advanced economies.

These measures of uncertainty are used widely in the empirical literature looking at the effects of uncertainty shocks but have been criticized, in particular because

[1]"In this article, I'll refer to a single concept of uncertainty, but it will typically be a stand-in for a mixture of risk and uncertainty" (Bloom 2014).

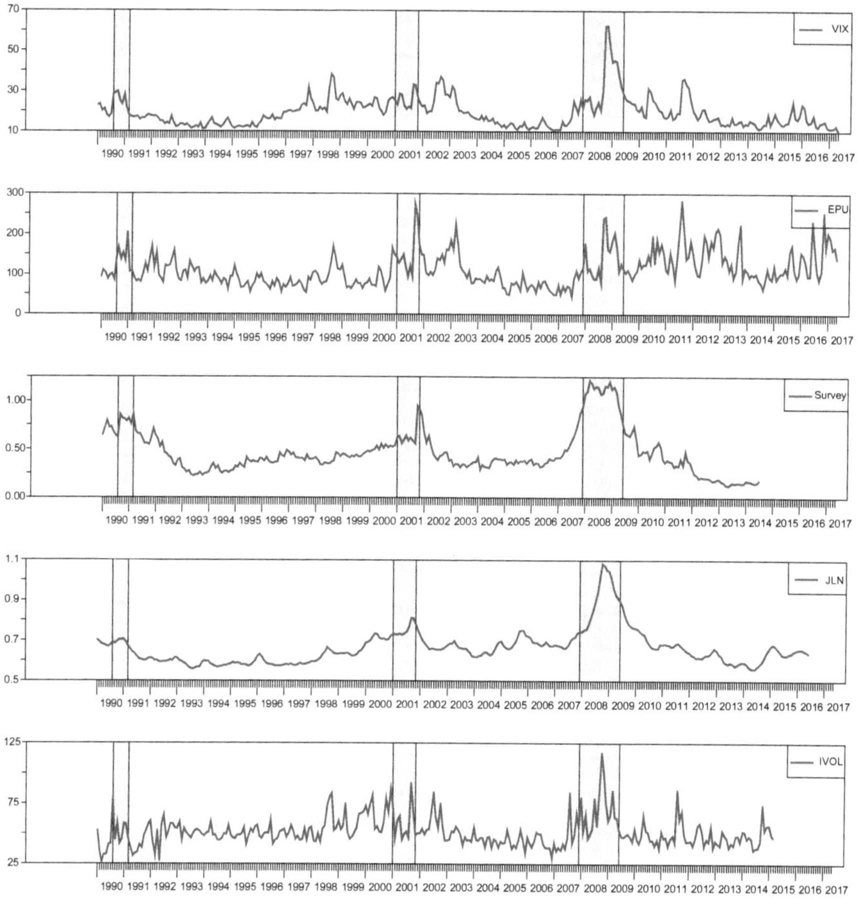

Fig. 1 Comparison of various measures of uncertainty for the US economy since 1990: VIX, EPU, Ozturk and Sheng (2017), Jurado et al. (2015) and Gilchrist et al. (2014). (Shaded areas corresponds to US recessions)

they integrate a time-varying risk premium which may not be directly related to uncertainty (e.g., depressed demand leads to an increase in the risk of business failure, and therefore, a higher risk premium). In this respect, Bekaert et al. (2013) propose an approach to decompose the VIX into two components, an uncertainty measure, and a proxy for risk aversion.

2.2 *Micro-level Measures of Uncertainty*

Uncertainty can be assessed also using micro-level approaches. Following the introduction of financial volatility measures, some authors have proposed the estimation

Table 1 Linear correlation coefficients between various monthly measures of uncertainty for the US economy since 1990: VIX, EPU, Survey (Ozturk and Sheng 2017), JLN (Jurado et al. 2015) and IVOL (Gilchrist et al. 2014)

Correlation	VIX	EPU	Survey	JLN	IVOL
VIX	1				
EPU	0.45	1			
Survey	0.58	0.19	1		
JLN	0.65	0.32	0.76	1	
IVOL	0.66	0.40	0.33	0.37	1

of uncertainty using high-frequency firm-level stock market returns. Typically, a standard deviation over a certain period of time is computed for a specific company. For example, Bloom et al. (2007) use daily stock prices for a large panel of UK manufacturing firms to compute annual uncertainty measures. Bloom (2009) uses the within month cross-sectional standard deviation of US firm-level stock returns from the Center for Research in Securities Prices (CRSP). Gilchrist et al. (2014) construct a proxy for idiosyncratic uncertainty using high-frequency firm-level stock market returns based on a panel of more than 11000 US non-financial corporations (see Fig. 1). First, they estimate daily excess returns purged of their forecastable component using a standard factor model, then in a second step, they calculate a quarterly firm-specific standard deviation of daily returns that is supposed to reflect idiosyncratic uncertainty.

In his seminal paper, Bloom (2009) proposed two other cross-sectional measures of uncertainty based on US micro data. First, he used the cross-sectional standard deviation of firms' pretax profit growth, from the quarterly national accounts of public companies. Those data are normalized by average sales for the period. Second, he computed the standard deviation of annual five-factor total factor productivity (TFP) growth taken from the NBER manufacturing industry database. He shows that those measures are strongly correlated to stock market return volatility (see Bloom 2009, Table 1, p. 629).

Similarly, Bloom et al. (2012) construct measures of uncertainty at various aggregate levels (establishment, firm, industry) by computing standard deviations of TFP shocks estimated as residuals of a first order autoregressive panel regression.

2.3 *Economic Policy Uncertainty*

Economic policy uncertainty (EPU) has been at the heart of recent major uncertainty shocks that have affected the global economy, ranging from suspicions of currency manipulation in China to the Brexit situation, through unexpected political elections outcomes. All those events are generating uncertainties about the implementation of economic and social programs. Measuring the influence of such events is not easy, and the recent literature focuses mainly on textual analysis and news-based metrics to assess this type of economic policy uncertainty- earlier work such as that by Julio and Yook (2012), use the election cycle to measure political uncertainty. Nick Bloom and co-authors have been at the forefront of this type of measurement. In a recent paper (Baker et al. 2016), they proposed monthly economy policy uncertainty (EPU) indices for the US, the UK, Japan, Canada, Australia, some European countries, and Brazil, Chile, India, China, South-Korea and Russia, constructed from news coverage about policy-related economic uncertainty[2] (see Fig. 1 for the US). The idea is based on counting the number of occurrences of specific words or a sequence of words, in certain newspapers in a given country. Typically, to be included in the count, the publication should simultaneously contain at least words referring to the economy (e.g. "economy" or "economics"), *and* to policy (e.g. "deficit" or "central bank" or "taxes"), *and* to uncertainty (e.g. "uncertain" or "uncertainty"). After some normalization steps an index is computed, allowing comparison over time. This set of EPU indexes constitutes the broadest worldwide database that can be used for international evaluations of uncertainty shocks. Davis (2016) used this database to create an index of global uncertainty by computing weighted averages of all those country-specific indexes to produce a single global measure. Note however, that for most of the countries (except the US and the UK), only two newspapers are considered to compute the indexes. Using the same methodology, on their website Baker, Bloom and Davis propose some specific EPU indicators. For example, they produce indexes for sub-sectors such as Brexit (for the UK), migration fears, health, trade, fiscal, monetary and regulatory policies. Another feature of interest is that they produce daily EPU indexes for both the US and the UK which allow investigation of the effects of high-frequency uncertainty shocks (for an application see Ferrara and Guérin 2016). Similarly, Alexopoulos and Cohen (2014) construct general economic uncertainty measures for the US based on a detailed textual analysis of some *New York Times* articles, and suggest using a broader set of keywords.

By applying a similar text-based approach, it is possible to develop indexes of monetary policy uncertainty (MPU). Husted et al. (2016) construct a daily news-based index of MPU to capture the uncertainty perceived by the public regarding the Federal Reserve's policy actions, based on counting words in ten large US newspapers. They search, in particular, for articles containing the combination (i) "uncertain" or "uncertainty", (ii) "monetary policy" or "interest rate" or "Federal Fund rates", and (iii) "Federal Reserve" or "Fed" or "Federal Open Market Committee" or "FOMC".

A global uncertainty measure was proposed by Caldara and Iacoviello (2016) who have constructed an index of global geopolitical risk resulting from a country's or region's political instability. This index is based on the frequency of words related to geopolitical tensions in leading international newspapers, and aims to capture events which perhaps are more exogenous to macroeconomic conditions. For example, they were able to identify events such as the Gulf War, the 2003 invasion of Iraq, the 9/11 terrorist attacks and more recently, the spikes during the Ukraine/Russia crisis, and around the Paris terrorist attacks. Similarly, Manela and Moreira (2017) suggest a

[2]Those indexes are downloadable at https://www.policyuncertainty.com.

news-based measure of US uncertainty, starting at the end of the 19th century, using front-page articles from the *Wall Street Journal*.

2.4 Macroeconomic Uncertainty Based on Forecasting

Beyond stock market volatility and economic policy, there is a growing literature aiming at measuring uncertainty based solely on macroeconomic information. The idea is to assume that uncertainty may be reflected in economic forecasting errors: the more uncertain the state of the economy the less accurate the forecasting.

In this context, Scotti (2016) develops a macroeconomic uncertainty index reflecting agents' uncertainty about the current state of the economy, defined as the weighted average of squared news surprises, for a set of macroeconomic variables and for a few advanced economies. Surprises are defined as differences between expected values from professional forecasters and realizations. The weights are estimated through a dynamic factor model applied to a set of macroeconomic variables. Those indexes are particularly interesting as they are available with daily frequency for the US, the UK, the euro area, Canada and Japan. Not surprisingly, the highest spikes in the indexes correspond to the latest financial crisis for both the US and euro area. Interestingly, the euro area uncertainty index reaches its highest values just before and just after the 2008–09 recession. While the uncertainty in the US appears subdued following this recession, it seems that the debt crisis kept uncertainty levels elevated in the case of the euro area.

In the same vein, Jurado et al. (2015) calculate an uncertainty index based on the unpredictable component in a large set of US macroeconomic and financial variables. This component is estimated by taking the difference between conditional forecasts stemming from a large dynamic factor model, and realizations (see Fig. 1). This index differs in its construction from Scotti's since it accounts for both macro and financial variables, and uses the conditional forecasts from an econometric model as the expected values. Since this index also integrates financial information, it is likely to have a stronger effect on economic activity when computing impulse response functions. This reflects the fact that uncertainty and financial shocks are often intertwined, and as Caldara et al. (2016) show, disentangling them is crucial in shock identification steps.

Rossi and Sekhposyan (2015) suggest measuring uncertainty as the distance between the realized value of a variable and its unconditional forecast error distribution, this latter being obtained either from a parametric model or from surveys. This differs from previous macro uncertainty measures in the sense that forecasts are unconditional, and are not conditioned by any information set.

Another approach to assessing macroeconomic uncertainty at any date in time is to adopt a model-based approach that relies on estimating econometric models with stochastic volatility, and to identify the estimated volatility to an uncertainty measure. Mumtaz and Theodoridis (2016) adopt this model and propose a dynamic factor model with stochastic volatility allowing for simultaneous estimation of a common global factor and country-specific factors for a set of 11 OECD countries. They show that global uncertainty goes a long way to explaining the variance of real and nominal variables. In similar vein, Carriero, Clark and Marcellino (2016) propose estimation of a large vector auto-regression (VAR) model on both macro and financial variables with errors following a stochastic volatility model. Estimated volatilities then are supposed to track macro and financial volatilities.

2.5 Macroeconomic Uncertainty Based on Surveys Among Forecasters

Macroeconomic uncertainty can be measured also by considering the disagreement among forecasters over selected macroeconomic variables in a specific opinion survey. The underlying idea is that the dispersion among forecasters should be high in periods of high uncertainty, and vice versa. This approach consists of evaluating the cross-sectional dispersion of forecasts obtained from a panel of economists, without necessarily investigating how the forecasts are formed. For example, Bachmann et al. (2013) proposed a measure of US uncertainty based on forecasting disagreements from the Philadelphia Federal Reserve Business Outlook Survey, and a measure of uncertainty in Germany based on disagreements among the IFO Business Climate Survey participants. Similarly, Bloom (2009) computes the standard deviation of US nominal GDP forecasts from the Philadelphia Federal Reserve survey.[3]

Lahiri and Sheng (2010) show that disagreement is only a fraction of uncertainty, and that the volatility of aggregate shocks must also be accounted for to obtain a complete picture of uncertainty. The idea is that uncertainty stemming from market participants can be decomposed into two factors: a common component reflecting the perceived variability of future aggregate shocks, and an idiosyncratic component reflecting the disagreement among professional forecasters. This kind of decomposition relies on the literature on capital asset pricing models which decomposes the volatility of a typical stock into market and firm-level volatility. This approach is used also by Ozturk and Sheng (2017) to propose various uncertainty indexes across three layers, namely (i) variable-specific uncertainty for a set of macroeconomic variables, (ii) country-specific uncertainty for a large panel of advanced and emerging countries, and (iii) a global uncertainty measure obtained from a weighted average of country-specific uncertainty indexes. For example, US-specific uncertainty estimated using this approach is presented in Fig. 1 (middle panel).

Within the dimension of monetary policy uncertainty, Istrefi and Mouabbi (2017) propose what they call a subjective measure of interest rate uncertainty, for several developed countries. This measure reflects market perceptions of interest rates as expressed by professional forecasters in the Consensus Economics survey, and

[3]Note that this approach can be implemented at a more micro-level by looking at managers' expectations about future demand growth (see Guiso and Parigi 1999, for an application using Italian data).

accounts for both disagreement among forecasters and the perceived variability of future aggregate shocks, in line with Lahiri and Sheng (2010). At the height of the global financial crisis, Istrefi and Mouabbi observed that while other macro and financial uncertainty measures used in the literature continued to rise, the uncertainty over interest rates fell. This reflects the reach of the zero lower bound (ZLB) on nominal interest rates and the forward guidance communication from several central banks to keep rates low for longer.

Ismailov and Rossi (2017) use the methodology in Rossi and Sekhposyan (2015) to construct an exchange rate uncertainty index based on fixed-horizon forecast errors from surveys conducted by Consensus Economics. This measure allows the author to establish a link between the deviations to the uncovered interest rate parity (UIRP) hypothesis and the level of uncertainty; ultimately it is shown that the UIRP condition holds when uncertainty is low.[4]

2.6 Discussion

Various measures of uncertainty have been proposed in the literature although they are not necessarily aimed at assessing the same concept. However, the various measures proposed for financial volatility are quite well correlated. Typically, the VIX and realized volatility show a strong correlation (between 0.8 and 0.9). In his seminal paper, Bloom (2009) shows that measures of financial volatility are strongly correlated to the disagreement among forecasters, and the firm profits and industry productivity growth distributions, leading researchers to use financial volatility, either implied or observed, quite widely as a proxy for uncertainty, in applied works.

However, the degree of correlation is lower in the case of other measures. Table 1 presents correlation coefficients of the five measures[5] depicted in Fig. 1. The start date is January 1990 but the ending date is dependent on the particular series (May 2017 for VIX and EPU, July 2014 for the survey measure in Ozrturk and Sheng 2017, June 2016 for the macro measure proposed by Jurado et al. 2015, and March 2015 for the micro measure in Gilchrist et al. 2014).

Overall, the VIX seems to be quite well correlated to other uncertainty measures but the EPU is poorly related to other measures. Over our sample going from January 1990 to May 2017, the correlation between VIX and EPU is 0.45, meaning that VIX and EPU often move together but also show distinct variations. By nature, VIX tends to react more strongly to financial events while the EPU is related more closely to policy events such as wars, elections or political battles over debt ceilings and

[4]See Husted et al. (2017) for an analysis of currency carry trade and uncertainty on foreign exchange markets.

[5]Charles et al. (2017) propose a comparative analysis of the effects of various measure of uncertainty in terms of impulse responses and variance decomposition. They also provide a synthetic indicator based on a dynamic factor model.

government fiscal policy. Also, by definition, the VIX tends to incorporate forward-looking information not embedded in the EPU.

Overall, the large number of uncertainty measures proposed in the burgeoning literature have a strong common component but do not capture exactly the same concept. In spite of a common behavior that can captured by estimating a factor model (see Haddow et al. 2013), idiosyncratic components of the uncertainty measures clearly play a role, and a distinction needs to be made between the concepts of financial uncertainty, macroeconomic uncertainty and economic policy uncertainty. In addition, due to the inherent unobservable nature of uncertainty, estimation methods may generate some differences in uncertainty measures for the same concept of uncertainty. In this respect, robustness checks for various measures appear necessary in empirical studies dealing with uncertainty.

Given this rich set of measures of uncertainty across time, countries and sectors, a key question is whether and how fluctuations in uncertainty impact the economy?

3 Understanding the Effects of Uncertainty Fluctuations

Following the Great Recession, the profession has paid much attention to the role of fluctuations in economic uncertainty as a source of business cycle fluctuations. Both theorists and empiricists have sought to better understand how such fluctuations can influence the economy, by offering numerous mechanisms through which an uncertainty shock—defined as an unexpected change in an uncertainty variable (see previous section)—is transmitted to the economy.

Although no consensus has been reached, the efforts made by economists to propose improved theories, and to examine new data has resulted in a growing body of knowledge on the macroeconomics of uncertainty. The purpose of this section is to provide readers with a comprehensive overview of how fluctuations in uncertainty affect the economy through three main mechanisms. First, we describe how fluctuations in uncertainty affect aggregate activity within the framework of irreversible investment. Second, we discuss the role of households' precautionary saving as a way to propagate uncertainty shocks. Third, we discuss the role of financial market frictions through which volatility fluctuations can influence aggregate activity. Throughout the discussion, we will continuously confront the theory with data via large macroeconomic models so as to assess the empirical relevance of transmission mechanisms.

3.1 Irreversible Investment

The first and best-known framework to study how fluctuations in uncertainty affect the economy is irreversible investment as discussed in the seminal contributions of Bernanke (1983) and Pindyck (1991). The basic idea is that, when investment projects are irreversible—that is, they cannot be "cancelled" or "modified" without very high costs—there exists a trade-off for investors between additional returns from the immediate launch of an investment project, and the benefits of waiting to gather more information in the future. The value of waiting is described in the literature as *real-option* value. At times, it can be preferable to postpone new investment projects, and at other times it might not. In such an environment, a rise in uncertainty clearly would tilt the balance in favor of *wait-and-see* behavior. Indeed, by pausing their investment and hiring, investors will obtain more information about the future which will increase the likelihood of their making a good decision, and thus, having a better understanding of long-run project returns. In the influential paper by Bloom (2009), the author highlights that "*increased uncertainty is depressing investment by fostering an increasingly widespread wait-and-see attitude about undertaking new investment expenditures*". Empirical results tend to show that the most irreversible investment categories, such as investment in infrastructure or equipment, react the most negatively to uncertainty shocks compared to for example, investment in intellectual property products (see Ferrara and Guérin 2016).

To provide evidence of this mechanism, Bloom (2009) introduces a firm-level model with time-varying second moments (uncertainty shocks) and non-convex (labor and capital) adjustments costs. The introduction of such costs in the model creates a threshold of inaction below which firms delay their investment projects. When uncertainty increases, the threshold becomes higher and firms freeze their economic activity as well as their hiring and investment activities. The simulated model reveals that, after a temporary positive shock to uncertainty, employment, output and productivity growth drop sharply, and the model implies that both hiring and investment rates decrease and reach their minimum four months after the shock. The *wait-and-see* behavior acts as a conduit to transmit fluctuations in uncertainty to the economy. Once the uncertainty is resolved, and the economic perspectives appear brighter, aggregate activity recovers quickly and then rebounds seven months after the shock (see Fig. 2). This pattern of overshooting—a short-lived period of above-normal growth—is explained by the massive come-back of the allocation of labor and capital to investment projects which previously was suspended. Recent empirical papers have highlighted the specific role of uncertainty during and after the Great Recession (see Fig. 3). For example, Bussière et al. (2015) assess the importance of uncertainty to explain the weakness in business investment observed since 2010 among a panel of OECD countries. While they conclude that the expected demand explains the main part of the investment slump, around 80%, they show also that uncertainty played a significant role, contributing around 17% (the rest being due to capital costs).

In spite of being a consensual channel of transmission, it should be noted that the role of wait-and-see behavior has been challenged by microeconomic data. For example, Bachmann and Bayer (2013) use a German firm-level data set to measure firms' profitability risk and cyclical fluctuations. In this context, they find that uncertainty shocks fed through the *wait-and-see* mechanism explain only a modest part of aggregate output variation. The authors rightly highlight that their findings

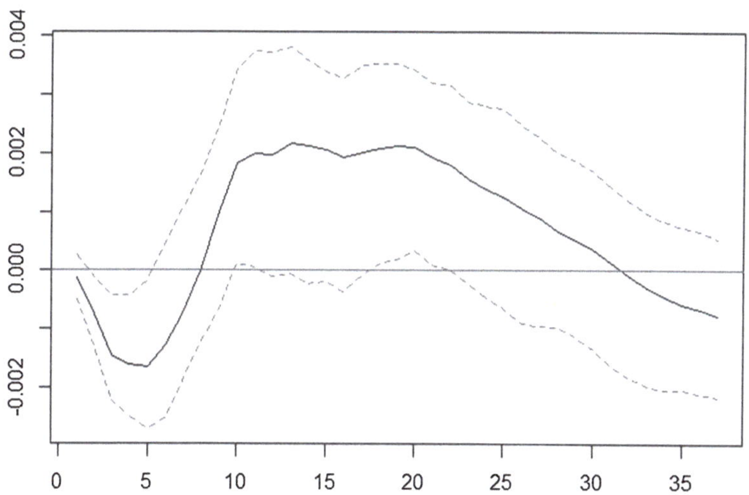

Fig. 2 Impulse response function of the monthly industrial production to an uncertainty shock (95% Bootstrap Confidence Interval). *Source* R-package provided by Nicholas Bloom to replicate the Bloom (2009)'s paper. https://people.stanford.edu/nbloom/sites/default/files/r.zip

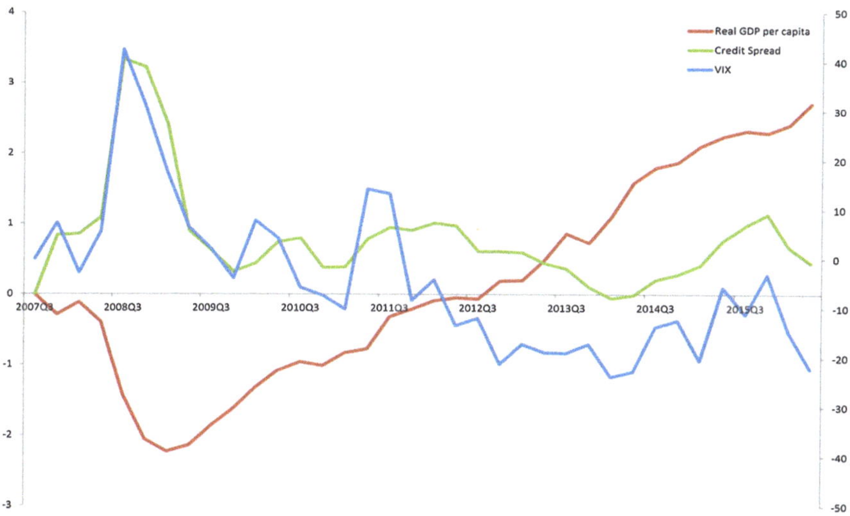

Fig. 3 Real GDP per capita, Credit spread, and the VIX during and after the great recession in the US economy. *Data source* https://macro.nomics.world/article/2016-06/cmr14-data/. Real GDP and VIX are in log deviation and Credit spread in deviation with respect to the 2007Q3 value

"*open up room for other (propagation) mechanisms that are currently discussed in the literature*", as we will see below.

3.2 Precautionary Saving

Precautionary saving is a well-known channel of influence of uncertainty on the economy, and is defined by Leland (1968) as "*the extra saving caused by future income being random rather than determinate*". Many economists have documented that heightened uncertainty during the Great Recession was accompanied by a surge in saving rates, suggesting that uncertainty can influence households' consumption decisions. For example, Mody et al. (2012) use a panel of OECD countries and establish a close and positive relationship between saving rates and labor income uncertainty between 2007 and 2009. The reason for this relationship is straightforward: When faced with a higher risk of bad outcomes, households seek to protect themselves by saving more. This *precautionary saving* results in a further reduction in consumption and an excess of desired saving. The authors show that more than two-fifths of the rise in the household saving rate between 2007 and 2009 is a response to a precautionary savings motive.

To support this intuition, Basu and Bundick (2017) use a simple VAR framework and show that a one-standard deviation unexpected change in uncertainty, measured by implied stock returns volatility, generates a large and persistent decline in output, consumption, investment and hours worked, with a trough for output of 0.2%. The ensuing co-movement among those macro variables is noteworthy since it means that the fall in consumption associated to precautionary saving is not necessarily compensated by a higher level of investment in the economy. In fact, most neoclassical models of precautionary saving fail to capture this and predict a negative co-movement between consumption and investment in response to uncertainty shocks. Heightened uncertainty induces precautionary saving, and thus, a decline in household consumption but an increased desire to supply labor (i.e., to increase the hours worked) for any given level of the real wage. This phenomenon is known as *precautionary labor supply.*[6] On the demand side, demand for labor remains unchanged because technology and capital stock are invariant to changes in uncertainty. As a consequence, hours worked, investment and output increase while consumption decreases. This unpleasant property proceeds from the assumption of price flexibility and can be overcome by considering nominal rigidities.

Basu and Bundick (2017) develop a New-Keynesian model with sticky prices, in which output is driven exclusively by demand in a short-run horizon. Basically, in a context of sticky prices, an increase in uncertainty[7] that causes a decline in consumption demand implies a drop in output and demand for labor and capital because prices cannot adjust quickly to changing conditions. To sum up, the difference between neoclassical models and New-Keynesian models for explaining the co-movement of aggregates lies in the demand for labor. Leduc and Liu (2016) pro-

[6] See Domeij and Floden (2006), Pijoan-Mas (2006) and Floden (2006) shows that households tend to adopt a "precautionary labor supply" attitude when facing idiosyncratic income risk.

[7] See Fernandez-Villaverde et al. (2015) for the effects of fiscal uncertainty via the aggregate demand channel.

pose a more detailed analysis of the labor market.[8] They examine the aggregate demand channel via labor search frictions. Again, under sticky prices, the authors show that the decline in aggregate demand reduces firms' incentives to post new job vacancies—i.e., a decrease in the value of a new match—causing a rise in unemployment. As fewer workers finds jobs, the incomes of households decrease further. The introduction of search frictions amplifies the effect of uncertainty shocks on aggregate activity via the aggregate demand channel and also via the irreversibility channel discussed in the previous section. Indeed, when uncertainty increases, *"the option value of waiting increases and the match value declines"* and firms reduce their hiring activity. Since the long-term employment contract between employer and employee is irreversible, firms prefer to wait for more information which is in line with the irreversible investment literature. Overall, the interactions of both the option-value channel and the demand channel, allow uncertainty shocks to represent 60 percent of unemployment variation, which is equivalent to what we see in the data. However, the data show that uncertainty fluctuations also impact on financial markets suggesting a specific channel associated to financial frictions.

3.3 *Financial Frictions*

Financial intermediaries play an important role in the propagation of fluctuations in uncertainty. When risk rises, they tend to protect themselves against default risk by charging a premium to cover the costs of a default. Arellano et al. (2016) and Christiano et al. (2014) were the first to use a general equilibrium framework to model the interaction between financial markets and fluctuations in uncertainty. The establishment of such a relationship via explicit theoretical models was motivated, not surprisingly, by the Great Recession of 2008–09.

To better understand why financial conditions are an important conduit for the transmission of uncertainty fluctuations to the economy, Christiano et al. (2014) augment the *financial accelerator mechanism* business cycle model developed initially by Bernanke et al. (1999) (hereafter BGG) to account for the presence of uncertainty shocks (described by the authors as "risk shocks").[9]

Entrepreneurs borrow externally to buy raw capital. Sometimes the allocation of this capital to the productive process is a success, sometimes it is not. In the model, the productivity level is decided independently by each entrepreneur. When the cross-sectional dispersion of productivities among entrepreneurs increases, the average

[8]Guglielminetti (2016) also shows the detrimental impact of uncertainty on the macroeconomy through frictional labor markets by using a DSGE model, and Caggiano et al. (2014) point out the non-linear impact of uncertainty on US unemployment.

[9]We focus our analysis on the BGG mechanism although there is a large class of business cycle models with financial frictions used in the literature to study the impact of uncertainty shocks but these financial frictions are not always modeled in the same way. For example, Arellano et al. (2016) differ greatly from Christiano et al. (2014) in the sense that uncertainty shocks imply large ranges of inaction by firms which decide to cut back investment projects to avoid default.

productivity of entrepreneurs remains unchanged but more extreme high and low productivity values are observed. As a consequence, financial intermediaries charge a higher premium to protect themselves since more entrepreneurs choose low levels of productivity and then are unable to repay their debts. This positive risk shock increases both the risk of default and the cost of external funds which leads to a fall in the economic activity of entrepreneurs, and in turn is transmitted to the overall economy in general equilibrium.

When the model is estimated, Christiano et al. (2014) conclude that fluctuations in risk constitute the most important shock driving the business cycle, much more than the real and nominal shocks usually considered in the literature. Brand and Tripier (2014) compare the predictions of this model for the US and the euro area, and conclude that risk shocks are a major source of business cycle fluctuations in both economies and explain a large part of their divergence in recent years.

This evidence based on the estimation of business cycles models is supported by empirical evidence from VAR models. In particular, Gilchrist et al. (2014) analyze this transmission channel in the US from 1963.Q3 to 2012.Q3 and provide strong evidence that credit spreads are a key conduit for the propagation of uncertainty shocks to the economy. To show this, they propose to identify their uncertainty shocks according to two distinct identification schemes à la Cholesky. In the first specification, there is no allowance for contemporaneous reaction to credit spread, other macroeconomic variables, changes to innovations under uncertainty (here measured as idiosyncratic at the aggregate level). Conversely, the second identification does not allow such an immediate reaction of credit spread to innovations in uncertainty but does still affect the rest of the economy with a lag. Given these two identifying restrictions, the authors show that, under both specifications, an uncertainty shock leads to a decline in investment, prices and output, with the drop in prices being small and persistent while the drops in investment and output being substantial and immediate. Although the patterns remain qualitatively similar across the two specifications, there are differences at the quantitative level. Indeed, the response of the macroeconomic variables is amplified dramatically under the second specification which allows an immediate response of credit spreads after the shock. Following an unanticipated increase in uncertainty, and in contrast to the first identification, credit spreads rise immediately and then return very slowly towards trend, suggesting that financial conditions are essential for the transmission mechanism of uncertainty shocks to the aggregate activity.

A very recent literature stream is focusing on the joint effects of uncertainty and other types of shocks that can affect the economy at the same time. For example, Caldara et al. (2016) use a penalty function approach to jointly identify uncertainty and financial shocks, and to assess the impact of those two types of shocks on the economy. They find that uncertainty shocks have a significant macroeconomic impact in situations where they elicit a tightening of financial conditions. Interestingly, they obtain also that the rise in the impact on uncertainty in response to a financial shock, suggests that the evolution of uncertainty is influenced by changes in financial conditions. From a policy perspective, those results suggest close monitoring of both uncertainty and financial stress measures since a common upward movement in both variables could lead to damaging effects on the economy. We refer also to Shim and Zhong (2016) for further empirical evidence on the links between financial and uncertainty in the context of a structural VAR framework. Choi et al. (2017) show how sectoral-level data can be used to identify the effects of uncertainty on productivity through a financial friction-based channel. Alessandri and Mumtaz (2014) and Lhuissier and Tripier (2016) have advanced this work by allowing time-variation in the way that the macroeconomic variables respond to uncertainty shocks over time. The severity and the duration of their impact on the economy depend crucially on the degree of financial frictions.

3.4 Discussion

Economic theory has for long provided theoretical channels to explain the economic effects of uncertainty as due to the presence of irreversible investment, precautionary saving and financial frictions. Combined with the rich empirical literature on uncertainty measurement, recent quantitative macroeconomic researchers have been able to quantity the respective relevance and importance of these mechanisms. Below, we discuss three recent areas of further research on the complex relationships between uncertainty and the economy.

First, so far, we have considered the mechanisms through which exogenous fluctuations in uncertainty influence the economy. However, not all fluctuations in uncertainty are exogenous, and it is particularly important to understand in more depth the mechanisms through which uncertainty reacts endogenously to changes in the economic environment. Working in environments where learning comes from market outcomes, several authors show that feedback mechanisms can occur when the economy is experiencing slowdown leading to heightened macroeconomic uncertainty. van Nieuwerburgh and Veldkamp (2006) develop a business cycle model with incomplete information about the economy's fundamental (i.e., the level of technology). They assume that the flow of information about the aggregate technology is time-varying and depends positively on the state of the economy. They show that recessions tend to generate less precise technological levels, leading in turn to more uncertainty and so further decline in investment projects and new hiring. Fajgelbaum et al. (2016) propose a similar learning framework in a model of irreversible investment with heterogeneous firms. The return from irreversible investment is a function of an imperfectly observed fundamental that follows an autoregressive process. Firms observe this return and update their beliefs appropriately. When the variance (i.e. uncertainty) of their beliefs about the fundamental is relatively lower, firms are more inclined to invest and produce. Furthermore, as the precision of these beliefs is procyclical and depends positively on the investment rate, a regime with low economic activity yields noisy estimates about fundamentals, leading in turn to a rise in uncertainty. During recessions, feedback mechanisms can result also from difficulties related to forecasting, as in the paper by Orlik and Veldkamp (2014). Indeed, recessions are rare events which are foreign to agents. As a consequence, it is more difficult to make accurate forecasts which induces large revisions in forecasting. Thus, poor accuracy in the probability of forthcoming extreme bad events—referred to by the authors to as the *black swan risk*—generates large fluctuations in uncertainty.

Second, so far, we have documented only how heightened fluctuations in uncertainty are able to generate macroeconomic contractionary effects. However, there is a channel through which uncertainty can stimulate investment, and which thus contrast with the channels described above and is referred to a *growth options* to use Bloom's (2014) terminology.[10] Bloom (2014), "*the growth options argument is based on the insight that uncertainty can encourage investment if it increases the size of the potential prize*". Typically, the *growth options* mechanism occurs when the decision process is very long. Bar-Ilan and Strange (1996) note that most investments take time, a phenomenon referred to as "investment lag". For example, Wheaton (1987) notes that "*the lag between issuing a construction permit and the completion of an office building is between 18 and 24 months*". Such lags tend to mitigate the negative effects of uncertainty on investment, and under some circumstances, even to stimulate investment. They act as negative real option phenomena since the investor can interrupt its decision and lose only the initial costs in the case of bad news, and keep its competitive advantage in the market in the case of good news. Krugman (2016) recalls this literature to explain why he was not convinced that the election of Donald Trump to US President would cause a recession because of the rising uncertainty. Future research should try to identify historical episodes (if they exist) when uncertainty stimulated economic activity.

Third, assessing and disentangling the joint effects of and the interplay among uncertainty shocks and various types of other shocks is a topic for future research (see Caldara et al. 2016, regarding the link between financial and uncertainty shocks). For example, Cascaldi-Garcia and Galvao (2016) try to evaluate the joint effect of technology news shocks à la Beaudry and Portier (2006), and uncertainty shocks, starting from empirical evidence that both are correlated. Indeed, when a news shock hits the economy, it is accompanied by increasing uncertainty about the interpretation of this news, though the effects are likely to differ overtime (news shocks are known to increase total factor productivity mainly over the medium-term). The authors find that the negative effects of uncertainty in the medium-term are attenuated by positive news shocks, in both amplitude and duration. Similarly, this attenuation bias means that news shocks have lower positive effects in the short-run than if news shocks were assumed to be orthogonal to uncertainty shocks.

4 Policy Implications: Three Lessons from the Literature

A better understanding of whether and how fluctuations in uncertainty affect the real economy is essential not only for academic economists but also for policymakers.

[10]Bloom (2014) also discusses the "Oi-Hartman-Abel" case in which firms are risk loving because of specific irreversibly.

Indeed, as explained in the previous sections, the recent literature tends to suggest that a disturbance originating from uncertainty is an important driver of economic fluctuations. In this respect, policy measures aimed at eliminating or mitigating periods of long-lasting volatility fluctuations and setting up defenses against the threat of future uncertainty fluctuations are thus appropriate. The traditional conception of stabilization policies needs to be extended to account for fluctuations in uncertainty. The corollary to this is that uncertainty needs to be monitored in real-time using the various available measures. Based on our own reading of the literature and our experience in this topic, to conclude the paper we suggest three policy implications.

#1 lesson: Macroeconomic policies have a direct role to play in stabilizing policy-related uncertainty

Stabilization policies traditionally are defined as monetary and fiscal policies implemented in response to supply or demand shocks to reduce the gap between the current level of economic activity, or inflation, and its long-term (or natural) level. Alongside the traditional supply and demand shocks, uncertainty fluctuations need also to be considered by the public authorities which may be directly responsible for them. Indeed, large fluctuations in the policy-based uncertainty measures can be interpreted as inefficient public management. Public authorities can be at the origins of policy uncertainty, e.g. through too frequent changes to fiscal policy as suggested by Fernández-Villaverde et al. (2015), or by amplifying uncertainty through lack of efficient national and international coordination in highly uncertain periods, e.g. the coincidence in 2013 of the US fiscal cliff issue and the European crisis. Thus, when implementing policies, public authorities should take into account their effects on the degree of uncertainty. This issue has been discussed intensively in the context of monetary policy; we can refer to the recent debates on the stance of monetary policy in all the advanced economies. However, it also concerns fiscal policy as suggested by Auerbach (2014) who focuses on long-term projections of the US federal budget, and by Alesina et al. (2015) who show that the output costs of fiscal consolidation plans are magnified when they consist of stop-and-go changes to taxes and spending.

#2 lesson: Financial uncertainty should be restrained trough financial regulations

However, policy-related uncertainty is only one among several sources of uncertainty fluctuations. The bulk of the evidence provided in the previous sections highlights the key role of financial markets as both the source of uncertainty and as mechanism amplifying uncertainty.[11] This suggests a new role for financial regulation: reducing the instability of financial markets which feed uncertainty in the economy as a whole. New institutions were implemented after the Great Recession to avoid a repetition of that financial turbulence. For example, in Europe, the European Systemic Risk Board's mission is precisely to monitor and assess financial risks. The potential interest of regulation deals also with cross-border capital flows

[11] Candelon et al. (2017) show that equity market spillovers are much stronger during periods of high uncertainty.

through which uncertainty can be transmitted and amplified among economies. The institutional view expressed by the IMF (2012) supports, in certain circumstances, a role for capital flows management, in accordance with adequate maroeconomic policies, to protect economies from the macroeconomic and financial stability risks associated to disruptive surges in inflows or outflows.[12]

#3 lesson: The effectiveness of economic stabilization policies depends on the state of uncertainty and should then be adapted accordingly

Beside the role of public authorities in stabilizing political, economic and financial uncertainty, the channel of transmission of macroeconomic policies is likely to be impaired by uncertainty. Under conditions of high uncertainty, the effectiveness of fiscal and monetary policies is damaged, and thus economic actors (households, firms, and investors) become less inclined to respond to policy impulses. Aastveit et al. (2013) provide strong empirical evidence to support this intuition. Estimating VAR models for the US, Canada, the UK and Norway, the authors show that, in periods of low uncertainty, an expansionary monetary policy that causes an unexpected decline in nominal interest rates would raise investment, consumption and GDP by more than twice as much as in a period of high uncertainty. Caggiano et al. (2017) show that the contractionary effects of uncertainty shocks are significantly larger when the Zero Lower Bound is binding, thereby justifying the use of unconventional monetary policy tools such as forward guidance, or large scale asset purchase programs since the onset of the Great Recession. Bloom et al. (2012) investigate the efficiency of policies in a "really uncertain business cycle" model with heterogeneous firms and factor adjustment costs. They show that the stimulating effect of a wage subsidy policy on output declines by over two-thirds when the level of uncertainty in the economy is high. As a result, policymakers should take into account the degree of uncertainty surrounding the economy.

References

Aastveit KA, Natvik GJ, Sola S (2013) Economic Uncertainty and the effectiveness of monetary policy. Norges bank working paper no 17/2013

Alesina A, Favero C, Giavazzi F (2015) The output effect of fiscal consolidation plans. J Int Econ 96:S19–S42

Alessandri P, Mumtaz H (2014) Financial Regimes and uncertainty shocks. Queen Mary, University of London, school of economics and finance, working papers no 729

Alexopoulos M, Cohen J (2014) The power of print: uncertainty shocks, markets, and the economy. Mimeo

Arellano C, Bai Y, Kehoe PJ (2016) Financial markets and fluctuations in volatility. Federal reserve bank of minneapolis, staff report no 466

[12]The importance of these risks for emerging economies was proposed by Rey (2013) in her Jackson Hole Conference and confirmed by much evidence in the literature, see among others Bruno and Shin (2015), Chinn et al. (2017) and Converse (2017).

Auerbach A (2014) Fiscal uncertainty and how to deal with it. Hutchins center on fiscal and monetary policies, working paper no 6
Bachmann R, Bayer C (2013) Wait-and-see business cycles. J Monet Econ 60:704–719
Bachmann R, Elstner S, Sims ER (2013) Uncertainty and economic activity: evidence from business survey data. Am Econ J Macroecon 5(2):217–249
Baker S, Bloom N, Davis S (2016) Measuring economic policy uncertainty. Q J Econ 131(4):1593–1636
Bar-Ilan A, Strange C (1996) Investment Lags? Am Econ Rev 86(3):610–622
Basu S, Bundick B (2017) Uncertainty shocks in a model of effective demand. Econometrica, forthcoming
Beaudry P, Portier F (2006) Stock prices, news and economic fluctuations. Am Econ Rev 96(4):1293–1307
Bekaert G, Hoerova M, lo Duca M (2013) Risk, uncertainty and monetary policy. J Monet Econ 60:771–788
Bernanke BS (1983) Irreversibility, uncertainty, and cyclical investment. Quart J Econ 98:85–106
Bernanke BS, Gertler M, Gilchrist S (1999) The financial accelerator in a quantitative business cycle framework. In: Taylor JB, Woodford M (eds) The handbook of macroeconomics. Elsevier Science BV, Amsterdam, pp 1341–1393
Bloom N (2009) The impact of uncertainty shocks. Econometrica 77(3):623–685
Bloom N (2014) Fluctuations in uncertainty. J Econ Perspect 28(2):153–176
Bloom N, Floetotto M, Jaimovich N, Saporta-Eksten I, Terry S (2012, July). Really uncertain business cycles. National bureau of economic research, working paper no 18245
Bloom N, Bond S, van Reenen J (2007) Uncertainty and Investment Dynamics. Review of Economic Studies, vol 74(2). Oxford University Press, pp 391–415
Brand T, Tripier F (2014) Risk shocks and divergence between the Euro area and the US. Centre d'Etudes prospectives et d'Information Internationales research center, working papers no 2014–11
Bruno V, Shin HS (2015) Capital flows and the risk-taking channel of monetary policy. J Monet Econ 71:119–132
Bussière M, Ferrara L, Milovich J (2015) Explaining the recent slump in investment: the role of expected demand and uncertainty. Banque de France, working papers no 571
Caggiano G, Castelnuovo E, Groshenny N (2014) Uncertainty shocks and unemployment dynamics in US recessions. J Monet Econ 67:78–92
Caggiano G, Castelnuovo E, Pellegrino G (2017) Estimating the real effects of uncertainty shocks at the zero lower bound. Bank of Finland research discussion paper no 6
Caldara D, Iacoviello M (2016) Measuring geopolitical risk. Board of governors of the federal reserve, working paper
Caldara D, Fuentes-Albero C, Gilchrist S, Zakrajsek E (2016) The macroeconomic impact of financial and uncertainty shocks. Eur Econ Rev 88:185–207
Candelon B, Ferrara L, Joëts M (2017) Global financial spillovers: a non-linear assessment of the uncertainty channel. Banque de France, working papers, forthcoming
Carriero A, Clark T, Marcellino M (2016) Measuring uncertainty and its impact on the economy. Federal reserve bank of Cleveland, working paper no 16–22
Cascaldi-Garcia D, Galvao AB (2016) News and uncertainty shocks. Economic modelling and forecasting research, working paper no 12
Charles A, Darné O, Tripier F (2017) Uncertainty and the Macroeconomy: evidence from an uncertainty composite indicator. Appl Econ forthcoming
Chinn M, Ferrara L, Giacomini R (2017) Impact of uncertainty shocks on the global economy. J Int Money Financ. forthcoming
Choi S, Furceri D, Huang Y, Loungani MP (2017) Aggregate uncertainty and sectoral productivity growth: the role of credit constraints. J Int Money Financ. forthcoming
Christiano LJ, Motto R, Rostagno M (2014) Risk Shocks. Am Econ Rev 104:27–65

Converse N (2017) Uncertainty, capital flows, and maturity mismatch. Author's Manuscript, J Int Money Financ. forthcoming
Domeij D, Floden M (2006) The labor-supply elasticity and borrowing constraints: why estimated are biased. Rev Econ Dyn 9:242–262
Fajgelbaum P, Schaal E, Taschereau-Dumouchel M (2016) Uncertainty traps. National bureau of economic research, working paper no 19973
Fernández-Villaverde J, Guerrón-Quintana P, Kuester K, Rubio-Ramírez J (2015) Fiscal volatility shocks and economic activity. Am Econ Rev 105(11):3352–3384
Ferrara L, Guérin P (2016) What are the macroeconomic effects of high-frequency uncertainty shocks?. Bank of Canada, staff working paper no 16–25
Ferrara L, Marsilli C, Ortega JP (2014) Forecasting growth during the great recession: is financial volatility the missing ingredient? Econ Model 36:44–50
Floden M (2006) Labour supply and saving under uncertainty. Econ J 116:721–737
Gilchrist S, Sim JW, Zakrajsek E (2014) Uncertainty, financial frictions, and investment dynamics. National bureau of economic research, working paper no 20038
Guglielminetti E (2016) The labor market channel of macroeconomic uncertainty. Bank of Italy, working paper no 1068
Guiso L, Parigi G (1999) Investment and demand uncertainty. Q J Econ 114:185–227
Haddow A, Hare J, Hooley J, Shakir T (2013) Macroeconomic uncertainty: what is it, how can we measure it and why does it matter? Bank Engl Q Bull 2013(Q2):100–109
Husted L, Rogers J, Sun B (2016) Measuring monetary policy uncertainty: the federal reserve, Jan 1985–2016. International finance discussion paper notes
Husted L, Rogers J, Sun B (2017) Uncertainty, currency excess returns, and risk reversals. J Int Money Financ. forthcoming
International Monetary Fund (2012) The liberalization and management of capital flows—an institutional view. IMF policy papers, 14 Nov 2012
International Monetary Fund (2016) Time for a supply-side boost? Macroeconomic effects of labor and product market reforms in advanced economies. In: World economic outlook, chapter 3, Apr 2016
Ismailov A, Rossi B (2017) Uncertainty and deviations from uncovered interest rate parity. J Int Money Financ. forthcoming
Istrefi K, Mouabbi S (2017) Subjective interest rate uncertainty and the macroeconomy: A cross-country analysis. J Int Money Financ. forthcoming
Jurado K, Ludvigson SC, Ng S (2015) Measuring uncertainty. Am Econ Rev 105(3):1177–1216
Julio B, Yook Y (2012) Political uncertainty and corporate investment cycles. J Financ 67:45–83
Knight F (1921) Risk, uncertainty and profit. Boston, MA, Hart, Schaffner & Marx, Houghton Mifflin Co
Krugman P (2016) Still confused about brexit macroeconomics. The New York times. https://krugman.blogs.nytimes.com/2016/07/12/still-confused-about-brexit-macroeconomics/
Lahiri K, Sheng X (2010) Measuring forecast uncertainty by disagreement: the missing link. J Appl Econom 25:514–538
Leduc S, Liu Z (2016) Uncertainty shocks and aggregate demand shocks. J Monet Econ 82(C):20–35
Leland H (1968) Saving and uncertainty: the precautionary demand for savings. Q J Econ 82(3)
Lhuissier S, Tripier F (2016, Juin) Do uncertainty shocks always matter for business cycles? Centre d'Etudes Prospectives et d'Informations Internationales research center
Manela A, Moreira A (2017) News implied volatility and disaster concerns. J Financ Econ 123:137–162
Mody A, Ohnsorge F, Sandri D (2012) Precautionary savings in the great recession. International monetary fund working paper 12/42, forthcoming in the IMF economic review
Mumtaz H, Theodoridis K (2016) Common and country-specific economic uncertainty. forthcoming
Orlik A, Veldkamp LL (2014) Understanding uncertainty shocks and the role of black swans. National bureau of economic research, working paper No 20445

Ozturk E, Sheng X (2017) Measuring global and country-specific uncertainty. J Int Money Financ. forthcoming
Pindyck RS (1991) Irreversibility, uncertainty, and investment. J Econ Lit 29(3):1110–1148
Pijoan-Mas J (2006) Precautionary savings or working longer hours? Rev Econ Dyn 9:326–352
Rey H (2013) Dilemma not trilemma: the global cycle and monetary policy independence. In: Proceedings—economic policy symposium-Jackson hole. Federal Reserve Bank of Kansas City, pp 1–2
Rossi B, Sekhposyan T (2015) Macroeconomic uncertainty indices based on now-cast and forecast error distributions. Am Econ Rev 105(5):650–655
Scotti C (2016) Surprise and uncertainty indexes: real-time aggregation of real-activity macro surprises. J Monet Econ 82:1–19
Senyuz Z, Yoldas E, Chauvet M (2015) What does financial volatility tell us about macroeconomic fluctuations? J Econ Dyn Control 52:340–360
Shin M, Zhong M (2016) A New Approach to Identifying the real effects of uncertainty shocks. Finance and economics discussion series 2016–040. Board of Governors of the Federal Reserve System, Washington. http://dx.doi.org/10.17016/FEDS.2016.040
van Nieuwerburgh S, Veldkamp LL (2006) Learning asymmetries in real business cycles. J Monet Econ 53:753–772
Wheaton W (1987) The cyclic behaviour of the national office market. AREUEA J 15(4):281–299
Yellen J (2017, September 26) Inflation, uncertainty and monetary policy. In: Speech at the 59th annual meeting of the national association for business economics

Determinants and Implications of Low Global Inflation Rates

Juan Carlos Berganza, Fructuoso Borrallo and Pedro del Río

Abstract In this chapter we look at global inflation trends over the last decade and try to disentangle factors that could explain the ultra-low levels of inflation during the recovery from the Great Recession. We review the literature on the subject, which points at possible structural shifts in price and wage setting processes in recent decades, such as changes in inflation's cyclical sensitivity to economic slack, in the role being played by forward-looking and backward-looking inflation expectations, or in the relevance of global factors. We then test empirically whether changes in the coefficients of the Phillips curve in the wake of the global financial crisis can explain the behaviour of inflation over this period for a large group of advanced economies. Our results show a wide range of variation between countries, and in some cases the findings are insufficiently robust to offer a satisfactory explanation of the recent course of inflation. Nevertheless, the persistence of inflation and the increased importance of backward-looking inflation expectations in some countries may pose risks for inflation-expectation anchoring and central bank credibility. Finally, we review the adverse effects on the real economy of ultra-low inflation over an extended period and analyse the policy options for addressing this problem.

This chapter is an updated version of the paper that was published under the same title in the Banco de España Occasional Working Paper Series.The authors would like to thank Marina Conesa, Roberto Pascual and Patricia Sánchez for their excellent research assistance. All the views are those of the authors and do not necessarily reflect the views of the Banco de España.

J. C. Berganza (✉) · F. Borrallo · P. del Río
Banco de España, Madrid, Spain
e-mail: jcberganza@bde.es

F. Borrallo
e-mail: fructuoso.borrallo@outlook.com

P. del Río
e-mail: pedrodelrio@bde.es

L. Ferrara et al. (eds.), *International Macroeconomics in the Wake of the Global Financial Crisis*, Financial and Monetary Policy Studies 46,
https://doi.org/10.1007/978-3-319-79075-6_10

1 Introduction

Over the past 5 years the world has witnessed an almost universal trend towards lower inflation rates, with rates often falling short of central bank targets. The decline steepened in mid-2014 with the oil-price slump, when inflation rates in the main advanced economies fell to extremely low—and in some cases negative—levels. This downward trend in inflation, apparently at odds with the context of economic recovery and highly expansionary monetary policies, followed a period in the immediate wake of the global financial crisis in which inflation proved surprisingly downwardly rigid and fell by less than expected, given the depth of the recession (the so-called "missing disinflation" puzzle). These developments have led to a search for the reasons why consumer prices should be behaving in this way.

One possible explanation is that the course of inflation has been closely linked to transitory factors, such as commodity prices, which have made a strongly negative contribution over the past 2 years. However, the drop in inflation is also apparent in core rates, where these more volatile factors ought to have less of an effect. Other alternative explanations have therefore been put forward that point to changes in the price formation process over the last few decades that are more structural in nature. Indeed, the economic literature has suggested the possibility that, at least in many advanced economies, the cyclical sensitivity of inflation (i.e. its response to the degree of economic slack in the economy) fell in the period up to the early 1990s, while the relative importance of the anchoring of economic agents' inflation expectations to central bank targets rose, thanks to the greater credibility they had achieved. At the same time, global factors became more important, as a result of the integration of world product and factor markets, lower production costs and increased international competition (all of which is reflected in inflation's heightened sensitivity to the degree of slack in the global economy).

Whatever the reason for unusually low levels of inflation, they can have harmful consequences for economies. For instance, low inflation rates tend to lead to higher real interest rates, and, therefore, tighter monetary conditions. Moreover, low inflation has a negative impact on public and private debt dynamics, making deleveraging harder in the most indebted countries, and making it more difficult for countries in a monetary union to restore competitiveness, thus forcing them to undergo internal devaluation. In the extreme case, there can be a de-anchoring of agents' inflation expectations, with the consequent risk of a deflationary spiral. Sub-target inflation can also have a negative impact on central banks' credibility.

This chapter starts with an overview of how inflation has progressed worldwide in recent years, distinguishing its behaviour in different geographical areas. It then examines the possible factors explaining this price behaviour, through a comprehensive review of the extensive literature on the topic and an empirical analysis examining various countries and periods.[1] The possible economic consequences of

[1] For a more comprehensive list of references see Berganza et al. (2016), "Determinants and implications of low global inflation rates", Banco de España Occasional Working Paper Series No. 1608.

ultra-low inflation rates are then discussed, along with the associated economic policy implications. The chapter ends with some concluding remarks.

2 Global Inflation Trends

Global inflation has fluctuated widely over the past ten years.[2] After climbing above 5% prior to the global financial crisis, as a consequence, in part, of strong commodity (mainly energy) prices, it declined sharply after the crisis to levels close to 0%. It began to gradually recover in mid-2009, and had reached 4% by mid-2011. Since then, global inflation was again on a downward trend, dropping to approximately 1% at the end of 2015 before slowly increasing to 2.5% in the first quarter of 2017 on the back of oil-price related base effects. However, global inflation dynamics seem to have lost momentum again and currently stands around 2%. Global core inflation—which excludes energy and unprocessed food prices, the most erratic components directly influenced by factors such as the weather—decreased from 3.4 to 1.2% during the crisis and, after a partial rebound, has again moderated in recent years, declining from 2.7% in mid-2011 to a minimum of 1.3% in the second half of 2015 and now stands slightly above 2% (Fig. 1).

Over the last 5 years, headline inflation in advanced economies (which had recorded negative rates during the crisis) dropped from a median rate of 3% to around 0% in the third quarter of 2015. It then increased gradually to 2% in the first quarter of 2017 before returning to around 1.5% in the last months, while in emerging market economies, it declined from 4.7 to 2.5% in mid-2015, value around which it has oscillated in the last quarters. Core inflation rates also fell in advanced economies in the wake of the crisis, dropping from 2 to 0.6%, although this drop was less than would have been expected given the depth of the recession. Subsequently core inflation rose to 1.9% at the end of 2011, and then declined again, hovering around 1% before gradually picking up, to reach 1.6% in June 2016 and moving sideways since then. In emerging market economies core inflation has also come down from 3.4% in mid-2011 to 1.7% before increasing again above 2% in the last months. Prices of industrial goods have been linked through the prices of imported goods, while services inflation has tended to remain higher.

Looking at the different countries in the most recent period, inflation rates had been on a downward trend in the main advanced economies until mid- 2016 (Fig. 2). Then the rebound in energy prices led to a gradual increase in inflation rates in the second half of that year, but during 2017 inflation rates have tended to recede again in line with the stabilisation of oil prices. Headline inflation in the United States increased from below 1% in mid-2016 to close to 3% in early 2017 but declined again to 1.6% by June 2017. In the euro area, inflation showed a similar pattern although at lower rates and after reaching the 2% target in February 2017 has declined again to 1.3%

[2]The global inflation rate has been constructed from a sample of 27 countries, representing 80% of global GDP.

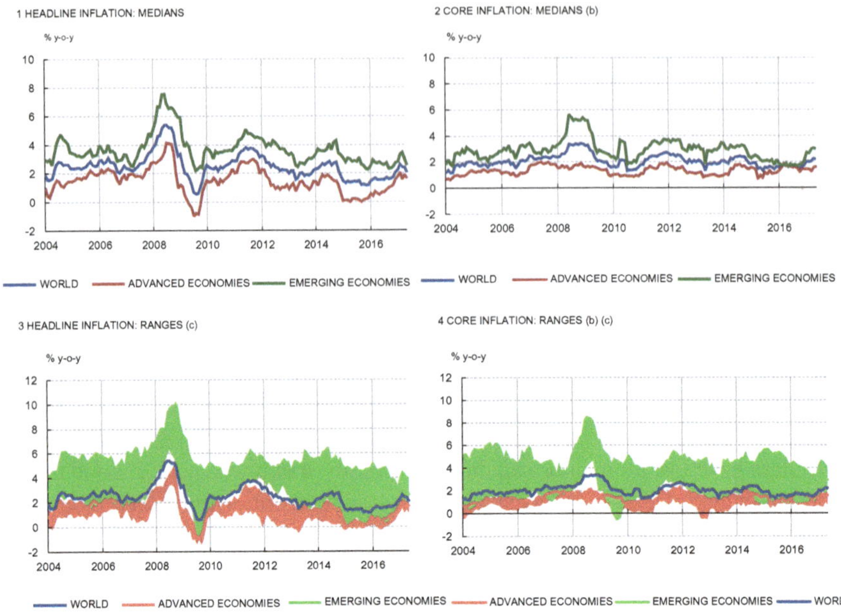

Fig. 1 Headline and core world inflation (**a**). *Sources* National Statistics, OECD and own calculations. **a** Includes: Canada, Euro area, Japan, Norway, Sweden, Switzerland, United Kingdom, and United States (advanced economies); and Brazil, Chile, China, Czech Republic, Hong Kong SAR, Hungary, India, Indonesia, Korea, Malaysia, Mexico, Peru, Philippines, Poland, Russia, Singapur, South Africa, Thailand, and Turkey (emerging economies). **b** Core inflation excludes food and energy. **c** First and third quartile

in June. In the United Kingdom the increase in inflation has continued unabated as a consequence of the depreciation of the pound, with inflation close to 3% in mid-2017. In the case of Japan, price trends have been driven by changes in economic policy in recent years (including the Bank of Japan's new inflation target and quantitative easing, and a consumption-tax increase),[3] such that the inflation rate rose from close to 0 to 2.5% in mid-2014, although it has subsequently dropped back to around 0% since mid-2015, even reaching negative values in mid-2016. The trend in core inflation has been fairly similar, at somewhat higher levels but falling short of central bank targets; only in the United Kingdom has climbed above 2.5%, as a result of the exchange rate depreciation, while in United States it has been above the 2% target since late-2015 before returning to lower rates more recently. In the euro area, core inflation has remained around 1%, and in Japan it has declined again below 0%.

[3]Changes in indirect taxes and administered prices have also made a big contribution to changes in inflation in other regions, with an impact on their apparently limited response to cyclical changes in the economy. In a number of euro area countries, for example, fiscal systems were reformed before the crisis to give indirect taxes a more central role, and if the impact of these tax increases is removed then inflation is seen to respond more strongly to the economic slowdown.

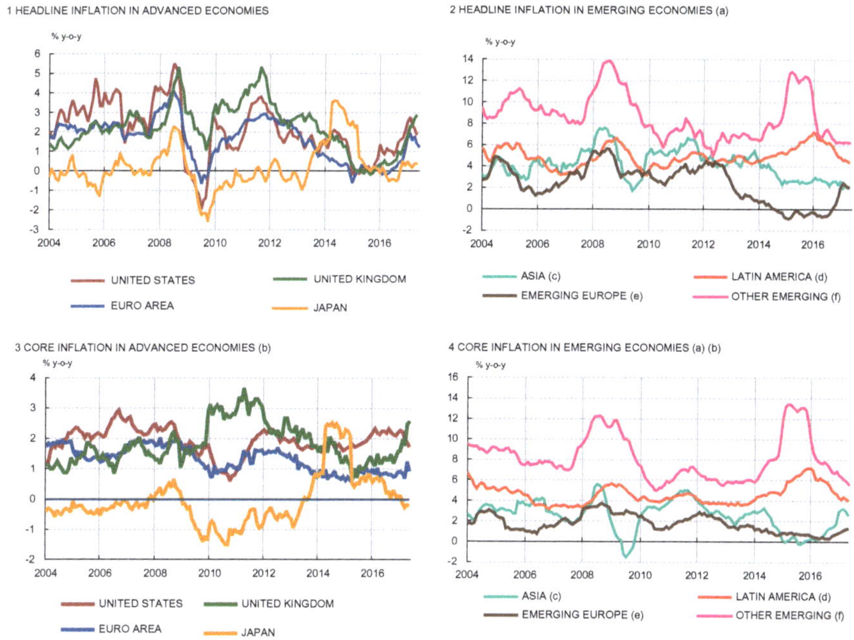

Fig. 2 Headline and core inflation by area. *Sources* Datastream, national statistics, OECD and own calculations. **a** Weigthed average of each country in 2005 by GDP in PPP. **b** Core inflation excludes food and energy. **c** China, Hong Kong SAR, India, Indonesia, Korea, Malaysia, Philippines, Singapore and Thailand. **d** Brazil, Chile, Colombia, Mexico and Peru. **e** Czech Republic, Hungary and Poland. **f** South Africa, Turkey and Russia

In some smaller advanced economies, such as Denmark, Sweden and Switzerland, inflation rates also moved into negative territory. These are small, open European economies, which have received large capital inflows as a result of spillovers from euro area problems and the ECB's low interest rates. In Denmark and Switzerland this has been exacerbated by their exchange rates' links to the euro. These countries have had to resort to negative policy rates and currency market interventions to stem the upward pressure on their currencies. Other advanced economies, such as Australia, Canada and New Zealand, have also experienced low inflation rates that have fallen short of their central banks' inflation targets. In the case of these commodity exporting countries, lower commodity prices affected negatively their income levels.

The trends in headline inflation rates in emerging economies have been more varied. Thus, while in some cases rates have been very low (particularly in the new EU Member States in Eastern Europe, and some emerging Asian economies, such as China and Korea), in some of the main emerging economies, such as Brazil, India, Indonesia, Russia and Turkey, inflation rates remained high, fuelled by currency depreciation. The same trends were apparent in core inflation, with very low levels in Asia and emerging European economies, and higher rates in Latin America and

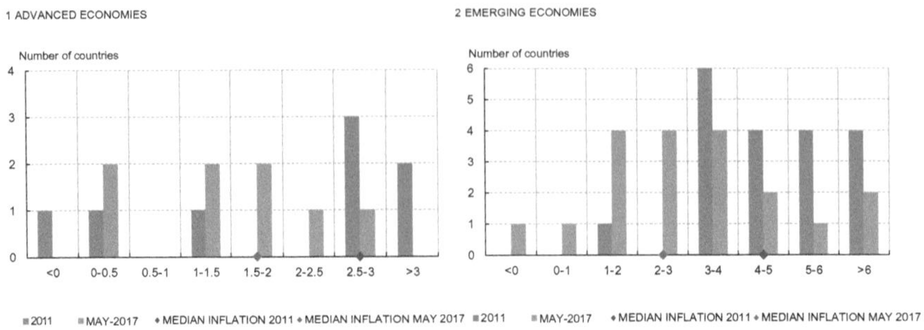

Fig. 3 Distribution of inflation rates (**a**). *Sources* Datastream, national statistics, OECD, own calculation. **a** Sample of 27 countries: Canada, the Euro area, Japan, Norway, Sweden, Switzerland, United Kingdom and United States (advanced) and Brazil, Chile, China, Czech Republic, Hong Kong SAR, Hungary, India, Indonesia, Korea, Malaysia, Mexico, Peru, Russia, the Philippines, Poland, Singapore, South Africa, Thailand and Turkey (emerging). Data is the average of the period

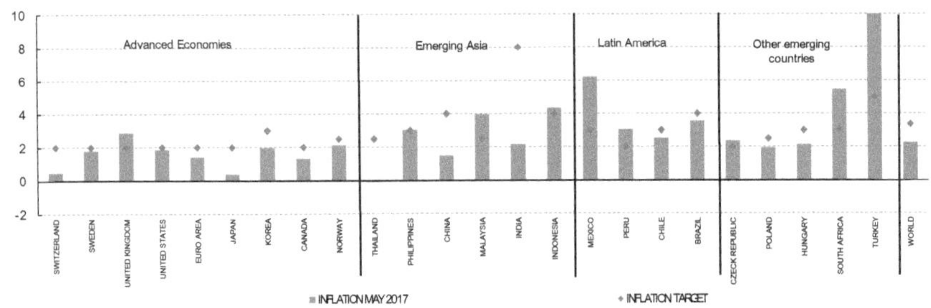

Fig. 4 Deviations from inflation targets (**a**). Sources: Datastream, national statistics, OECD, own calculation. **a** The bars show the annual inflation rate for May 2017 and the dots the price stability target of each Central Bank in the medium run (except for Turkey, which shows the target for the end of the year)

other emerging economies such as Russia and Turkey. In the last months, there has been a successful convergence on target ranges on the inflation front in some emerging countries once the past effects of depreciation have been absorbed (with the exception of some countries, most notably Mexico). Since 2011 the distribution of inflation rates worldwide has shifted downwards markedly (Fig. 3). And in many countries inflation rates are below the targets set by their central banks (Fig. 4). Similarly, there have been systematic downside errors in analysts' and central banks' inflation forecasts.

3 Determinants of Low Global Inflation

The standard framework for modelling inflation is the Phillips curve, according to which inflation is basically determined by economic agents' inflation expectations, which may comprise both backward- and forward-looking components. It is also affected by the degree of cyclical slack in the economy, so that a negative output gap (i.e. GDP below its potential level) or cyclical unemployment (defined as the extent to which the unemployment rate differs from its structural rate) will be associated with a lower inflation rate. Within this framework, low inflation could basically be explained by greater slack in the economy and/or by agents' lower inflation expectations.[4]

However, the Phillips-curve-based analysis has its limitations and remains controversial among economists. To start with, the degree of slack in the economy cannot be directly observed. Instead, various measures are used as proxies and, in exceptional circumstances, such as the global financial crisis, it is surrounded by higher uncertainty. Moreover, the empirical evidence shows that, at least in advanced economies, there were changes in the parameters of the Phillips curve between the 1970s and the early 1990s. First, in that period inflation became less sensitive to the cyclical situation of the economy (in terms of the Phillips curve, the curve flattened), although this sensitivity seems to have remained stable since then, not having diminished further during the crisis. Indeed, some studies have found it to have increased in recent years in some countries.[5] Second, some authors have also asserted that, as a consequence of the process of globalisation, inflation today depends less on each economy's cyclical position and more on the degree of slack in the global economy (a point of view stressed by the BIS; see for example Borio and Filardo 2007 and BIS 2014, 2015). Finally, other possible changes in the parameters of the Phillips curve have been highlighted, such as the fact that the inflation-expectations coefficient has risen as a result of central banks' greater credibility.

Additionally, the theoretical framework of the Phillips curve has sometimes been supplemented with other factors, which could play a significant role in price determination. These include supply shocks (affecting productivity or commodity prices, for example), labour market institutions, and the effects of exchange rates, indirect tax rates or demographic shifts.[6] This model, commonly known as the triangular

---

[4]Under this framework (see the formula below) inflation (π_t) would be determined by inflation expectations—possibly a combination of forward looking (LT_t) and backward looking elements (π_t')—and by the degree of cyclical slack in the economy ($slack_t$):

$$\pi_t = \lambda LT_t + (1 - \lambda)\,\pi_t' + \beta_1 slack_t + \varepsilon_t.$$

[5]See, for example, Stella and Stock (2013) for the case of the United States.

[6]A number of authors point to the deflationary effect of population ageing, particularly in the case of Japan, due primarily to the negative effect on economic growth and natural interest rates (Shirakawa 2012). For a more general discussion of the effects of ageing, see, for example, Nickel et al. (2017). These authors point to the greater preferencc of longer-lived generations for low inflation, as their income is mainly fixed, and their lower sensitivity to monetary policy. By contrast, Juselius and

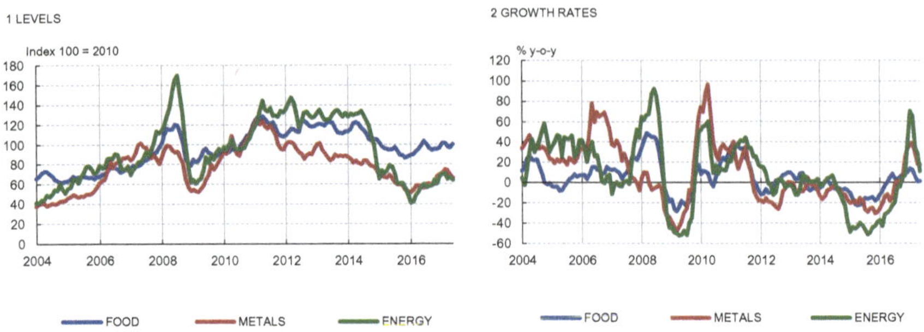

Fig. 5 Commodity prices. *Source* Datastream

model because it captures the effects of shifts in demand, supply and expectations, has been used by Gordon (2011), in particular. In the remainder of this section we explore how these factors have evolved and we undertake a comprehensive review of the extensive theoretical and empirical literature on the topic. The section concludes with an empirical exercise exploring the influence of each factor on inflation in advanced economies before and after the crisis.

3.1 *The Effect of Commodity Prices and Exchange Rates*

The way the main components of inflation have developed reveals that trends in commodity prices, particularly the oil price, have been among the main factors pushing down inflation worldwide (Table 1 and Fig. 5). The contribution of the oil price to global inflation has been shrinking since 2011 and was negative since 2014 until the middle of 2016. Since then much of the rise in inflation until the first months of 2017 was due to higher oil prices. Food prices have also fluctuated widely, contributing to the drop in inflation rates, particularly in emerging economies, where they account for a larger share of the basket of consumer goods. Core inflation, which excludes the energy and food components, has been somewhat more stable. As mentioned above, within core inflation, goods and services have performed differently. Inflation rates for goods, more directly linked to import prices, had tended to be negative until mid-2016 when production prices in China started to increase, whereas rates for services have remained higher. In some cases, such as the United States, the moderation of services inflation is also surprising when compared to previous recoveries, although this could reflect the moderation of health-care prices, after the country's recent health-care legislation, and other idiosyncratic factors.

Takáts (2015) find a positive correlation between the ratio of dependent population (young and elderly people) and a high inflation rate.

Table 1 Contributions to change in inflation[a] (Difference between Jun-16 and June-14, in pp)

	CPI energy	CPI food	CPI core	CPI general
Advanced economies				
United States	−1.2	−0.3	0.5	−1.1
Euro Area	−0.7	0.2	0.4	−0.2
Japan (a)	−1.7	−0.3	0.2	−1.8
Norway	1.6	0.0	0.6	2.1
Canada	−1.1	−0.2	0.5	−0.9
Sweden	0.2	0.1	0.7	1.1
Switzerland	−0.4	0.0	0.2	−0.2
United Kingdom	−0.6	−0.3	−0.1	−1.0
Emerging economies				
Brazil	0.4	1.1	0.8	2.3
China	−0.1	1.2	−1.7	−0.5
India	−0.2	0.0	−1.1	−1.4
Indonesia	−1.3	0.3	−0.2	−1.2
Mexico	−0.9	0.0	−0.5	−1.4
Korea	−1.0	−0.3	0.3	−0.9
Poland	−0.7	0.5	−0.8	−1.0
Czech Republic	0.2	−0.3	0.0	−0.1
South-Africa	−0.4	0.3	−0.2	−0.3
Turkey	−0.3	−1.7	1.7	−0.3

Source IMF, WEO database, April 2017
[a]For CPI energy, food and core columns, it is the variation of its contribution in the period. Japan data excludes the VAT effect

The direct effects of falling oil prices have varied between countries as a result of differences in oil's weight in the CPI, different levels of taxation on energy (usually in the form of unit tax rates), and changes in energy taxes and subsidies, as well as fluctuations in exchange rates. For example, oil prices have fallen by more in dollar than in euro terms, and less in other currencies that have depreciated against the dollar over the period. Similarly, the drop in the energy component of the CPI in the EU was smaller than in the United States, as a result of higher tax levels in Europe. In some emerging economies, such as Brazil and Indonesia, subsidy cuts caused an effective rise in fuel prices despite lower oil prices.

Another important point to consider when analysing the impact of falling commodity prices on inflation is whether the decline is being driven by supply- or demand-side factors. This is because the effects of a drop in the oil price caused by supply-side factors would be partially offset by the accompanying stimulus to activity, whereas a price drop driven by weak demand could have a bigger deflationary effect.

Finally, the impact of oil and other commodity prices on inflation, beyond the direct and indirect effects on production costs, will depend on how long the underlying shocks last. Thus, the likelihood of second-round effects on prices and wages will be greater if these shocks are persistent rather than short-lived. In this regard, there is extensive evidence that the degree of pass-through of commodity prices to core inflation has diminished over the past three decades. This is partly because the economy today makes less intensive use of commodities and also because the monetary authorities have gained credibility, which enables them to anchor inflation expectations more firmly. An additional factor is that wage indexing is less widespread.[7] In today's context, unless commodity prices continue to fall over the next few years, something not discounted by markets, the negative impacts on inflation can be expected to dissipate and are not likely to have significant second-round effects. However, the relative importance of demand from the emerging economies (in particular, China) in determining commodity prices has increased over time and events in large emerging economies (such as a possible slowdown in China while it makes the transition to a less investment- and more consumption-based model) may have a powerful impact on commodity prices over the next few years.

A large share of how inflation has developed in some countries can be explained by shifts in exchange rates. This is easy to confirm in the case of economies where a substantial depreciation in their currency has been linked to a subsequent rise in inflation. This was the case in Japan, following the launch of Abenomics, the United Kingdom, following the depreciation of the pound in the wake of the crisis, Mexico, explained by the election of Trump as President of the United States, and certain emerging economies confronted with the prospect of monetary policy tightening in the United States. By contrast, countries whose currencies have appreciated, such as Switzerland, the United States, China or, more recently, Japan, Brazil, and other emerging economies have experienced deflationary pressures via this route (see, for example, Fischer 2015 or Yellen 2015). This would explain why inflation has varied so widely around the world, as shown by the negative correlation between inflation rates and changes in nominal effective exchange rates in recent years (Fig. 6).

Nevertheless, as in the case of commodity prices, there is evidence that the exchange rate pass-through into inflation has decreased in recent decades. This has been particularly the case in the advanced economies, as well as in some emerging economies,[8] as a consequence of several factors, such as the better anchoring of inflation expectations, the development of global production chains that enable better absorption of exchange rate shifts by multinationals firms, the greater depth and liquidity of derivative markets, etc.[9]

---

[7]See, for example, Blanchard and Galí (2010) or BIS (2015). Álvarez et al. (2017) confirm the relevance of direct effects of oil prices on inflation in Spain while indirect and second-round effects are relatively smaller.

[8]See, for example, Campa and Goldberg (2008), or BIS (2014). Gopinath (2015) highlights, in the US case, the predominance of dollar-denominated imports as being a key factor in the reduced pass-through of the exchange rate into inflation. Factors such as exporters' pricing to market makes the extent of pass-through of exchange rate movements into import prices incomplete (see, for example, Bank of England 2015).

[9]For a contrasting opinion, see Hara et al. (2015) for the case of Japan since the 2000s. Moreover, Forbes (2015) and Forbes et al. (2015) also find that pass-through in the United Kingdom increased

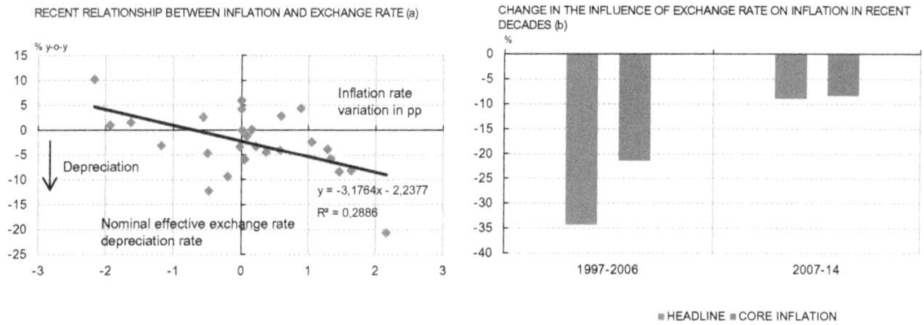

Fig. 6 Inflation and exchange rates. *Sources* Datastream, national statistics, BIS Annual Report (2015). **a** Variation between March 2015 and March 2016 in inflation and exchange rates for the following countries: Canada, Euro area, Japan, Norway, Sweden, Switzerland, United Kingdom, United States, Brazil, Chile, China, Czech Republic, Hong Kong, Hungary, India, Indonesia, Korea, Malaysia, Mexico, Peru, Philippines, Poland, Singapore, South Africa, Thailand and Turkey. **b** Correlation between headline inflation and the second lag of year on year change of nominal effective exchange rate. Simple average between Australia, Brazil, Canada, Chile, Colombia, Czech Republic, Denmark, Euro area, Hungary, India, Indonesia, Japan, Korea, Mexico, New Zealand, Norway, Peru, Philippines, Poland, Singapore, Sweden, Switzerland, Thailand, Turkey, United Kingdom and United States

In any event, the low levels of inflation recorded in recent years cannot be explained solely by relatively transitory movements of volatile variables, such as exchange rates, commodity prices, or indirect taxes. This raises the question of whether other factors have played a significant role in the price-formation process. The following sections examine some of these possible factors, from a theoretical viewpoint based on the Phillips curve.

3.2 *Cyclical Sensitivity of Inflation*

A high degree of economic slack is typically a driver of low inflation. However, measuring this slack is complicated by the difficulty of estimating potential GDP and the output gap. This measurement problem was exacerbated in the post-financial crisis global economic context. Although it seems clear that the financial crisis has substantially reduced potential GDP (and possibly potential growth as well), the precise extent to which it has done so is less clear. Indeed, potential growth prior to the

in the wake of the crisis. Furthermore, they highlight that to explain how this pass-through has evolved it is essential to distinguish the origin of the change in the exchange rate (i.e. whether it is due to domestic demand, global demand, domestic monetary policy, global supply shocks, domestic productivity, etc.). The largest degree of pass-through is found if the rise in the exchange rate is due to supply-side shocks, particularly domestic ones, while rising exchange rates linked to global or domestic demand shocks can cause price rises. Forbes et al. (2017) extend this analysis to a broad group of advanced and emerging market economies and Comunale and Kunovac (2017) apply the same methodology to the euro area.

crisis may have been overestimated as it was achieved by generating macro-financial imbalances that made it unsustainable, particularly in those advanced economies worst hit by the crisis (recent work on this line of research includes that by Alberola et al. 2013 and Borio et al. 2013).[10] There are also uncertainties about the point in the economic cycle reached by emerging economies. Insofar as part of these economies' growth in recent years is explained by strong capital inflows, credit booms and, in some cases, high commodity prices, potential GDP growth is likely to be lower now than previously estimated. Indeed, the main international organisations have cut their long term growth estimates for both the advanced and emerging economies.

An alternative to using the output gap as a measure of the cyclical position of the economy is to use the unemployment rate. However, identifying the cyclical and structural components of the unemployment rate is far from straightforward. The conceptual and practical difficulties in estimating NAIRU are analogous to those affecting potential GDP estimates (see, for example, Staiger et al. 1997). Moreover, changes in other labour market variables can give a different view of the degree of economic slack. For example, in the United States, some of the fundamental labour market variables, such as participation rates, unemployment rates, and long-term unemployment rates, have behaved in recent years in ways not in keeping with historical trends. At the same time, shifts in some statistical relationships that had remained stable over recent decades, such as the Beveridge curve (the relationship between the job-vacancy and unemployment rates) or Okun's law (the relationship between GDP growth and the unemployment rate) have become apparent. These shifts suggest the possible existence of structural changes in the labour market and/or in the relationships between the underlying economic variables. This has increased the uncertainty as to whether the unemployment rate is an accurate measure of the economy's idle capacity, especially when it has been close to what is considered the natural rate of unemployment and no wage pressure has been detected. In particular, it is not clear whether the natural rate of unemployment has changed, and if so, by how much. Moreover, it is unclear whether the unusual drop in the participation rate is partially reversible, and if so, to what extent. There is also uncertainty as to whether long-term unemployment is exhibiting hysteresis, a phenomenon that had been observed previously in other advanced economies, but not in the United States.[11]

All these uncertainties raise some difficult questions. Should economic slack be measured via GDP or unemployment? Should deviations from equilibrium levels or growth rates of the variables (as proposed by Orphanides and Van Norden 2005) be taken into account? Should financial factors and other macro-financial imbalances

---

[10]This situation is very different from that in the second half of the 1990 s, when there was a tendency to predict higher inflation than actually occurred in the advanced economies. Then, however, the technology revolution boosted productivity and potential growth, allowing greater slack and reducing inflationary pressures.

[11]For a detailed analysis of recent trends in the US labour market, see Berganza (2014). Some authors have suggested that the long-term unemployed disconnect from the labour market and do not exert the same pressure on wages as the short-term unemployed (Ball and Mazumder 2015). For a contrary view, see Kiley (2014).

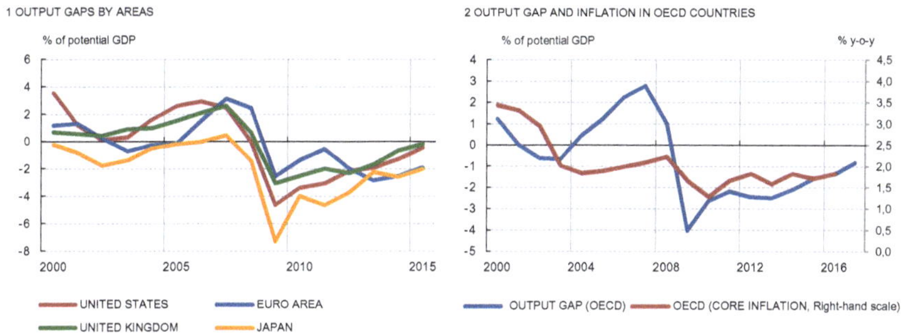

Fig. 7 Output gaps and inflation in advanced economies. *Sources* IMF, World Economic Outlook April 2017, OCDE Economic Outlook

be incorporated in the output gap estimates? In any event, existing estimates by international organisations suggest that although output (and unemployment) gaps in the main advanced economies (Fig. 7) are still significant, in general the degree of economic slack has decreased over the last few years, despite the moderation of inflation rates. Similarly, the wide output gaps that opened up in the aftermath of the crisis contrast with inflation's downward rigidity in that period (as highlighted, for example, by Ball and Mazumder 2011),[12] something that could be explained by the countercyclical behaviour of firms' margins, reinforced by financial constraints, as we will discuss below.

In any event, the fact that inflation rates have not responded as expected to economies' cyclical position in recent years is not something new. There is extensive empirical evidence in the literature showing that in advanced economies the Phillips curve flattened between the 1970s and the early 1990s.[13] Figure 8 shows the relationship between consumer price inflation and the output gap and between wage inflation and the cyclical component of the unemployment rate in different periods.[14]

[12]Ball and Mazumder (2011) find that according to traditional estimates of the Phillips curve core inflation in the US should have declined well below zero during the crisis (even reaching less than −3%, although it actually just fell to 0.6%). This contrasts with the historical evidence that pronounced and persistent negative output gaps tend to lead to significant deflation in terms of both prices and wages.

[13]See, for example, IMF (2013), BIS (2014), Blanchard et al. (2015). The empirical evidence for emerging economies is limited, although a similar trend seems to have been observed.

[14]For some authors, the Phillips curve presents non-linearities, being flatter when unemployment rates are higher, due to downward wage rigidities, and steeper when unemployment rates are very low (Linder et al. 2012 or Semmler and Gross 2017). For a contrasting view, see Musso et al. (2009) and for the case of the Spanish economy Álvarez et al. (2015) also find evidence that inflation responds differently in booms than in recessions, being higher in the contractionary phases of the cycle.

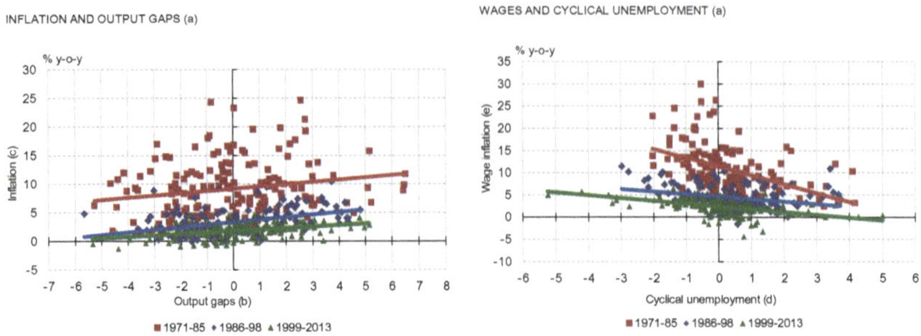

Fig. 8 Phillips curve in advanced economies. *Sources* BIS Annual Report (2014). **a** Annual data, regression lines estimated with panel data unbalanced regressions with individual fix effects, controlling with year on year changes on commodities prices. The countries are Australia, Canada, France, Germany, Italy, Japan, Spain, Sweden, Switzerland, United Kingdom, and United States. **b** Estimations using a Holdrick-Prescott filter. **c** Year on year change on the consumer price index. **d** Unemployment rate minus NAIRU. **e** Year on year change on wages

The reduced sensitivity of inflation to the degree of economic slack also means that it is much more difficult to predict inflation precisely.[15]

Another way of looking at the cyclical sensitivity of inflation is through changes in the coefficient of the Phillips curve that captures the effect of the economy's economic slack over time. A number of recent papers have shown that this parameter decreased in advanced economies between the 1970s and the 1990s, indicating a flattening of the Phillips curve during this period.[16] Nevertheless, there is also considerable evidence that this phenomenon has been reversed in some advanced economies in the wake of the crisis. For example, in some euro area countries, such as Spain, Finland and Italy,[17] this has come about as a result of greater market flexibility following a number of structural reforms.[18]

Turning to developments in labour markets, wage growth in the United States in the last few years has been weaker than in previous recoveries given the declining trend in the unemployment rate, and even bearing in mind the low rates of inflation. There could be various—not necessarily mutually compatible—reasons for this. First, as noted above, this wage behaviour could be a sign that the labour market conditions are actually weaker than the unemployment rate would suggest. However, the literature offers other possible reasons why wages have not risen more in some developed economies. For example, productivity gains in recent years have been low (a phenomenon also observed in other advanced economies). It could also be the case

---

[15]As indicated, for example, by Stock and Watson (2010).

[16]See, for example, IMF (2013), BIS (2014), Ball and Mazumder (2015), Blanchard et al. (2015).

[17]See, for example, Álvarez and Urtasun (2013), Oinonen and Paloviita (2014), Riggi and Venditti (2014), Álvarez et al. (2015), Banco de España (2015), Blanchard et al. (2015), IMF (2016) or Ciccarelli and Osbat (2017).

[18]For an analysis applied to the Spanish case, see Izquierdo and Puente (2015).

that productivity growth has been slow because wage growth has been slow; that is, faced with only tepid rises in labour costs, firms have had less incentive to invest in labour-saving technologies.

Muted wage growth could also be related to the composition of employment. For example, in the United Kingdom less productive workers earning lower wages bore the brunt of job losses during the crisis and experienced fastest job growth during the recovery, which could explain the slow growth of both productivity and wages (Broadbent 2015). This change in the composition of employment could be due to demand-side factors (less investment in physical and human capital in the wake of the crisis) or supply-side factors (increased immigration). Another explanation, which became popular following Yellen's speech at Jackson Hole in 2014 (Yellen 2014), was the concept of pent-up wage deflation developed by Daly and Hobjin (2014). Given workers' reluctance to accept cuts in nominal wages during a recession and the start of a recovery,[19] employees' real wages would remain above equilibrium levels; consequently, unemployment may fall during the recovery, thereby reducing the slack in the labour market, without pushing up nominal wages. This phenomenon would be temporary, so that once real wages reach equilibrium levels (and the pent-up wage deflation is absorbed) nominal wages should start rising again. This process may be abrupt, however.

Another interesting feature of price determination related to the reduced cyclical sensitivity of inflation is that in some advanced economies the close link between wage growth and CPI inflation seems to have dissipated. As Fig. 9 shows, in the US and UK economies this relationship was relatively tight in the 1970 and 1980s, whereas inflation seems to have become relatively insensitive to wage fluctuations since the 1990s. As mentioned above, one possible explanation for the looser relationship between wage growth and consumer price increases would be the existence of counter-cyclical mark-ups, such that inflation has become less sensitive to labour-market conditions because mark-ups have offset the effect of wages. If this is the case, increased mark-ups in many economies since the Great Recession would have partially offset the disinflationary effect of declining wages, helping explain inflation's more muted response. This phenomenon would have intensified in the aftermath of the financial crisis, as the financial constraints would reinforce the counter-cyclical trend in margins.[20]

Lastly, other possible explanations for inflation's potentially reduced cyclical sensitivity include the greater importance of global factors in determining prices or the effect of inflation-expectation anchoring. These issues will be addressed in the two following sections.

[19]There is extensive evidence of these downward rigidities in nominal wages, even in the US case (see, for example, Linder et al. 2012).

[20]As put forward by Gilchrist et al. (2015) or Montero and Urtasun (2014).

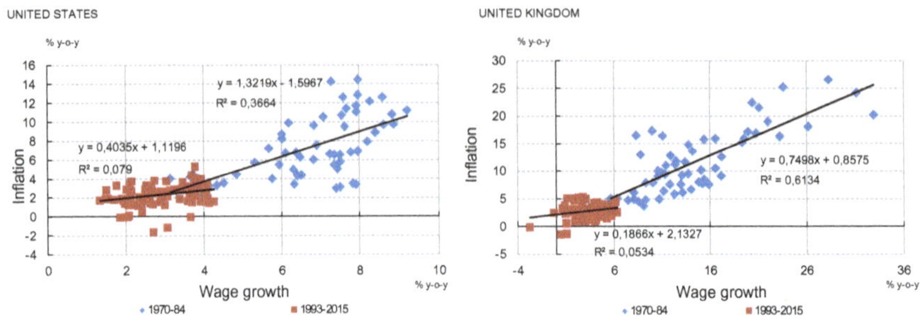

Fig. 9 Wage growth and inflation in the United States and the United Kingdom (**a**). *Sources* National Statistics **a** Quarterly data

3.3 Influence of Global Factors on Inflation

Some of the same studies that find inflation to have become less sensitive to domestic cyclical conditions argue that, by contrast, the significance of global factors has increased as a result of globalisation and the expansion of global value chains. This argument has been put forward in some BIS papers (see Borio and Filardo 2007 or Auer et al. 2017) and in BIS annual reports (2014, 2015, 2016, 2017). The estimates of the Phillips curve provided by these authors show the effects of variables such as the global output gap or import prices to be significant, while that of the domestic output gap to be small or even insignificant.[21] A recent IMF study has also highlighted the relevance of global factors (measured by the industrial slack in large exporters such as Japan, the United States, and especially China) in explaining low inflation by putting downward pressure on global prices of tradable goods (IMF 2016b). This study shows that the decline in goods inflation has been steeper than that in services, particularly in the case of tradable goods.

The process of globalisation has expanded the range of products and services that can be traded internationally. It has also led to tradable goods, particularly manufactured goods—but increasingly services too—becoming cheaper as a result of lower production costs in emerging economies, such as China, in particular.[22] Increased globalisation also influences prices through heightened international competition in both product and factor markets.[23] This competition also constrains workers' bargaining power and business margins.[24] At the same time, global supply and demand

[21]Many other studies seem to confirm the increased relevance of global factors in inflation. See, for example, IMF (2006, 2013) or Ciccarelli and Mojón (2010) and references therein.

[22]China's deflationary effect on the rest of the world has been highlighted, for example by ECB (2006) or Eickmeier and Kühnlenz (2013).

[23]Bentolila et al. (2007) highlight the importance of immigration in flattening the Phillips curve in Spain between 1995 and 2006.

[24]These competitive effects have been pointed out by a number of authors, such as Auer et al. (2011), BIS (2015) or Carney (2015).

conditions determine commodity prices, which have a direct impact on inflation. Strong growth in emerging economies—particularly China—in the years leading up to the crisis drove up prices of commodities, and this process has gone into reverse now these economies are slowing.

In line with the increased importance of global factors, inflation rates and wage growth have tended to be more closely synchronised among advanced economies in recent years and there is considerable evidence that a common factor, obtained empirically by principal component analysis, can explain a significant portion of the variability of inflation in advanced economies.[25] However, although it is accepted that global factors play a bigger role in determining inflation, there is considerable uncertainty as to the real significance of these factors in the recent drop in inflation.[26] And in the medium-to-long term, it is debatable to what extent globalisation will continue to exert a deflationary effect, as differences in labour costs between countries shrink.

3.4 *The Role of Inflation Expectations*

The other possible explanation given in the literature for inflation's reduced cyclical sensitivity is the stronger anchoring of agents' inflation expectations on central banks' targets and the increased significance of this factor in price and wage setting.[27] If agents remain confident of central banks' commitment to price stability, they will attach less importance to transient deviations in inflation and cyclical pressures on inflation will be more muted. The greater stability of inflation in recent decades, and its reluctance to drop further during the financial crisis, would be consistent with this hypothesis.[28] Several studies showing how the parameters of the Phillips curve have evolved over time confirm that the coefficient of inflation expectations has risen over the past decades (IMF 2013; Blanchard et al. 2015).

In this regard, it is particularly important that long-term inflation expectations remain well anchored, given that short-term expectations tend to be more volatile and more responsive to changes in inflation. As Yellen (2015) notes, the medium-

[25]The evidence of greater synchronisation between inflation rates in the advanced economies and the importance of common factors can be found in Ciccarelli and Mojón (2010), BIS (2014) or Gopinath (2015).

[26]Many authors, while not denying that global factors have a bigger influence, have questioned the centrality of global effects in explaining the recent episode of low inflation and the one prior to the global financial crisis. They also question the supposed inability of monetary authorities to control inflation for this reason. See, for example, Rogoff (2006), Ball (2006), Yellen (2006), Bernanke (2007), Woodford (2010), Carney (2015) or Mikolajun and Lodge (2016).

[27]See, for example, Ball and Mazumder (2011), IMF (2013), BIS (2014) or Yellen (2015).

[28]Particular importance is given to inflation-targeting regimes in explaining the greater importance of inflation expectations. See, for example, Gürkaynak et al. (2010) or Mehrotra and Yetman (2014). For a recent contrasting view, see Kumar et al. (2015).

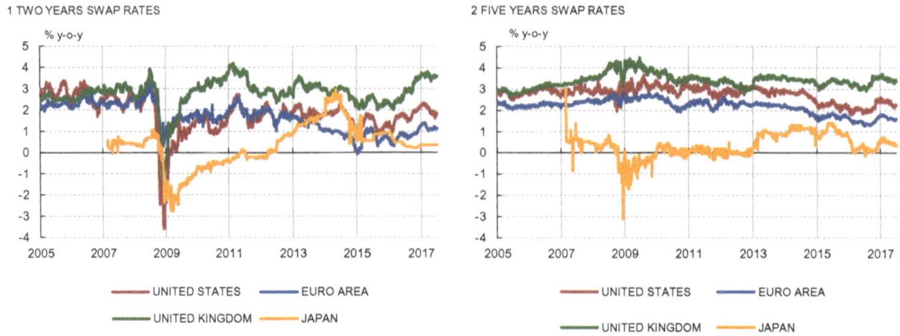

Fig. 10 Compensation by inflation. *Sources* Bloomberg

term effect on inflation of factors that are, in principle, transient (such as the amount of slack or energy prices) depends on whether long-term expectations are affected or not. In fact, in recent decades long-term expectations have remained much more stable and have barely been affected by changes in past inflation. However, in the most recent recovery the downward trend in inflation may have led to a drop in inflation expectations in some regions, particularly in the euro area, but also in the United States and the United Kingdom.[29] This is not just the case for short-term expectations but for medium- and long-term expectations too[30] (see Fig. 10). Indeed, this drop in inflation expectations triggered a reaction of monetary authorities, as they became aware of the risks of inflation expectations becoming unanchored and potentially leading to a deflationary spiral.

In particular, there is some evidence that the correlation between actual inflation and long-term expectations has become closer in advanced economies since the financial crisis (particularly when measures of inflation compensation obtained from financial markets are used)[31]; the correlation with oil prices appears to have increased

[29]See, for example, ECB (2015) or Yellen (2015). Ciccarelli and García (2015) find significant spillover effects since August 2014 from long-term inflation in the euro area on expectations in other regions, particularly the United States. This could explain the way market expectations were seen to drop at the same time.

[30]Several recent studies (Ciccarelli and Osbat 2017; Locarno et al. 2017) find that changes in short-term inflation expectations in the euro area have translated into long-term expectations since mid-2012.

[31]See, for example, BIS (2015), IMF (2016) or Ciccarelli and Osbat (2017). Nevertheless, the limitations of measures of inflation expectations derived from financial instruments (such as the existence of liquidity premiums) must be borne in mind, while, by contrast, expectations reported in surveys have remained much more stable (Yellen 2015). However, Lyziak and Paloviita (2016) find that in the euro area longer-term inflation expectations of professional forecasters and consumers have become somewhat more sensitive to shorter-term forecasts and to actual HICP inflation in the post-crisis period, which suggests that inflation expectations in the euro area have shown some signs of de-anchoring.

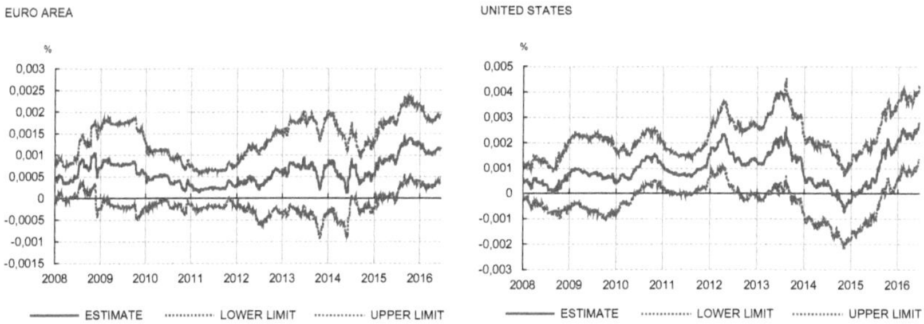

Fig. 11 Oil prices effect on long-term inflation expectations. *Sources* Bloomberg, own calculations. Coefficients are estimated by iterative regressions in a 2 year rolling window. The specification is: $D\_Z^{5y/5y} = a+b*D\_oil+c*D\_Z^{1y/1y}$, where $Z^{5y/5y}$ is the 5y/5y inflation expectations, $Z^{1y/1y}$ is the 1y/1y inflation expectations, and oil is the year on year change of oil price in national currency. Confidence intervals are calculated with robust residuals to heteroscedasticity, non-normality outliers using the Huber-White estimator.

as well[32] (see Fig. 11). This is particularly the case in economies experiencing slow growth, inflation rates persistently below targets and with policy interest rates close to the zero lower bound, like the US or the euro area, where long-term expectations seemed more firmly anchored than in some other countries such as Japan.[33] All this might indicate looser anchoring of expectations and possible second-round effects, which would be a matter of concern for monetary authorities.

Following the monetary policy decisions adopted in different areas in the last two years, long-term inflation expectations picked up again (ECB 2015; Ciccarelli et al. 2017), at least temporarily, but they have remained volatile and below inflation targets, which could indicate that markets are anticipating low inflation rates for a long time (Yellen 2015). Two recent studies by the IMF and the ECB have found that the coefficient of forward-looking inflation expectations estimated in a hybrid new Keynesian Phillips curve has diminished since the crisis, while the persistence of inflation (the coefficient of lagged inflation capturing the backward-looking component of expectations) has increased (IMF 2016; Ciccarelli and Osbat 2017), especially for countries at the effective lower bound.

---

[32]See, for example, ECB (2015) or IMF (2016). Kumar et al. (2015), for the case of New Zealand, indicate that business's price expectations are somewhat loosely anchored and respond mainly to developments in oil prices.

[33]The recent "Comprehensive Assessment" of the Quantitative and Qualitative Easing strategy by the Bank of Japan points to the adaptive character of inflation expectations as one of the main determinants of persistently very low inflation in Japan (Bank of Japan 2016). Locarno et al. (2017) point to the possibility of similar risks of deanchoring expectations for the euro area.

3.5 Empirical Analysis of the Factors Determining Inflation

The ultra-low inflation seen during the recent recovery has surprised both economic analysts and central banks, and numerous studies have been published analysing the role of various different factors in explaining why inflation is behaving in this way.[34] Most of these studies find that a large part of the decline in headline inflation can be attributed to transitory factors, such as lower energy prices, economic slack (both at the domestic and global level) and, in some cases, the effect of exchange rate movements. On the other hand, they usually find a wide degree of variation between countries in terms of the role of cyclical sensitivity and the relevance of forward-looking inflation expectations (whereas over recent decades the coefficient of slack has been declining gradually whilst the anchoring of inflation expectations has become more relevant). Nevertheless, overall, these studies are still unable to explain the recent decline in core inflation satisfactorily (not only due to heterogeneity alluded to above, but also to the lack of robust estimates of Phillips curves).

In our empirical exercise, we concentrated on the more recent period to try to discern whether there has been a change in the relative importance of those factors, based on the estimation of core inflation through a standard Phillips curve for 21 advanced economies.[35] In this specification, core CPI inflation (π_t) measured at quarterly annualised rates, is determined by inflation expectations—a combination of forward looking and backward looking elements—, the degree of cyclical slack and the role of import prices (the relative inflation of imports over consumer prices):

$$\pi_t = \lambda LT_t + (1 - \lambda)\,\pi_t' + \beta_1 slack_t + \beta_2 imp_t + \varepsilon_t$$

As in Ball and Mazumder (2011), the forward looking element of inflation expectations (LT_t) captures long term inflation expectations, measured by the Consensus forecast or proxied by the central bank targets, while the backward looking component (π_t') is constructed as the average core inflation rate of the last four quarters.[36] The degree of economic slack in each economy ($slack_t$) is proxied by the output gap (the difference between actual and potential GDP divided by potential output) or the unemployment gap (the difference between the unemployment rate and estimated NAIRU). Relative import prices (imp_t) are measured in domestic currency, to capture trends in prices of imported goods and services, as well as the effect of

[34]See, for instance, Banco de España (2015), BIS (2015), Blanchard et al. (2015), Carney (2015), Fischer (2015), Forbes (2015), Yellen (2015), IMF (2016) and a recent collection of ECB Working Papers prepared for a Low Inflation Task Force and summarised in Ciccarelli and Osbat (2017).

[35]Australia, Austria, Belgium, Canada, Denmark, the euro area, Finland, France, Germany, Ireland, Italy, Japan, the Netherlands, New Zealand, Norway, Portugal, South Korea, Spain, Sweden, Switzerland, the United Kingdom, and the United States.

[36]The sum of the coefficients of forward- and backward-looking inflation expectations is restricted to 1 in order to guarantee that the Phillips curve is vertical in the long run.

exchange rates.[37] The variables for slack and relative import prices are included contemporarily or lagged by one period, depending on which specification fits the data better. Finally, we added a dummy variable to account for VAT changes. (Definitions and sources can be found in the Appendix).

For each country in the sample we estimate the previous relation by OLS[38] for two periods: before the crisis, from 1997[39] to 2007, and after the crisis, from 2008 to 2015. Figure 12 reports the main results, in terms of changes in the coefficients of the Phillips curve between both periods, which, similarly to other studies show a wide degree of variation between countries; for some of them the results are not robust to alternative specifications of the slack—the output gap or the unemployment gap—or the backward-looking inflation expectations—different number of lags, for instance—.

In the case of inflation expectations, for some countries (Australia, Austria, Finland, the Netherlands, Norway, Ireland, Italy, the United Kingdom, and the United States), we find an increase in the relative role of the forward-looking component of expectations in the most recent period, although only in Italy and Finland there is a statistically significant difference between the coefficient in the two periods. For other countries it appears that the backward-looking component has increased (Canada, Denmark, the euro area, France, Germany, Japan, New Zealand, Portugal, South Korea, Spain, Sweden, and Switzerland), although this change is not statistically significant in a robust way in any of them.

Regarding the cyclical sensitivity of inflation, in line with other studies, there is also a high degree of heterogeneity. For some countries (Australia, Belgium, Canada, Finland, Ireland, Italy, Netherlands, Spain, Sweden and the United Kingdom), we find an increase in the coefficient of slack in the most recent period, while this is not the case in others (Austria, Denmark, the euro area, France, Germany, New Zealand, Norway, Japan, Portugal, Switzerland, and the United States). Again, most of these results are not simultaneously statistically significant and robust (except for Australia, Canada, Italy and Portugal).

Finally, the role of relative import prices on inflation varies also across countries. For some of them (Austria, Belgium, Denmark, the euro area, Germany Ireland, Japan, Norway, Portugal, Spain, South Korea and Switzerland) there is an increase in the coefficient, whereas for others (Australia, France, Finland, Italy, the Netherlands,

---

[37] Another variable typically used in the literature to capture global factors affecting inflation is the global output gap. We tried this variable (the OECD output gap) in our regressions, but it showed a high correlation with domestic output gaps and its coefficient was not significant.

[38] Estimation methods vary depending on the empirical approach and the definition of variables. Some authors (e.g., Blanchard et al. 2015) estimate jointly the evolution of inflation and the NAIRU (or potential output) obtaining time varying coefficients by applying the Kalman filter. Other studies, along the new Keynesian spirit, use the inflation rate in period t + 1 as the forward-looking component of inflation expectations and estimate by GMM, but this approach is subject to critiques due to the weakness of instruments. In line with studies such as Ball and Mazumder (2011) or Banco de España (2015), we use long-term inflation forecasts from Consensus or the central bank target which allow estimation by OLS for each country. Panel data settings are not considered due to the specific behaviour of inflation in each country.

[39] First quarter of 1999 for the euro area.

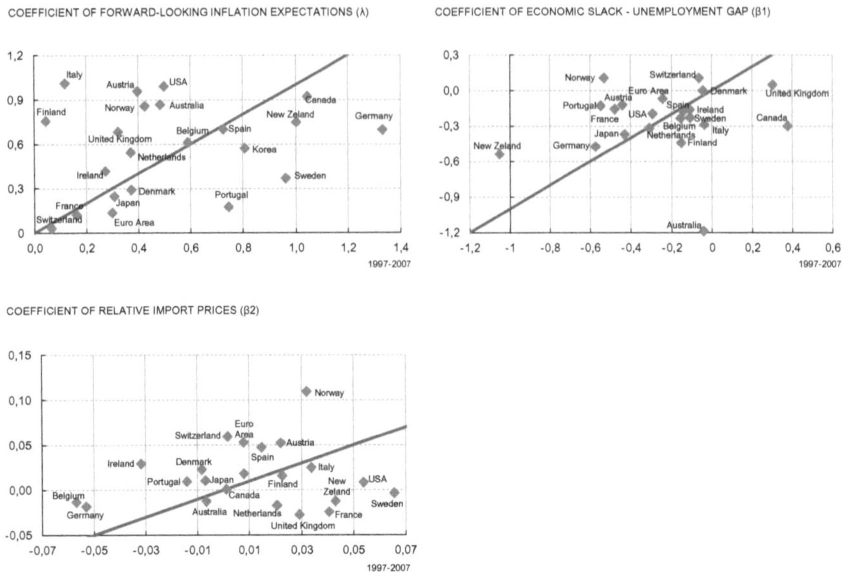

Fig. 12 Changes in the coefficients of the Phillips curve

New Zealand, Sweden, the United Kingdom and the United States) we observe a decrease. These results seem robust and statistically significant for a larger number of countries (Denmark, the euro area, France, New Zealand, Norway, Sweden, the United Kingdom and the United States).

Given the high degree of heterogeneity and lack of robustness of these results, instead of drawing general conclusions, we have tried to infer which factors might explain recent inflation trends in specific countries. In Fig. 13 we show the contribution of each factor to the year-on-year core inflation rate for the United States, the United Kingdom, the euro area and Japan.[40]

In the United States, forward-looking expectations seem to have taken on a more prominent role post-2008, while cyclical slack contributed to the decline in core inflation, although less powerfully since 2011. According to these estimates, if slack continues to diminish and long-term inflation expectations are well anchored, core inflation in the US should converge towards the Federal Reserve's inflation target. In the United Kingdom, the forward-looking component of inflation expectations also seems to have become more relevant since the crisis, but the coefficient of slack is not found to be significant (and has the opposite sign), and a large part of the recent decline in inflation remains unexplained. In the euro area and Japan—and keeping in mind the general lack of robustness of the results—it seems that the backward-looking inflation expectations component has taken a more central role when explaining inflation, in line with the findings in Bank of Japan (2016) and

[40]In Berganza, del Río and Borrallo (2016) the breakdown of inflation for the rest of countries is shown.

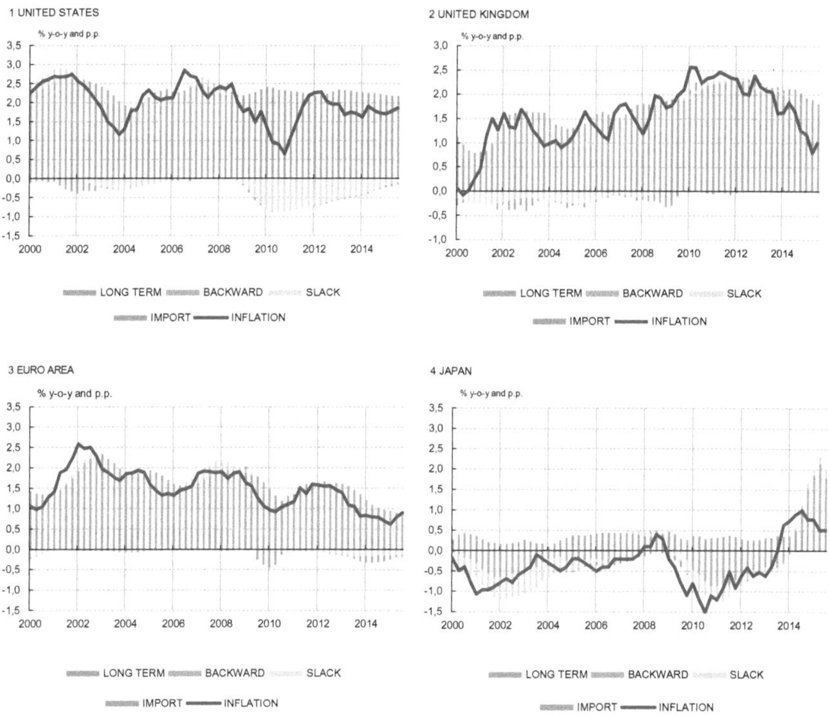

Fig. 13 Decomposition of core inflation. *Source* Own elaboration

Ciccarelli and Osbat (2017) for these economies. The relevance of import prices is relatively minor, except in the case of the euro area.

4 Implications of Low Inflation

4.1 Adverse Economic Effects of Low Inflation

Even if low inflation is the result of positive supply shocks, a context of excessively low inflation poses various risks. First of all, ultra-low inflation rates raise real interest rates, tightening monetary and financial conditions and weakening demand. In a recent study looking at the case of Sweden, Svensson (2015) estimates that, even with inflation expectations firmly anchored on the central bank's target, the effect of sub-target inflation has a cost in terms of unemployment.[41] Low inflation also

[41] Svensson estimates that with inflation 0.6 pp below target between 1997 and 2011 the unemployment rate was raised by 0.8 pp.

influences inequality: according to a recent study by Adam and Zhu (2014), an unexpected drop in prices increases the inequality in household wealth in the euro area, with younger middle class cohorts losing more, and older, wealthier households benefiting more.

Moreover, in the current context of high public and private debt in many countries, lower inflation makes deleveraging harder, as it reduces economic agents' nominal incomes (Yellen 2015). The channels through which lower inflation affects debt dynamics are diverse (for the classic treatment of the subject, see Fisher 1933). On the one hand, lower inflation reduces nominal GDP growth (to the extent that it is reflected in the GDP deflator), causing an automatic increase in the debt-to-GDP ratio. The paradigmatic case is that of Japan, where falling prices since the 1990s have accounted for a third of the over 100 pp increase in public debt since then. Moreover, the possible adverse effect of excessively low inflation on GDP growth would also worsen debt dynamics. Slower growth of prices and wages also has implications for both the public and private sectors' income available to meet debt servicing requirements. Lastly, in an environment of policy rates close to the lower bound, a drop in inflation cannot be accompanied by a proportional lowering of interest rates, which under normal circumstances would compensate for the higher debt ratio.

Similarly, a generalised drop in inflation can hinder macrofinancial adjustment and improvements to competitiveness in those countries belonging to a monetary area. This may force them to undergo a process of internal devaluation, as lower inflation across the area would oblige them to register even smaller—possibly negative—price and wage increases, which are more difficult to achieve in the presence of downward rigidities. This could potentially lead to a sharper adjustment through unemployment (Banco de España 2015; Yellen 2015).

The most harmful consequences of low inflation occur if it turns into deflation, particularly if this is persistent and accompanied by a de-anchoring of inflation expectations, as this can cause a drop in spending and a sharp economic slowdown.[42] Deflationary situations may be due to either supply or demand shocks. However, regardless of the origin, deflationary processes are rarely benign.[43] They cause a redistribution of income from debtors to creditors, incentives for credit intermediation are undermined by the loss of value of assets used for collateral, and if deflation persists, there is a tendency to fall into a spiral of lower prices, output, profits, and employment.

Finally, an environment of excessively low inflation, or even worse, a deflationary process, may undermine central banks' credibility and limit their ability to implement

[42]See, for example, Ahearne et al. (2002), Bernanke (2002), Buiter (2003), Kumar et al. (2003), Carney (2015).

[43]However, for some authors, mainly those associated with the BIS, the historical evidence shows that not all deflationary episodes are harmful, particularly in the case of those that result from positive supply shocks. See, for example, BIS (2015), Borio et al. (2015). Arias et al. (2015), for their part, indicate that the harmful effects of low inflation crucially derive from its origin, and the ability of monetary policy to respond. The effects are more positive if deflation is due to positive supply shocks and monetary policy is not limited by the effective lower bound.

counter-cyclical monetary policy (Ahearne et al. 2002; Yellen 2015). An environment in which interest rates are close to the effective lower bound further complicates matters, and a multiplicity of equilibrium situations may arise (Aruoba and Schorfheide 2015). The following section looks at the various challenges low inflation poses for economic policy, and monetary policy in particular, pointing out several policy alternatives that have been put forward in the literature.

4.2 Monetary Policy Implications

Central banks in the developed economies have responded to the environment of moderate economic growth and low inflation in recent years by trying to stimulate aggregate demand. Policy interest rates have remained close to zero in the United States, the United Kingdom, Japan and the euro area for over eight years. Indeed, more recently, official deposit rates have been brought below zero in some cases (Denmark the euro area, Japan, Sweden and Switzerland). Additionally central banks have adopted a series of unconventional monetary policy measures that have added extra stimulus, such as expanding their balance sheets by buying financial assets, or pursuing a policy of forward guidance to steer expectations regarding future monetary policy decisions. According to traditional instruments for measuring the degree of monetary policy easing, such as the Taylor rule, monetary policy has been highly accommodative in most developed economies. Therefore, notwithstanding the lags with which monetary policy operates, these policies should have resulted in higher inflation.

However, assessing the degree of monetary accommodation has become more difficult after the global financial crisis. The natural real interest rate, one of the key parameters of the Taylor rule, has dropped (Laubach and Williams 2015; Pescatori and Turunen 2015) and there is considerable uncertainty about how it will evolve over the next few years (Hernando et al. 2018; Rachel and Smith 2015). As mentioned in previous sections, there are serious doubts about economies' true cyclical slack (measured either via the output gap or unemployment rates), a variable also included in the Taylor rule. Furthermore, certain cyclical and structural characteristics—such as ageing, that increase the share of the population that is less sensitive to changes in interest rates (IMF 2013)—may have reduced the effectiveness of monetary policy. Moreover, given the flattening of the Phillips curve, central banks can only achieve their targets with more aggressive policies.[44]

The inability of central banks to control long-term inflation and provide a nominal anchor to the economy can have consequences for risk premia. Evidence of this can be found in the shifts experienced by medium- and long-term inflation swaps and the inflation expectations deriving from them, which should not have moved with oil prices, as over this time frame their effects should have disappeared.

[44] The same thing could happen when trying to control inflation when it starts to rise.

Moreover, recent experience has heightened central banks' concerns that the effective lower bound on interest rates may become a constraint again (Yellen 2016 or Neri et al. 2017), so that any shock could put the economy into an unfavourable equilibrium of low growth and inflation, with the space for monetary policy basically limited to unconventional measures (Reifschneider 2016). Monetary authorities are pondering the risks of the pace of normalisation of monetary policy in this context (Evans et al. 2015), as the possibilities of stimulating growth and employment would be limited, while there are a variety of tools to control inflationary pressures. This is all set in a context in which the experience of other central banks in recent years (Canada, the ECB, Norway and Sweden) has shown that when they have opted to raise policy interest rates, they have had to subsequently cut them again.

In order to obtain more leeway for action and to reduce the probability of reaching the lower bound of policy interest rates in periods of low inflation following adverse shocks, some authors, such as Blanchard et al. (2010a, b), Ball (2014) or Williams (2016) have suggested that central banks should raise their inflation targets, which would imply a higher average level of interest rates. In this regard, it is worth noting that the 2% target (the predominant target set in the developed economies) is the outcome of weighing up the efficiency costs of positive inflation rates (e.g. distortions in fluctuations in relative prices and increased uncertainty), against the costs associated with zero inflation, such as the downward rigidity of nominal wages and the possibility of reaching the effective lower bound (Bernanke 2002). Central banks considered that the probability of reaching the effective lower bound with the 2% inflation target was small.[45] This view may have changed since 2008, partly as a result of falling natural real interest rates (Chung et al. 2012; Canzoneri et al. 2015). Some analysts (e.g. Chung et al. 2012) therefore argue that the inflation target should depend on the natural real interest rate. Opponents of an increase in the inflation target argue that once the nominal anchor has been altered it may prove difficult and costly to anchor it at its new level, and that the change could undermine its credibility.

Some authors have proposed that inflation targeting be replaced by a flexible price level (Hatcher and Minford 2014 and the references therein) or nominal GDP (Woodford 2013; Williams 2016) targeting. In these frameworks, the central bank targets a steadily growing level of prices or nominal GDP, rather than the rate of inflation, automatically delivering the "lower for longer" policy prescription the situation calls for (Eggertsson and Woodford 2003).

[45]Reifschneider and Williams (2000) found that with a 2% inflation target monetary policy would be constrained by the effective lower bound only 5% of the time and that these episodes would have an average duration of a year.

Other authors have proposed avoiding the effective lower bound on policy interest rates by imposing a negative interest rate on physical cash (Haldane 2015). A series of options have been considered along these lines, such as: randomly eliminating banknotes based on their serial number (Mankiw 2009), abolishing physical currency (Rogoff 2016) or setting an explicit exchange rate between physical cash and electronic money (Agarwal and Kimball 2015). However, these proposals raise a number of logistic and behavioural issues. Therefore, if we accept that the effective lower bound will re-emerge as a constraint in the future, it will be necessary to deploy unconventional monetary policy measures—forward guidance and asset purchase operations—to stimulate demand and inflation (see, for example, Engel et al. 2015). Apart from the fact that asset purchases may be considered quasi-fiscal policy in some ways, they have expanded central banks' balance sheets considerably, but not stimulated private credit growth, which has led to an increase in excess bank reserves. In other words, the monetary base has expanded considerably, but the money supply has not.

As discussed above, another much more worrying situation than the persistence of low inflation, and one which has different implications for economic policy, would be deflation, which is defined as a persistent and widespread drop in price levels. In this regard, the lessons learned about deflation are: (i) it can become established very quickly; (ii) it can impose severe economic costs, unless it derives from a permanent positive supply shock (e.g. an increase in productivity); and (iii) vigorous and determined policies can make a rapid and decisive difference. Experience shows that it is essential that the authorities demonstrate they are fully ready to tackle deflation and that they are willing to take all the necessary measures to raise prices in the future as well as today (Eggertsson and Woodford 2003). Given the costs involved, it is also essential that deflationary risks be addressed in a forward-looking way, i.e. before they become established.

5 Concluding Remarks

In a context of a weak economic recovery accompanied by accommodative monetary policies, falling inflation rates in advanced economies may be due to transient factors—such as the slump in commodity prices or the effects of exchange-rate fluctuations—or to structural shifts in the price and wage setting process—such as shifts in the cyclical sensitivity of inflation to economic slack or in the relevance of forward-looking inflation expectations. These factors could also explain the inflation rate's surprising reluctance to drop in the immediate aftermath of the global financial crisis. Unfortunately, the empirical results in recent studies—including those in this chapter—are insufficiently consistent or robust to prove the existence of structural changes in the parameters of the Phillips curve. Although we cannot explain the recent trend in inflation in a completely satisfactory way, in some cases the recent drop in inflation might tentatively be ascribed to backward-looking inflation expectations playing a more important role, which could pose important challenges for central banks.

The lack of definite conclusions stemming from our estimated Phillips curves could simply reflect a misspecification of the model. For instance, there may be global factors depressing inflation rates that are perhaps are not adequately represented by the import prices included in the regressions. It could also be related to the difficulty of measuring the relevant variables (slack in the economy or the labour market). More worryingly, it could constitute a genuine failure of this type of model to explain inflation, something which deserves further investigation. In any case, any of these explanations would have serious implications for policymakers in that inflation may become more difficult to control.

We have also discussed how ultra-low inflation over an extended period can have adverse effects on the real economy, as it raises real interest rates, hampers public and private deleveraging, and hinders competitiveness adjustments in those monetary-union countries that are obliged to resort to internal devaluation. In the most extreme case, in which there is a de-anchoring of inflation expectations, there is the concomitant risk of slipping into a deflationary spiral, the consequences of which would be far worse still. In any event, the credibility of central banks' targets may be undermined if inflation rates fail to meet them for an extended period.

Against this backdrop, having reached the zero lower bound for policy interest rates, monetary policy sought to become more expansionary by resorting to unconventional measures. And more recently, several central banks in developed economies (including the ECB and the Bank of Japan) crossed this zero lower bound by setting negative interest rates on banks' reserves deposited with them, intensifying the debate on the scope for action and the marginal effectiveness and risks of monetary policies. This is an important debate as the lower equilibrium real interest rate suggests that in the future monetary policy may find itself in similar circumstances to today more often and for longer than in the past. In this scenario, support from other types of policies, such as fiscal policy or structural policies, is crucial in order to try to stimulate growth and inflation.

Appendix: Definitions and Sources of Variables

Variable	Definition	Sources
Core CPI	Annualized quarterly core inflation rate	Bureau of Economic Analysis (USA), European Central Bank (Euro Area), Ministry of Economics (Japan), OECD Economic Outlook (Canada, Germany, France, Italy, Denmark, Switzerland, Norway, Sweden, Spain, Finland, Austria, Netherlands, Belgium, Australia, Korea, United Kingdom, Portugal, Ireland, New Zealand), Datastream
Unemployment gap	The difference between the quarterly unemployment rate and the NAIRU	FRED (USA-unemployment rate), CBO (USA-NAIRU), Bank of Japan (Japan), OECD (Canada, Germany, France Italy, Denmark, Switzerland, Norway, Sweden, Spain, Finland, Austria, Netherlands, Belgium, Australia, Korea, Euro Area, United Kingdom, Portugal, Ireland, New Zealand-NAIRU), national statistics institutes (Canada, Germany, France Italy, Denmark, Switzerland, Norway, Sweden, Spain, Finland, Austria, Netherlands, Belgium, Australia, Korea, Euro Area, United Kingdom, Portugal, Ireland, New Zealand- unemployment rate), Datastream, Bloomberg
Long term expected inflation rate	The inflation expectations in 5–10 year or, alternatively, the objective of inflation of the central bank	Consensus (USA, Japan, Canada, Germany, France, Italy), Central Banks webpages (Denmark, Switzerland, Norway, Sweden, Spain, Finland, Austria, Netherlands, Belgium, Australia, Korea, Euro Area, United Kingdom, Portugal, Ireland, New Zealand)
Core import prices	Annualized quarterly import prices rate-excluding fuel-	Bureau of Economic Analysis (USA), European Central Bank (Euro Area), ONS (United Kingdom), Minisitry of Economics (Japan), Oxford Economics (Canada, Germany, France, Italy, Denmark, Switzerland, Norway, Sweden, Spain, Finland, Austria, Netherlands, Belgium, Australia, Korea, Portugal, Ireland, New Zealand), own calculations
Output gap	The difference between actual and potential GDP as a percentage of potential GDP	FRED (USA), Bank of Japan (Japan), Oxford Economics (Euro Area, United Kingdom, Australia, Canada, Denmark, Switzerland, Norway, Sweden, Korea, Germany, France, Italy, Spain, Ireland, Finland, Portugal, Austria, Netherlands, Belgium), WEO (New Zealand)

References

Adam K, J Zhu (2014) Price level changes and the redistribution of nominal wealth across the euro area. ECB working paper, 1853
Agarwal R, Kimball M (2015) Breaking through the zero lower bound. IMF working paper, 15/224
Ahearne A, Gagnon J, Haltmaier J, Kamin S, Erceg C, Faust J, Guerrieri L, Hemphill C, Kole L, Roush J, Rogers J, Sheets N, Wright J (2002) Preventing deflation: lessons from Japan's experience in the 1990s. Board of Governors of the Federal Reserve System, international finance discussion, paper 729
Alberola E, Estrada A, Santabárbara D (2013) Growth beyond imbalances. Sustainable growth rates and output gap reassessment. Banco de España, Documento de Trabajo 1313
Álvarez LJ, Urtasun A (2013) Variation in the cyclical sensitivity of Spanish inflation: an initial approximation. Banco de España Econ Bull July–Aug, 11–17
Álvarez LJ, Gómez A, Urtasun A (2015) Asymmetries in the relationship between inflation and activity. Banco de España Econ Bull Nov, 19–25
Álvarez LJ, Sánchez I, Urtasun A (2017) The effect of oil price fluctuations on Spanish inflation. Banco de España Anal Articles, May
Arias J, Erceg C, Trabandt M (2015) The macroeconomic risks of undesirably low inflation. In: Presented at the conference "The Post-Crisis Slump". European Commission, Brussels, 1–2 Oct
Aruoba SB, Schorfheide F (2015) Inflation during and after the zero lower bound. In: Presented at the Jackson Hole symposium, Federal Reserve Bank of Kansas City
Auer RA, Degen K, Fischer AM (2011) Low-wage import competition, inflationary pressure, and industry dynamics in Europe. Swiss National Bank working paper 2011/9
Auer RA, Borio C, Filardo A (2017) The globalisation of inflation: the growing importance of global value chains. BIS working papers 602
Ball LM (2006) Has globalization changed inflation? NBER working paper 12687
Ball LM (2014) The case for a long-run inflation target of four percent. IMF working paper 14/92
Ball LM, Mazumder S (2011) Inflation dynamics and the great recession. Brook Pap Econ Act, 337–381. Spring
Ball LM, Mazumder S (2015) A Phillips curve with anchored expectations and short-term unemployment. IMF working paper 15/39
Banco de España (2015) Inflationary dynamics of the Spanish economy in the context of the euro area. Chapter 4 of the annual report 2014, pp 99–123
Bank of England (2015) The effect of imported price pressures on UK consumer prices. Box in the inflation report, Nov, pp 28–29
Bank of Japan (2016) Comprehensive assessment: developments in economic activity and prices as well as policy effects since the introduction of quantitative and qualitative monetary easing (QQE). Background note, Sept 21, 2016
Bentolila S, Dolado JJ, Jimeno JF (2007) Does immigration affect the Phillips curve? Some evidence for Spain. IZA discussion paper 3249
Berganza JC (2014) El comportamiento del mercado de trabajo de Estados Unidos durante y después de la Gran Recesión. Banco de España, Boletín Económico, May, 67–79
Berganza JC, del Río P, Borrallo F (2016) Determinants and implications of low global inflation rates. Banco de España, Documento Ocasional 1608
Bernanke BS (2002) Deflation: making sure "it" doesn't happen here. In: Speech at the National Economists Club, Washington, 21 Nov
Bernanke BS (2007) Globalization and monetary policy. In: Speech at the 4th economic summit, Stanford Institute for Economic Policy Research, Stanford, California, 2 March
BIS (2014) Growth and inflation: drivers and prospects. In: Chapter 3, 84th annual report, pp 41–64
BIS (2015) Another year of monetary policy accommodation. In: Chapter 4, 85th annual report, pp 65–82
BIS (2016) Monetary policy: inching towards normalisation. In: Chapter 4, 86th annual report, pp 63–82

BIS (2017) Monetary policy: inching towards normalisation. In: Chapter 4, 87th annual report, pp 59–78
Blanchard OJ, Dell'Ariccia G, Mauro P (2010) Rethinking macro policy. J Money Credit Bank 42(Supplement s1):199–215
Blanchard OJ, Galí J (2010) The macroeconomic effects of oil price shocks: why are the 2000s so different from the 1970s? In: Galí J, Gertler MJ (eds) International dimensions of monetary policy. University of Chicago Press, pp 373–421
Blanchard O, Cerutti E, Summers L (2015) Inflation and activity—two explorations, and their monetary policy implications. IMF working paper 15/230
Borio C, Filardo A (2007) Globalisation and inflation: new cross-country evidence on the global determinants of domestic inflation. BIS working papers 227
Borio C, Disyatat P, Juselius M (2013) Rethinking potential output: embedding information about the financial cycle. BIS working papers 404
Borio C, Erdem M, Filardo A, Hofmann B (2015) The costs of deflations: a historical perspective. BIS Q Rev, 31–54
Broadbent B (2015) Compositional shifts in the labour market. In: Speech at the conference understanding the great recession: from micro to macro. Bank of England, 23 Sept
Buiter WH (2003) Deflation: prevention and cure. In: NBER working paper 9623
Campa JM, Goldberg LS (2008) Pass-through of exchange rates to consumption prices: what has changed and why? In: Ito T, Rose AK (eds) International financial issues in the Pacific Rim: global imbalances, financial liberalization, and exchange rate policy (NBER-EASE), vol 17. The University of Chicago Press, pp 139–176
Canzoneri M, Cumby R, Diba B (2015) Monetary policy and the natural rate of interest. J Money Credit Bank 47(2–3):383–414
Carney M (2015) Inflation in a globalised world. In: Speech at the Jackson Hole symposium, Federal Reserve Bank of Kansas City
Chung H, Laforte JP, Reifschneider D, Williams JC (2012) Have we underestimated the likelihood and severity of zero lower bound events? J Money Credit Bank 44:47–82
Ciccarelli M, Mojon B (2010) Global inflation. Rev Econ Stat 92(3):524–535
Ciccarelli M, García JA (2015) International spillovers in inflation expectations, ECB working paper 1857
Ciccarelli M, Osbat C (2017) Low inflation in the euro area: causes and consequences. ECB occasional paper 181
Ciccarelli M, García JA, Montes-Galdón C (2017) Unconventional monetary policy and the anchoring of inflation expectations. ECB working paper 1995
Comunale M, Kunovac D (2017) Exchange rate pass-through in the euro area. ECB working paper no 2003
Daly MC, Hobijn B (2014) Downward nominal wage rigidities bend the Phillips curve. Federal Reserve Bank of San Francisco working paper 2013-08
ECB (2006) Effects of the rising trade integration of low-cost countries on euro area. Box in the Monthly Bulletin, Aug, 56–57
ECB (2015) Developments in longer-term inflation expectations in the euro area. Box in the Economic Bulletin, 3:25–26
Eggertsson G, Woodford M (2003) The zero bound on interest rates and optimal monetary policy. Brook Pap Econ Act 1(2003), 139–233
Eickmeier S, Kühnlenz M (2013) China's role in global inflation dynamics. Deutsche Bundesbank discussion paper 07/2013
Engel E, Laubach T, Reifschneider D (2015) The macroeconomic effects of the Federal Reserve's unconventional monetary policies. Finance and economics discussion series 2015-005, Board of Governors of the Federal Reserve System, Washington
Evans C, Fisher J, Gourio F, Krane S (2015) Risk management for monetary policy near the zero lower bound. Federal Reserve Bank of Chicago, working paper 2015-03

Fischer S (2015) U.S. inflation developments. In: Speech at the Jackson Hole symposium, Federal Reserve Bank of Kansas City
Fisher I (1933) The debt-deflation theory of great depressions. Econometrica, Oct 337–57
Forbes K (2015) Much ado about something important: how do exchange rate movements affect inflation? In: Speech at the 7th money, macro and finance research group annual conference, Cardiff, 11 Sept 2015
Forbes K, Hjortsoe I, Nenova T (2015) The shocks matter: improving our estimates of exchange rate pass-through. Bank of England external MPC unit discussion paper 43
Forbes K, Hjortsoe I, Nenova T (2017) Shocks versus structure: explaining differences in exchange rate pass-through across countries and time. Bank of England external MPC unit discussion paper 50
Gilchrist S, Schoenle R, Sim J, Zakrajšek E (2015) Inflation dynamics during the financial crisis. Board of Governors of the Federal Reserve System, finance and economics discussion series paper, 2015-12
Gopinath G (2015) The international price system. In: Jackson Hole symposium, Federal Reserve Bank of Kansas City
Gordon RJ (2011) The history of the Phillips curve: consensus and bifurcation. Economica 78(1):10–50
Gürkaynak RS, Swanson E, Levin A (20) Does inflation targeting anchor long-run inflation expectations? Evidence from the U.S., UK, and Sweden. J Eur Econ Assoc 8(6):1208–1242
Haldane A (2015) How low can you go? In: Speech at portadown chamber of commerce, Northern Ireland, 18 Sept
Hara N, Hiraki K, Ichise Y (2015) Changing exchange rate pass-through in Japan: does it indicate changing pricing behavior? Bank of Japan working paper 15-E-4
Hatcher M, Minford P (2014) Inflation targeting vs. price-level targeting: a new survey of theory and empirics. https://voxeu.org
Hernando I, Santabárbara D, Vallés J (2018) The global real interest rate: past developments and outlook. Chapter 11 in this volume
IMF (2006) How has globalization affected inflation? Chapter 3, World Economic Outlook, Apr, pp 97–134
IMF (2013). The dog that didn't bark: has inflation been muzzled or was it just sleeping? Chapter 3, World Economic Outlook, Apr, pp 79–96
IMF (2016) Global disinflation in an era of constrained monetary policy. Chapter 3, World Economic Outlook, Oct, pp 121–170
Izquierdo M, Puente S (2015) Wage response to changes in the cyclical situation: an estimate based on MCVL social security administrative labour records. Banco de España Econ Bull June, pp 21–25
Juselius M, Takáts E (2015) Can demography affect inflation and monetary policy? BIS working papers 485
Kiley MT (2014) An evaluation of the inflationary pressure associated with short and long-term unemployment. Board of Governors of the Federal Reserve System, finance and economics discussion series, 2014-28
Kumar MS, Baig T, Decressin J, Faulkner-MacDonach C, Feyziogùlu T (2003) Deflation: determinants, risks, and policy options, IMF occasional paper 221
Kumar S, Afrouzi H, Coibion O, Gorodnichenko Y (2015) Inflation targeting does not anchor inflation expectations: evidence from firms in New Zealand. In: Brookings paper on economic activity, fall 2015 conference
Laubach T, Williams JC (2015) Measuring the natural rate of interest redux. Federal Reserve Bank of San Francisco, working paper 2015–16
Linder MH, Peach R, Rich R (2012) Compensation growth and slack in the current economic environment. Liberty Street Economics, Federal Reserve Bank of New York, 19 Nov
Locarno A, Delle Monache D, Busetti F, Gerali A (2017) Trust, but verify. De-anchoring of inflation expectations under learning and heterogeneity. ECB working paper 1994

Lyziak T, Paloviita M (2016) Anchoring of inflation expectations in the euro area: recent evidence based on survey data. ECB Working paper 1945
Mankiw NG (2009) It may be time for the Fed to go negative. New York Times, 18 Apr
Mehrotra A, Yetman J (2014) Decaying expectations: what inflation forecasts tell us about the anchoring of inflation expectations. BIS working papers 464
Mikolajun I, Lodge D (2016) Advanced economy inflation: the role of global factors. ECB working paper 1948
Montero JM, Urtasun A (2014) Price-cost mark-ups in the Spanish economy: a microeconomic perspective. Banco de España, Documentos de Trabajo 1407
Musso A, Stracca L, Van Dijk D (2009) Instability and nonlinearity in the euro-area Phillips curve. Int J Central Bank 5(2):181–212
Neri S, Nobili A, Conti AM (2017) Low inflation and monetary policy in the euro area. ECB working paper 2005
Nickel C, Bobeica E, Lis E, Sun Y (2017) Demographics and inflation. ECB working paper 2006
Oinonen S, Paloviita M (2014) Updating the euro area Phillips curve: the slope has increased. Bank of Finland research discussion papers 31–2014
Orphanides A, Van Norden S (2005) The reliability of inflation forecasts based on output gap estimates in real time. J Money Credit Bank 37(3):583–601
Pescatori A, Turunen J (2015) Lower for longer: neutral rates in the United States. IMF working paper 15/135
Rachel L, Smith TD (2015) Secular drivers of the global real interest rate. Bank of England staff working paper 571
Reifschneider D (2016) Gauging the ability of the FOMC to respond to future recessions. Finance and economics, discussion series 2016-068, Board of Governors of the Federal Reserve System, Washington
Reifschneider D, Williams JC (2000) Three lessons for monetary policy in a low inflation era. J Money Credit Bank 32(4):936–966
Riggi M, Venditti F (2014) Surprise! Euro area inflation has fallen. Bank of Italy, Questioni di Economia e Finanza, 237
Rogoff K (2006) Impact of globalization on monetary policy. In: Presented at the Jackson Hole symposium, Federal Reserve Bank of Kansas City
Rogoff K (2016) The curse of cash. Princeton University Press
Semmler W, Gross M (2017) Mind the output gap: the disconnect of growth and inflation during recessions and convex Phillips curves in the euro area. ECB working paper, 2004
Shirakawa M (2012) Demographic changes and macroeconomic performance—Japanese experiences. In: Speech at the conference BOJ-IMES, Institute for Monetary and Economic Studies, Bank of Japan, Tokyo, 30 May 2012
Staiger DO, Stock JH, Watson MW (1997) How precise are estimates of the natural rate of unemployment? In: Romer CD, Romer DH (eds) Reducing inflation: motivation and strategy. University of Chicago Press, pp 195–246
Stock JH, Watson MW (2010) Modeling inflation after the crisis. NBER working paper 16488
Stella A, Stock JH (2013) A state-dependent model for inflation forecasting. Board of Governors of the Federal Reserve System, International Finance Discussion Papers No 1062
Svensson LEO (2015) The possible unemployment cost of average inflation below a credible target. Am Econ J Macroecon 7(1):258–296
Williams JC (2016) Monetary policy in a low R-star world. FRBSF Economic Letter, 2016-23
Woodford M (2010) Globalization and monetary control. In: Gali J, Gertler MJ (eds) International dimensions of monetary policy. University of Chicago Press, pp 13–77
Woodford M (2013) Monetary policy targets after the crisis. In: Paper presented at the rethinking macro policy II: first steps and early lessons, conference hosted by the IMF
Yellen JL (2006) Monetary policy in a global environment. In: Speech at The Euro and the Dollar in a globalized economy conference, U.C. Santa Cruz, 27 May

Yellen JL (2014) Labor market dynamics and monetary policy. In: Speech at the Jackson Hole symposium, Federal Reserve Bank of Kansas City
Yellen JL (2015) Inflation dynamics and monetary policy. In: Speech at The Philip Gamble Memorial Lecture, University of Massachusetts, 24 September
Yellen JL (2016) The Federal Reserve's monetary policy toolkit: past, present and future. In: Speech at the Jackson Hole symposium, Federal Reserve Bank of Kansas City

The Global Real Interest Rate: Past Developments and Outlook

Ignacio Hernando, Daniel Santabárbara and Javier Vallés

Abstract There is ample evidence that real interest rates have progressively declined and converged since the 1980s in most advanced and emerging economies, to stand currently at very low levels. The persistence of this trend and its intensification during the global financial crisis have raised a series of highly relevant issues in different areas. We follow a conceptual framework where global real interest rates are determined by the supply of (saving) and the demand for (investment) loanable funds at the global level. Against this background, this chapter analyses the determinants of this trend from a global perspective highlighting how globalisation and increasing financial integration, contributed to increase the influence of the emerging market economies since the beginning of this century. In the wake of the global financial crisis other factors in place were the subsequent reduction in the propensity to invest, the increase in precautionary saving, the introduction of non-standard monetary policies or the increase in income inequality. Looking forward, this chapter argues that the normalisation of monetary policies, the change in the growth model of certain emerging countries and the socio-demographic and productivity trends would point to a gradual recovery in real interest rates over a medium-term horizon, albeit with a high degree of uncertainty. Over the longer term, this trend may tail off against a background of limited technological progress or a sharper-than-expected decline in investment in the emerging economies.

This chapter is an updated version of the article of the same title published in the Banco de España Economic Bulletin, January 2016.

I. Hernando (✉) · D. Santabárbara · J. Vallés
Banco de España, Madrid, Spain
e-mail: hernando@bde.es

D. Santabárbara
e-mail: daniel.santabarbara@bde.es

J. Vallés
e-mail: jvalles@bde.es

L. Ferrara et al. (eds.), *International Macroeconomics in the Wake of the Global Financial Crisis*, Financial and Monetary Policy Studies 46,
https://doi.org/10.1007/978-3-319-79075-6_11

1 Introduction

The real interest rate (i.e. the nominal return after discounting for expected inflation) is a key macroeconomic variable since it determines economic agents' intertemporal investment and consumption decisions. The equilibrium real interest rate is that which equates the supply (saving) and demand (investment) for loanable funds or, in other words, makes the marginal productivity of capital equal to the compensation that savers require to delay their consumption. This concept is closely linked to the real interest rate used in the business cycle literature, which is defined as that consistent with the use of all productive resources in an economy without any type of financial or real frictions (Wicksell 1898). This natural interest rate measures the return associated with the economy's potential growth and depends on fundamental parameters such as productivity and population growth, and the elasticity of intertemporal substitution, which measures consumers' readiness to delay their consumption.

The growing trade and financial integration of recent decades has seen real interest rates in every economy increasingly influenced by international developments. The progressive opening up of economies, with growing trade and financial flows, has enabled economies with investment requirements not covered by their domestic saving to resort to other countries' excess saving, such that financing flows towards countries where it is more profitable, generating global gains. Accordingly, a global real interest rate may be defined as that which equates the supply and demand for loanable funds at the global level. From this perspective, real interest rates are increasingly determined by factors common to all countries that depend on saving and investment at the global level.

There is a large evidence that real interest rates have progressively declined since the 1980s in most advanced and emerging market economies to stand currently at very low levels. The persistence and intensification of this trend during the global financial crisis led to consideration of a series of highly relevant issues in different areas (Teulings and Baldwin 2014). First, it can be asked to what extent the task of monetary policy of steering the interest rate towards its natural level is made more difficult by the fact that this natural interest rate may be very low (or even negative, if adverse macroeconomic shocks occur), given the current context of persistent low inflation rates, which means that nominal interest rates need to be significantly negative (Summers 2014). Further, the existence of excessively low interest rates for prolonged periods raises the question of the implications for financial stability. Lastly, there is the question of whether this situation is actually the reflection of a substantial reduction in potential growth at the global level.

Against this background, this chapter analyses the determinants of this trend from a global perspective, discussing the extent to which it is likely to continue in the medium and long term. In this connection, the following section reviews the main stylised facts relating to real interest rate developments. The third section discusses the determinants that the literature has related to the trends observed, differentiating between various time periods and highlighting the influence of the emerging market economies, since the beginning of this century, and of other factors that have operated

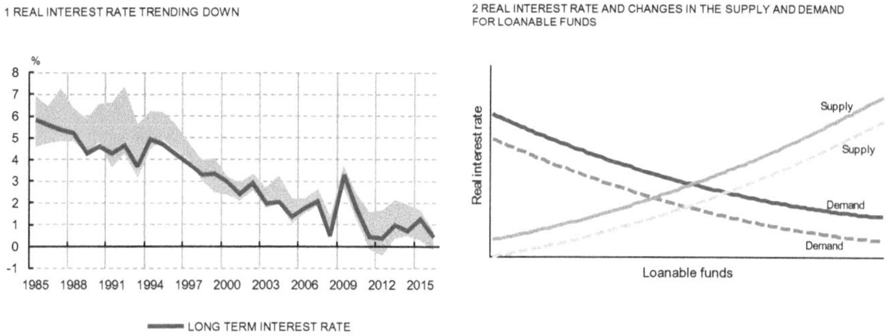

Fig. 1 Real interest rate *Source* Bank for International Settlements (BIS)

in the wake of the global financial crisis. The fourth section discusses some medium and long-term trends that may affect the future course of interest rates.

2 The Global Interest Rate

The equilibrium real interest rate is not a directly observable variable. As it is a key variable for understanding economic agents' decision-making, it is usually proxied at a specific term by the nominal return on public debt (considered as the safe asset in each economy) at that term less the inflation expectations over that same horizon.[1]

The left-hand panel of Fig. 1 tracks the average real interest rate (weighted by GDP) on the 10-year public debt of the main advanced economies since 1981. Two notable trends can be appreciated in the Figure (see also Blanchard et al. 2014).

The gradual decline in the real interest rate from levels around 5% in the mid-1980s to around 2% at the onset of the financial crisis, and ultimately approximately zero since 2012.

The reduction in the dispersion between the interest rates in an environment of greater financial integration, which heightens the importance of the common global factors in the determination of each country's real interest rates.

Indeed, assuming a high degree of financial integration between the main economies, global real interest rates will be determined by the supply of (saving) and the demand for (investment) loanable funds at the global level.[2] Under normal con-

[1]An alternative is to use the yields on inflation-indexed public debt instruments directly, but these are available only for a small number of economies and a very short period. Moreover, the markets for these assets are usually less liquid than those for traditional public debt, so that premiums may arise which complicate the interpretation of yields.

[2]Although financial integration had been increasing until the global financial crisis, during the period analysed there were significant restrictions on the mobility of capital flows, especially in emerging market economies, of which China is the best example. The consensus in the literature on international finance is that the advanced economies have closely interconnected capital markets,

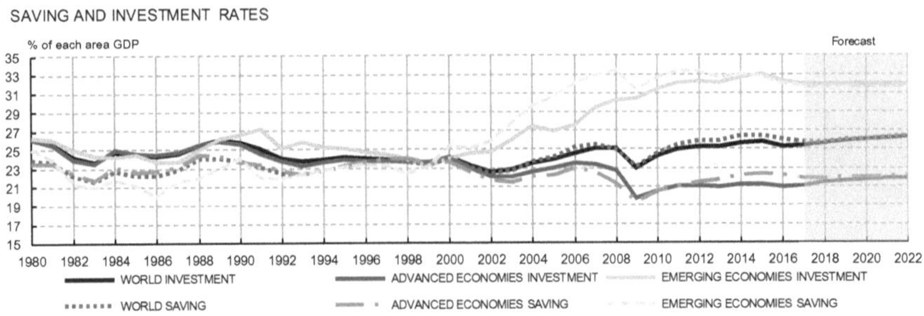

Fig. 2 Saving and investment rates *Source* IMF, WEO, April 2017

ditions, the supply of loanable funds increases with the interest rate, so that interest rate rises entail increases in saving and reductions in consumption (i.e. in consumption decisions, negative substitution and wealth effects predominate over the positive income effect), while the demand for funds will decline with the interest rate, so that interest rate rises entail falls in investment (see right-hand panel of Fig. 1).

In this conceptual framework, the fall in real interest rates may occur either due to a rightward shift in the saving curve (agents desire to save more at current rates) or to a leftward shift in global investment (agents prefer to invest less at current rates), or to a combination of both these developments. Figure 1 shows how positive shocks to global saving are associated with a decline in real interest rates accompanied by increases in global saving and investment. Negative shocks to investment also prompt falls in real interest rates, while global saving and investment diminish. The combination of a simultaneous increase in the propensity to save and decline in the propensity to invest would lead to a fall in real interest rates and an indeterminate effect on saving and investment.

Figure 2 shows saving and investment rates[3] for the global economy, the advanced economies and the emerging market economies.[4] The following stylised facts are apparent in this Figure:

- The relative stability of global saving and investment rates since the 1980s, despite the fall in interest rates over this period, although a mild upward trend is apparent from the early 2000s, which was only interrupted during the global financial crisis.

while the integration of the emerging market economies into the international financial system is more recent and limited. As a result, the implicit assumption of financial integration underlying the conceptual framework in which the interest rate is determined by the balance of the global supply and demand for funds needs to be considered with caution. Moreover, one possible side effect of the global financial crisis is an increase in financial fragmentation, which may reduce the importance of global factors in the determination of saving and investment at the global level.

[3]The differences between global saving and investment rates arise from statistical discrepancies.

[4]Saving and investment rates are calculated as nominal saving and investment, respectively, divided by nominal GDP. However, significant changes in relative prices must have occurred, since the price of investment goods shows a downward trend relative to the economy as a whole, which would lead to a higher investment rate at constant prices than in nominal terms.

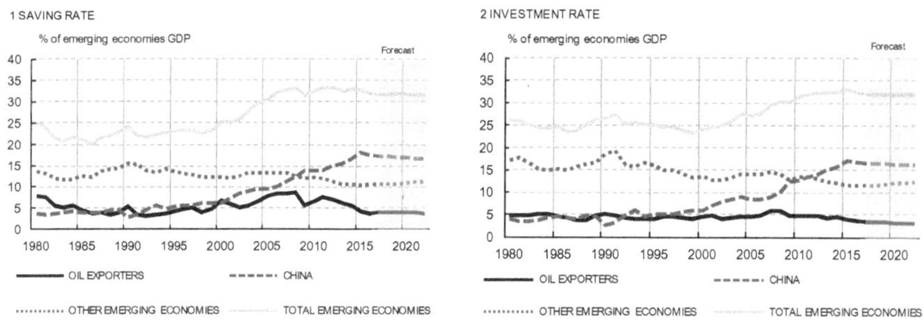

Fig. 3 Saving and investment in emerging economies *Source* IMF, WEO, April 2017

- In the advanced economies there was a fall in saving and investment rates from the start of the century, which intensified after the global financial crisis. Since then there has been a slight recovery, to rates of around 21% at present.
- By contrast, saving and investment rates in the emerging market economies increased substantially from the end of the 1990s, following certain significant regional crises and coinciding with the intensification of globalisation and greater financial integration. After the crisis, these ratios stabilised, but they remain above 30%.

In the early years of this century, the increase in saving in the emerging economies was much larger than the increase in investment, these economies providing net financing to the rest of the world, contradicting the simplest models of location of investment, which predicts that funds go where capital is scarcer. The saving rate of the emerging market economies increased notably after 2000. Consequently, the global saving rate increased between 2000 and 2007 by 1.6 percentage points (pp), of which 1.5 pp may be attributed to the increase in saving in the emerging economies, 0.8 pp to the increase in their weight in world GDP, and a negative contribution of −0.7 pp to the advanced economies. The increase in saving has been concentrated in a small number of economies, essentially China and commodity exporters (see Fig. 3). Nevertheless, the fall in commodity prices (in particular, in oil prices since mid-2014) has led to a significant reduction in the saving rates of commodity exporters.

3 Determinants of the Global Real Interest Rate

Since the real interest rate is the price that equates the desired supply and demand for loanable funds, its path is determined by those factors that influence agents' propensity to save and to invest. There is an abundance of theoretical and empirical literature that has studied the determinants of saving and investment decisions.[5] Among the

[5]See, for example, Desroches and Francis (2010), IMF (2014a), Grigoli et al. (2014), Bean et al. (2015), Rachel and Smith (2015), or the numerous references cited in these papers.

factors which explain the path of saving, may be distinguished those linked to structural factors and those associated with economic policies. In the first group, economic theory has highlighted the level and growth of income, demographics and uncertainty, which leads to saving for precautionary motives. Economic policies (for example, fiscal policy, the characteristics of the welfare state, inequality or the level of financial development, closely linked to regulation) may also influence the path of saving. Among the determinants of investment, besides standard variables like the marginal product of capital, the cost of capital or firms' profits, the literature has highlighted the uncertainty regarding future income, the demographic structure, the productive structure, urbanisation and financial development. In this case, economic policies can also play a notable role: directly, through public investment and the development of infrastructure, and, indirectly, by creating an environment conducive to the profitability of private investment.

Other factors also influence the path of the real interest rate, in addition to the determinants of saving and investment. On the one hand, the imbalance between the supply of and the demand for safe affects the profitability of safe assets. On the other, monetary policy through inflation expectations and the yield curve, affects long-term real interest rates, although the potential deviations from the natural interest rate will be temporary. Moreover, foreign policy rates may also affect the dynamics of local real long-term government bond yields.[6]

The conjunction of determinants that has led to the fall in the global real interest rate has prompted some debate, against a background of relatively stable global saving and investment rates, which is one of the stylised facts presented in the previous section. These trends would be compatible with an increase in the propensity to save, which would involve a rightward shift in the supply of loanable funds, taking place at the same time as a reduction in the propensity to invest, which would move the demand curve for funds leftward (see Fig. 1). However, other explanations are possible. For example, if the supply of funds (i.e. saving) is very insensitive to changes in interest rates (so that substitution and wealth effects are fully offset by the income effect), a reduction in the propensity to invest would give rise to a fall in the interest rate, with no effect on the amounts exchanged. Likewise, if investment were insensitive to changes in interest rates (as may have been the case, to some extent, following the global financial crisis), an increase in the propensity to save would lead to a fall in the real rate, with no change in equilibrium saving and investment.

The possible determinants of the path of real interest rates are reviewed below, highlighting the changes observed in the composition of saving and investment by geographical area and over time.

[6]Rawdanowicz et al. (2017) find little robust evidence about the role of proxies of the supply of and demand for government bonds to explain real interest rates. However, they find that real government bond yields are closely linked with real policy interest rates.

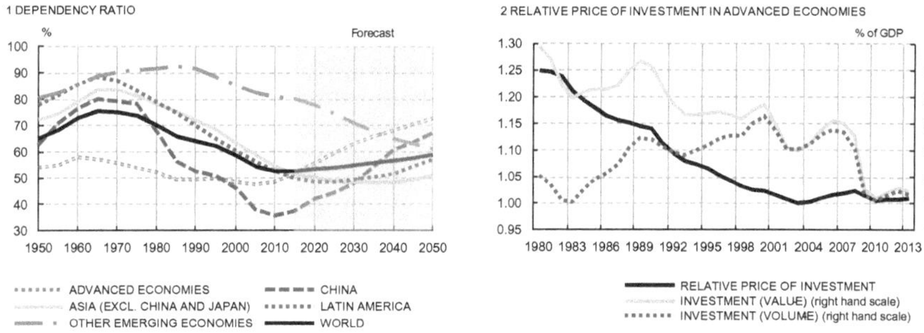

Fig. 4 Determinants of saving and investment *Source* UN and IMF (2014a)

3.1 Socio-Demographic Changes and Investment Shifts in the Advanced Economies (1980–2000)

In the last two decades of the 20th century, the advanced economies played a central role in global saving and investment developments. Limited financial integration at the global level and the low weight of the emerging market economies meant that their impact on global saving and investment decisions was small. As a result, the overall trend in real interest rates was determined by the increase in the readiness to save and the decline in the propensity to invest in the advanced economies.

In the 1980s, in most of the advanced economies longevity continued to rise and in some of them fertility began to fall. Against this background, the relative weight of the middle-aged segment of the population increased and, consequently, dependency ratios[7] fell (see left-hand panel of Fig. 4). According to life cycle theory, this segment has the highest wage income and the highest propensity to save for retirement, so that an increase in its relative weight boosts the aggregate propensity to save. In addition, technological progress and the start of globalisation would have led to an increase in wage dispersion, which may have increased the aggregate propensity to save, by increasing the income of richer people, who have higher saving rates (Bean et al. 2015). Low-skilled workers have suffered an erosion of their relative income in the advanced economies, deriving from the changes entailed by automation of many regular tasks and higher consumption of goods produced by the abundant labour available in the emerging economies. In conjunction with this, the increasing uncertainty regarding the sustainability of the welfare state led to an increase in individual protection. Conversely, financial deregulation would have helped eliminate liquidity constraints, limiting the increase in the readiness to save.

Among the factors that contributed to the decline in the propensity to invest in the period 1980–2000, the transformation of the productive structure of the advanced economies (with the weight of financial and business services growing, to the detriment of manufacturing) and the decline in the relative price of investment goods (see

[7]The ratio between the population aged under15 and over 64 and the population aged between 15 and 64.

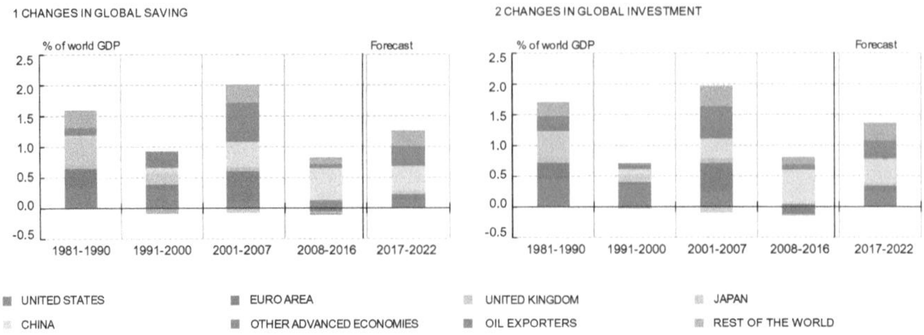

Fig. 5 Increase in saving and investment. Geographic distribution *Source* IMF, WEO, April 2017

right-hand panel of Fig. 4) may be highlighted.[8] Indeed, insofar as the investment content of services is more limited than that of industry, the shift in activity toward services contributed to reducing the rate of investment in the advanced economies, although the available evidence suggests that this composition effect is of limited quantitative importance (OECD 2015). The relative price of investment goods displayed a downward trend as a result of the technological progress incorporated into this type of goods, which has led to a gradual increase in their efficiency. Thus, although this development favoured the growth of investment in real terms, the nominal demand for funds to invest fell relative to GDP.[9] An additional factor was the downward trend in public investment in the advanced economies (IMF 2014b).

3.2 *The Growing Importance of the Emerging Market Economies (2000–2007)*

As mentioned in the second section, between 2000 and 2007 the emerging market economies, against a background of globalisation and increasing financial integration, contributed decisively to the increase in global saving and investment, playing a more important role in the evolution of global real interest rates. Figure 5 shows that China, along with the oil exporters, was the best example of these developments and, also, that the changes in saving were larger than those in investment, generating net lending by the emerging market economies. Indeed, Bernanke (2005) pointed to a "saving glut" in the emerging economies as the main determinant of the reduction in the real interest rate.

[8]See Berganza et al. (2015) for an analysis of the factors explaining the weakness of investment in the advanced economies.

[9]Problems related to the measurement of investment, stemming, for example, from the increasing importance of intangible assets and their possible undervaluation in the national accounts, would limit the decline in the observed investment rate.

The available empirical evidence suggests that sustained economic growth in the emerging market economies was the main determinant of the increase in the saving rate in this period (IMF 2014a). The determinants of saving in China, which accounts for approximately half of the saving of the emerging market economies, have a decisive influence on the behaviour of global saving. Bean et al. (2015) consider that the one child policy combined with limited social protection substantially boosted saving. Also, limited financial development and the protection of public corporations favoured the accumulation of retained earnings. The economic development strategy may also have played a role in the determination of saving. In this respect, China's exchange-rate policy throughout this period aimed to keep the renminbi exchange rate relatively stable and undervalued against the dollar. Upward pressures on the renminbi were countered, in order to stimulate exports and, consequently, economic growth. This resulted in the generation of very large current account surpluses. The pursuit of this strategy required restrictions on capital movements, which limited financial development and fostered a huge accumulation of international reserves.

At the same time, the increase in the prices of oil and other commodities from 2003, against a background of strong growth in the world economy, led to an increase in the saving of commodity exporters. An additional argument to explain the accumulation of reserves by the emerging market economies is that, following the financial crises of the 1990s, there was a tendency for self-insurance against possible future crises, given the limited development of global and regional institutional protection networks.

The increase in the foreign reserves of China and other emerging market economies, like the investments of the sovereign wealth funds of certain oil exporters (see left-hand panel of Fig. 6), mostly took the form of dollar-denominated fixed-income instruments, helping to finance the large US current account deficit. The limited development of the financial markets of the emerging market economies, along with the limited supply of safe assets, helps to explain this phenomenon (Caballero 2006). Thus, foreign holdings of US Treasury bonds increased considerably after 2000, largely due to the increase in the official holdings of these emerging market economies (see right-hand panel of Fig. 6). This phenomenon helps to explain the reduction in the real interest rate (Warnock and Warnock 2009; Bernanke et al. 2004; Beltran et al. 2013), and the increase in the equity premium, which may be associated with portfolio reallocation towards fixed-income instruments.

3.3 The Impact of the Global Financial Crisis (2008–2015)

As a result of the global financial crisis, various factors that are, to a greater or lesser extent, temporary, have continued to exert downward pressure on real interest rates. First, non-standard monetary policies have been geared towards reducing long-term interest rates, given the limited scope for changes in short-term rates. Specifically, sovereign bond purchases by the main central banks have had a composition effect on investors' portfolios, by reducing the return on safe assets and increasing the risk premia.

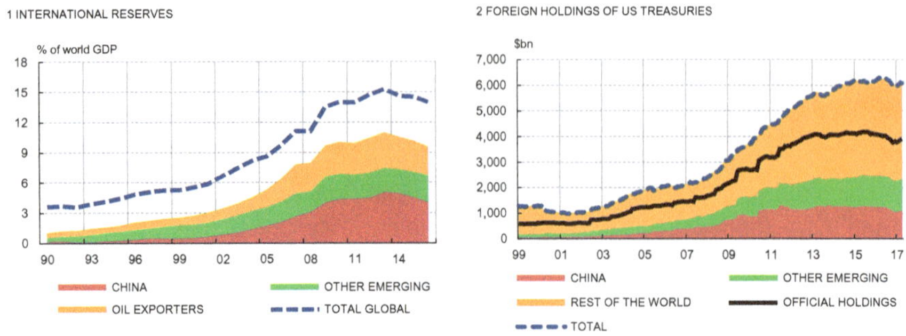

Fig. 6 Safe assets and portfolio shifts *Sources* IMF and US Department of the Treasury

Second, financial crises tend to reduce the propensity to invest, mainly as a result of the limited supply of financing and the more uncertain outlook (Berganza et al. 2015). Empirical evidence suggests that, three years after the start of a crisis, the ratio of investment to GDP will have fallen by between 3 and 3.5 pp (IMF 2014a). This is roughly the contraction recorded in the rate of investment in the developed countries following the global financial crisis. Moreover, in the euro area and in Japan, possibly due to their greater dependence on bank financing, business investment is recovering more slowly than in the United States and in the United Kingdom, and still stands below its pre-crisis level. Finally, those countries that have had to consolidate their public accounts following the crisis have, to some extent, used public investment as an item of adjustment.

The crisis also boosted the private sector's propensity to save for precautionary motives. First, because of the deterioration in income expectations and greater uncertainty; in addition, fiscal adjustment policies resulted in some cases in a limitation of the welfare state and, in particular, of public pensions, all of which led to an increase in private saving. At the same time, against a background of high corporate and household indebtedness in certain developed economies, the fall in the price of assets following the crisis obliged private agents to increase their saving rate in order to reduce the mismatches in their balance sheets and increase their ability to finance themselves, given the scarcity of credit. In parallel, the financial sector has tended to deleverage and increase the resources assigned to the creation of buffers to prevent the occurrence of crises and to reduce their cost if they do occur. These changes have, on aggregate, led to significant progress in the process of debt reduction in these economies since 2009 and to moderation in lending to finance investment. Also, fiscal consolidation has contributed to the increase in public saving in numerous economies.

Finally, changes in the distribution of income and wealth may also have boosted the propensity to save. The greater income inequality that had already been observed in the advanced economies since the 1980s, has been heightened in some countries following the crisis by higher and persistent unemployment rates and greater wage dispersion.

4 The Medium and Long-Term Outlook

As the recovery in the world economy takes hold, the effects of the financial crisis on the propensity to save and invest (partly linked to deleveraging) should ease, prompting some recovery in the real interest rate. Monetary policy will push nominal interest rates upwards as output gaps close and inflation rises. However, the application of the Basel III accords on capital and liquidity ratios will increase financial institutions' demand for safe assets in the coming years, exerting downward pressure on the real interest rate.

In the medium term, the propensity to save may decline as a result of China's policies to rebalance its economy and if oil prices remain low for a prolonged period. The Chinese authorities are currently pursuing a strategy to achieve more balanced growth, involving improvements in social protection, financial development and the liberalisation of cross-border flows, all of which should reduce saving arising from the precautionary motive and liquidity constraints. However, if the reforms lead to broad liberalisation of the capital account, China's high volume of savings will have a greater impact on the global real interest rate. In any event, the current account surplus of the Chinese economy has significantly decreased and the Chinese authorities have slowed down the process of removal of capital controls. The global propensity to save will also tend to decline if commodity prices remain at their current low levels, since the propensity to consume of oil importers tends to be greater than that of oil exporters. As regards investment in the emerging market economies, the slowdown in potential growth with respect to the period before the global financial crisis will entail less investment in infrastructure associated with industrialisation and urbanisation.

In the longer term, there is widespread agreement that two real factors will be important in the path of global saving and investment: demographics and technological change.

Increasing life expectancy and declining fertility are trends common to advanced and emerging market economies, albeit with somewhat different timing, which will tend to reduce the readiness to save. While population ageing began in the developed countries in the 1980s, in many emerging economies it is beginning at the moment, especially in Asia. In the initial stages of the ageing process, the aggregate propensity to save increases, as the middle-aged section of the population, which saves to finance lengthening retirement periods, increases in weight. In later stages, as the relative weight of the eldest groups increases, the propensity to save will tend to fall, while public saving will tend to be reduced due to the pressure on the health budget and public pension systems. These trends are clearly reflected in the path of the dependency ratio, as the UN projections to 2050 of population composition by geographical area (see left-hand panel of Fig. 4) indicate.

The reduction in the working-age population inherent in this process will also affect the propensity to invest. In principle, the decline in the labour force may generate an increase in wages and a substitution of capital for labour, intensifying productive processes with greater investment. However, the empirical evidence suggests that the relationship between these two factors of production at the aggregate level is positive, so that upward pressure on the rate of investment should not be expected in coming years.

These population ageing and labour force trends may be partially moderated by decisions such as those taken in certain European countries to raise the effective age of retirement in order to boost the sustainability of their pension systems. Possibly of greater importance will be the economic policy measures of countries such as China, given their greater weight at the global level. Notable in this respect is China's recent announcement of the end of the one child policy, to boost the birth rate.

A second decisive factor in determining the path of the long-term real interest rate, on account of its notable effect on the propensity to invest, is total factor productivity, which measures the level of technological progress of an economy. There is currently a debate regarding the level of innovation to be expected over the coming decades. On one hand, Gordon (2015) has argued that, at best, the United States will continue to post the low rates of technological change that have been recorded since 1980 (around 0.6% per annum), well below those of the period 1920–1970, when many of the advances of the second Industrial Revolution were incorporated. Other authors, however, maintain that the interaction between science and technology will involve a fresh boost to progress, through industries such as information and comunications, biotechnology and robotics, activities that are, in any case, still not adequately reflected in the measurement of GDP (Mokyr 2014). From an international perspective, European countries have on average failed to surpass the technological progress seen in the United States in recent decades and a large part of the progress in emerging countries stems from incorporating the innovations of the technologically most advanced countries. As discussed in Council of Economic Advisers (2015) on the basis of OECD's long-term projections, productivity growth in the long run is projected to be somewhat lower than in the recent past, what is more in line with the first hypothesis.

Accordingly, the normalisation of monetary policies, the change in the growth model of certain emerging countries and the socio-demographic and productivity trends would point to a gradual recovery in real interest rates, over a medium-term horizon, albeit with a high degree of uncertainty, both as regards the magnitude of the rise and its timing. Over the longer term, this trend may tail off against a background of limited technological progress, which fails to boost investment, or a sharper-than-expected decline in investment in the emerging economies.

References

Bean CR, Broda C, Ito T, Kroszner R (2015) Low for long? Causes and consequences of persistently low interest rates. Geneva report on the world economy 17. ICMB and London: CEPR Press Geneva

Beltran DO, Kretchmer M, Marquez J, Thomas CP (2013) Foreign holdings of U.S. treasuries and U.S. treasury yields. J Int Money Financ 32(1):1120–1143

Berganza JC, Romero M, Sastre T, Burriel P, Folch M (2015) La debilidad de la inversión empresarial en las economías desarrolladas. Boletín Económico, Banco de España, July

Bernanke BS (2005) The global saving glut and the U.S. current account deficit. Sandridge Lecture, Virginia Association of Economists, 14 Apr

Bernanke B, Reinhart V, Sack B (2004) Monetary policy alternatives at the zero bound: an empirical assessment. Finance and economics discussion series working paper no 48, Federal Reserve Board, Washington, DC

Blanchard OJ, Furceri D, Pescatori A (2014) A Prolonged Period of Low Interest Rates? In: Teulings C, Baldwin R (eds) Secular stagnation: facts. Causes and Cures, A VoxEU.org eBook

Caballero RJ (2006) On the macroeconomics of asset shortages. NBER working paper no 12753

Council of Economic Advisers (2015) Long-term interest rates: A survey. Executive Office of the President of the United States, Council of Economic Advisers, July.

Desroches B, Francis M (2010) World real interest rates: a global savings and investment perspective. Appl Econ 42:2801–2816

Grigoli F, Herman A, Schmidt-Hebbel YK (2014) World saving. IMF working papers 14/204

Gordon R (2015) US economic growth is over: the short run meets the long run. Mimeo

IMF (2014a) Prospective on global real interest rates, chapter 3. World Economic Outlook, April 2014

IMF (2014b) Is it time for an infrastructure push? The macroeconomic effects of public investment chapter 3. World Economic Outlook, October 2014

Mokyr J (2014) Secular stagnation? Not in your life. In: Teulings C, Baldwin R (eds) Secular stagnation: facts, causes and cures, A VoxEU.org eBook

OECD (2015) Lifting investment for higher sustainable growth. Chapter 3, Economic Outlook, v 2015/1

Rachel L, T Smith (2015) Secular drivers of the global real interest rate. Bank of England staff working papers, no 571

Rawdanowicz L, Hammouch M, Kasai M (2017) The fall in real long-term government bond yields: disentangling different drivers. OECD Economics Department working papers, no 1398, OECD Publishing, Paris

Summers LH (2014) US economic prospects: secular stagnation, hysteresis, and the zero lower bound. Bus Econ 49(2):65–73

Teulings C, Baldwin R (2014) Introduction. In: Teulings C, Baldwin R (eds) Secular stagnation: facts, causes and cures, A VoxEU.org eBook

Warnock F, Warnock V (2009) International capital flows and U.S. interest rates. J Int Money Financ 28(6):903–919

Wicksell K (1898) The influence of the rate of interest on commodity prices. In: Reprinted in Lindahl E (ed) Selected papers on economic theory by Knut Wicksell, 1958, pp 67–92

Part IV
Exchange Rate Shocks, Capital Flows and International Spillovers

The Nature of the Shock Matters: Some Model-Based Results on the Macroeconomic Effects of Exchange Rate

Sophie Haincourt

Abstract Exchange rate fluctuations have been particularly large since mid-2014, with the nominal effective exchange rate of the Dollar appreciating 22% between July 2014 and December 2016, well above normal fluctuation range. This article attempts to measure the impact of currency appreciation on domestic activity, accounting for the source of fluctuations. More specifically, by using the multi-country structural model NiGEM, we show that different types of exchange rate shocks can have different macroeconomic outcomes. Focusing on the period going from mid-2014 to December 2016, we show that the initial appreciation of the Dollar (from July 2014 to April 2015), coming from activity gaps and divergence in monetary policy expectations, choke 0.3 pp off US GDP growth, while the following phase of the currency appreciation, stemming from a fall in the Dollar risk premium would have been neutral, and even slightly positive, to US growth. When comparing the US with the euro area as regards the impact on growth, we get that the euro area is more sensitive than the US to a currency appreciation. As a result, a sustained rise in the currency could prove more challenging for the Euro area than for the US.

1 Motivation

Following the Global Financial Crisis, the central banks of the main advanced economies have strongly reacted to limit damages on economic activity by first cutting nominal short-term interest rates to reach the Zero Lower Bound. In a second step, various unconventional monetary policies have been implemented all over the world, ranging from large scale asset purchase programs to various forms of forward guidance. The common movement on short interest rates led to the fact that, for a while, the spread between interest rates of the US and other advanced countries was no more a driver of the bilateral exchange rate between the US Dollar and the currency of those countries (see for example Bussière et al. 2018 on this issue). As

S. Haincourt (✉)
Banque de France, Paris, France
e-mail: sophie.haincourt@banque-france.fr

L. Ferrara et al. (eds.), *International Macroeconomics in the Wake of the Global Financial Crisis*, Financial and Monetary Policy Studies 46,
https://doi.org/10.1007/978-3-319-79075-6_12

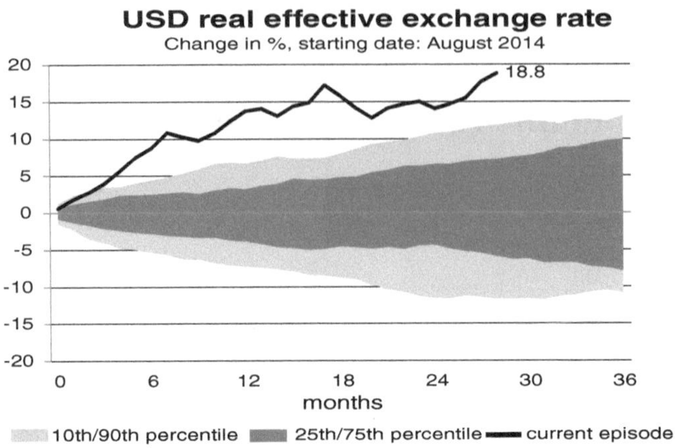

Fig. 1 Unusually large Dollar appreciation since mid-2014. *Source* Author's calculations based on BIS data (broad definition) as well as IMF calculation methodology described in the October 2015 WEO. Figures report Dollar and Euro historical fluctuation bands for real (consumer price adjusted) effective exchange rate based on all 36-month-long evolutions. Black lines indicate most recent exchange rate paths with no interruptions of more than 3 months. Last observation: December 2016

soon as the US economy started to recover, this led to expectations of tightening in the Fed monetary policy stance, leading in turn to a sharp US Dollar appreciation.

As a result, exchange rate fluctuations have been unusually large since mid-2014. The US Dollar, in particular, has appreciated by 22% between July 2014 and December 2016 in nominal effective terms and by 19% in real effective terms, while commodity currencies fell markedly in face of falling commodity prices and revised growth outlook. Although not unprecedented, such movements are well outside normal fluctuations ranges, in particular for the Dollar (see Fig. 1 as regards real evolutions).

Mirroring the US Dollar appreciation, the Euro depreciated by 5% in nominal effective terms and by 11% in real effective terms over the same period, consistent with the pursuing accommodative monetary policy carried out by the ECB (see Fig. 2 as regards real evolutions).

All the factors beyond this sharp US Dollar appreciation are not clearly identified. For example, by looking market-based measures of policy expectations, Fernald et al. (2017) do not find evidence that the Dollar has become more sensitive to interest rates since 2014. In spite of this, what is worrying is the impact of this appreciation on the domestic US economy. Indeed, exchange rate variations are important determinants of external positions, activity and inflation. But how are exchange rate fluctuations passed onto prices and volumes? The aim of this chapter is to assess the impact of exchange rate shocks in a context of a large-scale macroeconomic model. In particular, it seeks to show that different underlying causes of exchange rate fluctuations can lead to different outcomes for inflation and activity. We focus on the Dollar and

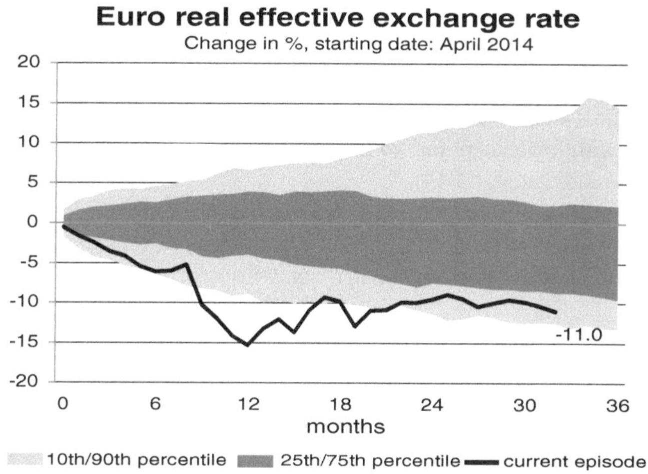

Fig. 2 Unusually large Euro depreciation since mid-2014. *Source* Author's calculations based on BIS data (broad definition) as well as IMF calculation methodology described in the October 2015 WEO. Figures report Dollar and Euro historical fluctuation bands for real (consumer price adjusted) effective exchange rate based on all 36-month-long evolutions. Black lines indicate most recent exchange rate paths with no interruptions of more than 3 months. Last observation: December 2016

Euro fluctuations over the period mid-2014 to end-2016 and their possible impact on inflation and activity in the US and the Euro area.

This chapter is organised as follows: after a brief overview of the literature, Sect. 1 presents simulation results of different types of exchange shocks using the global structural model NiGEM. Section 2 decomposes the fluctuations of the Dollar and Euro nominal effective exchange rates by the contributions of their currency counterparts, in an attempt to identify the types of exchange rate shocks. Based on these evidences, Sect. 3 builds a scenario reproducing the shocks experienced by the Dollar and the Euro over the period July 2014–December 2016. Using exchange rate pass-through estimates of the global NiGEM model, the article assesses the impact of the exchange rate shocks on prices and activity in the US and Euro area, accounting for spillovers across countries. Section 4 concludes.

2 'Good' Versus 'Bad' Currency Appreciations

The impact of exchange rate movements on inflation and activity has been the focus of numerous research studies, looking more particularly at the relationship between exchange rate movements and export and import prices (the so-called Exchange Rate Pass-Through, ERPT). Using firms' data, micro-economic studies focus on exporters' reaction of exchange rate changes in mark-ups and export volumes, with firm's productivity, currency invoicing and goods' homogeneity as main determinants. Macro-economic studies tend to look at the heterogeneity in countries' responses to exchange rate fluctuations, especially between advanced and emerging economies.

However, most studies tend to overlook the role played by the source of exchange rate changes, with few exceptions so far: Forbes (2014, 2015), Kirby and Meaning (2014), and Bussière et al. (2014).

In the first part of this section, we briefly review the literature on ERPT. In the second part, we assess how, in NiGEM, different types of exchange rate shocks can have distinct impacts on inflation and activity, with a focus on the US and the Euro area.

2.1 *Literature Review*

The ERPT refers to the elasticity of inflation to exchange rate changes and can be decomposed into two components: (i) the ERPT on import prices and (ii) the pass-through (PT) of import prices on inflation. The first PT is generally incomplete (lower than 1) and quite rapid, and differs among countries. It is related to microeconomic factors like margin behaviour or currency invoicing, but also to economic conditions. The second PT also varies across countries as it depends on the import-intensity of GDP, a structural feature of the economy.

Bussière et al. (2013) look at the issue of ERPT from a macroeconomic perspective. They find that (i) ERPTs are highly heterogeneous across countries: high for EMEs and very low for the U.S. and (ii) countries with a high elasticity on the export side also have a high elasticity on the import side. Both results are consistent with Gopinath's theory of the Internal Price System.

Gopinath (2015) emphasized the importance of the invoicing currency. She presents evidence that a disproportionate share of international transactions is invoiced in US Dollars and, to a lesser extent, in Euros. This matters a lot given that prices invoiced in foreign currencies are not very sensitive to exchange rates movements. As a matter of fact, in the case of the US, the empirical evidence shows that US exporters change their price by a very small amount (elasticity around 0.1), leading to an almost perfect pass-through.

The time-varying property of ERPT has been debated. In a chapter of its 2015 October World Economic Outlook (IMF 2015), the IMF investigates the relationship between exchange rate changes and trade for a large group of countries. The main finding is that, on average, a 10% real effective exchange rate depreciation increases domestic import prices by 6.1% and reduces export prices paid by foreigners by 5.5%. The results imply that a 10% depreciation of the currency is associated with a rise in real net exports of 1.5% of GDP, with substantial cross-country variation depending on GDP shares of exports and imports. The main finding is that exchange rate movements still have sizable effects on prices and volumes, consistent with Bussière et al. (2016) who, using a large dataset of disaggregated bilateral trade flows, underline that omitting unobserved marginal costs and competitor prices in the importing market could bias pass-through estimates. All countries in the sample satisfying the Marshall-Lerner conditions,[1] exchange rate changes can be said to play an important role in addressing global trade imbalances.

Because exchange rate fluctuations are not exogenous to the economy, Forbes (2014, 2015) looks at fluctuations in UK prices caused by different types of exchange rate shocks, stemming from global or domestic demand, global or domestic supply, as well as domestic monetary policy shocks. Using a SVAR model, Forbes shows that exchange rate appreciations are associated with lower import prices in all cases, except when the appreciation results from a positive shock to global demand (first stage of PT). The sharpest fall in inflation (second stage of PT) is associated with appreciation driven by supply shocks (such as productivity shocks). On the contrary, appreciations driven by (global or domestic) demand shocks have large positive effects on inflation. This is probably because stronger UK or global demand allows companies to avoid lowering prices despite a dearer currency. The model allows Forbes to break down the 2007–2008 sterling depreciation into different shocks. In particular, as depreciation occurred partly due to a sharp negative global supply shock (including in the UK), Forbes offers an explanation to the missing disinflation puzzle during that period.

Kirby and Meaning (2014) discuss Forbes using a global structural model, pointing at significantly different ERPT despite equivalent fluctuations in the exchange rate. Similarly to Forbes, they find that different exchange rate shocks can lead to different outcomes for prices and activity: supply-driven currency movements tend to generate higher ERPT than demand-driven shocks.

Similarly, Bussière et al. (2014) addresses the issue of the importance of the underlying ER shock, looking more specifically at productivity and capital flows shocks. Based on a large sample of emerging and advanced economies, they show that appreciations associated with higher productivity have a larger negative impact on growth than appreciations associated with capital inflows.

In a recent speech, ECB Executive Board member Benoit Coeuré (2017) looks at state-dependent ERPT, in order to explain why inflation in the euro area responded less than expected to the marked depreciation of the euro in 2014, followed by its appreciation in 2015. Beyond structural factors (such as trade integration and currency invoicing), weaker responsiveness of EA inflation to currency changes could be explained by cyclical reasons related to the type of shock hitting the economy. One of the main findings is that appreciations driven by positive demand shocks can lead to higher inflation, at odds with traditional thinking of the PT. As a result, although there is no empirical evidence that the exchange rate channel of monetary policy is inactive, its strength will depend on the state of the economy and more particularly of the factors at the source of the ER shock.

[1]The Marshall-Lerner condition is fulfilled if a currency depreciation results in an improvement of the trade balance. It generally implies that the absolute sum of the long-term export and import demand elasticities is greater than 1. The paper considers the full Marshall-Lerner conditions, i.e. taking into account not just the sum of the export and import quantity elasticities, but also the reaction of export and import prices.

2.2 *The 'Good' and the 'Bad' (in NiGEM): Model-Based Simulations*

With this literature in mind, we test in this chapter the hypothesis that different exchange shocks may lead to different ERPT and macroeconomic outcomes, using the global structural model NiGEM. The model will be used to assess the impact of the exchange rate shocks experienced by the US and the Euro area over the period July 2014–December 2016. So it is important to understand the determinants of exchange rates in NiGEM and the transmission channels of the exchange rate shocks. In this respect, following Kirby and Meaning (2014), we run in NiGEM three different types of exchange rate appreciation, stemming from two different sources:

- a 'good' appreciation due to a fall in the risk premium attached to the currency;
- a 'bad' appreciation, driven by a domestic monetary policy shock;
- a third appreciation due to a rise in interest rate differentials prompted by weaker foreign demand.

Let us now turn to the way exchange rates are modelled in NiGEM and the model simulation properties to exchange rate shocks. In NiGEM, the value of a currency of any country *n* for one US Dollar (*rx*) is determined via the uncovered interest rate parity condition given by:

$$E\left[\frac{rx_{t+1}^{n}}{rx_{t}^{n}}\right]=\left[\frac{1+\text{int}_{t}^{n}}{1+\text{usint}_{t}}\right]*\left(1+RP_{t}^{n}\right) \tag{1}$$

Equation (1) means that movements in bilateral exchange rate are determined by risk-adjusted interest rate differentials, with int^n the short term interest rate in the country n, *usint* the short-term interest rate in the US, and RP^n the risk premium attached to the currency of the country n. Effective exchange rates are calculated from a trade-weighted average of bilateral rates.[2] There are therefore several ways to introduce an exchange rate shock in NiGEM: directly, by acting on the UIP equation, changing either *int* or *RP* or both in (1); and indirectly, by generating an interest rate response to other shocks, with subsequent various responses in the exchange rates.

The 'good' appreciation: a fall in the risk premium

We run a risk premium shock (changing RP in Eq. (1)), generating a 5% appreciation in the nominal effective exchange rate (NEER) of the Dollar and the Euro.[3] In NiGEM, this is a direct endogenous shock to the floating exchange rate, with forward-looking agents. The fall in the risk premium will induce more investment and a higher equilibrium capital stock. This should lead to higher potential output

[2]In this article we use the 2010–2012 update of the trade matrix weights.

[3]The shocks are run independently. Exchange rate being calculated relative to the Dollar, the US risk premium shock is derived as a shock to all other economies in the model. The 5% subsequent rise in the NEER is equivalent to a 4% ex-post appreciation in real terms for both the Dollar and the Euro.

Table 1 Impact of different exchange rate shocks on GDP and CPI in the US and Euro area

A 5% appreciation of the nominal effective exchange rate prompted by	A fall in the domestic risk premium		A rise in domestic CB intervention rates		A fall in foreign demand and a rise in interest rate differentials	
	US	EA	US	EA	US	EA
N + 1						
GDP (diff. from baseline level)	+0.32	+0.15	−0.90	−1.10	+0.19	−0.59
CPI (diff. from baseline growth rates)	−0.77	−0.45	−1.42	−0.87	−1.11	−1.11
Long term						
GDP (diff. from baseline level)	+0.59	+1.11	−1.43	−0.38	+0.25	+1.02
CPI (diff. from baseline growth rates)	+0.03	−0.10	−0.02	−0.15	+0.37	+0.26

Source Author's calculations using NiGEM

and therefore more slack today, creating disinflationary pressure. Where monetary space is available, the Central Bank will respond by cutting its intervention rate.

Results are shown in Table 1 and point to a long-run pass-through to consumer prices close to 0 for the US and at around −0.1 for the EA. This is consistent with literature findings where the degree of ERPT to prices is lower in the US than in the EA, the reason being that foreign exporters prefer to keep constant the Dollar price of the goods they sell in the US (see Gopinath 2015, on the role of the Dollar as a transaction currency). The fall in the risk premium has an immediate positive impact on US GDP, twice the impact on EA GDP. The short-term pass-through to import prices is larger in the US than in the EA, pushing down inflation more significantly in the US (−0.8 pp on average the following year), than in the EA (−0.5 pp). Purchasing power improves, thus pushing up consumer spending.[4]

Results from the risk premium shock point to short term ERPT more pronounced in NiGEM than what most estimates would suggest. For example elasticities from the US Fed SIGMA model indicate that ERPT to inflation is large and instantaneous: a 10% dollar appreciation (in real effective terms) cuts core inflation by −0.5 pts after 1 year; while ERPT to activity is instantaneous but marginal (−0.2 to −0.3% after one year), rising to −0.7% after 2 years (Fisher 2015).

[4]Obviously the baseline is important for this type of exercise. At the time the simulations were implemented, the baseline scenario assumed a progressive rise in the FF rate, allowing some monetary space. As for the Euro area, official rates were assumed at zero over the simulation period, leaving no monetary space. The risk premium shock in the US leads to a 50 bp cut in policy rates, as the Central Bank responds to more slack in the economy. For a fair comparison with the EA (stuck at ZLB), we assume that interest rates are left unchanged in the risk premium shock. In the foreign demand shock scenario, US and EA official rates hardly move from the baseline; rather, the Dollar and Euro appreciation stems from lower official rates in shocked countries, pushing up the interest rate differentials in favour of the US and EA. The scenario described in Sect. 3, however, allows the Central Bank to react to the various shocks in order to reproduce in vivo the observed 2014–2016 episode.

This is an intended property of the model, where all non-commodity import price equations have been calibrated to adjust to the new equilibrium level over four quarters, leading to a full pass through after one year.

As regards export prices, elasticities are on average larger than most literature findings, pointing to a high pricing-to-market on the part of exporters (low PT). A factor which could explain the difference between NiGEM estimates and microeconomic estimates of the PT of the exchange rate to export prices is the acknowledgment of intermediate product prices, possible at a micro or sectoral level, but not within a macroeconomic model with one productive sector.

Demand elasticities are more in line with standard estimates, ranging from 0.1 to 0.4 for export demand and from 0.1 to 0.6 for import demand over the short run for a 1% deviation of the EER. Over the long term, elasticities are larger than standard estimates, notably for Italy and Spain, which pushes up the EA average. An explanation lies in a larger reaction of the user cost of capital and business investment in those two countries, perhaps more than warranted.

The 'bad' appreciation: a domestic monetary policy tightening

Here, we simulate a new path to the Central Bank intervention rate by changing the nominal target (NOMT) in the monetary policy rule. We use the two-pillar rule which brings the current nominal GDP back to its target level, as shown in Eq. (2) for the US:

$$\mathrm{u\ sin\,t}_t = \beta_1 \mathrm{u\ sin\,t}_{t-1} + \beta_2 \left[\frac{\mathrm{usnom}_t}{\mathrm{usnomt}_t}\right] + \beta_3 \left[\frac{\mathrm{u\ sin\ f}_t}{\mathrm{u\ sin\ ft}_t}\right] \tag{2}$$

With *usint*: Central Bank interest rate; usnom: nominal GDP; usnomt: nominal GDP target; usinf: inflation expectations; and usinft: inflation target. β_1 and β_2 are set equal to 0.5 and β_3 to 0.7 (as in the Euro area monetary policy rule).

We build a scenario where a faster-than-expected closing of the output gap puts a positive pressure on US interest rates, eventually pushing up the Dollar. We do a similar exercise for the Euro area.[5]

In a first stage, the monetary policy shock will change the short term interest rate and, as agents are forward-looking and rational, the long term interest rate. In a second stage, financial variables will act on the various components of demand, but will also affect supply through new expectations of real factor costs as inflation expectations will be affected by the monetary policy shock.

A monetary policy shock is expected to be more painful to activity than a risk premium shock, as the former implies an instantaneous rise in the Central Bank interest rate. In our scenario, the Fed Fund and 3-month Euribor rates increase by 50 bp and 57 bp respectively to generate a 5% appreciation in the Dollar and Euro nominal effective exchange rates. The transmission to consumer prices and growth is rapid and significant for both the US and Euro area (see Table 1). In both countries, the transmission of higher interest rates to investment explains most of the negative

[5]The shocks are run independently.

impact on activity, with negative spillovers to employment and wages. On average the following year, GDP is 0.9% and 1.1% below the baseline for the US and Euro area respectively.[6] As in a risk premium shock, the long-run implied pass-through of exchange rate appreciation to consumer prices is lower for the US than for the Euro area.

An appreciation due to a rise in interest rate differentials prompted by weaker foreign demand

Finally, for the use of the following empirical section, we implement a scenario where the Dollar and Euro appreciate due to a rise in interest rate differentials in favour of the US and EA, prompted by a downward revision of growth prospects outside the US and EA. Results are also shown in Table 1. They point to a larger sensitivity of the EA to changes in foreign demand, which, in this case, translates quickly into weaker GDP growth, contrary to the US. Indeed, the US benefits not only from a positive boost from net trade, but also from higher investment due to a lower user cost of capital.

To sum up, an ER appreciation originating in a fall in the currency risk premium tends to have a more benign impact on inflation than ER appreciations originating from changes in interest rate differentials. This is because a fall in the risk premium reflects improving agents' expectations on future growth, allowing companies to avoid lowering prices despite a dearer currency. This is consistent with afore mentioned results from K. Forbes and B. Coeuré. Moreover, NiGEM simulation results point to the possible occurrence of GDP increases as the fall in the risk premium induces more investment.

3 Lessons for the Recent Dollar and Euro Fluctuations (2014–16)

3.1 *Identification of the Shocks*

In this subsection, we decompose changes in the Dollar and Euro nominal effective exchange rates by the contributions of their currency counterparts, as shown in Fig. 3. This narrative identification of shocks behind exchange rate movements will help us to implement the NiGEM simulations to assess the macroeconomic impact of currency fluctuations.

The charts point to two distinct phases in Dollar and Euro fluctuations over the period going from July 2014 to December 2016:

- From July 2014 to April 2015 (when the Euro reached a trough): the significant contribution of the Euro, the Yen and the Canadian Dollar to the Dollar rise (7

[6]Again, this is stronger than simulation results from the Fed SIGMA model. But the results are not fully comparable as baseline scenarios may be different.

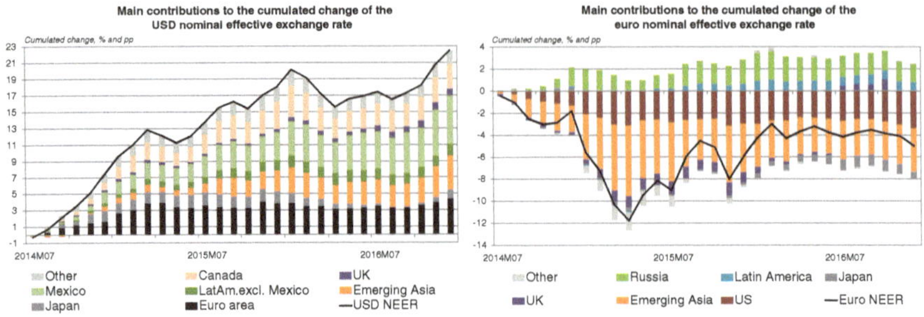

Fig. 3 Significant contrast between USD and Euro shock types by geographical sources. *Source* Author's calculations based on ECB and IFS data – data to December 2016

percentage points out of 12%) points to an appreciation triggered by business cycle gaps and different interest rates expectations between the US and its main advanced trading partners (left panel). The rising share of emerging countries in the Dollar appreciation, notably the Mexican peso, also points to a flight to the Dollar in face of falling commodity prices and lower growth forecasts for Emerging Market Economies (EMEs).
Over the same period, the NEER of the Euro (right panel) fell by 12%, mainly due to the US (contributing 3 pp) and emerging Asia (contributing 6.5 pp), the large contribution of the latter being explained by the peg of the Yuan to the Dollar. As a mirror image to the Dollar, the depreciation of the Euro appears to have been triggered by divergence in monetary policy expectations in respect to the US and China.

- From May 2015 to December 2016: this period was characterized by continued weakness in commodity prices, triggering downward revisions in expected growth for commodity exporters.[7] As a result, the flight to the Dollar, but also to other commodity-importers' currencies such as the Euro, intensified. The Dollar and the Euro appreciated by 10% and 7%, respectively, over the period, with mounting contributions from EMEs currencies. Divergence in interest rate paths between the US and its main trading partners contributed also to the renewed Dollar appreciation towards the end of the period.

To sum up, the decomposition of the Dollar and Euro changes points to two main evidences: first, identical forces appear to have been at the source of the Dollar and Euro fluctuations, albeit in opposite ways, during the first phase of the period under review; second, those forces have evolved over time. Of course, the distinction between the time phases is not so clear-cut, as the underlying forces causing exchange rate changes may have occurred alongside each other. We will get back to this in the following sub-section with a thorough description of the way exchange rate shocks

[7]For example, in June 2015 the US Energy Department revised down its forecast for world oil consumption in 2016. Likewise, 2015 and 2016 GDP growth forecasts for Emerging market and developing economies were revised by −1.3 pp on average between the April 2014 and the October 2016 WEO, and by the same magnitude over the medium term.

have been combined and implemented in the NiGEM model and our assessment of their impact on activity and prices in the US and the Euro area.

3.2 *Macroeconomic Impact of the Dollar and Euro Shocks*

Based on this decomposition of the Dollar and Euro fluctuations and NiGEM ERPT of different types of exchange shocks presented in Sect. 2, we can now build a scenario where the Dollar and the Euro experience different types of shocks and assess their impact on US and Euro area growth.

The shocks and their calibration are as follows[8]:

- From 2014Q3 to 2015Q1: a monetary policy shock leading to an appreciation of the Dollar and a depreciation of the Euro. Based on the approach described in Sect. 2.2, we build a scenario where a faster-than-expected closing of the output and employment gap puts a positive pressure on US interest rates, pushing up the NEER of the Dollar. Conversely, as inflation in the Euro area remains weak, making further monetary loosening likely, we postpone the closure of the output gap in the EA, pushing down short-term interest rates as well as the NEER of the Euro. The shocks are implemented simultaneously in the US and the Euro area. We add a negative risk premium shock to the Dollar assuming some fly-to-quality to the currency. Based on the respective contributions of the US trading partners, we assume that 75% of the observed appreciation of the Dollar over that period stemmed from monetary policy divergences (with the Euro area, UK and Japan in particular), and 25% from a flight-to-quality from emerging currencies to the Dollar, leading to a fall in the risk premium attached to the Dollar.
- From 2015Q2 to 2016Q4: a rise in the risk premium of commodity currencies due to a downward reassessment of growth prospects for commodity exporters, which materialised into lower demand spreading to other emerging countries. In practical terms, we implement two shocks: a negative real demand shock in China, Brazil, Russia, Turkey and South Africa (the main emerging economies found in NiGEM), prompting a rise in the risk premium on the currencies of the aforementioned countries, except China.[9]

---

[8]NiGEM being a quarterly model, shocks and model results are now expressed on a quarterly basis.

[9]A negative demand shock is implemented from 2015Q2 to 2016Q4 in China, Brazil, Russia, Turkey and South Africa, with domestic demand 2% lower than the baseline assumed at the time—amounting to a cumulated revision of −1.1% on GDP by the end of 2016, close to the revisions implemented by the IMF between April 2014 and October 2016 (see footnote 8). On top of the negative demand shock, higher currency risk premium are assumed on the aforementioned countries, excluding China (the Yuan being more or less pegged to the Dollar) but including other commodity producers such as Canada, Mexico and Norway. As a result, the risk premia on the Dollar and the Euro decline. Other assumptions for all simulation exercises are: agents are forward-looking; shocks are temporary; monetary policy reacts to changes in employment and activity gaps.

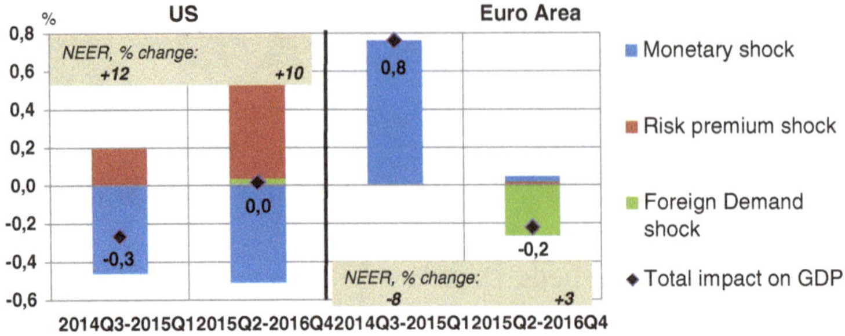

Fig. 4 EA less immune to a currency appreciation than the US. *Source* Author's calculations using NiGEM. NEER stands for Nominal Effective Exchange Rate.The bars show the respective contributions of the shocks (monetary, risk premia, foreign demand) to GDP growth

The shocks are calibrated so as to reproduce the Dollar and Euro fluctuations observed between 2014Q3 and 2016Q4, and are subsequently implemented in NiGEM.

According to our calculations and NiGEM simulations, the 22% appreciation of the Dollar since 2014Q3 choked 0.3pp off growth in the US (see Fig. 4). But as the source of the Dollar appreciation evolved over time, its transmission to the US economy has been quite distinct as well:

- During the first phase of the Dollar appreciation (2014Q3–2015Q1, up by 12% in nominal effective terms), a negative impact on GDP as growth and interest rates differentials led to diverging monetary expectations, not fully compensated by a fall in the risk premium attached to the Dollar;
- During the second phase of the Dollar appreciation (2015Q2–2016Q4, up by 10% in nominal effective terms), a rising positive impact on GDP of the fall in the Dollar risk premium (or rather, the rise in the risk premia of commodity currencies), compensating the negative impact of the sustained growth and interest rate gap between the US and its main trading partners. There are worries, however, that the rise in the Dollar prompted by the election of D. Trump in November 2016 might be a 'bad' kind of exchange rate shock, as it could re-open the interest rate gap between the US and its main trading partners due to stronger growth prospects in the US.[10] And as shown above, a Dollar appreciation driven by monetary decoupling could be more harmful to US growth than an appreciation driven by a fall in the Dollar risk premium.

The case for the Euro is different as the currency initially depreciated by 8% in nominal effective terms, boosting GDP growth by 0.8 pp over the period 2014Q3–2015Q1. The Euro subsequently appreciated (up 3% in nominal effective terms between 2015Q2 and 2016Q4). Interestingly, as both the Dollar and the Euro

[10]However, policy uncertainties on tax reforms and infrastructure spending have prompted some reconsideration on the probability of a US fiscal boost. Indeed, the June 2016 Article IV on the US economy has seen a revision by the IMF of the US growth forecasts.

were faced with the same type of shock from 2015Q2 onwards (namely, a negative shock to foreign demand and a positive shock to their currency risk premium), the estimated impact has been proportionally more negative for the Euro area than for the US. There are two main reasons for this:

- A higher openness of the Euro area economy, as well as a larger exposure to emerging countries, implies a higher sensitivity of the Euro area growth to negative shocks in the emerging world;
- Less leeway in terms of monetary accommodation as the Euro area policy rate is at zero in the baseline scenario, contrary to the Fed Fund Rate assumed to rise in the course of 2016 (see also footnote 5).

For these two reasons, a sustained rise in the currency could prove more challenging to activity in the Euro area than in the US.

4 Conclusions

The nature of the shock matters, indeed. According to our estimations, the appreciation of the Dollar has been more painful to the US economy during the early phase of the Dollar appreciation, when the shock was driven by divergence in growth and monetary cycles (July 2014 to April 2015). The following phase of the Dollar appreciation (+10% in nominal effective terms), turns out to have been more benign to US growth as the source of the appreciation appears to have been due to a fall in the Dollar risk premium, despite weaker global demand.

As for the EA, the depreciation experienced over July 2014 to April 2015 would have added 0.8 pp to growth. But the appreciation of the Euro afterwards has dented growth momentum while adding disinflationary pressures. Although the shocks faced by the US and the EA are assumed similar in nature, the Euro area appeared proportionally less immune than the US to the currency appreciation over that period. The Euro area being more open and exposed to emerging countries than the US, a loss in price-competitiveness could prove more challenging to the Euro area than to the US.

Another take-away of the study is that, according to our metrics, the Uncovered Interest rate Parity would have accounted for roughly 40% of the Dollar appreciation since mid-2014, leaving 60% unexplained or, rather, explained by other factors than UIP. This result appears to be in line with the empirical literature on UIP, see for example McDonald and Taylor (1992) or Bussière et al. (2018). This could also imply that the Dollar may not have been at its equilibrium level at the time of writing.[11]

There are numerous caveats to the results, however, and results should be interpreted with caution.

First, NiGEM being a structural model, the simulation results depend heavily on the model estimated elasticities and parameters. As a result, disparities in the ERPT

[11] According to equilibrium models of exchange rates, the Dollar would indeed be dis-aligned today, standing 10–20% above its equilibrium level according to the IMF June 2017 External Sector Report.

will derive not only from the type of the exchange rate shock, but also from two kinds of structural features: those reflecting modelling assumptions embedded in the model and those reproducing the structure of the economy (for example the weight of import prices in consumer prices). When comparing the pass-through of different types of ER shocks within a country, this is of minor significance. But this is less true when comparing ERPT across countries. Moreover, although reflecting observed economic features, this type of model suffers from the Lucas critique, as its structure is invariant to economic policies.

Second, the initial condition matters for the simulation results. Indeed, exchange rate depreciations tend to have more impact when economic slack and available capacity in the economy is high, giving scope for production and exports to expand following a rise in foreign demand associated with the fall in the currency. Third, the identification of the underlying sources of the Dollar and Euro fluctuations is based on the observation of the contributions of counterpart currencies and not on exchange rate models per se. The international role of the Dollar is another feature not accounted for in the study, which could leave unexplained a part of currency fluctuations linked to capital flows.

References

Bussière M, Chinn M, Ferrara L, Heipertz J (2018) The new Fama puzzle, NBER working paper No. 24342, February 2018

Bussière M, Delle Chiaie S, Peltonen TA (2013) Exchange rate pass-through in the global economy: the role of emerging market economies. Banque de France WP No. 424

Bussière M, Gaulier G, Steingress W (2016) Global trade flows: revisiting the exchange rate elasticities. Banque de France WP No. 608

Bussière M, Lopez C, Tille C (2014) Do real exchange rate appreciations matter for growth? CEPR Discussion Papers No. 9938

Coeuré B (2017) The transmission of the ECB's monetary policy in standard and non-standard times. Monetary policy in non-standard times workshop, Frankfurt am Main, 09/2017

Fernald J, Mertens T, Shultz P (2017) Has the Dollar become more sensitive to interest rates? FRBSF Econ Lett 2017–18

Fisher S (2015) The transmission of exchange rate changes to output and inflation. In: Remarks for the monetary policy implementation and transmission in the post-crisis period conference, Board of Governors of the Federal Reserve System, Nov 2015

Forbes K (2014) The economic impact of sterling's recent moves: more than a midsummer night's dream. Speech given in London, Oct 2014

Forbes K (2015) Much ado about something important: How do exchange rate movements affect inflation? In: Speech given at the 47th money, macro and finance research group annual conference, Cardiff, Sept 2015

Gopinath G (2015) The international price system. In: Federal Reserve Bank of Kansas City economic symposium, Jackson Hole, Aug 2015
International Monetary Fund (2015) Exchange rates and trade flows: disconnected? WEO Chapter 3, Oct 2015
Kirby S, Meaning J (2014) Exchange rate pass-through: a view from a global structural model. National Institute Economic Review No. 230, Nov 2014
MacDonald R, Taylor M (1992) Exchange rate economics: a survey. IMF Staff Pap 39(1):1–57

International Financial Flows in the New Normal: Key Patterns (and Why We Should Care)

Matthieu Bussière, Julia Schmidt and Natacha Valla

Abstract This chapter documents recent trends in international financial flows, based on a newly assembled dataset covering 40 advanced and emerging countries. Specifically, we compare the period since 2012 with the pre-crisis period and highlight three key stylized facts. First, the "Great Retrenchment" that took place during the crisis has proved very persistent, and world financial flows are now down to half their pre-crisis levels. Second, this fall can be related predominantly to advanced economies, especially those in Western Europe, while emerging markets, except Eastern European countries, have been less severely affected until recently. Third, not all types of flows have shown the same degree of resilience, resulting in a profound change in the composition of international financial flows: while banking flows, which used to account for the largest share of the total before 2008, have collapsed, foreign direct investment flows have been barely affected and now represent about half of global flows. Portfolio flows stand between these two extremes, and within them equity flows have proved more robust than debt flows. This should help to strengthen resilience and deliver genuine cross-border risk-sharing. Having high-

The views expressed in this document are those of the authors and do not necessarily reflect those of the Banque de France or the Eurosystem. We are very grateful to Valérie Ghiringhelli, Muriel Metais and Valérie Vogel for outstanding research assistance, and to Jonas Heipertz for additional help. We would like to thank Olivier Blanchard, John Bluedorn, Claudia Buch, Bruno Cabrillac, Menzie Chinn, Aitor Erce, Ludovic Gauvin, Jean-Baptiste Gossé, Pierre-Olivier Gourinchas, Galina Hale, Romain Lafarguette, Arnaud Mehl, Gian Maria Milesi-Ferretti, François Mouriaux, Damien Puy, Julio Ramos-Tallada, Romain Rancière, Cédric Tille, Miklos Vari and Frank Warnock for helpful comments and discussions.

M. Bussière · J. Schmidt (✉)
Banque de France, Paris, France
e-mail: Julia.schmidt@banque-france.fr

M. Bussière
e-mail: Matthieu.bussiere@banque-france.fr

N. Valla
European Central Bank and Paris School of Economics, Paris, France
e-mail: natacha.valla@ecb.europa.eu

L. Ferrara et al. (eds.), *International Macroeconomics in the Wake of the Global Financial Crisis*, Financial and Monetary Policy Studies 46,
https://doi.org/10.1007/978-3-319-79075-6_13

lighted these stylized facts, this chapter turns to possible explanations for and likely implications of these changes, regarding international financial stability issues.

1 Introduction

International financial flows play a central role in the international monetary system, not just because they represent the necessary counterpart to trade flows. In good times, they channel savings to the countries and regions of the world where they are most productive. In crisis times, they have the potential to disrupt the domestic financial systems of the most vulnerable countries and therefore constitute a key factor affecting global financial stability. Together with trade flows, international capital flows act as a powerful channel through which domestic shocks are transmitted across borders. International financial flows also represent one of the corner stones of the contemporary "dilemmas" and "trilemmas" that link monetary policy, exchange rates and the capital account (Rey 2013, or Aizenman et al. 2016). Finally, the composition of international capital flows underlines the concept of "global liquidity", which plays a central role in the international monetary system (CGFS 2011). For all these reasons, close monitoring of international financial flows is essential to assess the state of the global economic environment.

In recent years, international capital flows have registered profound changes, not only in terms of their magnitude but also their geographical patterns and composition by types of flows: foreign direct investment (FDI), portfolio (debt and equity) flows and *other investment* flows (which represent primarily bank flows; see Box 1 in Sect. 3 for more details). At this stage, the explanatory factors and implications of these changing patterns are not clear; they will likely trigger a debate in academic and policy circles alike. This chapter aims to contribute to this debate by presenting key stylized facts on international financial flows. We focus on gross rather than net flows, which tend to be more commonly analyzed. We outline likely explanatory factors for these developments and sketch out their implications, based on existing research.

The objective here is primarily to get the facts right, but this proves somewhat challenging, as international financial flows are reported for each country, but not for regional aggregates such as advanced and emerging economies or total world flows. Data gaps are a further challenge. The bulk of the analysis relies on the IMF Balance of Payments Statistics, which reports data at a quarterly frequency. We narrow down the analysis to 40 countries,[1] which represent more than 90% of world gross domestic product (GDP). Our focus is on recent evolutions (2012Q1–2016Q4)

[1] These countries are: Argentina, Australia, Austria, Belgium, Brazil, Canada, Chile, China, Czech Republic, Denmark, Finland, France, Germany, Greece, Hungary, India, Indonesia, Ireland, Israel, Italy, Japan, Luxembourg, Mexico, Netherlands, New Zealand, Norway, Poland, Portugal, Romania, Russia, South Africa, South Korea, Spain, Sweden, Switzerland, Taiwan, Thailand, Turkey, United Kingdom and the United States. The aggregate flows reported in Sects. 2 and 3 below are based on individual Euro area countries, thus taking into account intra-Euro area flows.

which we compare to the pre-crisis period.[2] The Global Financial Crisis and its immediate aftermath have already been analyzed extensively elsewhere (in particular by Milesi-Ferretti and Tille 2011). In the present chapter, we develop a "retrenchment indicator" which is computed for all countries and for all available sectors (FDI, portfolio equity, portfolio debt, and *other investment*). We also use long-run statistics for aggregate data to get a historical perspective, and we comment on short-run dynamics when they are particularly interesting.

Overall, three key stylized facts emerge from the exercise. First, gross international capital flows appear to be historically weak and have not recovered from the "Great Retrenchment" (Milesi-Ferretti and Tille 2011) observed in the wake of the Global Financial Crisis. This is true in absolute value (when flows are measured in US dollars) but also when expressed as a percentage of global GDP. The weakness of international capital flows, therefore, not only reflects the sluggishness of the world economy; it goes beyond this, mirroring the recent "global trade slowdown" (Hoekman 2015, or ECB 2016).[3] Though some might worry that such an evolution is alarming as it could mean, if it persists, that the global economy is becoming more fragmented than it used to be, another interpretation is possible: Given the large pre-crisis expansion in international capital flows, the "low" level observed in recent years could simply constitute a return to normal which is why we term the observed pattern the "New Normal".

The second stylized fact is that the weakness of international financial flows seems to affect all economic regions, albeit to a different extent. We provide in this chapter a battery of indicators that help monitor the evolution of international flows. Our "retrenchment indicator" is calculated as the difference between the value of these flows in the pre-crisis period (2005Q1–2007Q2) and the post-crisis period (2012Q1–2016Q4), scaled by GDP. The data show that the fall is very broad-based across countries, but it is more pronounced for advanced than for emerging market countries. Among advanced economies, the current level of inflows is back to the level that was registered in the mid-1990s. Among emerging economies, the fall is comparatively smaller, partly because the rise recorded in the decade preceding the Global Financial Crisis was smaller (which in turn could be related to the crises that affected emerging economies in the 1990s, to the lower level of financial development, overall, and to less open financial accounts). Euro area countries, especially those in the so-called periphery, recorded significantly lower flows as a percentage of GDP. This is consistent with the fact that the recovery was slower in these economies. A sectoral decomposition reveals that the fall in financial flows to and from Europe

[2]We define the pre-crisis period as 2005Q1–2007Q2 (2005 is the first year of the IMF BPM6 database). Taking this period as benchmark should not be interpreted in a normative way, especially given that this period was likely characterized by exceptional buoyancy of capital flows.

[3]International trade flows appear very weak compared to pre-crisis levels, which in itself is not very surprising given that economic activity is also less robust. More strikingly, global trade, which used to increase at twice the pace of global GDP, is now growing at roughly the same pace, suggesting that the relation between trade and GDP has changed, owing to a combination of cyclical and structural factors, as outlined in Hoekman (2015).

was particularly substantial for bank flows, which can be related to the fact that the European sovereign debt crisis markedly affected the banking sector.

Third, while all types of flows have been affected by the slowdown, some have been significantly more resilient than others, resulting in a marked change in the composition of financial flows. Specifically, FDI flows have fallen relatively less than other types of flows, while *other investment* flows have plummeted (even turning negative[4]). We will show below that *other investment* flows mainly consist of bank flows (and to a certain extent of flows by non-bank financial institutions). Portfolio flows are in the middle, and within this category, debt instruments have fallen much more than equities. As a result of these changes, the composition of international financial flows is now drastically different. Whereas the *other investment* category used to account for more than 40% of total flows before the crisis, these flows now constitute a small share of the total (14%). By contrast, the share of FDI has roughly doubled, from 24 to 48%. Within the portfolio category, we also see considerable reallocation: before the crisis, portfolio debt used to amount to more than twice the size of equity flows, whereas they are now of roughly equal magnitudes.

Building on existing research, several factors can be put forward regarding the likely causes of these evolutions. Bank flows may have been more strongly affected than other types of flows because of the problems that plagued the banking sector in advanced economies and led them to undertake a deleveraging process. As is well documented by now, the interbank market froze in the wake of the financial crisis, which affected cross-border lending by banks to other financial institutions. The changing composition of international financial flows may, therefore, reflect the disintermediation process that characterizes the global economy. Importantly, local lending by foreign bank affiliates may now substitute cross-border lending (IMF 2015). The role of European banks might be particularly important in explaining the slowdown: on the one hand, one observes a reversal of the so-called "banking glut" (Shin 2012), i.e. funding by European banks on US wholesale funding markets; on the other hand, cross-border intra-European financial intermediation has decreased substantially due to the reversal of flows from core to periphery countries. Another potential explanation that cannot be excluded is that regulatory (and political) pressure forced banks to concentrate on their core business and retrench from foreign markets.

These trends also have implications for financial stability issues. In particular, a stream of the literature has highlighted that the different types of flows typically exhibit different volatilities and do not show the same level of resilience during crises.[5] One can note that these differences in the volatility of financial flows have

[4]We consider here gross outflows (i.e. net purchases of foreign assets by domestic residents), and gross inflows (i.e. net purchases of domestic assets by foreign residents). As a result, gross flows may become negative. For instance, if foreign residents sell domestic assets massively, this will result in negative gross inflows.

[5]Conventional wisdom states that FDI flows represent a more stable source of external financing compared to portfolio and bank flows (in addition to other benefits, including the technology transfers they may entail); see e.g. Levchenko and Mauro (2007) or Albuquerque (2003). However, the extent to which they are indeed more stable is debated; see, for instance, Brukoff and Rother (2007),

been reflected in their respective evolutions since the crisis: noticeably, FDI flows proved more resilient than portfolio and especially banking flows. However, it is still an open question whether the volatility patterns observed previously will prevail in the "New Normal".

This chapter relates to existing studies that explored the recent evolution of international financial flows. Milesi-Ferretti and Tille (2011) provided an early analysis of the "Great Retrenchment" in international capital flows. They noted, in particular, that bank flows were hit the hardest, and that the retrenchment was shorter-lived for emerging economies. This chapter shows that this retrenchment continued and was even amplified beyond the early stage of the crisis. Bluedorn et al. (2013) have assembled a large database covering 147 countries since 1980 at an annual frequency and 58 countries at a quarterly frequency. They document and highlight the high volatility of international capital flows, with FDI flows being comparatively less volatile than bank and portfolio flows (but these last two types of flows are not fundamentally different in terms of volatility). While they do not find significant differences across country groups—advanced economies versus emerging economies—regarding the volatility of gross flows, they note that advanced economies "experience greater substitutability across the various types of net flows and greater complementarity of gross inflows and outflows". This chapter also relates to a large strand of the literature that sought to identify the determinants of international capital flows, including Broner et al. (2013), Forbes and Warnock (2012), Fratzscher (2011), Ghosh et al. (2014), Puy (2015), Erce and Riera-Crichton (2015)[6] and especially the papers that focus on the determinants of bank flows (see e.g. Buch and Goldberg 2015, and the literature reviewed therein). By focusing on gross and not net flows, we also contribute to the analysis put forward by Obstfeld (2012), who emphasizes the role of gross flows. Importantly, however, we focus here predominantly on international capital flows and not stocks (i.e. the international investment position). This is not to say that stocks do not matter, as clearly they do, but flows provide an early evaluation of where stocks are going and catch substantial attention in themselves. This chapter also echoes the analysis of Borio and Disyatat (2015), who emphasize the importance of financing in the analysis of the external sector. We complement recent contributions that focus on the vulnerability of emerging economies to sudden stops of capital flows. Among others, this literature analyzes the role of gross flows separately, aiming to distinguish the impact of inflows from that of outflows (see e.g. Alberola et al. 2016, and the references therein). Finally, while we do not aim to evaluate the impact of capital flows on growth, this chapter relates to the strand of the literature that looks at the short- and long-run effects of capital flows on growth (see, for instance, Blanchard

Bluedorn et al. (2013) and the references cited therein. The relative stability of different types of capital flows has crucial implications for capital account openness and in particular its sequencing (see e.g. Kaminsky and Schmukler 2003, or Bussière and Fratzscher 2008).

[6]These papers take mostly an empirical approach; see Tille and Van Wincoop (2010) for a theoretical view.

et al. 2015; Reinhart and Reinhart 2009 and the references cited in these papers). We hope that the stylized facts presented here will feed into this debate.[7]

The rest of this chapter is organized as follows. Section 2 focuses on total gross flows (lumping together portfolio, FDI and *other investment*) for the world as a whole and for the world's largest countries and regions. Section 3 turns to the composition of financial flows. It outlines some of the possible factors that may explain why some components have been more resilient than others, and suggests the likely implications, for the global economy, of the new composition of financial flows.

2 Global Financial Flows: Dwindling to a Trickle

2.1 The Rise and Fall of Global Financial Flows

The decade preceding the crisis has been one of financial globalization. The ramping-up of international capital flows and the accumulation of external assets and liabilities in the decades preceding the Global Financial Crisis were perhaps even more dramatic than the already impressive acceleration of trade flows and the development of current account imbalances that took place over this period. This can be related to greater capital account openness. Overall, the magnitude of gross inflows in advanced and emerging countries rose markedly up to the 2008–09 Global Financial Crisis, especially for the former (Fig. 1). Comparing the current period with the period immediately before the Global Financial Crisis may be biased, as capital flows were historically high, especially for advanced economies (for emerging economies the rise was less pronounced and the level was lower, partly because of the crises that plagued emerging economies in the 1990s and early 2000s). If one takes a longer perspective, capital flows appear to be back to their mid-1990s level.

When financial globalization matured before the onset of the Global Financial Crisis, orders of magnitude had changed relative to a decade earlier (Milesi-Ferretti and Tille 2011) along various lines:

- Foreign assets constituted a significantly bigger share of portfolios; the value of those assets also rose relative to GDP generally.
- Financial globalization had been more pronounced in advanced than in emerging economies, the former receiving more gross inflows than the latter (Fig. 1).
- The size of current account imbalances and of creditor/debtor positions had become more dispersed (Bracke et al. 2008).
- The banking sector in advanced economies had been one of the key drivers of financial globalization. Banks extended their international activities during this process, either through cross-border lending or via foreign affiliates, which played

[7] We do not touch upon the issue of capital controls and other tools aimed at managing international capital flows. Interested readers may check IMF (2012), Ostry et al. (2011, 2012), Pasricha et al. (2015), Forbes et al. (2015a), as well as the references therein.

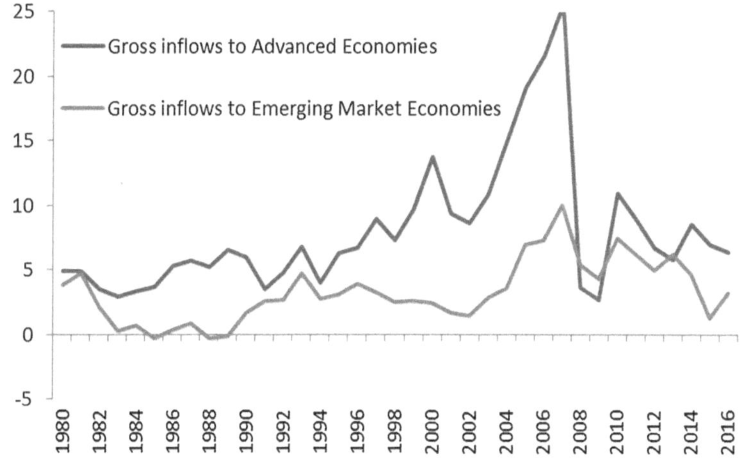

Fig. 1 Gross inflows in advanced and emerging market economies, 1980–2014 (% GDP). *Source* IMF Balance of Payments Statistics (BoPS) and authors' calculations

an important role in the subsequent period (see Cetorelli and Goldberg 2011, 2012, and the references therein).

With this pre-2008 snapshot in mind, this section offers a bird's eye review of major stylized facts that emerged since 2008. We document international financial interdependencies by focusing on gross quarterly capital flows—outflows and inflows—since 2005. We deliberately choose to remain mainly at an aggregate level of description in this section, allowing only for a geographical split between advanced economies and emerging economies. Section 3 will dig deeper into sectoral categories of capital flows, breaking down aggregates into foreign direct investment (FDI), portfolio investment and *other investment*. Based on Balance of Payments data as of the last quarter of 2016, three key stylized facts emerge.

Stylized fact no. 1: The "Great Retrenchment" that took place during the crisis has proved very persistent and international capital flows are now at a lower level than the one observed prior to the crisis.

In the years preceding 2008, gross international financial flows were very substantial, hovering around a quarterly aggregate of around 10–15% of global GDP. That was equivalent, back then, to about USD 2,000 bn. The onset of the financial crisis in the summer of 2007 put a "sudden stop" to that flourishing regime: in the first quarter of 2008, these flows were suddenly reduced to nil (Fig. 2).[8] Aggregate gross flows massively retrenched in the third quarter of 2008, as visible in Fig. 2, when Lehman Brothers collapsed. In that quarter alone, their reversal was equivalent to −10% of global GDP.

[8]In this section and in the rest of the paper (except where otherwise indicated), we use quarterly data from the IMF BoP Statistics, which start in 2005.

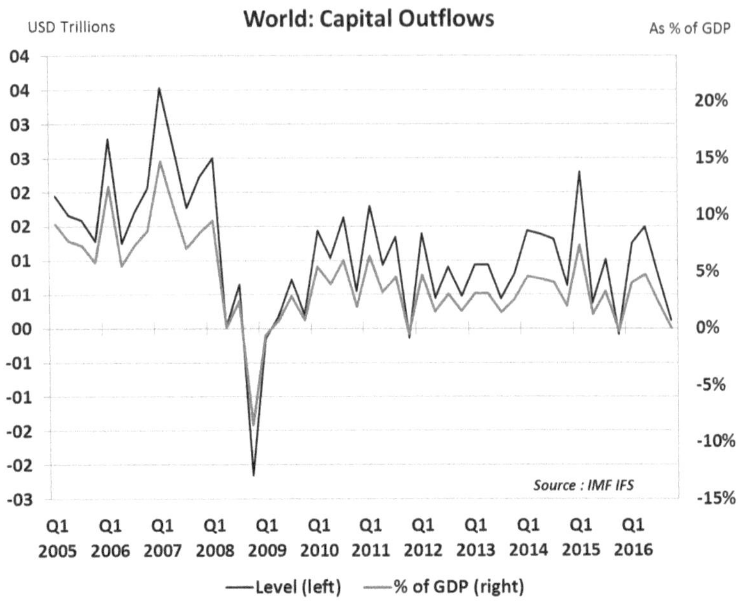

Fig. 2 Global gross financial flows. *Source* IMF Balance of Payments Statistics (BoPS) and authors' calculations

Since 2010, gross cross-border financial flows have not returned to the buoyancy of the pre-crisis period. Instead, as of the end of 2016, they seemed to have settled at a "new average" that looks to be below 5% of GDP (Fig. 2). This muted revival raises questions about whether the pre-crisis intensification of global financial linkages, summarized above, was too exuberant.

2.2 The Geographical Pattern of Global Financial Flows: Stylized Facts

Stylized fact no. 2: Advanced economies have been the most affected by the retrenchment in international financial flows.

The retrenchment of global financial flows after the 2008 sudden stop turns out to be predominantly an advanced economy story. In fact, a sharp contrast between advanced and emerging economies emerged after the sudden stop in 2008. Since then, flows to and from advanced countries seemed to have stabilized around an average that was significantly lower than what prevailed before 2008 (Fig. 3).

In emerging markets, gross capital flows were significantly more resilient than in advanced economies already in the early phase of the crisis (Fig. 3). After 2008, capital inflows into emerging economies recovered quickly and even outpaced pre-

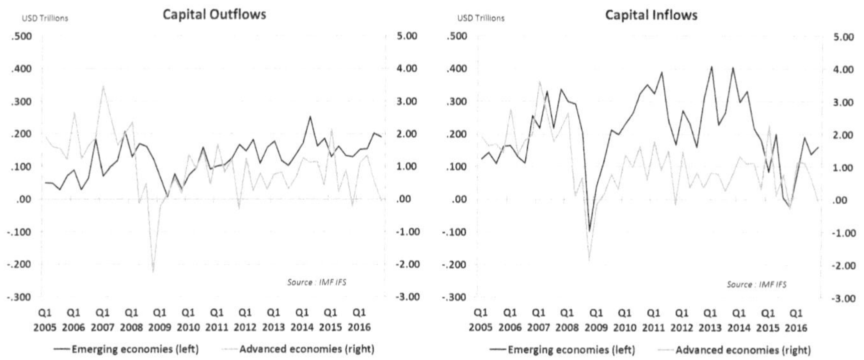

Fig. 3 Gross capital outflows and inflows for emerging and advanced economies. *Source* IMF Balance of Payments Statistics (BoPS) and authors' calculations

crisis levels, although the most recent numbers show a downward trend. This is likely related to the underlying drivers of these inflows, namely monetary policy in industrialized countries, in particular the US. While liquidity abundance in advanced economies pushed investors towards emerging economies, this trend has dwindled lately as signals of monetary policy normalization became more apparent.

While emerging economies fared much better than advanced economies after the Global Financial Crisis, the latter account for a much larger share of total flows than emerging markets (the ratio is about 1:10).[9] As a result, the fall recorded by the former could not be offset by the recovery of the latter, and global flows are now smaller than they were before the crisis.

Looking at capital outflows more closely (left-hand side panel of Fig. 3) suggests that capital outflows from emerging countries have been more resilient than those originating from advanced economies. Within the block of emerging countries, this resilience in international exposure of investors holds less true in Eastern Europe, as shown in the regional breakdown of flows (Fig. 4). The most plausible explanation of the fact that Eastern Europe remains the hardest-hit when it comes to emerging economies is its close relationship with Western Europe, in particular through the banking sector. In contrast to Eastern Europe, Asia and Latin-America generally recorded a rise in both their outflows and inflows (Fig. 4).

We now look beyond aggregate facts and investigate country-level developments. To that purpose, we developed a simple metric, which we call a "retrenchment indicator". This indicator compares the level at which capital flows settled after the 2008 sudden stop (since the first quarter of 2012 until the last quarter of 2016) with their pre-crisis average over the period 2005Q1 to 2007Q2. We scale this difference by GDP. In particular, we calculate:

[9]The difference partly reflects the fact that several advanced economies, like the UK and Luxembourg, are financial hubs, such that flows to and from these centers are hard to attribute to specific countries. In addition, advanced economies comprise the Euro area where cross-border financial integration is particularly high.

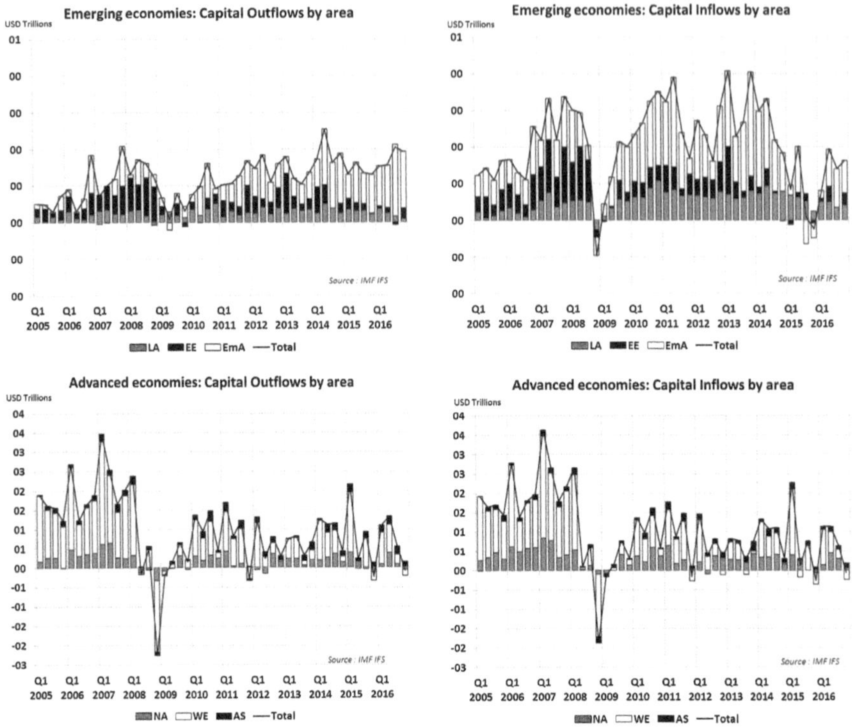

Fig. 4 Gross capital outflows and inflows, by regional aggregates. *Note* NA North America, LA Latin America, EE Eastern Europe, WE Western Europe, EmA Emerging Asia, AS Asia. *Source* IMF Balance of Payments Statistics (BoPS) and authors' calculations

$$Retrenchment\ (rel.) = \frac{\frac{4}{10}\sum_{t=2005Q1}^{2007Q2} K_t - \frac{4}{20}\sum_{t=2012Q1}^{2016Q4} K_t}{\frac{4}{10}\sum_{t=2005Q1}^{2007Q2} Y_t}$$

The top and bottom 10 countries are presented in Table 1. *First*, capital flows indeed intensified in many emerging economies and in some "safe havens" such as Luxembourg. As a matter of fact, the intensification of inflows to Luxembourg suggests that "financial centers" have continued to cater to the redistribution of flows across countries. *Second*, by contrast, the retrenchment of capital flows turns out to be the most severe in Western European countries, including the UK, peripheral Euro area countries and France. Euro area periphery countries such as Spain, Portugal and Ireland were among those economies that received a large amount of inflows prior to the crisis and were therefore subject to a large degree of retrenchment (see also Hale and Obstfeld 2014). Another pattern that seems to emerge is that a large number of countries that were subject to retrenchment are the ones that have large banking systems. We will investigate this issue further in Sect. 3.2 by disaggregating

Table 1 Retrenchment indicators, as a percentage of GDP, top and bottom 10 countries (Top and bottom 10 countries ranked by size of difference between post and pre-crisis outflows and inflows, % of GDP)

Outflows			Inflows		
LX	Luxembourg	57.1	LX	Luxembourg	58.5
CH	China	8.0	CL	Chile	11.7
TH	Thailand	4.4	CH	China	8.7
KO	South Korea	3.9	ID	Indonesia	7.6
IN	India	3.8	BR	Brazil	6.0
CL	Chile	3.5	IN	India	5.9
NZ	New Zealand	3.0	CA	Canada	5.3
BR	Brazil	2.6	JP	Japan	2.8
JP	Japan	1.9	AU	Australia	2.2
RS	Russia	1.6	MX	Mexico	1.2
PT	Portugal	−15.6	DK	Denmark	−19.1
FN	Finland	−17.1	ES	Spain	−20.9
NW	Norway	−18.1	FR	France	−24.5
FR	France	−24.5	PT	Portugal	−24.5
SW	Switzerland	−44.5	SW	Switzerland	−26.9
BG	Belgium	−45.6	BG	Belgium	−43.3
AT	Austria	−49.4	AT	Austria	−49.2
NL	Netherlands	−60.0	UK	United Kingdom	−56.5
UK	United Kingdom	−60.1	NL	Netherlands	−65.1
IR	Ireland	−98.9	IR	Ireland	−96.6

Source IMF Balance of Payments Statistics (BoPS) and authors' calculations
Note Periods: Pre-crisis: 2005Q1–2007Q2, Post-crisis: 2012Q1–2016Q4

international capital flows by the type of flow to investigate the particular role played by banks.

3 When the Composition of Capital Flows Matters

3.1 Different Components, Different Degrees of Resilience

Stylized fact no. 3: The composition of international capital flows has shifted away from other investment *flows (which comprise bank flows) towards more FDI. Portfolio flows have also retrenched; this is mainly due to a contraction in debt flows.*

While the previous section focused on aggregate flows, we now turn to the decomposition by the main types of flows. This exercise reveals that the collapse of international financial flows has been very uneven (Fig. 5).[10] Strikingly, FDI has been very resilient (flows in the post-crisis period are just one notch below their pre-crisis level), whereas flows in the "*other investment*" category—which comprises bank flows (see Box 1)—have been almost completely wiped out.

Box 1: Other investment in the financial account

In the text, we refer broadly to the *other investment* category as bank flows as it is generally assumed that they constitute the bulk of this category. This box briefly explains this association by highlighting the differences between banking flows and other subcategories of *other investment*.

Other investment comprises the following types of financial flows: (1) Other equity, (2) Loans, (3) Currency and deposits, (4) Trade credit and advances and (5) Other accounts receivable/payable. The last four components are categorized as debt instruments. It is not only possible to disaggregate these instruments by the type of flow, but also by the counterparty, notably: (1) Central bank, (2) Deposit-taking corporations, except the central bank ("banks"), (3) General government and (4) Other sectors.

For typical industrialized economies, banks constitute the most important counterparty. Looking at stocks (rather than flows) which are by definition non-negative, International Investment Position (IIP) data show that assets held by banks make up for example 71% in the United Kingdom or 69% in France (data for 2013). However, in economies such as Ireland, United States or Luxemburg, they make up respectively 30%, 41% and 43%. In these cases, the sub-category *Other sectors* also constitutes a large part. *Other sectors* can be disaggregated into (1) financial (non-bank) corporations as well as (2) non-financial corporations and households. In most industrialized countries, the former outnumbers the latter to a large extent. Thus, while bank flows do constitute a large fraction of other investment, the importance of non-bank financial flows can be quite substantial in some economies and therefore explains the smaller share of banks in these cases.

Portfolio flows come somewhat between these two extremes, but even there, significant heterogeneity prevails: portfolio equity flows have been much more resilient than debt flows, which have halved between the pre- and the post-crisis periods. The

[10] In this section we focus on international capital outflows. In principle, the data should match the data series for inflows at the world level. However, due to statistical errors and since our database does not include all countries in the world, global outflows and inflows do not match exactly. In spite of these discrepancies, the data for global inflows lead to the same conclusions, in terms of which flows have been the most resilient. Another challenge is that not all countries report the split between debt and equity in the "portfolio" category, or at least not since 2005. To provide a meaningful comparison, we have therefore split Figs. 5 and 6 in two, showing first the broad "portfolio" category for the whole sample, and then the debt/equity split for the restricted sample of countries, losing in the process Argentina, China, India, Mexico and Turkey. We also omitted Saudi Arabia for data availability reasons related to *other investment* flows.

(a)

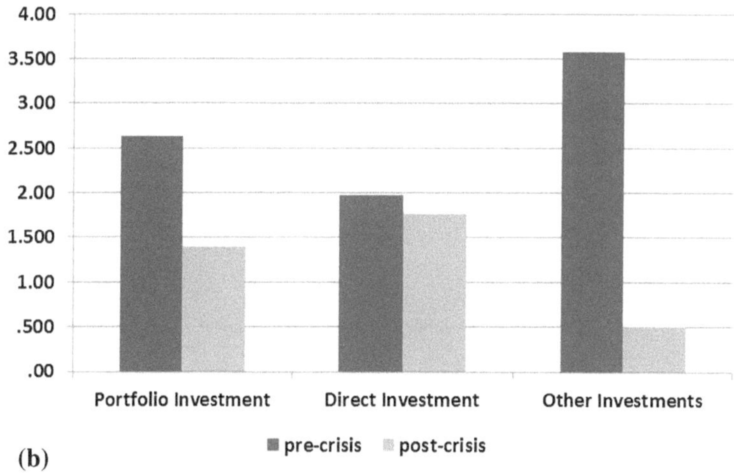

(b)

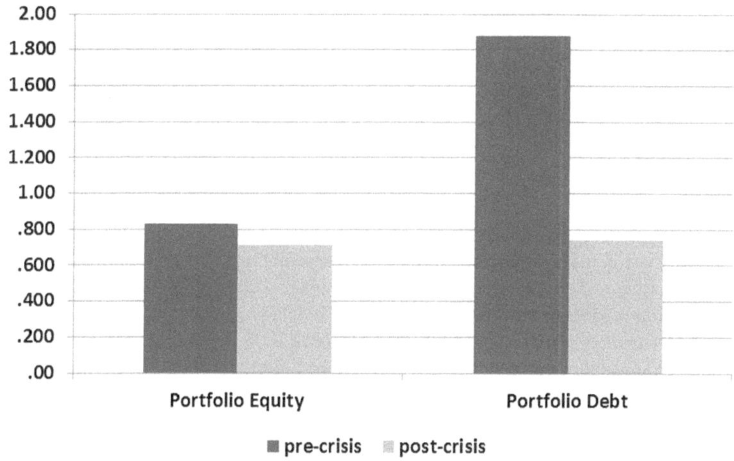

Fig. 5 Comparison of capital flows before and after the crisis, by financial instrument (% GDP). **a** Breakdown between portfolio, FDI and other investment (full sample). **b** Breakdown of the portfolio investment category between debt and equity (restricted sample of the countries reporting the debt and equity categories separately since 2005). This figure shows two sets of figures corresponding to different sample composition. The upper panel reports data for the full sample for the broad categories FDI, portfolio and other investment. The lower panel reports the composition of debt and equity within the portfolio category, for the restricted sample of countries reporting this split since 2005. *Source* IMF Balance of Payments Statistics (BoPS) and authors' calculations. *Note* Periods: Pre-crisis: 2005Q1–2007Q2, Post-crisis: 2012Q1–2016Q4

resilience of equity flows bodes well for the ability of the economy to withstand forthcoming shocks as it has better risk-sharing properties than debt (Albuquerque 2003). One should underline, nonetheless, that there has not been a substitution between types of flows: all flows have fallen, but in different proportions.

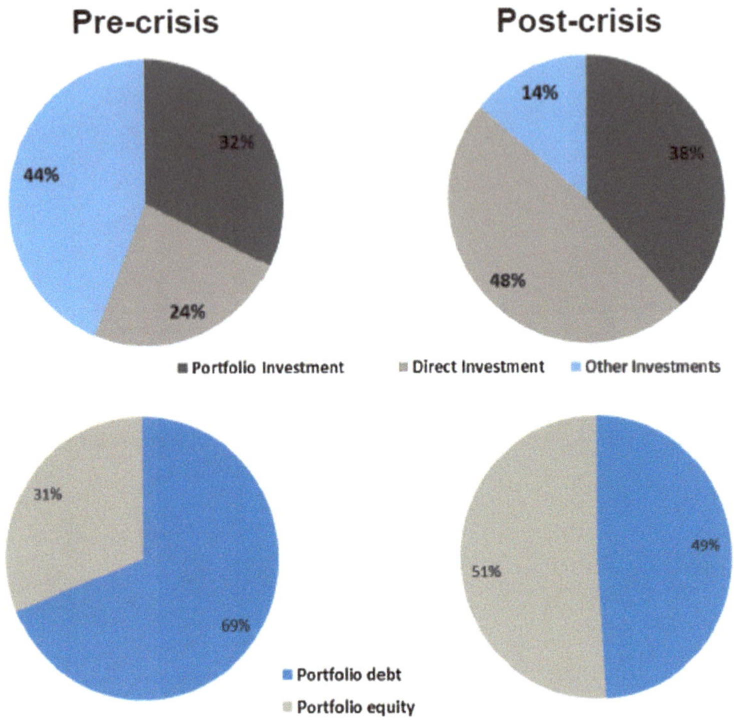

Fig. 6 Composition of global financial flows by categories before and after the crisis. As in the previous figure, this figure shows two sets of figures corresponding to different sample composition. The upper panel reports data for the full sample for the broad categories FDI, portfolio and other investment. The lower panel reports the composition of debt and equity within the portfolio category, for the restricted sample of countries reporting this split since 2005. *Source* IMF Balance of Payments Statistics (BoPS) and authors' calculations. *Note* Periods: Pre-crisis: 2005Q1–2007Q2, Post-crisis: 2012Q1–2016Q4

As a result of these different evolutions, the composition of world flows is now fundamentally different from what it used to be before the crisis (Fig. 6). In the pre-crisis period, the *other investment* category used to constitute the bulk of global flows, with a share of 44%, whereas this share is now about 14%. By contrast, whereas FDI used to represent less than a fourth of the total, in the post-crisis period FDI amounts to 48% of total flows. Finally, the share of portfolio investment has slightly increased, from 32 to 38%. Within the portfolio category, the share of debt has fallen, from two-thirds to about half, compared to the share of equity, which has risen correspondingly (as shown in the lower panel of Fig. 6).

Before turning to possible explanations for this dramatic change in the composition of global financial flows and its likely implications for the global economy, it is worth exploring the geographical breakdown of the flows. To that aim, we once again use our "retrenchment indicator" which reflects the change in in- and outflows in percentage of GDP. To recall, it is expressed as the difference between the value of these flows in the pre-crisis period (2005Q1–2007Q2) and the post-crisis period (2012Q1–2016Q4), scaled by GDP in the pre-crisis period. Table 2 reports the difference of the post-crisis flows with the pre-crisis flows for the main regions of the world for both inflows and outflows.

Several key findings stand out:

- First, the collapse of the *other investment* category can be predominantly attributed to advanced economies: the fall is particularly pronounced for Western Europe. For this region, the flows have been negative in the post-crisis period. This is consistent with the fact that the European crisis affected the banking sector, and led to substantial deleveraging and disintermediation thereafter.
- For other regions, the evolution of this *other investment* category has been very different. In particular in Asia, flows in both directions have increased between the two periods. For Eastern European countries, the *other investment* category has been characterized by retrenchment in both outflows and inflows, with the latter being more pronounced. Overall, the collapse in *other investment* flows originating from and going to advanced countries (North America and especially Western Europe) was less than compensated by the rise recorded in other regions because the size of these regions in the pre-crisis flows was overwhelming for advanced countries (international financial flows are much larger for advanced economies than for emerging economies).
- Turning to the other types of flows, one can note that FDI flows have been fairly resilient for most regions of the world; they even show an increase for all regions except Europe. Overall, FDI has retrenched in advanced economies and this is entirely due to the retrenchment in Western Europe.
- Finally, concerning the portfolio category, we need to distinguish between debt and equity (the former has fallen much more than the latter at the global level). Portfolio debt flows have fallen substantially for Western Europe. By contrast, equity flows have fallen to a smaller extent.

Figure 7 shows the composition of gross flows for outflows and inflows for advanced and for emerging market economies over time. In advanced economies, overall swings into positive or negative territory are mainly driven by the *other investment* category. A similar pattern can also be observed for inflows into emerging economies. FDI and portfolio flows remain rather stable over time. Whenever one observes large increases or decreases of total flows, this can often be traced back to movements in *other investment* flows. As this category plays a particular role for total flows, we discuss its behavior in more detail in the next section.

3.2 Changing Composition of International Financial Flows: Explanatory Factors and Implications

The changing composition of international financial flows documented above is a striking feature of the global economic environment. One may wonder what could

Table 2 Difference between sum of flows 2012Q1–2016Q4 and sum of flows 2005Q1–2007Q2 (% GDP)

Outflows						Inflows				
	Portfolio Equity	Portfolio Debt	Direct Investment	Other Investment	Total	Portfolio Equity	Portfolio Debt	Direct Investment	Other Investment	Total
NA	0.06	−0.32	0.23	−1.39	−1.42	−0.24	−0.70	0.10	−1.17	−2.01
LA	0.07	−0.22	0.23	0.78	0.86	0.10	0.89	1.36	−0.10	2.25
EE	−0.17	0.13	−0.15	−0.64	−0.83	−0.39	0.05	−1.51	−3.83	−5.69
WE	−0.96	−6.08	−3.66	−16.70	−27.40	−0.23	−8.56	−1.93	−17.53	−28.25
EmA	−0.24	−1.17	2.82	5.76	7.73	−0.99	0.92	3.71	−0.37	3.53
AS	0.15	0.32	1.51	0.12	2.10	−0.81	−0.43	0.65	2.10	1.51
EME	−0.08	−0.44	0.96	2.04	2.65	−0.34	0.71	1.49	−0.92	1.02
ADV	−0.13	−1.40	−0.43	−4.28	−6.24	−0.29	−2.22	−0.25	−4.12	−6.88
WD	−0.13	−1.26	−0.23	−3.39	−4.97	−0.30	−1.80	−0.09	−3.58	−5.77

Source IMF Balance of Payments Statistics (BoPS) and authors' calculations (restricted sample)
Note NA North America, LA Latin America, EE Eastern Europe, WE Western Europe, EmA Emerging Asia, AS Asia, EME emerging Market Economy, ADV advanced economies, WD World

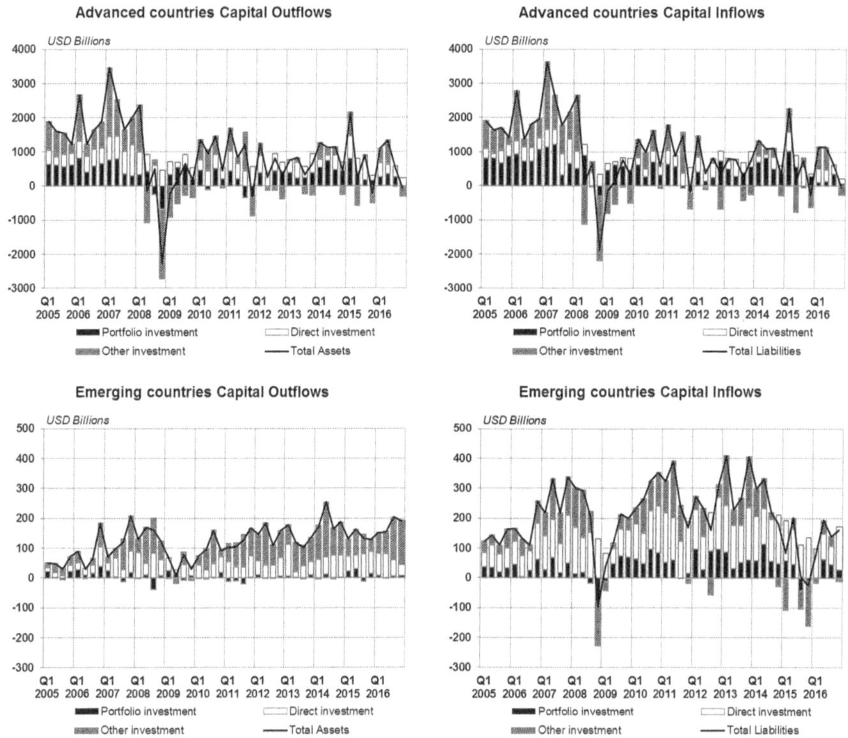

Fig. 7 International financial flows by type of flow. *Source* IMF Balance of Payments Statistics (BoPS) and authors' calculations

have triggered this change and what are the likely implications for the world economy. While it is usual to list separately the causes and the consequences for expositional purposes, several factors can be seen both as a cause and a consequence. One obvious factor to underline in this respect is the fact that economic activity has been weak since the Global Financial Crisis; the recovery has regularly disappointed, and international organizations such as the International Monetary Fund (IMF) have repeatedly revised their global growth forecasts downwards (see Chap. 1). Weak economic activity is both an explanatory factor for weak financial flows, and, since negative shocks are transmitted through financial linkages, a consequence. In this respect, the European crisis has played an important role.

Another key factor to underline is that some types of international financial flows seem to be inherently more volatile than others. In this respect, bank flows and portfolio flows are often described as "hot money" (see, for instance, Bluedorn et al. 2013). By contrast, FDI flows are typically more stable over time, which is why they are generally considered as a safer form of financing (in addition to other benefits they carry, such as technological transfers). Also, within portfolio flows, equity flows have been more resilient than debt flows. Yet, overall, the behavior of international

Table 3 Volatility of flows by sector and by subperiods (coefficient of variation)

	Portfolio equity	Portfolio debt	Direct investment	Other investment
Pre-crisis	0.33	0.25	0.24	0.58
Post-crisis	0.80	0.65	0.33	6.09
Total period	0.80	0.66	0.31	2.34

Source IMF Balance of Payments Statistics (BoPS) and authors' calculations
Note Periods: Pre-crisis: 2005Q1–2007Q2, Post-crisis: 2012Q1–2016Q4

financial flows after the Global Financial Crisis reflects the traditional wisdom: the flows that are considered to be the most volatile are precisely those that saw the largest decline.

The different components of financial flows have therefore been faithful to their reputation: "hot money" (with the exception of equity flows) has evaporated quickly, whereas FDI has been more robust. Looking forward, this may suggest more stable flows as the resulting composition is composed mainly of FDI flows. However, other elements need to be considered as well to get a full assessment. Table 3, which presents key statistics on the volatility of the main categories of financial flows during the main subperiods considered here (and for the whole sample), confirm these established stylized facts (bearing in mind of course that both sub-periods are short, thus enabling few observations to calculate these statistics). For instance, FDI, which was less volatile than *other investment* before the crisis, was also less volatile after the crisis.

The factors behind the collapse in cross-border banking flows have been analyzed in CGFS (2011), which investigates the question of global liquidity and focuses on bank flows as the prime measure of global liquidity. Among the possible explanatory factors, the paper by CGFS (2011) highlights the role of risk aversion for the retrenchment observed in the years following the crisis. High levels of uncertainty have likely contributed to the observed patterns in recent years (see for example Converse 2017, on this topic).

To some extent, the fall in bank flows could be interpreted as a correction from the "global banking glut" that prevailed in the pre-crisis period (Shin 2012), through which European banks helped to enhance intermediation capacities in the US. These considerations represent a convincing argument as to why it is important to look at gross and not just net international financial flows. Meanwhile, recently, McQuade and Schmitz (2017) have looked into the cross-country heterogeneity of gross capital flows. They found, in particular, that gross inflows in the post-crisis period (which is defined slightly differently from ours) were higher for the countries with smaller external and internal imbalances in the pre-crisis period.

The fact that international banking flows have fallen dramatically could also reflect the disintermediation process that intensified in the wake of the Global Financial Crisis. In turn, this process could result from different factors. Several prominent observers have pointed out the effect of tighter financial regulation, which could explain why the banking sector seems to be losing ground, compared to financial markets (see, for instance, Tarullo 2012, 2014; CGFS 2010; Gambacorta and Van Rixtel 2013, etc.). Several studies have also pointed out that the exceptional measures put in place after the crisis have a substantial domestic bias, which could have played a role in the global retrenchment process (see e.g. Beck et al. 2015; Forbes et al. 2015b). Moreover, it is also possible that local lending by affiliates has (partly) replaced cross-border lending. In this respect, the shift from cross-border banking to more activities by foreign affiliates might have a positive impact on financial stability (IMF 2015). Another potential explanatory factor could lie in the recent weakness of international trade flows (as documented, for instance, by Hoekman 2015). Indeed, trade credits are included in the *other investment* category, such that the weakness of international trade would mechanically affect this type of flow. Indeed, trade credit issues have been highlighted as one of the potential causes of weak trade (see, for instance, Amity and Weinstein, 2011, or Chor and Manova 2012). This notwithstanding, trade credits amount to fairly low levels and cannot account for the fall in investment flows.

4 Conclusion

This chapter has presented three main stylized facts on international financial flows in recent times, focusing on the comparison with the pre-crisis period. (i) Overall, international capital flows have dried up, now averaging at barely half of their pre-crisis level in percentage of world GDP. (ii) In terms of geographical distribution, this fall has mainly affected advanced countries, especially Western Europe, while for emerging market economies flows have actually increased. (iii) The composition of international capital flows has changed dramatically, due to the heterogeneous change in their sectoral composition: bank flows have been very markedly affected, whereas FDI has remained roughly unchanged at the global level. Within portfolio investments, debt flows have fallen much more than equity flows (Western Europe being again the region of the world where debt flows have fallen most).

Several factors can be put forward to explain these changes. They range from general factors, such as the weakness in the global recovery and the associated degree of uncertainty, to more specific factors, affecting certain regions and sectors more than others. Among the latter, the European crisis in 2011–13 seems to have played a key role, as it is really flows to and from Western Europe that decreased the most. Regarding the sectoral composition, several explanations can be put forward for the collapse in bank flows. The need to repair bank balance sheets and the substitution of cross-border flows by local lending by affiliates have been documented extensively. In addition, regulation may have played an important role (see IMF 2015, for instance).

The consequences of these changes for financial stability are not clear at this stage. The changes that have taken place since the Global Financial Crisis may correspond to a simple normalization, as suggested for instance by Coeuré (2015), after rather "exuberant" times in the pre-crisis period. The fact that the share of "hot money" has gone down while that of FDI has increased may lead to a more stable international monetary system, but the concept of "hot money" remains somewhat elusive (bearing in mind that many operations under the *other investment* flows contribute to the liquidity of markets) and it is hard to gauge if the pre-crisis properties and specificities of the various types of flows that we focused on will prevail in the "New Normal".

References

Aizenman J, Chinn MD, Hiro I (2016) Monetary policy spillovers and the trilemma in the new normal: Periphery country sensitivity to core country conditions. J Int Money Finance 68(C):298–330
Albuquerque R (2003) The composition of international capital flows: risk sharing through foreign direct investment. J Int Econ 61(2):353–383
Alberola E, Erce A, María Serena J (2016) International reserves and gross capital flows dynamics. J Int Money Finance 60(C):151–171
Amiti M, Weinstein D (2011) Exports and financial shocks. Q J Econ 126(4):1841–1877
Beck R, Beirne J, Paternò F, Peeters J, Ramos-Tallada J, Rebillard C, Reinhardt D, Weissenseel L and Wörz J (2015) The side effects of national financial sector policies: framing the debate on financial protectionism, Occasional Paper Series, No 166, September 2015
Blanchard OJ, Chamon M, Ghosh AR, Ostry JD (2015) Are capital inflows expansionary or contractionary? Theory, policy implications, and some evidence. Centre for Economic Policy Research Discussion Papers, DP10909
Bluedorn JC, Duttagupta R, Guajardo J, Topalova P (2013) Capital flows are fickle: anytime, anywhere. International Monetary Fund, working papers 13/183
Borio C, Disyatat P (2015) Capital flows and the current account: taking financing (more) seriously. Bank for International Settlements, working paper No. 525
Bracke T, Bussière M, Fidora M, Straub R (2008) A framework for assessing global imbalances. European Central Bank, occasional paper series 78
Broner F, Didier T, Erce A, Schmukler SL (2013) Gross capital flows: dynamics and crises. J Monetary Econ Elsevier 60(1):113–133
Brukoff P, Rother B (2007) FDI may not be as stable as governments think. Magazine. International Monetary Fund Survey. https://www.imf.org/external/pubs/ft/survey/so/2007/RES051A.htm
Buch CM, Goldberg LS (2015) International banking and liquidity risk transmission: lessons from across countries. Int Monetary Fund Econ Rev 63(3)
Bussière M, Fratzscher M (2008) Financial openness and growth: short-run gain, long-run pain? Rev Int Econ 16(1):69–95
Cetorelli N, Goldberg L (2011) Global banks and international shock transmission: evidence from the crisis. Int Monetary Fund Econ Rev 9(1):41–76
Cetorelli N, Goldberg L (2012) Liquidity management of U.S. Global Banks: internal capital markets in the great recession. J Int Econ 88(2):299–311
Chor D, Manova K (2012) Off the cliff and back? Credit conditions and international trade during the global financial crisis. J Int Econ 87:117–133
Coeuré B (2015) Paradigm lost: rethinking international adjustments. Egon and Joan von Kashnitz Lecture, Clausen Center for International Business and Policy, Berkeley
Committee on the Global Financial System (CGFS) (2010) Funding patterns and liquidity management of internationally active banks. Committee on the Global Financial System Papers No 39
Committee on the Global Financial System (CGFS) (2011) Global liquidity—concept, measurement and policy implications. Committee on the Global Financial System Papers, 45
Converse N (2017) Uncertainty, capital flows and maturity mismatch. J Int Money Finance (forthcoming)
European Central Bank (ECB) (2016) Understanding the weakness in global trade—what is the new normal? European Central Bank, Occasional Paper Series 178

Erce A, Riera-Crichton D (2015) Catalytic IMF? A gross flows approach. European stability mechanism, working paper 9
Forbes K, Fratzscher M, Straub R (2015a) Capital-flow management measures: what are they good for? J Int Econ 96(S1):S76–S97
Forbes KJ, Reinhardt D, Wiedalek T (2015b) The spillovers, interactions, and (un)intended consequences of monetary and regulatory policies. In: 16th Jacques Polak annual research conference
Forbes KJ, Warnock FE (2012) Capital flow waves: surges, stops, flight, and retrenchment. J Int Econ 88(2):235–251
Fratzscher M (2011) Capital flows, push versus pull factors and the global financial crisis. J Int Econ 88(2):341–356
Gambacorta L, Van Rixtel A (2013) Structural bank regulation initiatives: approaches and implications. Bank for International Settlements, working papers No 412
Ghosh AR, Qureshi MS, Kim JI, Zalduendo J (2014) Surges. J Int Econ 92(2):266–285
Hale G, Obstfeld M (2014) The Euro and the geography of international debt flows. National bureau of economic research, working papers 20033
Hoekman B (2015) The global trade slowdown: a new normal? Centre for Economic Policy Research eBook. http://www.voxeu.org/content/global-trade-slowdown-new-normal. Accessed 24 June 2015
International Monetary Fund (IMF) (2012) The liberalization and management of capital flows: an institutional view. http://www.imf.org/external/np/pp/eng/2012/111412.pdf
International Monetary Fund (IMF) (2015) Global financial stability report—navigating monetary policy challenges and managing risks. International Monetary Fund, Washington, DC
Kaminsky G, Schmukler S (2003) Short-run pain, long-run gain: the effects of financial liberalization. National Bureau of Economic Research, working papers 9787
Levchenko AA, Mauro P (2007) Do some forms of financial flows help protect against 'sudden stops'? World Bank Econ Rev 21(3):389–411
McQuade P, Schmitz M (2017) The great moderation in international capital flows: a global phenomenon? J Int Money Finance 73(A):188–212
Milesi-Ferretti GM, Tille C (2011) The great retrenchment: international capital flows during the global financial crisis. Econ Policy 66:28–346
Obstfeld M (2012) Does the current account still matter? Am Econ Rev 102(3):1–23
Ostry JD, Ghosh AR, Chamon M, Qureshi MS (2011) Capital controls: when and why? Int Monetary Fund Econ Rev 59:562–580
Ostry JD, Ghosh AR, Chamon M, Qureshi MS (2012) Tools for managing financial-stability risks from capital inflows. J Int Econ 88(2):407–421
Pasricha G, Falagiarda M, Bijsterbosch M, Aizenman J (2015) Domestic and multilateral effects of capital controls in emerging markets. Working Paper 2015-37
Puy D (2015) Mutual funds flows and the geography of contagion. J Int Money Finance 60(C):73–93
Reinhart C, Reinhart V (2009) Capital flow bonanzas: an encompassing view of the past and present. National Bureau of Economic Research Chapters, National Bureau of Economic Research International Seminar on Macroeconomics 2008, 9-62
Rey H (2013) Dilemma not trilemma: the global financial cycle and monetary policy independence. Jackson Hole Paper August 2013
Shin HS (2012) Global banking glut and loan risk premium. Int Monetary Fund Econ Rev 60(2):155–192
Tarullo D (2012) Regulation of foreign banking organizations. Board of Governors of the Federal Reserve System. Speech at the Yale School of Management Leaders Forum
Tarullo D (2014) Enhanced prudential standards for bank holding companies and foreign banking organizations. Opening Statement by Gov. Daniel K. Tarullo
Tille C, Van Wincoop E (2010) International capital flows. J Int Econ 80:157–175

International Spillovers of Non-standard Monetary Policy: Evidence From Central and Eastern Europe

Alessio Ciarlone and Andrea Colabella

Abstract Among the non-standard monetary measures used by the European Central Bank (ECB), asset purchase programmes (APPs) have been gaining increasing importance in the last couple of years, accounting for about half of total assets in the Eurosystem's balance sheet as of late 2016. This chapter aims to gauge the impact of the ECB's APPs on the financial markets of a set of Central, Eastern and South Eastern European (CESEE) economies. We find that the APPs implementation contributed to supporting cross-border portfolio investment flows to, and foreign bank claims into, CESEE economies mainly in an indirect way—i.e. through their impact on certain liquidity and financial condition indicators in the euro area—therefore revealing the existence of both a portfolio rebalancing and a banking liquidity channel of transmission. Without such non-standard monetary measures, both types of cross-border capital flows would have been weaker and financial conditions in CESEE economies more stringent than they actually were. In fact, we also show that the implementation of the ECB's APPs had the effect of lowering both policy and long-term interest rates to levels well below those predicted on the basis of similarities in business cycles or global risk factors. These effects may not have been entirely unwelcome during the recent period of sub-par growth and unusually low inflation, but may pose relevant policy challenges going forward, against the background of a cyclical divergence between CESEE countries and the euro area economy.

The authors would like to thank Giuseppe Parigi, Pietro Catte, Valeria Rolli, Giorgio Merlonghi, Emidio Cocozza, Daniela Marconi, Martina Cecioni, Urszula Szczerbowicz and participants of the seminar organised by the Department of Economics at the University of Oxford and of the 14th Emerging Markets Workshop organised by Banco de España. The views expressed here are those of the authors and do not necessarily reflect those of the Bank of Italy. All errors and omissions remain our own.

A. Ciarlone (✉) · A. Colabella
Bank of Italy, Directorate General for Economics, Statistics and Research, International Relations and Economics Directorate, Rome, Italy
e-mail: alessio.ciarlone@bancaditalia.it

A. Colabella
e-mail: andrea.colabella@bancaditalia.it

L. Ferrara et al. (eds.), *International Macroeconomics in the Wake of the Global Financial Crisis*, Financial and Monetary Policy Studies 46,
https://doi.org/10.1007/978-3-319-79075-6_14

1 Introduction and Main Conclusions

Since the eruption of the 2008–2009 global financial crisis, the ECB has resorted to various kinds of non-standard monetary measures to address a range of unprecedented and unusual risks caused by liquidity shortages in certain financial markets, fears of a euro area break-up and ensuing 'redenomination risk' and, more recently, a prolonged period of excessively low inflation. Among such non-standard measures, asset purchase programmes (APPs) have gained increasing importance, accounting for around 45% of total assets in the Eurosystem's balance sheet as of late 2016 (from less than 10% at end-2014).[1] While most of the existing research on the international spillover effects of unconventional monetary policies (UMPs) has focused on the US Fed's quantitative easing (QE) measures, the available evidence about the ECB's non-standard policies in general—and APPs in particular—is relatively scant so far.

In an attempt to fill these analytical gaps, we gauge the impact of the ECB's APPs on the financial markets of a set of Central, Eastern and South Eastern European (CESEE) economies.[2] This is done, first, by means of a fixed-effect panel regression *event study* analysis, aimed at highlighting the likely existence of short-run spillover effects of the APPs on a set of financial market indicators. In addition, and more importantly from a policy perspective, we check for more persistent financial spillover effects on the dynamics of cross-border capital flows, by looking separately at both portfolio investment (through a *portfolio rebalancing* channel) and international bank lending (through a *banking liquidity* channel). Finally, we also look at whether the implementation of non-standard policies helped ease financial conditions in the CESEE economies—proxied by movements in policy, short- and long-term interest rates—through international monetary spillovers.

The main conclusions of our analysis are the following. APPs *announcements* appear to have been accompanied, in the very short-run, by a broad-based appreciation of CESEE currencies *vis-à-vis* the euro, an increase in the value of domestic stock market indices, a moderate compression of their respective long-term sovereign yields and a positive impact on mutual fund investment flows. As regards the channels through which the spillovers were transmitted, our results show that the outright purchases of financial assets by the ECB ultimately translated into both stronger cross-border portfolio investment flows to, and larger foreign bank claims into our sample CESEE economies. Ultimately, the implementation of non-standard measures by the ECB also turned out to be an economically and statistically significant factor behind the compression of both policy and long-term interest rates in CESEE economies to levels well below those predicted on the basis of similarities in business cycles or global risk factors.

[1]Throughout the paper we will refer without distinction to the ECB's or the Eurosystem's non-standard tools, though these measures are actually decided and implemented by the Eurosystem as a whole.

[2]The CESEE economies analysed here include both non-euro area EU countries—Bulgaria, Croatia, the Czech Republic, Hungary, Poland and Romania—and a number of EU candidates and potential candidates—Albania, Bosnia-Herzegovina, the FYR of Macedonia, Montenegro and Serbia.

The chapter is organized as follows. First, we will sketch the main transmission channels of outright asset purchases and identify a few stylized facts about the ECB's APPs. Then, we will illustrate our empirical strategy to quantify the international spillover effects of these non-standard monetary measures onto CESEE economies and show the main results of our estimation exercise. A few policy considerations are presented in the concluding section.

2 Transmission Channels of UMPs

The literature has broadly identified three main channels through which APPs can transmit their effects to the financial system (and to the real economy), both domestically and internationally: the *portfolio rebalancing*, *banking liquidity* and *signalling* channels (see, for example, Cova and Ferrero 2015; Bluwstein and Canova 2016).

Outright purchases of public and private securities modify the size and composition of the balance sheet of both the central bank and the private sector, and therefore may affect the economy through a *portfolio rebalancing* channel. As these measures involve the purchase of longer-duration assets, they increase the liquidity holdings of the sellers, inducing a rebalancing of investors' portfolios towards the preferred risk-return configuration. A necessary condition for this channel to be effective is an imperfect substitutability among different assets due to the presence of economic frictions.[3] By purchasing a particular security, the central bank reduces the relative amount held by private agents, usually in exchange for risk-free reserves. As a result, asset prices increase and long-term interest rates fall, creating more favourable conditions for economic recovery.

Outright asset purchases may also directly ease financial conditions and support bank lending to the private sector by improving the availability of funds through a *banking liquidity* channel. The counterpart of the purchase of long-term assets on private banks' balance sheets is typically an increase in reserves. Since such reserves are more easily traded in secondary markets than long-term securities, there would be a decline in the liquidity premium which, in turn, would enable previously liquidity-constrained banks to extend credit to investors. This would result in a decline of borrowing costs and an increase in overall bank lending, including cross-border lending to emerging and developing countries (Lim et al. 2014). The importance of this channel largely depends on the business cycle and on the conditions of the domestic banking sector.

The *signalling* channel operates when the central bank, through its unconventional measures, conveys information to the public about its intentions regarding the future evolution of monetary policy. If this communication is perceived by market participants as a signal of lower-than-previously-expected future policy rates, long-term yields may decline (via a lower risk-neutral component in interest rates). This

[3]For instance, asymmetric information, limited commitment and limited participation (Cecioni et al. 2011; Falagiarda and Reitz 2015).

channel may also be complemented by a sort of *confidence* channel whereby the announcements, or actual operations, of the central bank may contribute to reducing economic uncertainty, reducing risk premia and bolstering activity (Ferrara et al. 2018). In this case, the credibility of the central bank plays a crucial factor.

This classification, of course, makes no claim of being exhaustive; in practice, there is actually a substantial degree of overlap among the different channels, as shown by the existing literature.[4] For this reason, it is often impossible to unambiguously identify which channels may be at play.

3 Some Stylized Facts

3.1 *The ECB's Asset Purchase Programmes*

Since mid-2009, the ECB has implemented a number of APPs as part of its non-standard monetary policy toolkit with a view to dealing with the emergence of unprecedented problems and risks. The Enhanced Credit Support (ECS) contained the first programme of outright asset purchases, i.e. the Covered Bond Purchase Programme (CBPP1), with the explicit goal of rekindling the functioning of the covered bond market, an essential source of refinancing for banks. This programme was renewed in November 2011 (CBPP2) and in October 2014 (CBPP3).[5]

In May 2010, as tensions on the sovereign debt markets of certain euro area countries emerged, the ECB introduced an additional APP, the Securities Market Programme (SMP), involving purchases of euro area government bonds to ensure adequate depth and liquidity in secondary markets.[6]

In July 2012, at the height of the European sovereign debt crisis, President Draghi's 'whatever it takes' speech in London paved the way for the adoption, in September 2012, of Outright Monetary Transactions (OMT). Within this programme, the ECB could purchase an unlimited amount of sovereign bonds maturing in 1–3 years on

[4]In the extant literature there is a very long series of transmission channels. To name but a few examples: Krishnamurthy and Vissing-Jorgensen (2011) proposed a *duration risk* channel, a *safety* channel, a *prepayment risk premium* channel, a *default risk* channel and an *inflation* channel; Fratzscher et al. (2014) added a *risk aversion* channel, a *bank credit risk* channel and a *sovereign credit risk* channel; Cova and Ferrero (2015) an *asset pricing* channel and a *government budget constraint* channel.

[5]The CBPP1 ended, as planned, on 30 June 2010 when it reached the originally announced target of €60 billion in nominal terms. The CBPP2 terminated on 31 October 2012 when it reached a nominal amount of €16.4 billion, below the original targeted amount of €40 billion. The CBPP3, on the contrary, was not launched with a pre-established targeted nominal amount; as a matter of fact, as of end-2016, it reached €203.5 billion.

[6]SMP purchases were made in two big waves, one in the first half of 2010 and the other in the second half of 2011, with their liquidity impact sterilized through specific operations. The purchases were conducted on a discretionary basis, according to daily market conditions. Following the ECB Governing Council decision of 6 September 2012 to initiate outright monetary transactions, the SMP was terminated.

request by a government asking for financial assistance, provided that the bond-issuing country implemented the specific measures (the conditionality principle) agreed under an adjustment programme to be signed with the European Financial Stability Facility, later the European Stability Mechanism. The OMT was introduced to combat monetary and financial fragmentation in the euro area by removing the redenomination risk related to its possible break-up, though tensions in euro area sovereign markets eased significantly immediately following the announcement. The OMT has never been activated.

In June 2014, the ECB announced a credit easing package to support lending to the real economy, including intensifying preparatory work for outright purchases of asset-backed securities (ABSPP), which started in October 2014 in parallel with the launch of the third wave of the CBPP.

In January 2015, the Governing Council announced the Expanded Asset Purchase Programme (EAPP), which adds a purchase programme for public sector securities (PSPP) to the existing private sector asset purchase programmes (CBPP3 and ABSPP), in order to address the risk of an overly long period of low inflation. Under the EAPP, the ECB has expanded its purchases to include bonds issued by euro area central governments, agencies and European institutions, with combined monthly asset purchases amounting to €60 billion on average (from March 2016 until March 2017 this average monthly figure was €80 billion).

The purchases are intended to be carried out until the end of 2017 or until the adjustment in the path of inflation is consistent with the objective of monetary policy. Since June 2016, investment grade euro-denominated bonds issued by non-bank corporations established in the euro area have been included in the list of eligible assets for regular purchases (i.e. the Corporate Sector Purchase Programme—CSPP).

The overall stock of securities purchased under all programmes increased steadily to 10% of the Eurosystem's total assets between 2009Q3 and 2010Q3, hovered around this level until the end of 2014, and then started increasing again following the launch of the EAPP to reach a share of almost 45% of total assets as of late-2016 (see Fig. 3 in Appendix 2 for greater detail).

3.2 *The Impact on CESEE Economies of the Series of Shocks Hitting the Euro Area*

The 2008–2009 global financial crisis spread to most emerging economies, including those in the CESEE region, through both real and financial channels. After the collapse of Lehman Brothers in September 2008 and the ensuing increase in global risk aversion, capital inflows to the CESEE region came to a sudden stop and global trade collapsed, placing the region at the epicentre of the emerging market fallout. Not only the CESEE region was particularly hard hit, it was the hardest hit, and this 'recoupling' with advanced economies continued throughout the euro area's sovereign debt crisis.

Standard explanations of the plausible different transmission mechanisms of a crisis emphasises trade and financial integration channels. CESEE countries are in general much more open than other emerging regions and trade links with the euro area are very intense, hence the fall in euro area demand for their exports was a major drag on output in the region. As for the financial channels, bank-linked capital outflows initially played a major role, reflecting the global retrenchment of Western European banks. This was lately accompanied by the outflow of other categories of capital, as other financial investors became more risk-averse and decided to reduce their exposure in CESEE countries and fly to 'safe havens'. As a matter of fact, net private capital inflows dropped from about 11% of GDP in 2007 to practically zero in 2009, with the magnitude of this fall being much larger than that recorded in Latin America at the time of the debt crisis in the early 1980s (where it fell from about 5% of GDP to −3%) and in developing Asia after 1997 (where it fell from about 6% of GDP to −1%). Such a huge fall in capital inflows along with the resulting credit crunch necessitated strong adjustment in domestic demand, weighing heavily on macroeconomic and financial developments in the CESEE region, which was pitched into recession. Such an adverse impact was further exacerbated by the subsequent export and investment declines, the latter resulting from increased overall uncertainty about future growth prospects.

Local governments responded to the collapse in economic activity with varying degrees of monetary and fiscal accommodation, as well as by adopting a wide range of emergency measures to ensure adequate liquidity in the market. Monetary policy responses had to craft a fair compromise between sustaining growth and preserving financial stability by avoiding excessive exchange rate depreciation. The varying degree of monetary stimuli across countries reflected differences in exchange rate regimes, external funding costs, and the level of pre-crisis policy rates: on the one hand, there were countries where risks of significant balance sheet effects due to sharp exchange rate depreciations prevented policy rate cuts (such as Croatia and FYR of Macedonia); on the other hand, there were countries perceived by markets as safer that were able to provide more monetary policy stimulus (such as the Czech Republic and Poland). The fiscal space available varied across countries, too. Higher pre-crisis primary balances and lower public debt levels allowed for greater fiscal accommodation during the crisis (again, in the Czech Republic and Poland). Conversely, countries with limited fiscal space (such as Hungary) were forced to adopt fiscal adjustment measures to boost market confidence in their policy frameworks. A handful of CESEE economies officially applied for IMF support,[7] often jointly

[7]The programmes signed for Bosnia-Herzegovina, Hungary and Romania, were approved in the immediate aftermath of the global crisis, and took the form of large and front-loaded support packages designed to avoid crippling recessions. An arrangement with Serbia was first treated as precautionary but was quickly augmented and drawn upon. In 2009, Poland qualified for the newly-introduced Flexible Credit Line, a precautionary arrangement with no requirement to take additional measures, underscoring its very sound economic fundamentals and policy frameworks. Additionally, FYR of Macedonia adopted a Precautionary and liquidity line (which it later drew upon), an arrangement that recognized its sound fundamentals with focused and limited conditionality.

with the EU.[8] At the same time, major Western European banks with a significant presence throughout the CESEE region committed to rolling over their exposures under the aegis of the Vienna Initiative, further contributing to avoiding a meltdown of financial systems in host countries.[9]

These measures sowed the seeds of a strong cyclical rebound, which led many CESEE economies to recover almost all the GDP losses recorded in the aftermath of the 2008–2009 financial crisis and 2011–2012 euro area's sovereign debt crisis and, in some cases, to close existing output gaps. Against this background, it has been acknowledged (IMF 2015a, b) that the announcement and subsequent actual implementation of non-standard monetary measures by the ECB played an important role in this sense by positively affecting euro area growth prospects while boosting the confidence of global investors, who started to rebalance their portfolios towards this area in search of higher yields.

4 Empirical Results

4.1 Event Study Analysis

In order to identify the effects of the ECB's APPs on financial market variables in CESEE countries, we first replicate the event study approach contained in many examples of the empirical literature on the topic.[10] Our econometric procedure implies the estimation of a panel model with country fixed-effects where the dependent variable is, alternately: (i) the one-day percentage change in each country's currency bilateral foreign exchange rate *vis-à-vis* the euro, in percentage points; (ii) the one-day change in each country's ten-year government bond yield, in basis points; (iii) the one-day return on each country's major stock market index, in percentage points; (iv) the weekly amount of portfolio inflows into, respectively, each country's bond and equity sectors. We regress each of these dependent variables against a set of controls, including surprises related to the release of macroeconomic indicators

[8]The EU offers balance of payments assistance to member countries outside the euro area that are experiencing, or threatened by, difficulties in financing external imbalances. This kind of financial assistance takes the form of medium-term loans, which are conditional on the implementation of policies designed to address underlying macroeconomic imbalances. Typically, balance of payments assistance from the EU is offered in cooperation with the IMF and other international financial institutions.

[9]The European Bank Coordination 'Vienna' Initiative is a framework for safeguarding the financial stability of emerging Europe. The Initiative was launched at the height of the first wave of the global financial crisis in January 2009. It brought together all the relevant public and private sector stakeholders of EU-based cross-border banks, which own much of the banking sectors in that region and also hold a significant portion of government securities. It was reactivated in late 2011, when signs of a severe credit crunch within the eurozone, and of rapid deleveraging in emerging Europe, resurfaced.

[10]All the following subsections except for Sect. 4.2.2 are drawn from Ciarlone and Colabella (2016), to which the interested reader is referred for the actual estimation results.

Table 1 Event study analysis

	Nominal spot FX	LT yield	Equity	Portfolio flows		
				All	Stock	Bond
ECB indicator dummy	$+^{*}$	$-^{*}$	$+^{**}$	$+^{**}$	$+^{*}$	$+^{**}$
Surprise index (Citi)						
US	+	$+^{*}$	$+^{**}$	+	$+^{*}$	$-^{**}$
Euro area	$+^{**}$	+	$+^{***}$	+	$+^{*}$	+
Volatility measures						
JPMorgan	$-^{*}$					
MOVE		$+^{**}$				
VIX			$-^{***}$	$-^{**}$	$-^{**}$	$-^{**}$

Note the sample of 11 CESEE economies includes: Albania, Bosnia-Herzegovina, Bulgaria, Croatia, Czech Republic, Hungary, FYR of Macedonia, Montenegro, Poland, Romania and Serbia. Robust standard errors, with ***p < 0.01, **p<0.05, *p<0.1. The estimated equation is $y_{i,t} = \alpha_i + \beta_1 APP_{EA,t} + \beta_2 F_t + \varepsilon_t$, where the dependent variable $y_{i,t}$ represents, alternatively: (i) **Nominal spot FX**, the (one-day) percentage change in country *i*'s currency bilateral exchange rate *vis-à-vis* the euro; (ii) **LT yield**, the (one-day) change in country *i*'s ten-year government bond yield; (iii) **Equity**, the (one-day) percentage change in country *i*'s major stock market index; (iv) **Portfolio flows**, the weekly amount of portfolio inflows into country *i*'s bond and equity sectors. The list of independent variables hosts: (i) **Surprise index (Citi)**, a measure of the contemporaneous surprises related to the release of macroeconomic indicators in the US and the euro area; (ii) **JPMorgan**, a volatility index for EMEs changes; (iii) **MOVE**, a volatility index for long-term bond yields; (iv) **VIX**, the Chicago board option volatility index exchange rate, a popular measure of the implied volatility of S&P 500 index options. The different specifications are estimated by means of an OLS country-fixed effect panel procedure on a daily frequency except for the portfolio flows one, which is estimated on a weekly basis, for the period January 2009 to June 2016

both in the euro area and in the US as well as changes in certain global volatility indices. More importantly, we include a dummy indicator to capture the *surprise* effect related to the release of news regarding the non-standard monetary measures announced and adopted by the ECB.[11]

The results are in line with those reported in other pieces of research focused on the experience of the US Fed. Table 1, in fact, shows that the estimated coefficient of the dummy indicator turns out to be statistically significant, and with the expected sign, in all the different model specifications: APPs *announcements* caused a broad-based appreciation of CESEE currencies *vis-à-vis* the euro, an increase in the value of domestic stock market indices and a moderate compression of their respective long-term sovereign yields. These findings seem to support the hypothesis of a sort of international *portfolio rebalancing* mechanism at play (Falagiarde et al. 2015), as shown by the positive impact on portfolio capital flows to CESEE economies in both the equity and debt compartments.

[11]The dummy indicator includes the 18 positive occurrences recorded from January 2009 to March 2016 and is contained in Table 6 in Appendix 1.

4.2 Longer-Term Analysis: The Portfolio Rebalancing and Banking Liquidity Channels

However, event study techniques can only provide a limited representation of the spillover effects from non-standard monetary measures, since they cannot capture longer-lasting financial impacts or shed light on the subsequent transmission. It is therefore important to combine this approach with other methodologies, which take into account longer time spans and control for a wider set of macroeconomic and financial variables. In this way, we are able to analyse other important transmission channels including the *banking liquidity* one, which we suspect would be more relevant than the *portfolio rebalancing* channel for CESEE economies in light of these countries' close banking interlinkages with the euro area.

Our estimation approach builds upon two strands of research.

On the one hand, we refer to the large body of literature according to which the surge of cross-border international capital flows was largely attributable to global liquidity and funding conditions, which in turn was mainly determined by the very accommodative conventional and unconventional monetary policies implemented by central banks across advanced economies in recent years (Bruno and Shin 2012, 2013, 2014, 2015; Rey 2013, 2015).[12] To capture this impact we select a standard array of both *quantity* and *price* indicators to properly describe the state of liquidity and financing conditions in the euro area, namely: the yearly changes in the M2 (as in IMF 2010) and in credit to the private sector (as in Cerutti et al. 2014) aggregates, among the former; the average level of 10-year yields on AAA rated government bonds (as in Korniyenko and Loukoianova 2015), the average term spread (as in Cerutti et al. 2014; IMF 2016),[13] and, finally, the average spread between Italian and Spanish long-term yields and the German Bund (our innovation),[14] among the latter.

On the other hand, we follow the procedure originally proposed by Ahmed and Zlate (2014) and Korniyenko and Loukoianova (2015) to adequately isolate those

[12]Although the assumption in the literature has been that factors driving global liquidity originate predominantly in the US, some more recent results (Cerutti et al. 2014; Korniyenko and Loukoianova 2015) suggest that euro area supply factors are both regionally and globally important too.

[13]The average term spread is calculated as the difference between 10-year yields of AAA euro area government bonds and the 3-month Euribor rate.

[14]The average spread between Italian and Spanish long-term yields and the German Bund is intended to capture those phases in which the 'redenomination' risk related to the break-up of the euro area and the ensuing fragmentation of its financial system became particularly acute. As documented in Albertazzi et al. (2012), Neri (2013) and Zoli (2013), in fact, at the height of the euro area sovereign debt crisis adverse movements in the Italian and other peripheral euro area countries sovereign spreads were unfavourably transmitted to bank funding costs, lending conditions and the availability of credit for the real economy. Against the background of the strong banking linkages between the euro area and CESEE economies—Italian, Austrian and, to a lesser extent, French banking groups are dominant players in these countries' banking sectors—we believe that this variable would be able to capture quite well the transmission of the shock stemming from the outbreak of the euro area's sovereign debt crisis to CESEE economies.

Table 2 The ECB's asset purchases and euro area financial and liquidity conditions

	M2 in %	Nominal credit in %	LT yield in %	Term spread (in basis points)	Average spread (in basis points)
Observations	$+^{***}$	$+^{***}$	$-^{***}$	$-^{***}$	$-^{***}$

Note robust standard errors, with ***p<0.01, **p< 0.05, *p < 0.1. The estimated equation is $y_t = \alpha + \beta_1$ $Asset\ purchases_{t+1} + \varepsilon_t$, where the dependent variable$y_{i,t}$ represents, alternatively: (i) **M2**, the yearly change in the euro area M2 aggregate; (ii) **Nominal credit**, the yearly change in the stock of euro area credit to the private sector; (iii) **LT yield**, the average level of 10-year yields on euro area AAA rated government bonds; (iv) **Term spread**, the difference between the 10-year yields of euro area AAA rated government bonds and the 3-month Euribor rate; (v) **Average spread**, the average spread between Italian and Spanish 10-year yields and the corresponding German Bund. The independent variable $Asset\ purchases_{t+1}$ measures the one-quarter ahead ECB's actual gross asset purchases. The models are estimated by OLS on a monthly basis for M2 and nominal credit and on a weekly basis for the remaining dependent variable from January 2009 to June 2016

changes in euro area liquidity and financing conditions that could be considered as directly attributable to the implementation of the ECB's non–standard monetary measures; although, in fact, the state of liquidity and financing conditions may depend on a large set of factors—among which both standard and non-standard monetary measures played a relevant role—we are actually interested only in the latter. Therefore, our testable hypothesis is that the outright purchases of public and private financial assets carried out between 2009Q3 and 2016Q2 translated into a gradual easing of liquidity and financing conditions in the euro area which, in turn, ultimately impacted on the cross-border portfolio and banking flows to CESEE economies.[15]

Against this background, our estimation strategy foresees two different steps.

First of all, we test whether the implementation of the ECB's APPs actually translated into more favourable liquidity and financing conditions in the euro area. By running simple OLS regressions—where the ECB's one-quarter ahead actual gross asset purchases are used as an explicit determinant of the different variables used to measure euro area liquidity and financing conditions—Table 2 shows that the actual realization of these non-standard programmes translated into: (a) an acceleration in the growth of the M2 aggregate and credit to the private sector; (b) a reduction in long-term government yields; (c) a flattening of the yield curve; and (d) a compression in the sovereign spreads of peripheral euro area countries. These estimation results are relevant not only per se, but also because the ensuing fitted values will represent an essential ingredient for the longer-term models aimed at highlighting the existence of two important channels of transmission for the ECB's non-standard monetary measures into CESEE economies.

As a second step, we run two separate regressions, one for each of the two types of cross-border capital flows: for portfolio flows our model follows the basic tenets of portfolio theory, according to which expected returns, risk and risk preferences mat-

[15]See Ciarlone and Colabella (2016) for greater details.

ter for international investors' asset allocations (Ahmed and Zlate 2014); for banking flows we start with a traditional model based upon a set of standard control variables describing country-specific characteristics and time-varying global financial conditions (McGuire and Tarashev 2008; Buch et al. 2009; Herrmann and Mihaljek 2010; García-Herrero and Martinez-Peria 2005). In order to quantify the specific influence of the ECB's APPs, we then augment each of the two basic specifications for the two types of capital flows with some additional explanatory variables, such as: the actual measures of euro area liquidity conditions; the portion of them actually accounted for by the working of the ECB's outright asset purchases; and, finally, a dummy indicator to investigate the behaviour of these flows during the quarters when the different rounds of asset purchase programmes were first announced or subsequently implemented and extended. As regards the signs of the estimated coefficients, we expect to see a direct (i.e. positive) relationship between cross-border capital inflows and *quantity* indicators of euro area's liquidity and financing conditions, an inverse (i.e. negative) relationship with the *price* indicators and again a direct (i.e. positive) relationship with the dummy indicator.

In the case of the *portfolio rebalancing* channel, the estimation results reported in Table 3 clearly point to a significantly positive influence on portfolio flows from euro area financial and liquidity conditions, confirming the results of the available literature for the US on a larger sample of emerging economies (IMF 2010; Cerutti et al. 2014). The coefficient of the growth rate of the M2 monetary aggregate shows the expected positive sign, and is statistically significant. Similar conclusions hold for the *price* indicator: a fall in euro area long-term yields brings about larger portfolio flows to CESEE economies (as in Ahmed and Zlate 2014). Once these actual indicators are supplanted by the fitted values obtained by recurring to the procedure described in Ahmed and Zlate (2014), their respective coefficients continue to have the expected sign and to be highly statistically significant. Turning to the effect of the *announcement* of the ECB's APPs, the coefficient of the dummy indicator suggests a positive and statistically significant impact on portfolio capital inflows, again as expected.

In the case of the *banking liquidity* channel, the estimation results contained in Table 4 suggest that cross-border banking flows towards CESEE economies seem to be positively related, as expected, to the euro area M2 dynamics. Secondly, the coefficient of the average sovereign spread in stressed peripheral euro area countries *vis-à-vis* the German Bund is negative and statistically significant, suggesting that fragmentation and redenomination risks have brought about a reduction in cross-border banking flows towards CESEE economies. Lastly, a fall in euro area long-term yields is estimated to deliver larger cross-border banking flows to CESEE economies. Turning to the announcement episodes captured by the dummy indicator, the related coefficient suggests a positive impact on banking flows, though it comes out as not statistically significant. Finally, once all the indicators of actual liquidity and financial conditions in the euro area are replaced by their fitted counterparts accounted for by

Table 3 The *portfolio rebalancing* channel

Category	Name of variable	(1)	(2)	(3)	(4)	(5)	(6)
Growth							
	Domestic real GDP growth	+**	+*	+**	+*	+	+
	Euro area real GDP growth	+	+**	+*	+	+	+
Short-term rates							
	Domestic interbank rates	+*	+*	+*	+*	+	+
	Euro area interbank rates	−**	−***	−***	−***	−***	−***
VIX index		−***	−	−	−***	−***	−***
Time trend		−*	−***	−***	−***	−***	−***
Euro area liquidity indicators							
Non-price	Growth of Euro area M2		+***				
Price	Long-term bond yields			−***			
Asset purchases							
	Announcements				+***		
Asset purchases' impact on							
	Growth of Euro area M2					+**	
	Long-term bond yields						−**

Note The sample of 11 CESEE economies includes: Albania, Bosnia-Herzegovina, Bulgaria, Croatia, Czech Republic, Hungary, FYR of Macedonia, Montenegro, Poland, Romania and Serbia. Bootstrapped (1,000 replications) standard errors, with ***p < 0.01, **p < 0.05, *p < 0.1. The estimated equation is $PORT_{i,t} = \alpha_i + \beta_1 Gi + \beta_2 G_{EA} + \beta_3 R_i + \beta_4 R_{EA} + \beta_5 VIX + \beta_6 LIQ_{EA} + \beta_7 t + \varepsilon_{i,t}$, where the dependent variable $PORT_{i,t}$ measures the ratio between portfolio flows to country *i* to the respective GDP. The list of independent variables includes: (i) $\boldsymbol{G_i}$ and $\boldsymbol{G_{EA}}$, the real GDP growth rates in country *i* and the euro area, respectively; (ii) $\boldsymbol{R_i}$ and $\boldsymbol{R_{EA}}$, the respective short-term interest rates to capture the relative attractiveness of domestic versus foreign assets and thus capital flows; (iii) **VIX**, a measure of global risk aversion; (iv) $\boldsymbol{LIQ_{EA}}$ a series of measures for euro area liquidity and financing conditions; (v) $\boldsymbol{t}$, a time trend. The different specifications are estimated by means of an OLS country-fixed effect panel procedure on a quarterly basis from 2009Q3 to 2016Q2

the working of the ECB's APPs, their respective coefficients again have the expected sign and are all statistically significant at conventional levels.[16]

Hence, the more accommodative financial and liquidity conditions in the euro area resulting from the actual implementation of the ECB's programmes of outright asset purchases, along with the easing of the tensions on sovereign bond markets

[16]To explore the sensitivity of our results, we conducted an extensive series of robustness checks. To begin with, we replicated the event study analysis using two-day and one-week windows instead of the one-day reported before. For both the models relative to the portfolio rebalancing and banking liquidity channels, we experimented with different indicators of liquidity and financing conditions, substituting the growth rate of credit to the private sector with the M2 growth rate and the average term spread with the 10-year yields on euro area AAA rated government bonds. For the portfolio rebalancing channel, we also investigated the robustness of our results for the bond rather than the stock compartments. Overall, the results turned out to be broadly consistent with those reported in the main tables and confirm the role played by the ECB's APPs.

Table 4 The *banking liquidity* channel

Category	Name of variable	(1)	(2)	(3)	(4)	(5)	(6)	(7)	(8)
Domestic									
	Real GDP growth	$+^{***}$	$+^{*}$	$+^{***}$	$+^{***}$	$+^{***}$	+	+	+
	Interbank rates	+	–	+	+	+	–	–	–
	Exchange rates	$-^{***}$	$+^{*}$	$+^{***}$	$+^{*}$	$+^{**}$	$+^{*}$	$+^{*}$	$+^{*}$
	M2 growth	$+^{***}$	+	$+^{***}$	$+^{**}$	$+^{**}$	–	–	–
Global									
	VIX index	$-^{*}$	$-^{**}$	–	$-^{***}$	–	$-^{**}$	$-^{**}$	$-^{**}$
Time trend		$-^{*}$	$-^{*}$	$-^{*}$	–	$-^{*}$	$-^{***}$	$-^{***}$	$-^{***}$
Euro area liquidity indicators									
Non-Price									
	M2 growth		$+^{**}$						
Price									
	Long-term bond yields			$-^{**}$					
	Average spread				$-^{**}$				
Asset purchases									
	Announcements					+			
Asset purchases' impact on									
	Growth of Euro area M2						$+^{***}$		
	Long-term bond yields							$-^{***}$	
	Average spread								$-^{***}$

Note The sample of 11 CESEE economies includes: Albania, Bosnia-Herzegovina, Bulgaria, Croatia, Czech Republic, Hungary, FYR of Macedonia, Montenegro, Poland, Romania and Serbia. Bootstrapped (1,000 replications) standard errors, with $^{***}p < 0.01$, $^{**}p < 0.05$, $^{*}p < 0.1$. The estimated equation is $BANK_{i,t} = \alpha_i + \beta_1 Gi + \beta_2 R_i + \beta_3 NEER_i + \beta_4 M2_i + \beta_5 VIX + \beta_6 LIQ_{EA} + \beta_7 t + \varepsilon_{i,t}$, where the dependent variable $BANK_{i,t}$ measures the ratio between BIS reporting banks flows to country i to the respective GDP. The list of independent variables includes: (i) $\boldsymbol{G_i}$, the real GDP growth rates in country i; (ii) $\boldsymbol{R_i}$, the reference interest rate in country i; (iii) $\boldsymbol{NEER_i}$, the nominal effective interest rate in country i; (iv) $\boldsymbol{M2_i}$, the year-on-year change in the M2 aggregates in country i; (v) **VIX**, as a measure of global risk aversion; (vi) $\boldsymbol{LIQ_{EA}}$, a series of measures for euro area liquidity and financing conditions; (vii) $\boldsymbol{t}$, a time trend. The different specifications are estimated by means of an OLS country-fixed effect panel procedure on a quarterly basis from 2009Q3 to 2016Q2 of peripheral euro area countries, seem to have had a positive effect overall on both portfolio and cross-border banking flows towards CESEE economies. In the absence of these non-standard monetary measures, both cross-border portfolio and banking flows would have been weaker—especially in the most recent quarters of the sample and regarding cross-border banking flows—and these countries' financial conditions probably more stringent than it was actually the case.

4.2.1 Counterfactual Analysis

To illustrate the first point, in Fig. 1 we report the fitted values from each of the full models and the model predictions under the counterfactual that keeps one of the explanatory variables—in particular, that related to the ECB's APPs—at a certain initial level. For instance, the series depicted in the left-hand (right-hand) panels describe the results for the *portfolio rebalancing* (*banking liquidity*) channel: the solid line represents the quarterly country average of the fitted values stemming from the estimation of a model with no role for the impact of the ECB's APPs on M2 in the euro area; the dashed line represents the quarterly country average of the fitted values stemming from the model that accounts for the direct impact of the ECB's APPs on the growth rate of M2 in the euro area. Overall, the two panels clearly show that these non-standard monetary measures positively affected both types of inflows to CESEE economies, with particularly in recent years the introduction of an extended and enlarged programme of financial asset purchases to explicitly address the risks of a too prolonged period of low inflation.

4.2.2 The Easing of Domestic Financial Conditions

To illustrate the second point we analyse whether, and to what extent, the implementation of non-standard policies by the ECB might have had an impact on the evolution of CESEE interest rates, used here as a natural proxy for the state of domestic financial conditions. Figure 2, for instance, clearly shows that interest rates at different maturities in CESEE economies have tended to move closely together with those prevailing in the euro area: while the co-movement appears to be the closest for long-term interest rates (Fig. 2, right-hand panel), it seems to be also present for policy rates (Fig. 2, left-hand panel) and short-term market rates (Fig. 2, centre panel), although in a less pronounced fashion. As a matter of fact, the average correlation of long-term yields in CESEE economies with those of the euro area at monthly frequencies turned out to be 88%, while the average correlation between policy rates was 79% and that of short-term market rates 74%.

These unconditional correlations may reflect common economic and financial factors driving interest rates in a similar direction. For instance, shifts in international investors' willingness to take risks could move monetary conditions in a similar direction globally. The evolution of the euro area business cycle is expected to directly affect global macroeconomic conditions, via for example, trade channels,

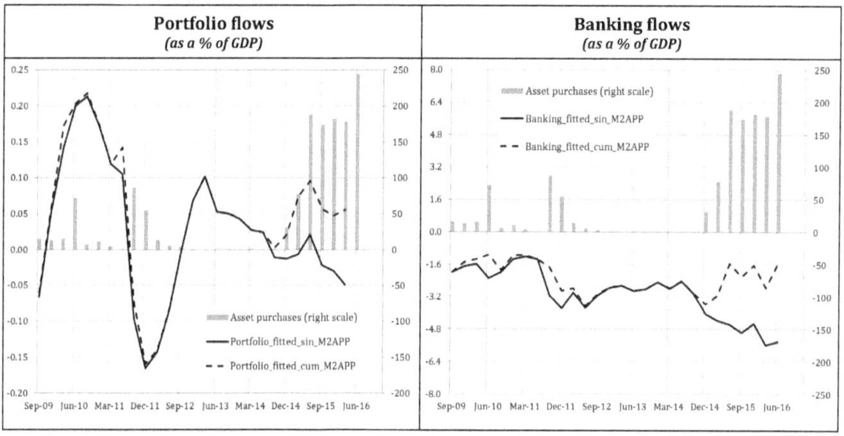

Fig. 1 Gauging the impact of the ECB's APPs: counterfactual analysis. *Note* in the figures, the solid lines represent the quarterly country average of the fitted values stemming from the estimation of models with no role for the impact of the ECB's APPs on M2 in the euro area (i.e., the impact of the ECB's asset purchases on the growth rate of the M2 aggregate was kept equal to zero over the whole estimation period); instead, the dashed lines represent the quarterly country average of the fitted values stemming from the model that account for the direct impact of the ECB's APPs on the growth rate of M2 in the euro area. The fitted values and counterfactuals are based on the model with country fixed effects. Bars represent the volume of asset purchased by the ECB

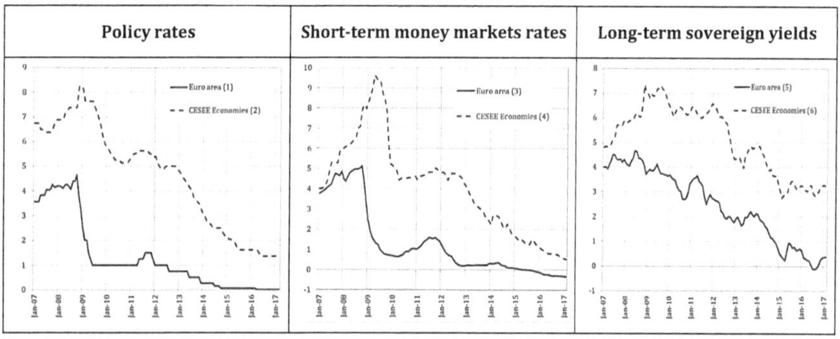

Fig. 2 Interest rates in CESEE economies are strongly correlated with those in the euro area. *Notes* (1) interest rate on the main refinancing operations of the Eurosystem, end-of-period; (2) median across reference rates of Albania, Czech Republic, Hungary, Poland, Romania and Serbia, end-of-period; (3) 3-month euribor rate, monthlyaverage; (4) median across 3-month interbank rates of Bulgaria, Croatia, Czech Republic, Hungary, the FYR of Macedonia, Poland, Romania and Serbia, monthlyaverage; (5) 10-year yields on euro area AAA rated government bonds, monthly average; (6) median across 10-year sovereign yields of Bulgaria, Croatia, Czech Republic, Hungary and Romania, monthly average

implying monetary responses in CESEE economies that are similar to those in the euro area. Yet, beyond these channels, these correlations could also reflect genuine monetary spillovers. On the one hand, investors behaviour could tie interest rates together: global investors portfolio reallocations—following, for instance, the implementation of non-standard policies represented by the purchase of financial assets—might link the long-term rates of CESEE economies to those of the core financial centres. Reflecting the existence of the portfolio rebalancing channel, search for yield might shift funds from low-yielding bonds in the core economies to higher-yielding bonds elsewhere, pushing the latter yields down. On the other hand, monetary policies in the CESEE countries might closely mirror those in the euro area; in other words, there might also be policy spillovers. For instance, central banks might want to prevent the emergence of large interest rate differentials to avoid exchange rate appreciation, which could have undesirable effects on inflation or result in a loss of trade competitiveness. Alternatively, they might be concerned that large interest rate differentials could induce speculative short-term capital inflows that could increase, in turn, financial stability risks. To avoid the emergence of these interest rate differentials, policy makers in CESEE economies would tend to 'shadow' euro area policy rates and, if market expectations project this linkage into the future, other short- and long-term interest rates would likely follow.

Of course, the high observed unconditional correlations shown in Fig. 2 do not necessarily imply that price or policy spillovers are at play. In order to check for them, one needs to estimate the residual correlations after controlling for other potential economic and financial drivers of domestic interest rates; in technical terms, to go from unconditional to conditional correlations. To do this, we follow the examples provided in other pieces of literature on the topic (Gray 2013; Takáts and Vela 2014; Edwards 2015; Hoffmann and Takáts 2015; Obstfeld 2015) in using panel regression techniques to analyse international monetary spillovers, which we define as spillovers in policy and short- and long-term interest rates. More precisely, we run fully-modified OLS panel regressions to take into account the existence of any likely co-integrating relationship among variables on quarterly data spanning from 2007Q1 to 2016Q4. In all our specifications, domestic policy rates, 3-month interbank rates and 10-year government bond yields prevailing in our sample of CESEE economies are regressed on: (i) a vector of domestic macroeconomic variables (comprising the output gap in the case of policy rates or the year-on-year real GDP growth rate for short- and long-term rates, and the year-on-year inflation rate throughout all the specifications) to capture the impact of country-specific business cycle conditions; (ii) a vector of euro area macroeconomic variables (comprising the year-on-year real GDP growth and inflation rate) to control for the impact of the euro area's business cycle conditions and (iii) the (log of the) VIX index—a widely used measure of stock market volatility—to take into account changes in international investor sentiment as a potential common financial factor. To adequately control for the domestic monetary transmission mechanism, we also include (the level of) domestic policy rates in the specifications for both short- and long-term rates.

The results of the estimation exercise are contained in Table 5. The first column clearly shows the existence of economically and statistically significant spillovers from policy rates in the euro area to those in CESEE economies: in particular, a 100 bp change in the rate on the ECB's main refinancing operations is associated with a 56 bp shift in the policy rate of CESEE economies—which is in line with the results obtained by Gray (2013), Takáts and Vela (2014) and Edwards (2015) for the US on a larger sample of emerging economies. Such spillovers seem to be also at play for long-term rates: the results contained in the third column, in fact, would suggest an even larger (74 bp) variation in CESEE 10-year yields following a 100 bp change in the euro area AAA-rated government bond yields. In contrast, there appears to be no significant spillovers in short-term rates (as in Obstfeld 2015): the estimates contained in the second column, in fact, would suggest that the impact of changes in the 3-month Euribor rate turns out not to be statistically significant in affecting CESEE economies short-term rates. Presumably, this is because the influence of euro area rates on short-term market rates is already fully captured by CESEE policy rates, which are included among the regressors. All in all, these initial results would point to the conclusion that interest rates in the euro area affect interest rates (at least the policy and the long-term ones) in CESEE economies well beyond what similarities in business cycles or global risk factors would predict, clearly indicating the existence of international monetary spillovers.

Up to now we have focused on generic monetary spillovers between the euro area and CESEE economies. However, we would like to take one step further and analyse the impact that is more directly related to the ECB's non-standard monetary measures. To adequately delve into this more important aspect—from the point of view of the main theme of this chapter—we depart from the basic model specification relative to long-term rates, supplanting the 10-year yield on euro area AAA rated government bonds with a battery of variables which has already been used to describe the impact of these non-standard policies. The first three measures are taken from IMF (2016), and are represented by: (i) the Wu and Xia (2016) 'shadow rate' calculated for the euro area, to summarise the term structure of interest rates;[17] (ii) the term spread (calculated as the difference between the 10-year yield on euro area AAA rated government bonds and the 3-month Euribor rate, in basis points) to give another representation of the price impact of non-standard policies; and (iii) the increase in the ECB's holdings of securities held for monetary policy purposes as a quantity, rather than a price, indicator of such non-standard measures. Moreover, to be consistent with the approach already used in the regressions run for the portfolio and banking liquidity channels, we also used a dummy indicator—related to the release of news regarding the announcement, or subsequent modifications, of non-standard monetary measures—as well as the changes in both the euro area 10-year yield on AAA rated government bonds and the term spread that could be considered as directly attributable to the actual implementation of financial asset purchases by the ECB (as in Ahmed and Zlate 2014; Korniyenko and Loukoianova 2015; Ciarlone and Colabella 2016). The estimation results of this further battery of specifications are contained in columns (b)–(g) of Table 5. All of them seem to

[17]In a zero lower bound environment, a number of researchers have started designing shadow rate models to characterize the term structure of interest rates or quantify the stance of monetary policy. The Wu and Xia (2016) shadow rate builds on an options model for interest rates to find implied values of segments of the term structure. In short, the shadow rate is assumed to be a linear function of three latent variables called factors, which follow a VAR (1) process; the latent factors and the shadow rate are estimated with an extended Kalman filter.

Table 5 International monetary spillovers

		Policy rates	Short-term rates	Long-term rates						
				(a)	(b)	(c)	(d)	(e)	(f)	(g)
Base representation										
Euro area variables	Policy rate	**0.558 (0.146)*****								
	Short-term rate		−0.035 (−0.101)							
	Long-term rate			**0.736 (0.099)*****						
	Real GDP growth	**−0.233 (0.077)*****	−0.033 (−0.059)	**−0.093 (−0.047)****	−0.016 (0.046)	**−0.137 (0.060)****	0.009 (0.063)	**−0.112 (0.060)****	0.009 (0.063)	0.009 (0.063)
	Inflation	−0.143 (−0.176)	−0.068 (−0.115)	**0.196 (0.094)****	**0.321 (0.089)*****	**0.267 (0.119)****	**0.218 (0.103)****	**0.310 (0.119)*****	**0.218 (0.103)****	**0.218 (0.103)****
Domestic variables	Policy rate		**1.004 (0.085)*****	**0.279 (0.078)*****	**0.658 (0.070)*****	**0.373 (0.102)*****	**0.426 (0.097)*****	**0.492 (0.090)*****	**0.426 (0.097)*****	**0.426 (0.097)*****
	Output gap	−0.043 (−0.078)								
	Real GDP growth		0.023 (0.038)	**−0.095 (0.029)*****	0.032 (0.030)	**−0.085 (0.039)****	−0.054 (0.037)	−0.054 (0.037)	−0.054 (0.037)	−0.054 (0.037)
	Inflation	**0.451 (0.068)*****	**0.125 (0.057)****	−0.063 (0.058)	**−0.091 (0.055)***	0.016 (0.072)	−0.033 (0.062)	0.017 (0.072)	−0.033 (0.062)	−0.033 (0.062)

(continued)

Table 5 (continued)

		Policy rates	Short-term rates	Long-term rates						
				(a)	(b)	(c)	(d)	(e)	(f)	(g)
Global	VIX index	0.004 (0.005)	**0.007 (0.003)****	**0.006 (0.003)****	**0.011 (0.003)*****	**0.013 (0.003)*****	**0.023 (0.003)*****	**0.023 (0.003)*****	**0.023 (0.003)*****	**0.023 (0.003)*****
Proxies for ECB's non-standard measures										
Other euro area's liquidity	Term spread				**0.646 (0.081)*****					
	Shadow rate					**0.175 (0.063)*****				
Asset purchases	Flows						**−0.006 (0.001)*****			
	Dummy							**−0.318 (0.207)***		
Asset purchases impact on	Long-term rates								**0.619 (0.116)*****	
	Term spread									**0.961 (0.179)*****
Observations		190	185	151	151	151	112	151	112	112
R-squared (adj.)		0.92	0.96	0.94	0.94	0.89	0.92	0.89	0.92	0.92

Note sample of 11 CESEE economies includes: Albania, Bosnia-Herzegovina, Bulgaria, Croatia, Czech Republic, Hungary, FYR of Macedonia, Montenegro, Poland, Romania and Serbia. Robust standard errors are provided in parenthesis, ***p < 0.01, **p < 0.05, *p < 0.1. The estimated equation is $RATE_{i,t}=\alpha_i + \Gamma_1 X_{EA,t} + \Gamma_2 X_{i,t} + \beta_1 VIX + \beta_2 LIQ_{EA} + \varepsilon_{i,t}$ where the dependent variable $RATE_{i,t}$ is, alternatively, the level of the reference, the short- and long-term interest rates in CESEE economies. The list of independent variables includes: (i) $\boldsymbol{RATE_i}$ and $\boldsymbol{RATE_{EA}}$, the level of policy rates in country *i* and the level of the reference, the short- and long-term interest rates for the euro area, respectively; (ii) $\boldsymbol{G_i}$ and $\boldsymbol{G_{EA}}$, the real GDP growth rates in country *i* and the euro area, respectively; (iii) $\boldsymbol{INFL_i}$ and $\boldsymbol{INFL_{EA}}$, the annual inflation rates in country *i* and the euro area, respectively; (iv) $\boldsymbol{GAP_i}$, the output gap in country *i*; (v) $\boldsymbol{LIQ_{EA}}$, a series of measures for euro area liquidity and financing conditions. The different specifications are estimated by means of fully-modified OLS panel regressions on a quarterly basis from 2009Q3 to 2016Q4 point to the same conclusion: whichever way the impact of the ECB's non-standard policies is measured, there always appears to be economically and statistically significant spillovers stemming from the implementation of these policies on CESEE economies' long-term rates, thereby helping to ease domestic financial conditions.[18] As it was the case for the euro area's AAA-rated government bond yield, in fact, the direction of the estimated relationship is always as expected: a compression in the term spread, or a reduction in the shadow rate, is accompanied by similar movements in CESEE economies' long-term rates, which also decrease in correspondence with both the announcement and the actual realisation of asset purchases by the ECB. The changes in the euro area's AAA-rated government bond yields and term spread, which can be accounted for by the implementation of APPs, generates changes in the same direction in CESEE economies' long-term rates.

5 Conclusion and Policy Considerations

In the context of the relatively weak economic conjuncture of recent years, most CESEE economies seem to have benefitted from the spillover effects arising from the ECB's non-standard monetary policies. APPs *announcements* appear to have been accompanied, in the very short-run, by a broad-based appreciation of CESEE currencies *vis-à-vis* the euro, an increase in the value of domestic stock market indices, a moderate compression of their respective long-term sovereign yields and a positive impact on mutual fund investment flows. As regards the channels through which the spillovers were transmitted, our results show that the outright purchases of financial assets by the ECB ultimately translated into both stronger cross-border portfolio investment flows to, and larger foreign bank claims on, our sample of CESEE economies. Ultimately, the implementation of non-standard measures by the ECB also turned out to be an economically and statistically significant factor behind the compression of both policy and long-term interest rates in CESEE economies to levels well below those predicted on the basis of similarities in business cycles or global risk factors.

Looking forward, however, the desirability of the cross-border effects of non-standard monetary policies may change if the cyclical position of recipient CESEE economies gradually diverges from the euro area's one, as currently projected. After several years of growth near 3%, there are signs that in most CESEE economies output gaps are closing, with unemployment rates falling to pre-crisis levels, real wage growth picking up and credit growth gradually gathering pace. In spite of this, inflation is still subdued and monetary policy stances have remained accommodative throughout the region. However, should a monetary tightening become necessary prior to the ECB's unwinding of its ultra-accommodative stance, the boost

[18] As a robustness test, we replicated the same set of estimates by recurring to panel feasible generalized least squares, as in Grey (2013). The results, not reported here for the sake of brevity but available from the authors upon request, are in line with those reported in the main text.

to cross-border portfolio and banking flows from continuing asset purchases could be amplified. This may pose relevant challenges to macro-financial and monetary policy management in CESEE economies. Against this background, policymakers would need to stand ready to adapt their macroeconomic and prudential policies to safeguard domestic macro and financial stability.

There has been considerable debate in recent years on the policy implications of capital flow surges for emerging economies, and on the effectiveness of alternative strategies for offsetting their undesired effects. An important contribution has come from the IMF with the publication of its 'institutional view' on the liberalization and management of capital flows (IMF 2012). One general lesson seems to be that both the risks associated with capital flows and the appropriate measures to deal with them depend heavily on the specific economic and financial conditions in the individual recipient countries and on their policy frameworks. A few points seem potentially relevant for CESEE countries. If allowed to move flexibly, the exchange rate can act as an important shock absorber, even though it may not fully insulate domestic financial markets from capital inflows. However, vulnerabilities due to foreign currency exposures need to be properly monitored and addressed in advance, also with a view to avoiding the re-accumulation of past imbalances. And large, persistent exchange rate movements may have undesired effects on trade competitiveness. The options to limit an undesired exchange rate appreciation include a more accommodative monetary policy stance (conventional or unconventional) than what would be justified on strictly domestic grounds—which however would exacerbate the expansionary effects of capital inflows on domestic demand and credit—and sterilized intervention which, however, tends to be only temporarily effective and, if substantial, can prove costly. Fiscal policy can be deployed counter-cyclically to dampen undesired effects on domestic demand and asset prices, thus relieving part of the pressure on monetary policy and the exchange rate. A flexible use of fiscal policy is even more important in countries which, having a fixed exchange rate, have no autonomous monetary policy. Macro-prudential tools can be used to offset some of the risks of a low interest rate environment, dealing with the specific areas or sectors exposed to the greatest risks, but they cannot be regarded as a full substitute for monetary policy. They can serve both to prevent the accumulation of vulnerabilities and to enhance the resilience of the financial system in case the risks materialize.

Andrea Colabella worked on this research while visiting the Department of Economics of the Oxford University.

Appendix 1: The ECB's Asset Purchase Programmes

Table 6 Chronology of main events

Announcement date	Quarter	Non-standard monetary policy decision	Note
7-May-09	2009Q2	A covered bond purchase programme (CBPP1) announced	"The Governing Council has decided in principle that the Eurosystem **will purchase euro-denominated covered bonds issued in the euro area**. The detailed modalities will be announced after the Governing Council meeting of 4 June 2009"
4-Jun-09	2009Q2	CBPP1 starts	"Following-up on its decision of 7 May 2009 to purchase euro-denominated covered bonds issued in the euro area, the Governing Council of the European Central Bank decided upon the technical modalities today"
10-May-10	2010Q2	Securities market programme (SMP) announced (plus the first 6-month LTRO and the reactivation of fixed-rate tender procedures with full allotment)	"The Governing Council of the European Central Bank decided on **several measures** to address the severe tensions in certain market segments which are hampering the monetary policy transmission mechanism and thereby the effective conduct of monetary policy oriented towards price stability in the medium term"
6-Oct-11	2011Q4	A new covered bond purchase programme (CBPP2) announced (plus one 12- and one 13-month LTROs)	"The governing council of the European central bank decided (…) to **launch a second covered bond purchase programme** (CBPP2)"
3-Nov-11		CBPP2 starts	"Further to its decision of 6 October 2011 to launch a new covered bond purchase programme (CBPP2), the governing council of the European central bank decided today upon the technical modalities of the programme"
26-Jul-12	2012Q3	President Draghi's "whatever it takes" London speech	

(continued)

Table 6 (continued)

Announcement date	Quarter	Non-standard monetary policy decision	Note
2-Aug-12		Outright monetary transaction (OMT) announced	"The governing council (…) **may undertake outright open market operations** of a size adequate to reach its objective. (…) Furthermore, the Governing Council may consider undertaking further non-standard monetary policy measures according to what is required to repair monetary policy transmission"
6-Sep-12		Technical features of OMT	"As announced on 2 August 2012, the governing council of the European central bank has today taken decisions on **a number of technical features regarding the Eurosystem's outright transactions** in secondary sovereign bond markets that aim at safeguarding an appropriate monetary policy transmission and the singleness of the monetary policy"
5-Jun-14	2014Q2	Outright purchases of asset-backed securities announced (plus a series of targeted longer-term refinancing operations T-LTROs).	"In pursuing its price stability mandate, the Governing Council of the ECB has today announced measures to enhance the functioning of the monetary policy transmission mechanism by supporting lending to the real economy. In particular, the Governing Council has decided: (…) 2. **To intensify preparatory work related to outright purchases of asset-backed securities** (ABS)"
4-Sep-14	2014Q3	ABS purchase programme (ABSPP) and a new Covered Bond Purchase Programme (CBPP3) announced	"(…) The governing council decided to **start purchasing non-financial private sector assets**. (…) The Eurosystem will purchase a broad portfolio of simple and transparent asset-backed securities (ABSs) (…) **under an ABS purchase programme** (ABSPP). (…) In parallel, the Eurosystem will also **purchase a broad portfolio of euro-denominated covered bonds** issued by MFIs domiciled in the euro area **under a new covered bond purchase programme (CBPP3)**"

(continued)

Table 6 (continued)

Announcement date	Quarter	Non-standard monetary policy decision	Note
2-Oct-14	2014Q4	Operational details of ABSPP and CBPP3	"The governing council of the European central bank today agreed key details regarding the operation of its new programmes to buy simple and transparent asset-backed securities (ABSs) and a broad portfolio of euro-denominated covered bonds. Together with the targeted longer-term refinancing operations, the purchase programmes will further enhance the transmission of monetary policy"
17-Nov-14		President Draghi's testimony to the European Parliament set the stage for purchases of sovereign bonds	"If necessary to further address risks of too prolonged a period of low inflation, the Governing Council is unanimous in its commitment to using additional unconventional instruments within its mandate. (…) We have also tasked relevant ECB staff and Eurosystem committees with the timely preparation of further measures to be implemented, if needed. **Such measures could include might entail the purchase of a variety of assets, one of which is sovereign bonds**"
26-Nov-14		Vice President Constancio's speech in London confirms this intention	"(…) we will have to consider buying other assets, **including sovereign bonds in the secondary market**"
4-Dec-14		President Draghi's introductory statement to the press conference fully endorse the purchase of sovereign bonds	"Evidently we are convinced that a **QE programme which could include sovereign bonds falls within our mandate**, or better, is an eligible instrument that we could use in the pursuit of our mandate. Not to pursue our mandate would be illegal"
22-Jan-15	2015Q1	Expanded Asset Purchase Programme (EAPP)—comprising the ABSPP, the CBPP3 and a new Public Sector Purchase Programme (PSPP)—announced	"The governing council of the European central bank today **announced an expanded asset purchase programme**. (...) This programme will see **the ECB add the purchase of sovereign bonds to its existing private sector asset purchase programmes** in order to address the risks of a too prolonged period of low inflation". Combined monthly asset purchases **will amount to €60 billion** and are intended **to be carried out until at least September 2016**

(continued)

Table 6 (continued)

Announcement date	Quarter	Non-standard monetary policy decision	Note
9-Nov-15	2015Q4	Increase in PSPP issue share limit announced	Increase in PSPP issue share limit (from 25 to 33%) enlarges purchasable universe of sovereign assets
4-Dec-15		Reassessment of the appropriateness of the ECB's monetary policy stance	"The Governing Council decided **to extend the asset purchase programme** (APP) and carry out monthly purchases of €60 billion **until the end of March 2017, or beyond, if necessary**. (…) The governing council decided **to include,** in the public sector purchase programme, **euro-denominated marketable debt instruments issued by regional and local governments located in the euro area** in the list of assets that are eligible for regular purchases"
10-Mar-16	2016Q1	Reassessment of the appropriateness of the ECB's monetary policy stance	"At today's meeting the governing council of the ECB took the following monetary policy decisions: (…) (4) The monthly purchases under the asset purchase programme **will be expanded to €80 billion starting in April**. (5) **Investment grade euro-denominated bonds issued by non-bank corporations established in the euro area** will be included in the list of assets that are eligible for regular purchases

Note This table displays a chronology of all the events related to the announcement (and further modifications and extensions) of the ECB's non-standard monetary measures implying the purchase of public and private financial assets on primary and secondary markets: for each event, the day of the announcement is reported as well as the type of adopted measure and a brief description of the main features of each programme

Appendix 2: The ECB's Asset Purchase Programmes

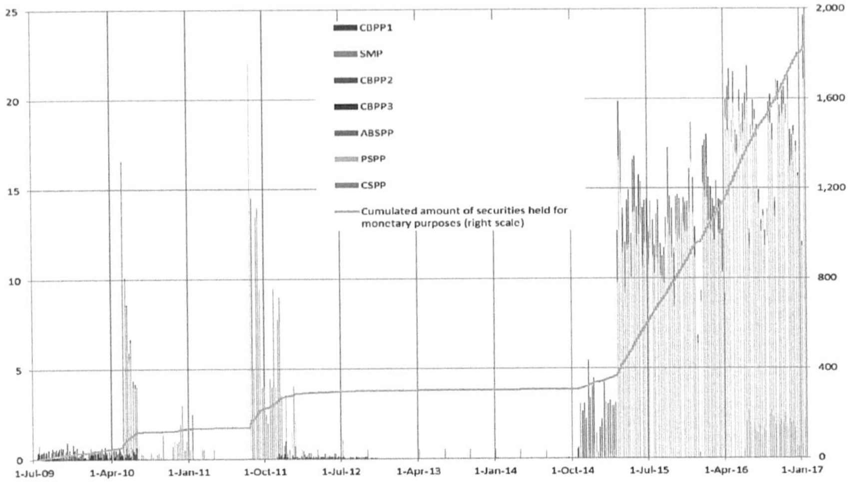

Fig. 3 Timeline of the ECB's asset purchase programmes (*weekly data, billions of euros*). *Note* the figure shows the amounts of financial assets purchased on a weekly basis by the ECB since autumn 2009 under the different programmes, as well as the cumulated stock held for monetary policy purposes. Source: European Central Bank

References

Albertazzi U, Ropele T, Sene G, Signoretti FM (2012) The impact of the sovereign debt crisis on the activity of Italian banks. Bank of Italy occasional paper, 133, September

Ahmed S, Zlate A (2014) Capital flows to emerging market economies: a brave new world? J Int Money Finance 48:221–248

Bluwstein K, Canova F (2016) Beggar-thy-neighbour? The international effects of ECB unconventional monetary policy measures. Int J Central Banking, September

Bruno V, Shin HS (2015) Cross-border banking and global liquidity. Rev Econ Stud 82:535–564

Bruno V, Shin HS (2014) Cross-border banking and global liquidity. BIS working paper, 458, August

Bruno V, Shin HS (2013) Capital flows, cross-border banking and global liquidity. NBER working paper, 19038, May

Bruno V, Shin HS (2012) Capital flows and the risk-taking channel of monetary policy. BIS working paper, 400, December

Buch CM, Koch CT, Koetter M (2009) Margins of international banking: is there a productivity pecking order in banking, too? Deutsche Bundesbank discussion paper series 2. Banking Financial Stud 12

Cecioni M, Ferrero G, Secchi A (2011) Unconventional monetary policy in theory and in practice? Bank of Italy occasional paper, 102, September
Cerutti E, Claessens S, Ratnovski L (2014) Global liquidity and drivers of cross-border bank flows. IMF working paper WP/14/69, April
Ciarlone A, Colabella A (2016) Spillovers of the ECB's non-standard monetary policy into CESEE economies. Ensayos sobre Política Económica 34:175–190
Cova P, Ferrero G (2015) Il programma di acquisto di attività finanziarie per fini di politica monetaria dell'Eurosistema. Bank of Italy occasional paper, 270, April
Edwards S (2015) Monetary policy independence under flexible exchange rates: an illusion? World Econ 38(5):773–787
Falagiarda M, McQuade P, Tirpák M (2015) Spillovers from the ECB's non-standard monetary policies on non-euro area EU countries: evidence from an event-study analysis. ECB working paper, 1869, November
Falagiarda M, Reitz S (2015) Announcements of ECB unconventional programs: implications for the sovereign spreads of stressed euro area countries. J Int Money Finance 53:276–295
Ferrara L, Lhuissier S, Tripier F (2018) The challenges of rising uncertainty for macroeconomic policy. In: Ferrara et al (eds) International macroeconomics in the wake of the global financial crisis. Springer, Berlin
Fratzscher M, Lo Duca M, Straub R (2014) ECB unconventional monetary policy actions: market impact, international spillovers and transmission channels. Paper presented at the 15th Jacques Polak annual research conference, 13–14 Nov 2014
García-Herrero A, Martínez Pería MS (2005) The mix of international bank's foreign claims: determinants and implications. Working papers, 0502, BBVA Bank
Gray C (2013) Responding to a monetary superpower: investigating the behavioural spillovers of US monetary policy. Atlantic Econ J 41(2):173–184
Herrmann S, Mihaljek D (2010) The determinants of cross-border bank flows to emerging markets: new empirical evidence on the spread of financial crises. BIS working paper, 315, July
Hoffmann B, Takáts E (2015) International monetary spillovers. BIS Q Rev, September
IMF (2016) Cross country report on spillovers, July
IMF (2015a) Reconciling fiscal consolidation and growth. Central, Eastern, and Southeastern Europe, November, Regional Economic Issues
IMF (2015b) Mind the credit gap. Central, Eastern, and Southeastern Europe, May, Regional Economic Issues
IMF (2012) The liberalization and management of capital flows—an institutional view. November
IMF (2010) Global financial stability report, April
Korniyenko Y, Loukoianova E (2015) The impact of unconventional monetary policy measures by the systemic four on global liquidity and monetary conditions. IMF working paper WP/15/287, December
Krishnamurthy A, Vissing-Jorgensen A (2011) The effects of quantitative easing on interest rates: channels and implications for policy. Brookings Papers Econ Act 43(2), Fall
Lim JJ, Mohapatra S, Stocker M (2014) Tinker, taper, QE, bye? The effect of quantitative easing on financial flows to developing countries. World Bank policy research working paper, 6820, March
McGuire P, Tarashev NA (2008) Bank health and lending to emerging markets. BIS Q Rev, December
Neri A (2013) The impact of the sovereign debt crisis on bank lending rates in the euro area. Bank of Italy occasional paper, 170, June
Obstfeld M (2015) Trilemmas and trade-offs: living with financial globalisation. BIS working paper, 480, January
Rey H (2015) Dilemma not trilemma: the global financial cycle and monetary policy independence. CEPR discussion paper, 10591, May

Rey H (2013) Dilemma not trilemma: the global financial cycle and monetary policy independence. Paper presented at the Jackson Hole symposium, August. http://www.kansascityfed.org/publications/research/escp/escp-2013.cfm
Takáts E, Vela A (2014) International monetary policy transmission. BIS paper, 78, August
Wu J, Xia F (2016) Measuring the macroeconomic impact of monetary policy at the zero lower bound. J Money Credit Banking 48(2–3):253–291
Zoli E (2013) Italian sovereign spreads: their determinants and pass-through to bank funding costs and lending conditions. IMF working paper WP/13/84, April

FSC
www.fsc.org
MIX
Papier | Fördert
gute Waldnutzung
FSC® C083411

Kolibri 360 GmbH
Ferdinand-Jühlke-Straße 7
99095 Erfurt, Deutschland
produktsicherheit@kolibri360.de

Financial and Monetary Policy Studies

Volume 46

Series Editor
Ansgar Belke, Fakultät für Wirtschaftswiss, University of Duisburg-Essen, Essen, Germany

More information about this series at http://www.springer.com/series/5982